for Pete and Gill

READ THIS FIRST

It's frightening how some people, though adept at walking and scrambling, have none of the mountain sense usually learned through decades of mountain wandering, problem solving and familiarity with mountains in all weather.

Learn to read topo maps and be able to find a grid reference. Turn back if it looks too hard for you, if you can't handle loose rock, if the river is too high, if you can't hack a 10-hour day, or if the route finding is out of your league. Turn back from a summit or ridge if a thunderstorm is approaching or if conditions are made dangerous by rain, snow or ice. ***At all times use your own judgment.*** The author and publisher are not responsible if you have a horrible day or you get yourself into a fix.

In this book there are no do's and don'ts. It is assumed that users of this book are caring, intelligent people who will respect the country they are travelling through.

Be aware that in Kananaskis Country, trails can change in an instant owing to logging and the search for oil and gas. Please notify me of any changes you find so I can make revisions in future editions. Use **Contact Us** under the **About** tab at kananaskistrails.com.

Just before Volume 3 went to press, Kananaskis Country experienced severe flooding which damaged some trailheads and sections of trail. Expect a few changes.

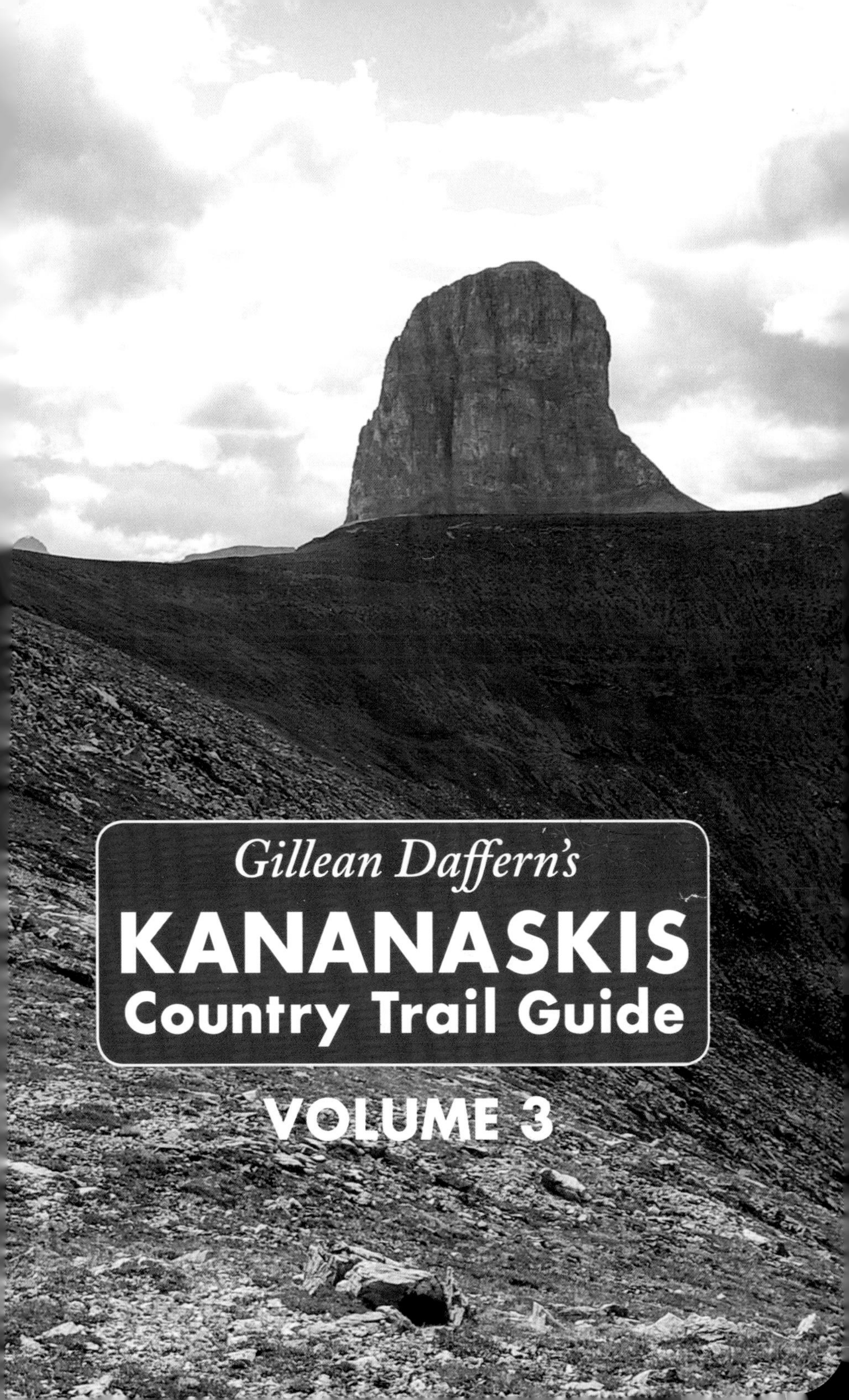

Gillean Daffern's
KANANASKIS
Country Trail Guide
VOLUME 3

RMB | Rocky Mountain Books Ltd.

rmbooks.com

@rmbooks

facebook.com/rmbooks

Cataloguing data available from Library and Archives Canada

ISBN 978-1-897522-76-9 (v. 1).—ISBN 978-1-897522-77-6 (v. 2)

ISBN 978-1-927330-03-6 (v. 3).—ISBN 978-1-927330-09-8 (v. 4)

Book design and layout by Gillean Daffern

Cover design by Chyla Cardinal

Interior photographs by Gillean Daffern unless otherwise noted

Maps by Tony and Gillean Daffern

Topographical maps Her Majesty the Queen in right of Canada.

Printed and bound in Canada

Distributed in Canada by Heritage Group Distribution and in the U.S. by Publishers Group West

For information on purchasing bulk quantities of this book, or to obtain media excerpts or invite the author to speak at an event, please visit rmbooks.com and select the "Contact Us" tab.

RMB | Rocky Mountain Books is dedicated to the environment and committed to reducing the destruction of old-growth forests. Our books are produced with respect for the future and consideration for the past.

We acknowledge the financial support of the Government of Canada through the Canada Book Fund and the Canada Council for the Arts, and of the province of British Columbia through the British Columbia Arts Council and the Book Publishing Tax Credit.

Nous reconnaissons l'aide financière du gouvernement du Canada par l'entremise du Fonds du livre du Canada et le Conseil des arts du Canada, et de la province de la Colombie-Britannique par le Conseil des arts de la Colombie-Britannique et le Crédit d'impôt pour l'édition de livres.

Disclaimer

The actions described in this book may be considered inherently dangerous activities. Individuals undertake these activities at their own risk. The information put forth in this guide has been collected from a variety of sources and is not guaranteed to be completely accurate or reliable. Many conditions and some information may change owing to weather and numerous other factors beyond the control of the authors and publishers. Individual climbers and/or hikers must determine the risks, use their own judgment, and take full responsibility for their actions. Do not depend on any information found in this book for your own personal safety. Your safety depends on your own good judgment based on your skills, education, and experience.

It is up to the users of this guidebook to acquire the necessary skills for safe experiences and to exercise caution in potentially hazardous areas. The authors and publishers of this guide accept no responsibility for your actions or the results that occur from another's actions, choices, or judgments. If you have any doubt as to your safety or your ability to attempt anything described in this guidebook, do not attempt it.

CONTENTS

TRAILS

Changes in the 4th edition

The big news is that the guide now extends to 5 volumes. The reasons are all advantageous to the reader: to keep the number of pages down (who wants to tote around a 1000-page guide book); to allow for a more user-friendly layout where trails are arranged by access road; to make room for more maps; and for ease of adding new trails and subtracting old ones.

There have been major changes to access roads, trails and trailheads, the extraordinary growth of Canmore and the proliferation of golf courses being the major factor in the Bow Valley. New trails have been built for mountain bikers, some of which double as hiking trails, and older trails decommissioned in an effort to leave corridors for wildlife. Some trails are closed at certain times of the year. In other areas such as the Ghost, trails and access continue to be affected by logging, the search for gas, OHV use and management plans.

Since the last edition K Country has become a collection of parks: wildland parks, provincial parks, provincial recreation parks, Don Getty parks, ecological reserves, preservation zones, wildland zones, cultural and facility zones etc., each with a different level of protection and with different sets of rules. This makes things tricky for us guidebook writers. We have also been introduced to seasonal closures, permits, user fees and substantial fines for non-compliance. As if to sum it up, the word "ranger" has been replaced by the less friendly-sounding "conservation officer." However, as of 2012, officers who don't tote firearms are called Parks Services Rangers.

Further reading

Some trails in the Ghost abut against Banff National Park. For description of ongoing routes read the *Canadian Rockies Trail Guide*, by Brian Patton & Bart Robinson, and *Backcountry Banff*, by Mike Potter.

ACKNOWLEDGEMENTS

For this edition the following three people have been extremely helpful and supportive: Don Cockerton (as always over many editions through the years), Brian Carter and Alf Skrastins. I also wish to acknowledge Doug Campbell, Tyler Dixon, Jeff Eamon, Alaric Fish, Gill Ford, Gary Hunt, Gord Hurlburt, Ed Latvala, Peter Oprsal, Michael Roycroft, Doug Saul, Jim Stanton, Kevin Stanton, Gerry Stephenson, Heinz Unger, David Wasserman, Len Webber, Geoff Williams and the late Bill Baxter.

All photos are by the author unless credited otherwise. Special thank you to Alf Skrastins and Bob Spirko, who have provided many photos for this volume. In the effort to get the best photos possible I also wish to thank Matthew Clay, Eric Coulthard, Cal Damen, Gord Dobson, Rob Eastick, Blake Edwards, Andy Genereux, Rick Green, Tanya Koob, Dinah Kruze, Shawn Lawrence, Roy Millar, John Miller, Rachel Oggy, Rod Plasman, Mike Potter, Derek Ryder, Bob Truman, Heinz Unger, Cole Warawa and Geoff Williams. Thank you all for taking the time to search through your files and albums.

PHOTO CAPTIONS

Front cover: #41 Heart Mountain Circuit, approaching Grant MacEwan Peak. Photo Alf Skrastins

Page 1: Crossing the Ghost River.

Title Page: #16 Bastion Ridge. Devils Head from side trip no. 2.

Contents page: #51E Upper Spray Falls in spate.

Page 10: Helicopter. Photo Derek Ryder

Page 17: #61B Waterfall below Grassi Lakes.

Page 344: "Totem" off the TransAlta Road.

Back cover: #84 Sparrowhawk Creek tarns. Photo Alf Skrastins

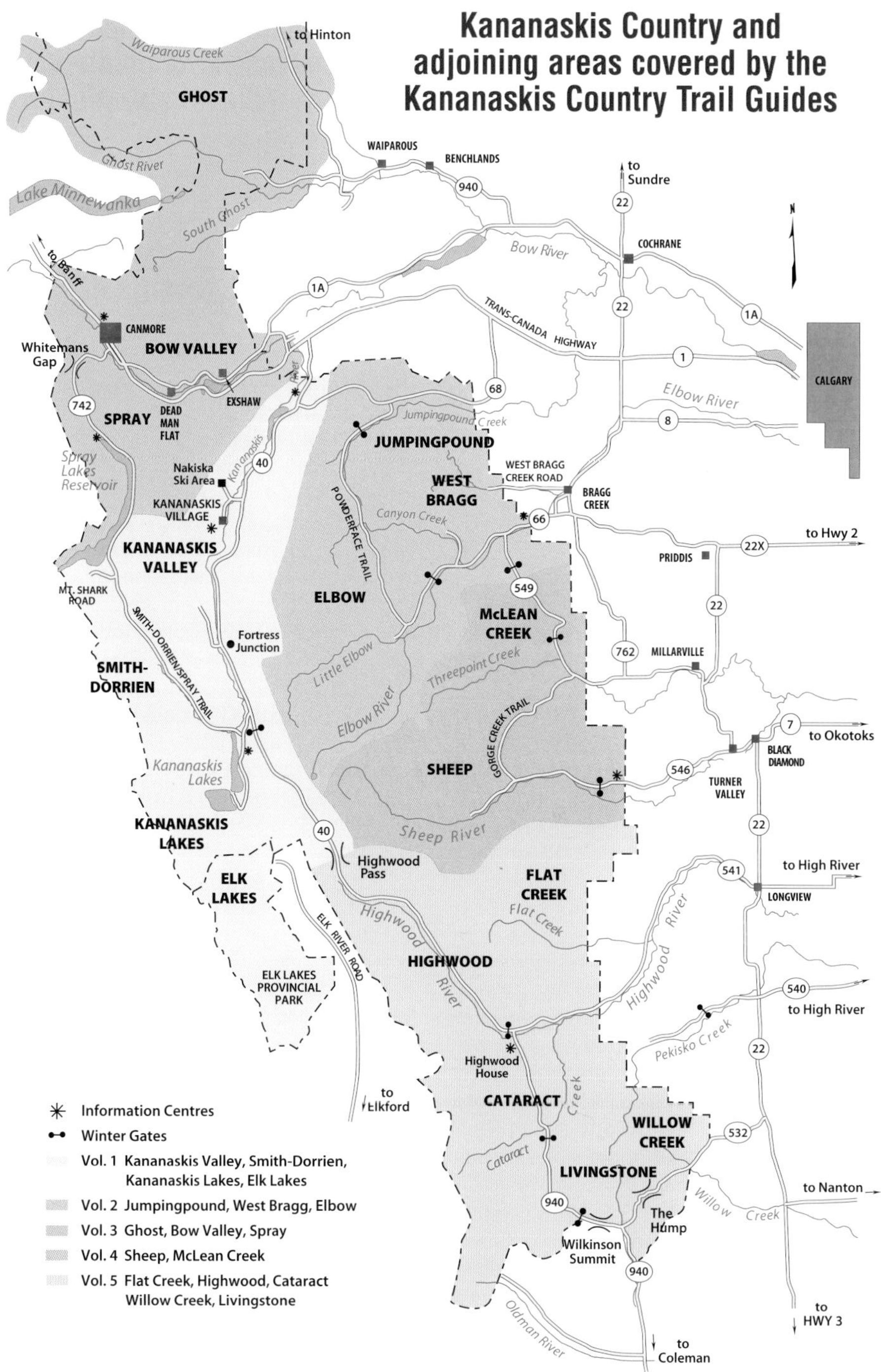
Kananaskis Country and adjoining areas covered by the Kananaskis Country Trail Guides
to Hinton
Waiparous Creek
GHOST
Ghost River
Lake Minnewanka
South Ghost
WAIPAROUS
BENCHLANDS
940
to Sundre
22
COCHRANE
Bow River
to Banff
1A
TRANS-CANADA HIGHWAY
22
1A
CANMORE
BOW VALLEY
Whitemans Gap
EXSHAW
1
CALGARY
742
SPRAY
DEAD MAN FLAT
68
Elbow River
Jumpingpound Creek
8
JUMPINGPOUND
Spray Lakes Reservoir
40
Nakiska Ski Area
Kananaskis
WEST BRAGG CREEK ROAD
WEST BRAGG
BRAGG CREEK
POWDERFACE TRAIL
KANANASKIS VILLAGE
Canyon Creek
66
to Hwy 2
22X
KANANASKIS VALLEY
PRIDDIS
549
ELBOW
MT. SHARK ROAD
McLEAN CREEK
22
Fortress Junction
SMITH-DORRIEN/SPRAY TRAIL
762
MILLARVILLE
SMITH-DORRIEN
Little Elbow
Threepoint Creek
Elbow River
GORGE CREEK TRAIL
7
to Okotoks
BLACK DIAMOND
Kananaskis Lakes
SHEEP
546
TURNER VALLEY
KANANASKIS LAKES
40
Sheep River
22
Highwood Pass
FLAT CREEK
to High River
541
LONGVIEW
ELK LAKES
Flat Creek
Highwood
ELK RIVER ROAD
Highwood River
HIGHWOOD
River
540
ELK LAKES PROVINCIAL PARK
to High River
Pekisko Creek
22
Highwood House
to Elkford
CATARACT
Creek
WILLOW CREEK
532
Cataract
LIVINGSTONE
to Nanton
940
The Hump
Willow Creek
Wilkinson Summit
940
Oldman River
to HWY 3
to Coleman
Information Centres
Winter Gates
Vol. 1 Kananaskis Valley, Smith-Dorrien, Kananaskis Lakes, Elk Lakes
Vol. 2 Jumpingpound, West Bragg, Elbow
Vol. 3 Ghost, Bow Valley, Spray
Vol. 4 Sheep, McLean Creek
Vol. 5 Flat Creek, Highwood, Cataract Willow Creek, Livingstone

KANANASKIS COUNTRY

THE NAME

Since the last edition of these guidebooks, it seems the whole world has learned to pronounce the name "Kananaskis": CBC's Lloyd Robertson, American President Bush, British prime minister Tony Blair, Russian president Putin. One wonders what explorer John Palliser would have thought of it all. The strange name dates back to 1858 when Palliser named the pass he was about to cross "Kananaskis, after the name of an Indian, of whom there is a legend, giving an account of his most wonderful recovery from the blow of an axe, which had stunned but had failed to kill him, and the river, which flows through this gorge also bears his name." Possibly the Indian in question was the great Cree Koominakoos who lost an eye and part of his scalp in a battle with the Blackfoot in the Willow Creek area but made a miraculous recovery and showed up at Fort Edmonton some weeks later "ready to take to the warpath again."

THE CONCEPT

Today, the Kananaskis Passes, Kananaskis Lakes and the Kananaskis River form the heart of Kananaskis Country (or K Country as it is more commonly called), a provincial recreation area owned by Albertans and established on October 7, 1977, to "alleviate congestion in national parks, and to provide greater recreation opportunities for Albertans."

Let's give credit to architect Bill Milne, who got the ball rolling. Alberta Premier Peter Lougheed and his Minister of Highways, Clarence Copithorne, quickly came on board and a new Hwy. 40 was built. Their vision for the Kananaskis Valley was one of strenuous physical outdoor activity accessible from a good road but with minimal services. As we all know, that simple idea turned into the grand plan called Kananaskis Country, encompassing a lot more country (over 4000 square kilometres) and a lot more development and trails for every conceivable outdoor sport.

Many people forget that K Country has always been multi-use, meaning it is also open to logging, cattle grazing and oil and gas exploration. Lately it's been divvied up into various parks with different levels of environmental protection.

LOCATION

K Country is located on the eastern slopes of the Canadian Rockies, west and south of the Olympic city of Calgary, Alberta. From the city outskirts the eastern boundary is a mere 20-minute drive away.

The west boundary adjoins Banff National Park, then runs down the Continental Divide. The northern boundary is delineated by Hwy. 1 and the fringe communities of Exshaw, Dead Man's Flats and Canmore. The eastern boundary coincides neatly with the Bow–Crow Forest reserve boundary, while the southern boundary is marked by Hwy. 732 (Johnson Creek Trail). While not technically a part of K Country, the adjoining areas of the Ghost, the Bow Valley and the northern bit of Elk Lakes Provincial Park (which is usually accessed from Peter Lougheed Provincial Park) are also included in the trail descriptions.

GETTING THERE

Calgary is served by major airlines, several bus companies and by train from the east. Greyhound buses run west along the Trans-Canada Hwy. to Canmore, but stops are infrequent. That's it as far as public transportation goes. You need a car.

The area described in Volume 3 is accessed by either Hwy. 1 (the Trans-Canada Hwy.) or by Hwy. 1A (Bow Valley Trail) to Canmore. Hwy. 940N leaves the 1A 13.2 km west of the town of Cochrane. The Ghost River Road and the Waiparous Creek Road head west from Hwy. 940. Connecting Hwy. 1 and the 1A is Hwy. 1X. The Spray area is accessed from Canmore via Hwy. 742 (Smith-Dorrien/Spray Trail).

WHAT TO EXPECT

This volume covers the Bow River Valley between the gates to the mountains and Canmore, and its tributaries the Ghost and Waiparous rivers. It also takes in the Spray Lakes Reservoir area, which is accessed from Canmore and is part of the hydroelectric scheme for the Bow.

Scenically, this is a very diverse area. The Ghost, for instance, comprised of the Ghost, the South Ghost and the North Ghost (Waiparous Creek), is unlike anywhere else with its canyons, big cliffs and wide valley bottoms where the rivers tend to run underground. Although it is a low snow area, it's famous for the size and quality of its ice climbs.

The eastern portion of the Bow Valley is a unique mix of features resulting from past ice ages, most of which are displayed in Bow Valley Provincial Park. Farther west the valley bottom is a floodplain unsuitable for trails. In this area the trails follow side valleys that tend to be stony and arid. Scattered throughout are several popular ridge walks and easy scrambles such as the Heart Mountain Horseshoe.

Around Canmore itself is a big network of mountain biking trails that double as hiking trails. At the other extreme, a large number of surrounding peaks offer easy ways up.

The Spray Valley high above Canmore is a complexity of canals and lakes, the largest of which is Spray Lakes Reservoir. Most of the hikes take off from the east side of Hwy. 742 and lead to passes.

WEATHER TRENDS

Hiking season starts as early as March in the east and can continue until the end of November or beyond. As the snow clears, the areas farther west open up.

However, snow can fall in any month of the year, as campers well know. Just as likely, temperatures can rise to the mid-30s Celsius. Rain most often falls in June or is associated with late afternoon thunderstorms that have accounted for a number of fatalities in K Country. Should it occur, Indian summer can be glorious through October. Warm days, cold nights, no thunderstorms, no flies, no mosquitoes and no flowers, but then you can't have everything.

NATURAL HISTORY IN A NUTSHELL

I urge you to buy the appropriate field guides or Ben Gadd's all-in-one *Handbook of the Canadian Rockies*.

Mammals Most commonly seen in this area: bighorn sheep (north side of Hwy. 1A), mule and whitetail deer, elk, moose, wolves, coyotes, cougars, black bears and grizzlies. Then there's the usual bevy of beavers and muskrats in every foothills valley, plus squirrels. Chipmunks, picas, marmots and porcupines are found more to the west.

Wild horses inhabit various areas in the Ghost but are rarely seen.

Birds Most common: whisky jacks (the ones that gather around when you stop to eat), Clark's nutcracker, hummingbirds (wear red), ravens, crows, chickadees, kinglets, swallows, flycatchers, warblers, owls, grouse, migrating eagles and ospreys nesting on telephone poles. Lac des Arcs is the place to see tundra and trumpeter swans early in the spring. Spring-fed creeks around Canmore are well known for overwintering mallards.

Fish Trout (cutthroat, rainbow, brown, bull) in small man-made ponds and in the spring creeks around Canmore.

Vegetation Trees range through fire-succession lodgepole pine and aspen in the east to spruce and fir on north- and east-facing slopes in the west.

For flowers you'll need two field guides, one for the prairies and one for the mountains. Apart from the area at the head of the South Ghost, this is not a huge alpine meadow area. Best pocket meadows to aim for include the Mt. Allan/Pigeon Mountain/Wind Ridge area, the head of Exshaw Creek and the upper valleys and passes on the east side of Hwy. 742. Look for orchids of many kinds in the Bow Valley and around Canmore.

POSSIBLE HAZARDS

River crossings Large rivers like the Waiparous and the Ghost are impassable during runoff and after prolonged rain, Caribbean water it is not; this water is often numbing even if it's only knee deep. Consider carrying neoprene booties.

Bears, cougars and other beasts At all times be aware of bears, but particularly in early spring and during berry season in August/September. Often K Country will close a trail until a bear has moved out of the area, so be sure to read their trail report on the web before setting out. Carry a bear repellent and bear bangers where you can reach them in a hurry.

You might think yourself safer in the Canmore area next to civilization, but this is not so. This place is a magnet for cougars and bears (both black and grizzly) attracted by pets, bird feeders, man-made ponds and ungulates feeding on golf course grasses. Development has spread right across the valley and up the hillsides, impinging on traditional game routes up and down the valley. Designated wildlife corridors crossed by some trails are not nearly wide enough, according to experts. Other bear places are Wind Valley, the upper Ghost and the South Ghost.

Elk and moose should be given a wide berth, especially in spring when with young and in fall during the mating season.

Hunters Hunting is allowed everywhere except in provincial recreation areas. September to December is the time to dress in psychedelic shades of orange and pink. In November, hunting is allowed on Sundays. Before and after that month, Sunday is a "safe" day, but I wouldn't bet on it.

Ticks etc. Between about March and mid-June ticks are abroad and are found mainly in areas where there are lots of sheep, i.e., the south slopes of Grotto Mountain and Lady Macdonald and in the arid valleys north of Hwy. 1A. Having said that, I once picked up a tick on Grotto in November.

Loose rock This refers mainly to the sedimentary limestone of the Front Ranges. Of course, there *is* firm limestone but it's safer to expect the worst. On scrambling pitches, develop the technique of pushing back handholds. Be extra careful of rockfall in gullies. On some routes you'll run into scree—lots of it. Use game trails, where the scree is more stabilized.

Logging trucks The Ghost is a heavily logged area. Be alert for trucks on logging roads *and* on public roads. Usually signs go up.

Other users Very often in the Bow Valley you'll be sharing the trails with mountain bikers (both DHS, or downhill specific, and cross-country) so be prepared to step off the trail. In the Ghost be alert for equestrians and reckless OHVers.

Helicopters In the annoyance category are sightseeing helicopters that in season fly to and fro over the passes south of Canmore and around Yamnuska.

FACILITIES

Hwy. 940N
An information kiosk is located at the South Ghost Recreation area.

TransAlta Road
Trapper's Hill Lodges, run by the Lazy H Trail Company, offers upscale camping and trail rides.

Hwy. 1X
In Bow Valley Provincial Park, **Bow River Campground** has a small store selling snacks and trail food.

The Kananaskis Guest Ranch offers accommodation, barbecues, 18-hole golf course, trail rides and overnight trips.

NOTE Since the last edition the company hamlet of Seebe (and therefore the general store) has been shut down.

Hwy. 1A (Bow Valley Parkway)
The town of **Cochrane** has all amenities, including an eclectic selection of eateries, both western and ethnic. MacKay's famous ice cream shop is located in the centre of town.

In the village of **Exshaw**, Heart Mountain Cafe has a gas station. The cafe is open weekdays from 7 am to 3 pm; closed on weekends. However, a variety of savoury snacks can be zapped in the microwave. Hot drinks are always on hand.

The **Alpine Club of Canada's Clubhouse** near Canmore is open to nonmembers.

Hwy. 1 (Trans-Canada Hwy.)
Rafter Six Ranch Resort offers accommodation in the lodge and cabins and has a camping field with picnic tables and outhouses. Bring your own water. Facilities, which are also open to day visitors, include a restaurant, coffee shop, bar and gift shop. Evening meals must be reserved ahead of time. From May to October Sunday brunches are available by pre-booking. Other attractions include trail rides, a ropes course, a museum and Teton the white buffalo. While May to October are the peak months, the resort is open all year.

The hamlet of **Dead Man's Flats** has motels, B&Bs, an Esso gas station with small grocery store, and a Husky station with restaurant that sells an excellent selection of trail foods. The Junction House restaurant is open evenings and weekends from noon to 10 pm. Closed on Mondays.

The hamlet of **Harvie Heights** west of Canmore has motels, but no eateries. The nearby **Cross Zee Ranch** not only offers trail rides, but hosts private gatherings like dances, weddings and corporate functions.

Canmore
Canmore, the location of K Country's head office, has everything for all budgets: hotels (with convention facilities), motels, inns, B&Bs, campgrounds, gourmet restaurants, pubs and fast food outlets, grocery stores, sports shops, two great book stores, and bike rentals. Most of it is centred downtown or along Hwy. 1A. The town information centre is located on Hwy. 1A. Alberta Tourism, Parks & Recreation Office is located in Suite 201 at 800 Railway Avenue.

Nearby, **Three Sisters Mountain Village** has a bistro. **Silvertip Golf Course** features Stoney's Bar & Grill and Rustica Steakhouse.

Up the hill on Spray Lakes Road is the **Canmore Nordic Centre** day lodge, open 9 am–5:30 pm daily year-round, including an information centre and full-service cafeteria. Banquet or meeting room space can be reserved in the day lodge. Trail Sports is a full-service bike shop for rentals, repairs, sales and lessons.

Bike 'n' Hike Shuttle runs a shuttle for hikers and bikers between Canmore and Banff and to Grassi Lakes, Goat Creek and Ha-Ling trailheads.

Hwy. 742 (Smith-Dorrien/Spray Trail)
Below **Three Sisters Dam** is a biffy and a telephone that takes coins only.

CAMPING

HIGHWAY ACCESSIBLE CAMPING

Campgrounds fill up quickly in the summer. It's galling to find every campsite full of people whose idea of exercise is the walk to the biffy, so book ahead if you can. After Labour Day the situation eases. Use the phone numbers and email addresses to check on opening and closing dates, make reservations etc. Prices vary depending on amenities offered and the number of vehicles in your party. An RV and a tent counts as one vehicle. Generally, Alberta seniors receive a discount.

Hwy. 940N
North Ghost (May–mid Oct)
Waiparous Creek (May–mid Oct)
Group campgrounds at **Waiparous Creek**, **North Ghost** and **Air Strip** (open year round).
Call 403-637-2198.

TransAlta Road
Trapper's Hill Lodges Welcomes tents and RVs. On site you can stay in comfortable camping lodges that house 4 people. Call 403-851-0074 (or 8120). horseandrider@lazyhtrailco.com.

Hwy. 1A
Ghost Reservoir (May–end of Oct)
Call 403-851-0766.

Hwy. 1X Bow Valley Provincial Park
Willow Rock (Apr–end of Oct)
Bow River (May–end of Sep)
Elk Flats group (May–end of Oct)
Call Bow Valley Park Campgrounds 403-673-2163.

Hwy. 1
Three Sisters (mid Apr–end of Nov)
Group campgrounds at **Owl** and **Grouse** in Bow Valley Provincial Park South (May–end of Oct).
Call Bow Valley Park Campgrounds 403-673-2163.
Bow Valley (May–mid Oct)
Lac des Arcs (May to the Sep long weekend.) Call 403-537-2757.
Rafter Six Ranch Resort 403-673-3622 provides picnic tables and primitive outhouses. Bring your own water.

Canmore
Spring Creek RV Campground 3 Ave. (mid Apr–mid Oct) No tents. Call 403-678-5111.
Rundle Mountain 1734 Bow Valley Trail (May–Oct). Call 403-678-2131.
Wapiti 100 Ray McBride St. Call 403-678-9511.

Hwy. 742, north end
Spray Lake West (Jun–mid Oct). Call 1-866-366-2267.

BACKCOUNTRY CAMPING

Quaite Valley in Quaite Creek off Hwy. 1 is the only backcountry campground.

For official sites you need permits costing $12 per person plus a $12 reservation fee plus GST applied to all telephone and advance bookings. Children under 16 are free but still require a permit. Permits can be picked up from visitor centres elsewhere in K Country. The most hassle-free way is to call the Backcountry Permit Desk at 403-678-3136. In Alberta the number is toll free if you dial 310-0000 first. It will have occurred to you that camping at such sites can cost considerably more than highway-accessible camping.

Random camping is allowed almost anywhere except in provincial parks and provincial recreation areas.

Random camping is further broken down into random with permit; restricted random with no access Apr 15–Sep 30; no random camping and no access Dec 15–Jun 15; bivouac random Apr 15–Sep 30; bivouac random Apr 15–Sep 30 but with no access Dec 15–Jun 15. If totally in the dark as to which of these areas you hope to camp in, call the above number for elucidation.

INFO

SEASONAL ROAD CLOSURES

Roads in this area are open year-round. However, be aware that the two gravel roads up the Ghost River and Waiparous Creek are often in rough shape and you may not get where you are aiming for. A 4 wheel drive, high-clearance vehicle is recommended.

A FEW RULES

- Respect seasonal trail closures.
- No registration is necessary for overnight trips. However, registration books are available at information centres and at some trailheads.
- Respect open-fire bans. Should you wish to report a fire, telephone numbers are listed on trailhead kiosks.
- Dogs must be on a leash.
- Anglers require an Alberta or BC fishing licence.
- There are some restrictions on backcountry camping. See under Backcountry Camping.
- There are some restrictions for mountain bikers. Read the trail description or contact an information centre.

"Closed" sign on Montane trail above Canmore.

CHECK THE K COUNTRY WEBSITE

Check the K Country trail report for conditions. Especially useful are the "Important Notes," which among other things give warnings about bear or cougar sightings and temporary trail closures. See www.albertaparks.ca/kananaskis-country.aspx.

CHECK OUR BLOG

KananaskisTrails.com is a blog site maintained by Gillean and Tony Daffern. It covers all things Kananaskis, including notification of new trails, trail changes and trail issues.

K COUNTRY PUBLICATIONS

For up-to-date specific info pick up the *Explore Kananaskis Country* map and the *Explore Alberta Parks* publication. Copies are available at all information centres in K Country and across Alberta.

THE GHOST WATERSHED ALLIANCE SOCIETY (GWAS)

Founded to identify ecosystem and environmental issues. Conducts walks into the Ghost River area. See www.ghostwatershed.ca/GWAS/Home.html.

FRIENDS OF KANANASKIS COUNTRY

is a not-for-profit registered charity that works to preserve "the ecological integrity of Kananaskis Country through educational programming, increased public awareness and leading by example." Volunteers are needed for work parties. Call 403-678-5593 or trails@kananaskis.org.

VOLUNTEERS NEEDED FOR:

Bow Valley Volunteer Stewards;
Canmore Nordic Centre Provincial Park;
Push To Open Nature Initiative;
Researching Amphibian Numbers in Alberta (RANA);
Wildlife Ambassador Program (Bow Valley WildSmart).

To learn more about each organization, visit www.albertaparks.ca/kananaskis-country/volunteering.aspx.

USING THE BOOK

ARRANGEMENT OF TRAILS

Trails are arranged by highway and are colour coded. Refer to the map on page 16.

TYPES OF TRAILS

Official trails, maintained by Kananaskis Country, Alberta Tourism, Parks & Recreation (TPR) and Alberta Environment & Sustainable Resource Development (ESRD), are a mix of new and old trails, logging and exploration roads, fire roads and cutlines. Expect parking lots at trailheads, biffies and the occasional picnic table. Junctions are marked with signage of the "You are here" variety. Some trails have directional arrows or coloured markers on trees or posts. Unless the trail is equestrian, expect bridges over creeks.

Unofficial trails are similar to the above, but sometimes have no obvious trailhead and are neither signposted nor marked in any way except perhaps for the occasional piece of flagging, cairn or trimmed branches. Creek crossings are the norm. For the first time, this category includes trails demoted from official status.

Routes either have no trails or have long trail-less sections where you have to navigate from one intermittent game trail to another. Often there is some bushwhacking.

Scrambles can be official or unofficial trails or can be routes. They range from ridge walks to gruelling uphill flogs in excess of 1000 m to the top of a mountain. You can be sure of scree and possibly a pitch or two of easy scrambling. There may be mild exposure. Special equipment is unnecessary in optimum conditions when the mountain is devoid of snow and the weather is good.

HEIGHTS, HEIGHT GAINS

are given in both metric and imperial.

RATING TRAILS

No attempt has been made to classify trails. What's difficult for one person is easy for another. It's all relative. Also coming into play is the length of a trail, its gradient, its remoteness from a trailhead, conditions underfoot and so on. Read the introductory description carefully. If you're having a horrible time, it's up to you to turn back and try something easier.

RATING TIMES

Times are dependent on too many variables—everybody chugs along at a different rate. Some will be carrying heavy packs; some people, like me, want to make frequent flower stops. And then there are the underfoot conditions to consider, the weather and so on.

- Half-day, up to 3 hours.
- Day, up to 6 hours.
- Long-day, up to 10 hours plus. (Take headlamps.)
- Backpack, overnight camping.

Some of the trips are designated "bike 'n' hike" and "bike 'n' scramble." Biking the first part of the trail can cut down the time considerably. In this way I've often squeezed a weekend trip into one day.

DISTANCES

Distances are given in kilometres. Distances shown between each segment of trail are not cumulative; they show the distance of that segment only.

TRAIL DESCRIPTIONS

Trail descriptions are arranged according to the character of the trail. Most trails lead to a single destination. But sometimes the destination is the springboard for further options under headings like "going farther," "side trip," "optional descent route" etc. I sometimes describe the same mountain with different ways up and down, or an area with a number of trails or peaks radiating out from the same access. Occasionally loop trails can be extended into longer loops. Long-distance trails, rarely hiked in their entirety, are described by segment.

DIRECTIONS

Left and right refer to the direction of travel as described.

GRID REFERENCES AND GPS RECEIVERS

Topo maps have blue grid lines running east–west and north–south. Each line is numbered. The first two numbers indicate the grid line forming the west boundary of the kilometre square in which your point is located, and the third digit is the estimated number of tenths of a kilometre your point is east of that line. The fourth and fifth numbers indicate the south boundary of the square, and the last digit is the estimated number of tenths of a kilometre your point is north of that line.

Where I give grid references, you can follow along on your topo map. Just know that the values can be out by up to 100 m in either direction and that topo maps of mountain areas are inaccurate anyway.

GPS receivers are useful when bushwhacking or for finding your way back to a trail or a trailhead. Most grid references given in the book are accurate. Those references preceded by a tilde symbol (~), indicate the grid reference is approximate, usually because the receiver used was an older or cheaper model unable to pick up all the satellites.

MAPS IN THE BOOK

Sketch maps in the text are not always to scale and serve only to clarify complex areas where you might go wrong. Maps at the back of the book are based on today's topo maps, which come in a mix of imperial and metric. Therefore, contour intervals vary. Trails and routes are drawn on as accurately as possible, and missing or wrongly placed features on the underlying topo map have been rectified.

In the book :

- Red line: a trail, official or unofficial.
- Red dash: a route.
- Black line: trail in other volumes, or trail not used.
- Dashed black line: route in other volumes of this series.

BUYING MAPS

The latest editions of Gem Trek maps come close to being the perfect maps for the area, with contour intervals of 25 m. They show grid lines, up-to-date road alignments, official trails, some unofficial trails, and major powerlines.

Government topo maps, depending on the edition, are in both imperial and metric, with contour lines at 100 ft. intervals and 40 m intervals respectively (not so good). Occasionally, features like small lakes, streams, glaciers and even mountains are omitted, which leads to exciting discoveries. Generally, road alignments are corrected on maps newer than 1983.

Provincial Resource Base Maps from Alberta Energy are updated fairly regularly and show what the other maps don't: all cutlines, all powerlines and exploration and logging roads. Unfortunately, the reality is sometimes nothing like what is shown on the map.

MAPS FOR VOLUME 3

Gem Trek

- Best of Canmore: scale 1:35,000, contour interval 25 m.
- Canmore & Kananaskis Village scale 1:50,000, contour interval 25 m.

Government Topo Maps

Scale 1:50,000

- 82 O/6 Lake Minnewanka
- 82 O/7 Wildcat Hills
- 82 O/3 Canmore
- 82 J/14 Spray Lakes Reservoir

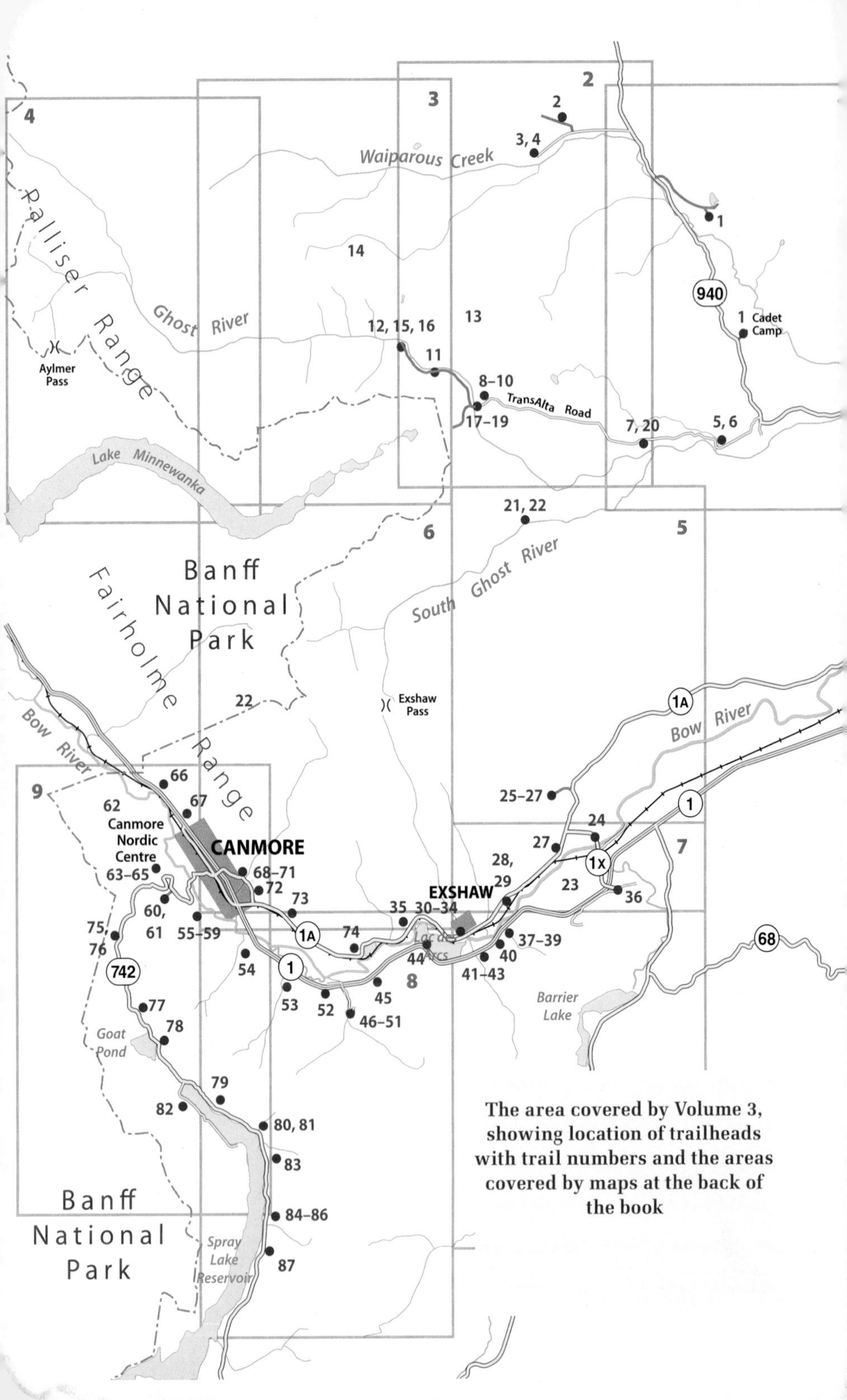

The area covered by Volume 3, showing location of trailheads with trail numbers and the areas covered by maps at the back of the book

TRAIL DESCRIPTIONS

1 AURA CREEK SAND DUNES—map 1

In the sand forest.

Day hike, bike 'n' hike
Unofficial trails, river crossing via route 1
Distance 9.3 km return via route 1;
9.1 km return via route 2
Height gain 140 m (460 ft.) via route 1;
61 m (200 ft.) via route 2
High point 1475 m (4840 ft.)
Map 82 O/7 Wildcat Hills

Access Hwy. 940.
South for route 1. At 1.5 km north of the forest boundary turn right (east) at the kiosk and on a gravel road drive for 990 m through a gate (usually kept open) to the entrance gate of the Rocky Mountain National Army Cadet Summer Training Centre. Park off road before the second gate.
North for route 2. At 9.1 km north of the forest boundary and just north of Waiparous Creek bridge turn right (east) onto a side road signed "Whispering Pines Bible Camp." Drive the road for 2.2 km, past a kiosk in a meadow and through a gate. Climb steeply up a hill, then drift gently downhill to a T-junction at marker 103. Park at 413920. The road to left leads to the bible camp at Cow Lake. Your route is the dirt track ahead.

There are many sandy areas to the east of Waiparous Creek. The best known are the Aura Creek dunes, which cover both sides of a low ridge, and though anchored by vegetation, they provide plenty of sheltered bowls for sunbathing and chutes steep enough for rolling down. Unfortunately, I can't guarantee your peace won't be shattered by dirt bikers straying far from official OHV trails.

There are two routes to choose from. Route 1 is a very pleasant walk, but involves wading Waiparous Creek, which on a hot summer day is no hardship at all—by August the crossing is easy. Route 2 follows the Eau Claire tote road and can be biked. On the downside it's now an official OHV route with puddles.

TRAIL NOTE The simple start to Route 1 of previous editions has been stymied by the building of the Rocky Mountain National Army Cadet Summer Training Centre (RMNACSTC) right across the valley. It's an incredibly sprawling complex ringed by the usual military paranoia of barbed wire fences within fences and "No Trespassing" signs. How to bypass it? In the end, I decided on a route that follows the fenceline but involves extraneous ascent and descent of a hill.

HISTORY NOTE Route 1 takes you past the RMNACSTC and fire man-up building that's replaced the old ranger station. This land once belonged to the Bar C Ranch. At the time I'm talking about it was owned by George Creighton, who agreed to lease the Forestry Department some land at Aura Spring for a ranger station under condition that no one was to cut his timber. In all innocence, Forestry sent out a man called Flack to build a cabin, which in those days was done by axing a few nearby trees. Incensed, Creighton promptly razed the cabin and scared the wits out of Flack with his six-shooter. Undeterred, Forestry then sent in Archie Howard to build another cabin. He borrowed Laurie Johnson's .32 revolver, all unknowing that Johnson, who must surely have been hiding behind a tree to watch the fun, had also provided Creighton with black ammunition for his .45, which made a hell of a noise and emitted lots of smoke. The ruse, if that was what it was—no one was ever too sure about Creighton's intentions—worked and no further attempt to build a ranger station was made until after Creighton's death. Can't help but think what he would have thought of the RMNACSTC.

Route 2 follows the tote road built in 1906 by the Eau Claire Lumber Company to its logging camps on the Waiparous. It started from Cochrane and went more or less on the line of today's Hwy. 940, but then diverted to the east bank of Waiparous Creek. Later, another tote road started west of Morley and on the line of Richards Road gained the Bar C Ranch, after which it followed the route of today's highway, and required heavy-duty trestle bridges. So today's Hwy. 940 is an amalgamation of both tote roads.

Crossing the Waiparous.

Route 1 in the forest.

Route 1 via trail 4 km

First, know there's a more direct start using bit trails between the outer and inner fences (red dash on the map), that takes advantage of gaps in the fences, and bushes over head height. Unfortunately, the meadow section right at the start is in full sight of the cadet camp parade ground. We've used it as the return route about four times now and so far no one has used us as target practice or even shouted at us—as far as we know. The last time, we were deafened by bagpipes playing *Scotland the Brave* over and over. Nevertheless, I though it discretionary to direct you onto the out-of-sight route, as follows:

On a grassy track head left across meadow and through a gap in the E–W fence. Ahead is a N–S fence climbing a hill. Transfer to a trail following the right side of this fence to a kissing gate. Cross to the left side. After the fence turns east, continue north on the trail that undulates to a T-junction with a grassy old road. Turn right, then almost straightaway left on a trail that takes you out to an open banktop. Leave the trail that's veering left; it's simpler to wade around the banktop in long grasses to an intersection with the direct start. Turn left and follow this trail through meadow, then steeply down hills to a meadow bordering Waiparous Creek. Turn left.

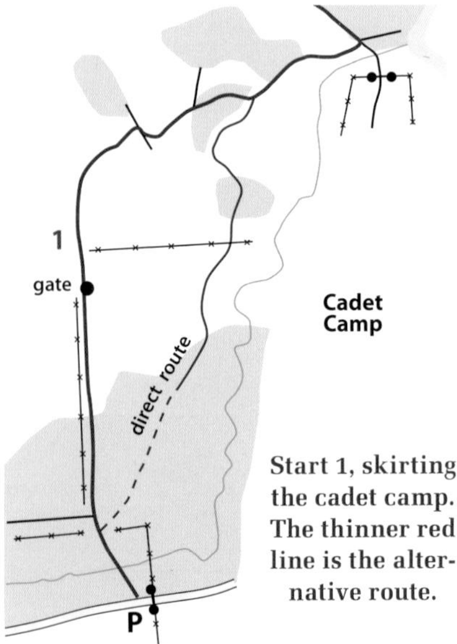

Start 1, skirting the cadet camp. The thinner red line is the alternative route.

On entering forest the trail improves. Cross a side creek close to the Waiparous, then walk open pine forest past a trailer with four flats into a meadow where you intersect an OHV track at 437887.

Sans trail, continue ahead through open forest to gain the Waiparous River banktop. Turn left and follow the bank. When opposite the Aura Creek confluence, wade the Waiparous.

Pick up a steep trail on the left bank of Aura Creek that soon moderates and climbs a sandy rib. Entering pine forest at flagging, the trail levels and it's an easy walk to the NE–SW cutline at 439900 where you pick up route 2 coming in from the left.

Cross the cutline onto the trail climbing hillside.

Route 2 via tote road 3.9 km

At marker 103 go straight on a dirt road (orange OHV signs) that parallels Waiparous Creek within sound of the Bumble Bee ice cream van doing the rounds of Waiparous Creek campground. At first it's all downhill. Intersect an OHV cutline at marker 99. Continue straight and dip steeply to cross Cow Lake's effluent where there used to be a cabin with a rusted Edwards Coffee can.

Next up is the flat, wet section downstream of willowy bogs, where generations of corduroy lie rotting, sinking in the muskeg. At one point where the road gets in a muddy groove, follow the trail to its left. It's a relief to find the track rising into dry pine forest once more. Wend left at a Y-junction and arrive at a T-junction with a NE–SW cutline at 435898. Turn left.

Where the cutline is on the rise, it is crossed by a trail at 439900. Right is route 1. Turn left up a trail climbing the hillside.

Sand Dunes loop 1.3 km

After the uphill, the trail descends a little and heads right to the bottom of the west-slope sand dunes. Walk up the right side of them to the ridgetop. Turn right and follow the trail that swings back left along the east side of the ridge to a big bowl from where steep chutes of sand splay down the hillside into the forest.

To return to the tote road, find the sandy track starting at 441903. At a split go left if heading for Horse Lake, right if returning to one or the other of the trailheads. In the latter case, climb over a hill to the intersecting trail at 439900.

GOING FARTHER

1A Horse Lake (Aura Lake)

Add 1.6 km one way
Extra height gain 24 m (80 ft.)

The area around the lake is home to bands of wild horses and coexisting wolf packs. To know more, read *Wild Horses, Wild Wolves*, by Maureen Enns.

Back on the cutline access road (still tote road) turn left and descend to a T-junction at Aura Creek, which was called Lunch Creek in Eau Claire's time. Don't cross. Keep left on another track that climbs into meadows. The track parallels the creek, falling, then rising to another junction. Keep left on a grassy track, then go straight at the next junction.

Walk through a large, flat, willowy, boggy meadow with Horse Lake somewhere in the middle of it. Where the track starts veering left for the trees, a faint trail heads off to the soggy west shore. Cross a creek downstream of the lake to the south and east shores, which are muddy and stamped with the distinctive hooves of the wildies. Look for fringed gentians in August.

Horse Lake, looking north to Camp Ridge.

2 MOCKINGBIRD LOOKOUT—map 2

Half-day, short-day hike
Unofficial fire road
Distance 5.6 km return
Height gain 354 m (1160 ft.)
High point 1902 m (6241 ft.)
Map 82 O/6 Lake Minnewanka

Access Hwy. 940 (Forestry Trunk Road) north of Hwy. 1A. Follow it through the hamlets of Benchlands and Waiparous to Richards Road junction and turn right. At 16.1 km north of the junction turn left (west) onto Waiparous Valley Road.

Drive past Camp Mockingbird to a junction 2.8 km in from the Hwy. Keep right here on the better road. In 1 km, just past marker 121, look for the fire road on the right at 342970. It is positively identified by a sign "Dangerous road closed to all vehicles with 4 or more wheels." Park here. NOTE that access roads, while easy to drive, have stretches of wood mats (boardwalk for vehicles) that require concentration.

An easy walk on fire road up Mockingbird Hill to a lookout where you are treated to a 360 degree panorama. Obviously this trail is very popular because of its short length and proximity to campgrounds and youth camps.

LOOKOUT HISTORY The present building, dating from 1973/4, replaced the old box-like structure that had stood on this spot for over 20 years. In turn the first Mockingbird Lookout superseded the one on nearby Black Rock Mountain that was abandoned in 1952. Its name came about during the survey for the first lookout in July of 1950? Must have been 1951, because the song playing on the transistor radio the guys had with them was *Mockin' Bird Hill.*

Walk up the fire road. Beyond the gate, you start winding through dense pine forest, intersecting and brushing against assorted cutlines, the rather boring nature of the walk relieved by sampling raspberries, blackcurrants and strawberries growing along the verge. On gaining the south ridge the road levels a little, following the ridgeline through a fence to a lush summit meadow with more paraphernalia than previously, including two masts, a solar panel, shed and helipad. This modest hilltop, far distant from the Front Ranges, is one panoramic viewpoint, the kind of place where you expect John Wayne to come riding through the meadow to a stirring score by John Williams.

Look southwest across Waiparous Creek to a solitary mountain closer in than the Front Ranges and about 600 m higher than Mockingbird. This is Black Rock Mountain, and the pimple on top is the old lookout, the objective of route #11. To its right, the rock obelisk of Devils Head is unmistakable and can be used as a reference point. So, going clockwise from Devils Head, pick out Castle Rock and the bare mountains around the head of the Red Deer River.

Closer in, the eyes travel over forest and cutblocks through which wind the Burnt Timber, Fallen Timber and Little Red Deer rivers. A little north of east the eye is stayed by large areas of open ground near the edge of the forest. These are the Greasy Plains, a name with a fine Tolkienesque ring to it. In reality, the Greasy Plains on Grease Creek were named by James Hector, who called them "Pré de graisse" after the black birch, or greasewood, that grows along the creekbed. They were a well-known feature of the Indian trail between Morley and the Red Deer River. Right of the plains and beyond diminishing waves of forested ridges with cutblocks—Salter, Keystone, Swanson and Wildcat—you can spot a few of Calgary's skyscrapers. Completing the 360 degree panorama is the view to the south of Moose Mountain, whose summit is occupied by the next lookout in the chain running south to the U.S. border.

The view west.

Above: Mockingbird Lookout.

Below: Walking the fire road.

Crossing the mouth of the north fork below The Prow and Waiparous Wall. Photo Andy Genereux from Ghost River Rock Climbs

3 WAIPAROUS CREEK—maps 2, 3

Backpack, bike 'n' hike
Official OHV trails, unofficial trails, river crossings
Distance to chasm 12.4 km; to valley head 17.9 km
Height gain to chasm 305 m (1000 ft.)
High point at chasm 1875 m (6150 ft.)
Map 82 O/6 Lake Minnewanka

Access Hwy. 940 m (Forestry Trunk Road) north of Hwy. 1A. Follow it through the hamlets of Benchlands and Waiparous to Richards Road junction and turn right. At 16.1 km north of the junction turn left (west) onto Waiparous Valley Road.

Drive past Camp Mockingbird to a junction 2.8 km in from the Hwy. In this section of road, stretches of wood mats (boardwalk for vehicles) require concentration.

NOTE Beyond this point, Waiparous Valley Road gets progressively worse. Most vehicles can get to Camp Chamisall entrance. After this you need high clearance and 4 wheel drive. If at any point you don't like the road, park and continue on foot or on bike. We notice that bikers can navigate the rough roads at twice the speed of a creeping vehicle!

In detail: At the 2.8 km junction keep leftish on a stony road that follows the north bank of Waiparous Creek, descending all the while, past marker 119 to the bridge over a side creek at 3.9 km. Now on river flats, you pass Camp Howard on your right at 4 km. Shortly after is an important 4-way junction.

There are three different ways to reach marker 123.

1. A sign points to Waiparous Valley Road to right. This is a new road, built since the last edition, that detours around Camp Chamisall. Unfortunately, it is extremely soft in places, with wall-to-wall mud puddles. Unless frozen, it requires an OHV.

2. The stony road to left is the original road, which the river has washed out near Camp Chamisall. This section is nip and tuck and we decided to back off rather than risk getting hung up. Your choice.

3. Ahead is a straight, stony cutline with a sign for Camp Chamisall. On both sides are "No Trespassing" signs (the camp is on your left). Puddles have a hard base, so no worries there. Where the cutline intersects the new road, turn left for the 3-way junction at marker 123.

Turn right and continue on hard, stony road, evident in the midst of minor roads twining about it, to marker 127 at an important OHV junction. Go straight. (Road to left crosses the Waiparous to Meadow Creek, Lesueur Creek and Lost Knife Creek.) Only a little farther on, at the foot of a definite uphill, turn left into a parking area at 316952. It's the end of the orange road as shown on the topo map.

Also accessible from #12 Ghost River to Waiparous Creek via Johnson Lakes.

The most accessible of the three Ghost Rivers has an exploration road, then 4×4 trail, then cutline that takes you easily into the head of the valley. Unfortunately, you'll be sharing a large part of the route with OHVers to the chasm, where most people call it a day. Don't let this put you off. The cliff scenery is superb and it's easy enough to get off the beaten track. Six fords can be problematical early in the season, particularly the first one at the Margaret Lake turnoff.

HISTORY NOTE The north fork of the Ghost River was named Waiparous Creek by James Hector on December 10, 1858. It translates roughly to Crow Indian Scalp,

---

To Margaret Lake turnoff 6.5 km

This section can be easily biked. Apart from the first uphill, the going is flat with occasional wall-to-wall puddles you can safely bike through without sinking up to your handlebars.

From the parking area return to the "road" and follow it up a deeply trenched hill. Traverse a side hill, then descend steeply to a side creek where you can wash off the mud. On the flats the road twines around the cutline. The scenery is the same whichever route you take: lodgepole pines. I prefer keeping right—whether road or cutline doesn't matter—all the way along to the end of the twining section. After this, follow the road, enjoying enticing views of Devils Head and to its right the square block of Castle Rock, which was shown as early as 1910 on sectional maps issued by the Department of the Interior showing timber belts. Its last official appearance was in 1930.

A cutline crossing the river is NOT the ongoing route. The junction lies another half kilometre on at marker 129.

To Ghost River turnoff 340 m

Turn left (ahead is #4 to Margaret Lake) and wade the Waiparous between riffles. The road continues and shortly intersects a major NE–SW cutline where route #12 to Johnson Creek and the Ghost River turns off to the left on an OHV trail. Go straight.

To the chasm 5.5 km

The road curves around a river bend, fading out temporarily where the stream from Castle Rock cirque enters the Waiparous. At crossing no. 2, the road is joined by a cutline access road coming in from the NE–SW cutline on your left. Now on the north bank, follow the road over a low, forested ridge to crossing no. 3 at the

Sunrise Wall in early morning. Photo Andy Genereux from Ghost River Rock Climbs

Approaching the canyon. Photo Robert Lampard

The chasm marks the usual end of a trip up the Waiparous.

confluence of the Waiparous with its spectacular north fork. Except at high water, it's possible to edge along the south bank between the last two fords. Watch for a cairn and survey marker en route.

The north fork is bounded on the west by The Prow, a 300-metre-high frontage for a remarkable line of cliffs extending halfway along the valley, and on the east side by the two summits of "Sheep Meadow" Mountain, which appear to have been bombarded by rocks hurled from a trebuchet.

The main valley is no less interesting. You wind past a popular camping spot by the side of a small waterfall, then, reversing the S-bend, travel below a cliff rivalling that of the north fork. By midday Sunrise Wall sends forth long shadows. On windy days, water seeping over the edge drifts in a fine spray across its black-streaked walls. See if you can spot the 130-metre-high Waiparous Tower.

Cross the creek for the fourth time and climb steeply over a side ridge below Pinto Wall to creek crossing no. 5, the final one before the chasm. Both crossings can be avoided by an unsuspected traverse along the south bank.

A gloomy stretch of road, often muddy from rills running off the hillside, ends at a viewpoint overlooking a free-falling waterfall across the valley. Zig down to the valley floor, cross a major side creek and arrive at a road junction.

Either take the road to the left, which wastes no time in climbing to get above the upcoming canyon, or continue along the riverbank to where the road ends at a campsite, then climb a well-trodden trail up the bank to a continuation of the road above and turn right.

The canyon lies 200 metres farther on at about 204954. Clearings in trees to the right indicate the entry point into meadows above the river's plunge into a chasm, a delightful spot that is usually the culmination of a trip up the Waiparous. The prominent mountain come into view ahead is Mt. Davidson, at 2941 m (9650 ft.).

GOING FARTHER

3A Upper Waiparous Creek

Distance 5.6 km from chasm
Extra height gain 259 m (850 ft.)
High point 2134 m (7000 ft.)

A more strenuous option.

Continue along the road to its end in about 1 km. Although it can't be seen from road's end, a cutline carries on to the very end of the valley along the north bank. To get to the start of it, descend the bank and wade the river, aiming for the left-hand bank of the side stream with the waterfall called Indian Scalp.

The cutline, which climbs high above the river (closeted once more in a canyon), is serpentine in nature, with the annoying habit of traversing steep sidehills on the slant and additionally is clogged with windfall requiring lengthy detours at many points. Two deeply cut side streams may be difficult to cross during their tumultuous headlong rush to join the Waiparous at runoff. Eventually the cutline makes a gradual descent to flat meadows at the valley head under Mt. Davidson.

MOUNTAIN NOTE Mount Davidson was named back in 1935 after James Wheeler Davidson (1872–1933), a journalist, diplomat, businessman and explorer. (He was a member of the Peary expedition to see if Greenland was an island, and was with Admiral Byrd on his second attempt to reach the North Pole.) As a Calgarian he established 23 Rotary clubs "from Banff to Bangkok," developed the Alberta Motor Association, was president of Crown Lumber and a founder of the Calgary Philharmonic. To know more about Davidson's remarkable life read *The Life and Times of James and Lillian Davidson in Rotary International*, by fellow Rotarian and climber Robert Lampard.

The mountain had its first documented ascent on August 2, 2003, by 24 Rotarians, friends and family members who held a Rotary meeting on the summit, drank champagne, buried a time capsule and logbook and sang *O Canada*. Bob, who had climbed the mountain previously with his son Geoffrey, was so determined to get this diverse group of non-climbers to the summit, he organized a helicopter to ferry people about. However, everyone made the summit under their own steam from the saddle to the southeast.

Mount Davidson from the valley above the chasm.

4 MARGARET LAKE—maps 2, 3

Day hike, bike 'n' hike
Official OHV trails
Distance 4.5 km return from marker 129; 17.5 km return from parking area
Height gain 162 m (530 ft.) return
High point 1716 m (5630 ft.)
Map 82 O/6 Lake Minnewanka

Access Via #3 Waiparous Creek trail at 6.5 km. Marker 129 denotes the Margaret Lake turnoff.

This gem of a lake has the misfortune to lie smack in the middle of OHV land. Expect a roller-coaster walk on cutlines for the most part, with a bit of flat trail in the middle. Biking is strongly recommended to the Margaret Lake turnoff, after which the hills are way too towering.

NAMING NOTE "Margaret" was Margaret Hill, the wife of Ray Hill, one time chief ranger at the Canmore Ranger Station.

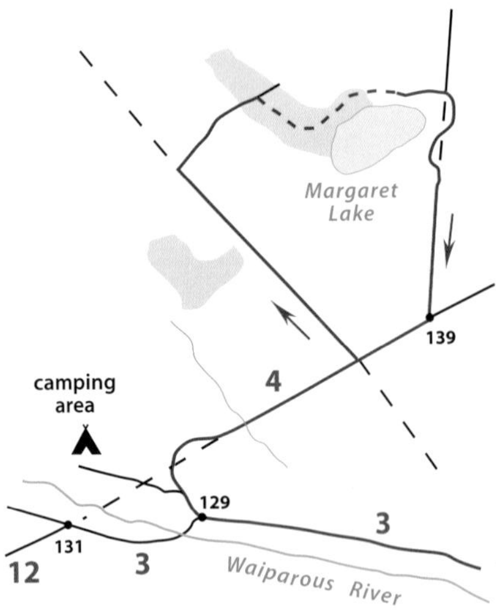

Margaret Lake from Waiparous Creek trail

To the loop 1 km

Follow #3 Waiparous Creek trail to the junction above the first ford at marker 129.

Continue ahead on the Margaret Lake OHV trail. It shortly curves right (ahead is a camping area), crosses a NE–SW cutline and climbs a steep bank. At the top it joins the NE–SW cutline and turns left. Dip to cross a small creek, then climb one of those towering hills to a T-junction with a NW–SE cutline at ~262954.

The loop 2.5 km

Turn left on the NW–SE cutline. A slight uphill precedes a roller-coaster ride down the other side that even dirt bikers have trouble with. At the second dip, look for flagging on the right side. This indicates the flagged trail to Margaret Lake.

On reaching a meadow, turn right to gain the southwest corner of the lake. Not too scenic, you may think. But follow the shoreline trail around to the left to gain the north shore where glades slope down to the water at sunbathing angle. Now look back. The lake is all blue and glittery in the afternoon sun, all the most spectacular peaks of The Ghost lined up as backdrop. It's a grand sight. Almost as amazing is the sight of OHVers walking along the shore in appreciation of the scenery.

I'm glad to report a huge improvement at the east end where most OHVers access the lake. Nowadays a good trail crosses a bridge over the south fork of Hidden Creek and heads through a gate in a fence to a parking lot!

Back on the Margaret Lake OHV trail at a NNE–SSW cutline, follow a detour road around to the right, back to the cutline. Then climb to the T-junction with Mockingbird OHV trail to left (the NE–SW cutline) at marker 139.

Turn right. A down-up brings you back to the start of the loop at the T-junction with the NW–SE cutline. Go straight and return the same way you came.

Margaret Lake, looking west to Devils Head and Castle Rock.

The NW–SE cutline road, typical of OHV roads in the area.

5 LESUEUR CREEK—map 1

Half-day, short-day hike
Unofficial trail, possible creek crossing
Distance 5.7 km
Height gain 122 m (400 ft.)
High point 1466 m (4810 ft.)
Maps 82 O/7 Wildcat Hills, 82 O/6 Lake Minnewanka

Access Hwy. 940 (Forestry Trunk Road) north of Hwy. 1A. Drive 25.4 km to Richards Road junction (sign). Keep right, then in 150 m take the first left (west) onto a gravel road signed "Trapper's Hill Lodges 8." This is the TransAlta Road built by TransAlta Utilities into the forest reserve. It can be further identified by a metal gate and a kiosk. NOTE This road is good to the bridge over Lesueur Creek (main east access), but it's in poor shape after that, with waves of potholes to the west access.

There are 3 accesses off this road to lower Lesueur Creek.

Main east access The TransAlta Road at 2.65 km. Park on the right side of the road between the texas gate and the bridge over Lesueur Creek. Further identified by a kiosk and a "No OHVs" sign.

Well road access The TransAlta Road at 6 km. Turn right onto an old well road that curves to the right of a line heater and ends on the banktop at an intersecting cutline and sign riddled with bullet holes. Park here.

West access The TransAlta Road at 6.4 km. Either park at the junction with a dirt road on the right side of the road, or turn right and drive 1.2 km to Lesueur Creek crossing.

The Lesueur Creek trail connects Bar C lands to the headwaters of Meadow Creek at Bagley's cabin. It falls naturally into three sections. The middle section is a dirt road so messed up by OHVs that it's not worth doing (after rain the dirt turns to mud the consistency of peanut butter), and the upper section is a nebulous horse trail through "the great bog"—both of which were described in the 3rd edition. Most hikers nowadays just do lower Lesueur Creek, an easy and beautiful traverse of open hillside and verdant valley bottom touted by ESRD as the trail to do next after Black Rock Mountain.

The traverse below the ridge.

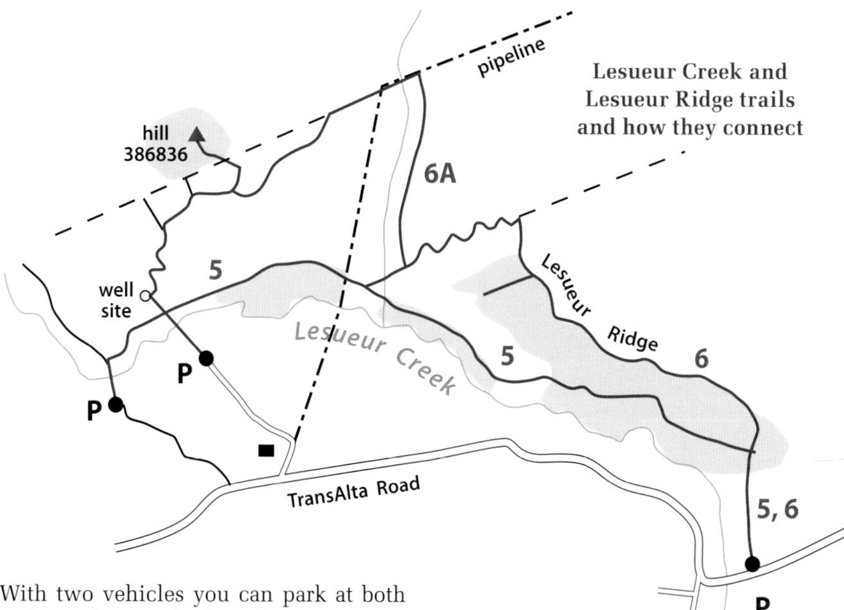

With two vehicles you can park at both ends. With one vehicle at the main access consider making a loop with #6 Lesueur Ridge.

NAMING NOTE Bar C was formerly the Le Sueur Ranch. The Le Sueurs hailed from the Isle of Guernsey, and possibly their only claim to fame is that this is where Ralph Connor wrote *Black Rock: A Tale of the Selkirks* in 1896, the first of a hugely successful string of books mixing adventure and religion. The outfitters call it Beaver Creek.

EAST TO WEST

The traverse to access 2, 5.1 km

Heading north, follow a trail along the fenceline past logged areas and up a short hill to a T-junction at 620 m. Turn left. (Ahead is #6 Lesueur Ridge.)

Some distance above Lesueur Creek, the trail traverses the grassy, south-facing slopes of Lesueur Ridge, winding in and out of its folds through patches of aspens and the odd stand of Douglas fir.

At a Y-junction, keep straight. (The lesser-used trail to left criss-crosses the creek back to the road bridge.) Shortly your own trail descends to the valley bottom. En route, Devils Head and other mountains of the Ghost come into view ahead.

After crossing a drift fence, start keeping a beaver watch, the trail passing to left and right of beaver ponds and dams of all ages. Cross a cutline and its access road at 392829 and then a pipeline right-of-way constructed in 2004. (The cutline access road is the route off/on #6, Lesueur Ridge.)

At the next lot of ponds, a sign indicating no motorbikes occurs at a 4-way with an old well road (track) at 382828. If headed for access 2, turn left and follow the track, soon to be trail, across Lesueur Creek between ponds and up the bank to the parking area.

To access 3, 610 m

At the 4-way continue ahead on the trail, passing through an area of beaver devastation. Go either way at a split and arrive at a T-junction with a dirt OHV road at 377825.

Turn left and cross Lesueur Creek, perhaps finding logs downstream of the ford. If your vehicle isn't waiting here, walk another 1.2 km along the road to the TransAlta Road.

6 LESUEUR RIDGE—map 1

The trail along the ridgeline.

Short-day hike
Unofficial trails, minor creek crossings
Distance 4.9 km to Lesueur Creek
Height gain E–W 229 m (750 ft.)
Height loss E–W 146 m (480 ft.)
High point 1630 m (5200 ft.)
Maps 82 O/7 Wildcat Hills, 82 O/6 Lake Minnewanka

Access Via #5 Lesueur Creek starting from the main east access.

This is the grassy ridge above Lesueur Creek, which can be combined with Lesueur Creek to make an 8.7 km loop back to the trailhead. A longer version adds in the hill at 385838, which gives you a panoramic view to the west. I recommend travelling east to west for views.

FROM MAIN ACCESS

To NE–SW cutline 3.5 km

From the main access, follow #5 Lesueur Creek trail north along the fenceline and up a short hill to a T-junction. Continue uphill. (Lesueur Creek trail turns left.)

The trail soon turns left into a grove of aspens offering a brief respite before tackling the long, rolling climb along the ridge crest between forest on the right and grassy slopes sweeping down to Lesueur Creek on the left. Rocky outcrops make fine seats from which to look south over forest and cutblocks to Kangienos Lake, and to follow the winding of the Ghost rivers and the TransAlta Road as they head west to the mountains. Watch for a side trail winging out left to a promontory—a really good viewpoint for the ridge you have walked thus far. Devils Head now comes into sight, and down below you can spot the gas well road crossing the valley.

Shortly the trail turns away from the escarpment and into the forest. It climbs a little to reach what is probably the high point of this trip, then a few minutes later intersects a NE–SW cutline.

To hill turnoff 1.3 km

Turn left down the cutline, which is your route to Lesueur Creek. The descent is much nicer than you might think. To avoid steep hills, use three snippets of grassy cutline access road to the right. The fourth one crosses a wee side creek. Back on cutline, climb over a small ridge. On the other side is a 4-way junction at 394830. Turn left on the cutline access road. (Straight is the descending cutline; to right, the trail to #6A.)

To Lesueur Creek 120 m
The access road curves back right to join the cutline at a second side creek crossing. On the far side, again use the cutline access road to left, which intersects Lesueur Creek trail at 392829.

To return to main access, turn left on the valley trail and keep going.

GOING FARTHER

6A Hill 385838

Distance 4.4 km to Lesueur Creek
Added height gain E–W 186 m (610 ft.)
High point 1649 m (5410 ft.)

This add-on crosses the hill west of Lesueur Ridge on pleasant old cutline access roads. Combined with Lesueur Ridge and creek, it makes a loop of 14.2 km back to the trailhead.

To summit 2.8 km
At the 4-way 394830, turn right following a good trail along the banktop of the second side creek in the pines. On reaching a pipeline right-of-way turn left onto the right-of-way and cross the side creek. Where the right-of-way wends left, keep straight on a NE–SW cutline aiming for the hill, here presenting its forested side.

At the bottom of the rise, turn left onto the cutline access road that climbs above meadows on the hill's south slope. High up, reach a T-junction with another access road at 386835.

Detour to the summit by turning right. The track curves round to the left, briefly joins the NE–SW cutline, then cuts rightward to the summit meadow. To the west is a panoramic view of the Front Ranges, the Moose Mountain massif from this vantage point showing itself as an isolated island of summits.

To Lesueur Creek 1.6 km
Return to the last junction at 386835 and keep straight. A very pleasant track descends through aspen forest to a T-junction. Turn left. Shortly, cross a spring on corduroy to another junction. Turn left, travelling through open pine forest and then aspens to a second corduroy bridge over a side creek. Climb a short hill into a well site meadow. If doing this trip in reverse, look for flagging at the start of the track in the trees.

Cross the meadow in the downhill direction. An access road materializes and descends to Lesueur Creek Valley. Intersect the valley trail at 382828.

Turn left and follow the trail back to the main east trailhead.

#6A Descent through aspen forest.

7 SPRINGS OF THE GHOST trail—maps 1, 2

Short-day hike
Unofficial trail, minor creek crossings
Distance 4 km to end of loop;
6.3 km total return distance
Height gain E–W 24 m (80 ft.)
Height loss E–W ~61 m (~200 ft.)
High point 1469 m (4820 ft.)
Map 82 O/6 Lake Minnewanka

Access Hwy. 940 (Forestry Trunk Road) north of Hwy. 1A. Drive 25.4 km to Richards Road junction (sign). Keep right, then in 150 m take the first left (west) onto a gravel road signed "Trapper's Hill Lodges 8." This is the TransAlta Road built by TransAlta Utilities into the forest reserve. It can be further identified by a metal gate and a kiosk. NOTE This road is good to the bridge over Lesueur Creek, but it's in poor shape after that, with waves of potholes.

In more detail: Turn right up the hill after the bridge over Lesueur Creek. In 7.2 km from the gate, at an intersecting cutline, turn left and drive to the top of the steep slope down to the Ghost River Valley. Park.

Also accessible from Trapper's Hill Lodges and from #8 The Lower Ghost.

The trail just west of Trapper's Hill junction.

An easily followed forest trail that wanders up and down the north bank of the Ghost River, crossing many year-round springs. There is the option of carrying on to the valley bottom and of making loops with trails used by #8 The Lower Ghost.

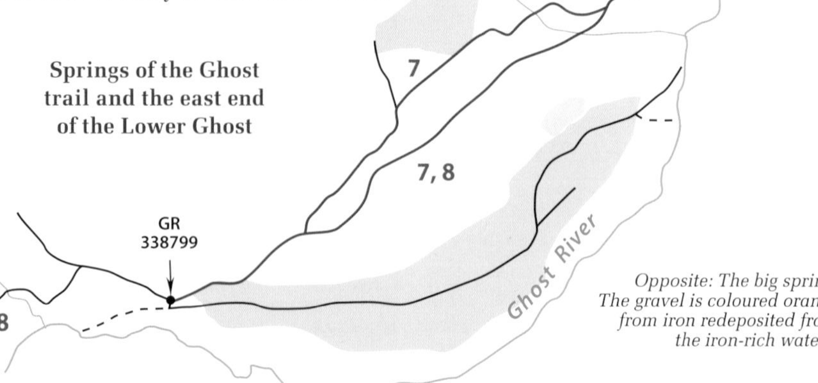

Springs of the Ghost trail and the east end of the Lower Ghost

Opposite: The big spring. The gravel is coloured orange from iron redeposited from the iron-rich waters.

To Trapper's Hill junctions 890 m
Walk west along the top of the steep slope and into the trees. At a split keep left, then left down a hill. Cross spring no. 1. Two undulations lead to important T-junction 372814. Keep right on a horse trail. (Horse trail to left descends to the Ghost River and is #8 The Lower Ghost.)

At the next junction a few metres on keep straight. (Trail to right makes a beeline for the gate of Trapper's Hill Lodges.)

To the biggest spring 1.4 km
A pleasant walk through aspen ends with a climb across an open slope, followed by a steep descent to cross spring no. 2, which flows in multiple channels down the hillside. In only a couple of metres turn left off the main trail at 368813 onto a narrow ditch-like trail that avoids an exceedingly steep drop. Where you join the main trail turn left and cross spring no 3.

Climb to a high point with spring trickle, then turn sharp left down a hill, near the bottom veering right to cross a dry gully. The trail splits just before the crossing. Use the better, right-hand trail and climb to a Y-junction. Go left, then keep right. At the following T-junction 364810 go straight across spring no. 4. (Trail to left is #8 the Lower Ghost.) A stretch through pines brings you to the east bank of spring no. 5 at 362808.

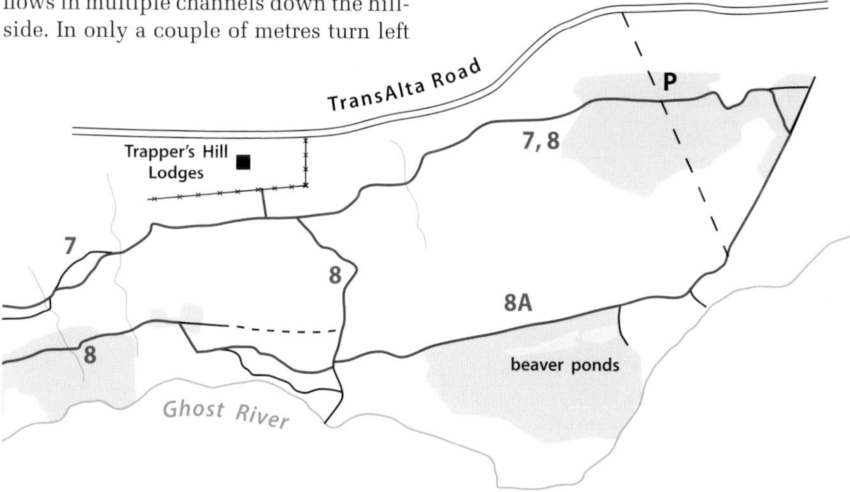

The loop 1.7 km
The biggest spring of them all rushes down a wide swath of gravel sprinkled with tufa. Turn right on a trail that climbs up the right side of the creek a way and then crosses it and meanders through aspens below a steep grass slope. At a T-junction turn left and descend slightly to T-junction 355804. Turn left. (The trail ahead leads to the flats of the Ghost River Valley. See #8.)

A walk through pine forest takes you back to the big spring. Cross the creek to 362808 and return the same way you came. Alternatively, try one of the routes used by #8.

8 LOWER GHOST—maps 2, 1

The downhill between cutlines no. 2 and 3 gives a great view across the valley to End Mountain.

Day hike
Unofficial trails, possible river crossing
Distance 12.7 km
Height gain N–S 76 m (250 ft.)
Height loss N–S 192 m (630 ft.)
High point 1594 m (5230 ft.)
Map 82 O/6 Lake Minnewanka

Access Hwy. 940 (Forestry Trunk Road) north of Hwy. 1A. Drive 25.4 km to Richards Road junction (sign). Keep right, then in 150 m take the first left (west) onto a gravel road signed "Trapper's Hill Lodges 8." This is the TransAlta Road built by TransAlta Utilities into the forest reserve. It can be further identified by a metal gate and a kiosk.

READ BEFORE YOU GO This road is good to the bridge over Lesueur Creek, then in poor shape with waves of potholes all the way to the top of the big hill. Overall, expect a slow drive.

West access Drive the road for 16.6 km to the top of the big hill down to the Ghost River. En route turn right up the hill after the bridge over Lesueur Creek; keep straight at red marker 15 (Enviros access road to right) and straight where the access road to a Sutton Energy well turns left. For the final few kilometres, you drive through cutblocks. Come to the top of the big hill down to the Ghost River. Turn right into an unsigned parking area.

East access Drive the road for 7.2 km to an intersecting cutline. Turn left and drive to the top of the steep slope down to the Ghost River valley. Park.

Also accessible from #20 Lower South Ghost and from #7 Springs of the Ghost.

"The Lower Ghost" refers to the Ghost River Valley between the top of the big hill on the TransAlta Road and the South Ghost confluence. While it's possible to hike the entire valley on a stony track that follows the middle of river flats, there's no reason to do so when there are soft sandy trails along the north bank that are much more interesting. At the east end there is a choice of routes back to access 2, and it's here where you might run into guided horse trips from Trapper's Hill Lodges. To sort out the complexity of trails in this area see the sketch map for #7 on pages 34/35.

To do the whole trail you need vehicles at both ends. Conversely, just hike the western section to the first or second cutline, or the eastern section in combination with Springs of the Ghost trail.

I find the lower Ghost especially enjoyable in spring when the grass is greening on the open slopes, the sand is dried out and fit for scuffing, and yet to the west the mountains are still covered in snow.

RIVER NOTE The Ghost River surfaces somewhere around the bend near the drift fence (most of it having been siphoned off to the Minnewanka reservoir). However, the actual place varies from month to month. For hikers who don't want to get their feet wet, a non-paddling detour is available at a small cost.

TRAIL NOTE Dirt bike riders are still riding the trails and since I last walked the route may have made even more trails I am unaware of. To date they have done a thorough job of scarring every available ridge and hillside.

WEST TO EAST

West access to cutline no. 2, 3.1 km

From the parking area, it's easier to walk down the big hill on the TransAlta Road to where a trail intersects it, then turn left.

Very shortly, come to the banktop above the Ghost River. A soft, sandy trail links big sandy areas with views across the valley to Devils Gap. To your left is a vast 2008 cutblock that is finally greening up. Just don't try walking in it.

Cross NE–SW cutline no. 1.

The next section, again flirting with the edge of the cutblock, is slightly uphill above grassy banks with limber pines. Accompanying you to the west are the cliffs of Orient Point. Steeper climbs lead to a T- junction. Turn left. (To right, a moderate trail winds round no. 2 cutline to the Ghost River Valley bottom.) Your trail climbs, turns right and crosses NE–SW cutline no. 2 at 311816 on a downhill.

Sandy trail between the start and cutline no. 1.

To cutline no. 3, ~2.3 km

Continue down, then climb a steep, stony hill, at the top passing through a gap to the left of a big open hill. Descend grassy slopes of "the big hill" that give a fabulous view of the valley and End Mountain. Ahead of you is the knoll with the conglomerate cliff at its base.

Another steep uphill (look back for view of the big hill) leads into an undulating section of steep little hills. Keep right at splits. A sandy chute deposits you in a meadow. Climb out of this to a gap between the knoll and a grassy slope to left. A long, easy descent with views brings you to NE–SW cutline no. 3.

To the narrows 2.6 km

Cross cutline no. 3, which is staggered—a steep hill down right, then a hill down left. Immediately after, your trail follows a small ridge, then heads off left slightly downhill to a T-junction. Keep left. After passing two trails climbing the hillside to your left, keep left at a second T-junction.

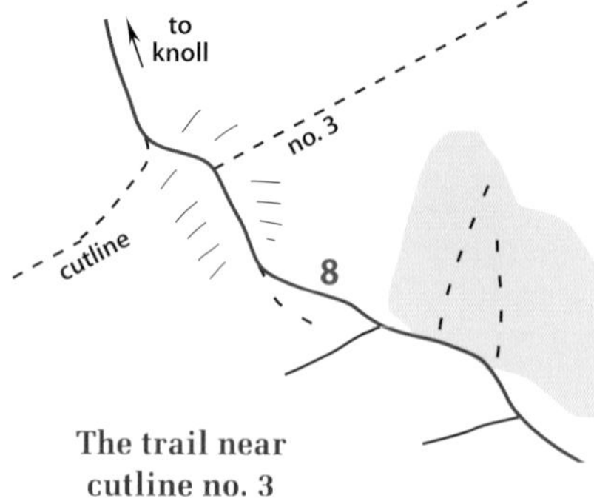

The trail near cutline no. 3

(Both trails to right descend to the valley bottom.) See the sketch map above.

From the junction a gradual climb leads into a lovely traverse of open hillside with limber pines. Below you is a rock tower and a line of crags. To left, steep grassy slopes are scarred with dirt bike tracks. Not far over the top lies a Sutton Energy well that can be driven to from the TransAlta Road but offers no good connector trail into this section of valley.

In this way you turn the big bend, changing direction from southeast to northeast. The mountains have been left far behind. Ahead are the narrows. Start a gradual descent to valley bottom above springs and sand pockets. (Trails heading down the bank are horse trails.)

Arriving in trees, where the trail splinters, keep right 'twixt trees and a stony river channel. Back in trees, intersect a NW–SE cutline. Out on the flat, cross the stony channel, which usually holds a little water in pockets. A few metres ahead, at 347801, is the broken-down drift fence gate at the so-called narrows and the convergence with the valley's stony track.

To 353803, 790 m both ways

Waypoint 353803 is your next objective—the place on the left (northeast) bank where you can pick up a good trail.

A beautiful section of trail between cutline no. 3 and the narrows.

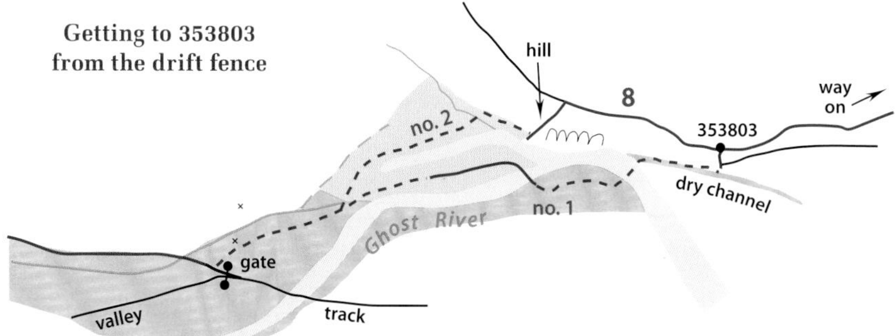

You are probably thinking, "Why not just continue ahead on the valley track?" As mentioned, this is where the water rises and with every ford going east the river deepens and quickens. Like Richard III you'd soon be calling for a horse.

There are two ways of getting there from the drift fence:

1. The direct route takes in two river crossings, the water at this point usually just above boot level. Before you get to the gate, go leftish through a gap in the fence and head for where the stony channel you just crossed reaches the river. Recross the channel. Then follow the piece of land between the river and a narrow channel with water to its left. You should find an old track. At the end of the land where the channel on the left flows into the Ghost below crags, wade the river.

When past the crags and opposite a dry, stony channel, recross to the east bank. Follow the channel, looking for a narrow, sandy trail to left that leads in a minute or two to a T-junction below a bank. Climb the bank to T-junction 353803 and turn right. (Trail to right below the bank appears very promising as a way on, but ultimately it and its offshoots lead back to the river.)

2. While there are no river crossings, there is a steep little hill to climb. Before you get to the gate, go leftish through a gap in the fence and head for where the stony channel you just crossed reaches the river. Recross the channel. Walk the LEFT side of a narrow channel starting up that has water in it. On reaching the northeast bank, jump a wee creek emanating from beaver ponds, then turn right, following a strip of grass below a steep bank past an old beaver dam. Just before crags halt progress, climb a shaley trail straight up the bank to a T-junction with a good trail. Turn right (trail to left climbs above a side valley) and descend to junction 353803. Go straight.

To horse trail junction 2.6 km

Follow the trail along the banktop, keeping left. It soon heads inland into the trees. At T-junction 355804 turn right. (Trail ahead is part of the loop at the end of Springs of the Ghost trail.)

Walk though pine and aspen forest to mineral spring no. 5, cross, and pick up the trail on the far side. Continue through pines and cross spring no 4. Immediately after, turn right at 364810.

Descend alongside the spring to a T-junction just above the river and turn left. After crossing a small gully the trail turns sharp left uphill, then sharp right into a traverse of aspen meadow hillside. Cross spring no. 3 and the three channels of spring no. 2. A stint through pines brings you to an indistinct junction at 370812 in a small clearing.

The trail ahead may look better, but it fades badly. I prefer to turn right. Just beyond a bit of deadfall a good trail develops and heads for the bank of the Ghost River. Go either way at the muddy bit. Then stay on the banktop. Reach the horse trail between Trapper's Hill Lodges and the Ghost River at staggered 4-way 373811. Turn left.

NOTE It's worth making a side trip down to the river at the horse crossing place just to inspect the deep, swift-flowing water.

To east access 1.3 km

Keep straight. (Trail to right is OPTIONAL RETURN Beaver Ponds trail.)

Continue straight into a bit of a meadow from where the horse trail winds and climbs to junction 372814 not far below Trapper's Hill Lodges. Turn right onto what is also Springs of the Ghost trail.

The trail undulates, crosses spring no. 1 then climbs toward the TransAlta Road. Just before reaching it, take the first right and keep right, emerging from trees onto the top of the steep slope plunging down to the Ghost River. Walk along the edge to your parked vehicle.

OPTIONAL RETURN

8A Beaver Ponds trail

Distance 1.5 km

At staggered T-junction 373811 turn left, then right. A nice flat trail returns to the banktop above beaver ponds set in a wet meadow dotted with scraggly-looking spruce. (The river is looping around the other side of the valley at this point.) After a dip, note a trail heading right, down the bank. This is #20 Lower South Ghost.

Shortly, come to a cutline access road arisen out of the river at a fast-flowing bend. Go straight, following the road around to the left. Pass below a NNW–SSE cutline seen zooming up an excessively steep hill—even for cutlines—to east access. Continue along the road, which soon enough turns left and climbs the slope a little less steeply. Thankfully, just below the top, escape left on a traversing trail.

On reaching the top, turn left and follow a track past the top of the cutline to East access.

#8A Beaver ponds below the trail.

9 INDIAN SPRINGS LOOP—map 2

The meadows of upper Meadow Creek, looking toward Phantom Crag and the Anti-Ghost.

Day hike, bike 'n' hike
Unofficial trail
Distance of loop 10.1 km return
Height gain 60 m (50 ft.) to cabin
Height loss 34 m (110 ft.)
High point 1609 m (5280 ft.)
Map 82 O/6 Lake Minnewanka

Main access Hwy. 940 (Forestry Trunk Road) north of Hwy. 1A. Drive 25.4 km to Richards Road junction (sign). Keep right, then in 150 m take the first left (west) onto a gravel road signed "Trapper's Hill Lodges 8." This is the TransAlta Road built by TransAlta Utilities into the forest reserve. It can be further identified by a metal gate and a kiosk.

READ BEFORE YOU GO This road is good to the bridge over Lesueur Creek, then in poor shape with waves of potholes all the way to the top of the big hill. Overall, expect a slow drive.

In detail: Drive the road for 16.6 km to the top of the big hill down to the Ghost River. En route turn right up the hill after the first bridge; keep straight at red marker 15 (Enviros access road to right) and straight where a Sutton Energy well access road turns off to the left. For the final few km you drive through cutblocks. Come to the top of the big hill down to the Ghost River. Turn right into an unsigned parking area.

CAR CAMPING The short-lived road beyond the parking area is a popular camping area. You can also drive up the start of Indian Springs trail (a stony track) to camping areas on the left side and at the Y-junction.

East access Follow the TransAlta Road for 12.3 km to red marker 15. Turn right here onto the Enviros access road which can be driven by the public for 2.7 km. A little way in, keep right and through a forested gap in Enviros Ridge. Cross a fence with double gate at a cutline and descend to a meadow. Keep left at the first T-junction once signed with marker 19. (OHV track to right leads to marker 17 at a camping area near Lesueur Creek.) A few metres on is another T-junction where you park ~339853. The better road to left accesses Enviros Wilderness School and the lake. The "road" to right continues to Meadow Creek Cabins but is off limits to private vehicles. Walk or bike 920 m to where you can pick up the loop at intersecting NE–SW cutline 339861.

Also accessible from #10A Anti-Ghost traverse.

This trail (old track) runs between the Ghost River Road at the top of the big hill and upper Meadow Creek. The walking is flat, easy and pleasant if the meadow and pine country of the foothills appeals. The middle section in the trees is slow to dry out after snow melt.

This trail serves as a base for trails onto the Anti-Ghost. See the sketch map on page 45. At the far end or from East access you can connect up with old roads and horse trails leading to Enviros Lake and Lesueur Creek.

HISTORY At the end of the trail is a forestry cabin and Meadow Creek Cabins built by Brewster Adventures for clients on overnight horse riding trips. The old cabin near the pond is Bagley's Cabin built in 1926 by the legendary Bill Bagley and Jim and Pat Brewster as the focal point of Devils Head Ranch that was used for pasturing horses during the winter.

FROM MAIN ACCESS

To Indian Springs 1.6 km

Walk back along the road a few metres to where a stoney track turns off to the left (north). Follow it uphill. At a Y-junction in a sandy meadow keep right. (Track to left connects with Anti-Ghost traverse and West Side trail.) Cross a cutline, then keep straight. Continue through open pine forest and meadows offering spectacular views behind you of Devils Gap and Orient Point. Next up is a Y-junction at 303845 where the track veers right. (Trail to left connects with Anti-Ghost traverse. In spring, open hillsides above the trail are crammed with yellow lady slipper orchids.)

Only a short distance on, arrive at Indian Springs on the left. A rickety boardwalk leads to a flume that conveys water from a mossy bank. Indian Springs is not much to look at but it's guaranteed-fresh water. On the right side of the track hereabouts are camping sites.

To loop junction 670 m

In denser trees enter the narrows and cross a drift fence. The next stretch over the watershed into Meadow Creek country is flat, boring and fast. At T-junction 307853 turn right onto a less defined track. (Indian Springs track ahead is your return loop.)

To Meadow Creek cabins 4.1 km

The new track meanders along through one or two glades, then runs parallel to the drift fence to a T-junction. Keep right. (Trail to left leads back to Indian Springs track just east of the Anti-Ghost traverse T-junction.)

Continue heading northeast through open pine forest and one big meadow, eventually joining a NE–SW cutline where you keep left. Cross a NW–SE cutline shortly, before hitting the "road" at 339861 between Enviros and Meadow Creek Cabins that we used to drive. NOTE To reach East access, walk right for 920 m.

Turn left and walk the "road" alongside a fence to Y-junction 336866. Turn left. (Track to right goes through a gate, across a slough and through another gate to the cabins. Kevin tells me the "moat" is intentional, meant to deter straying OHVers from entering private property or risk getting lassoed. It's okay for us hikers, though, to go and take a closer look at historic Bagley's Cabin.)

Indian Springs.

Return to loop junction 1.5 km
On the way back now, cross a beautiful flat meadow that will have horses if you're lucky, and a vista to the west of ghostly mountains: Orient Point to the left, the peculiar outline of Phantom Crag straight ahead and Anti-Ghost Ridge backdropped by Black Rock Mountain to your right.

Just after passing to the left of ponds, you enter trees where the track divides. Keep right on a stony track (track to left joins the loop near the drift fence) and descend back into meadows. At T-junction 324863 keep straight. (Trail to right is #10A Anti-Ghost traverse.)

Shortly enter trees, the track rounding the bottom of a forested hill into denser forest. On reaching junction 307853 again, go straight and return the same way to the trailhead.

SIDE TRIP

9A Enviros Lake

Distance 650 m from East access

At East access, turn left and walk the access road through a gate to Enviros Wilderness School. Relying on their good will, you can walk through leased land to the lake, a pale beauty of clearest lime green and azure rippling over a marl bottom.

From the loop you can access the other shores of the lake, but the going is not pleasant, with much bog to tramp through, and of course you don't get the mountain view.

Below top: historic Bagley's Cabin.

Below bottom: Enviros Lake backdropped by the Anti-Ghost, Devils Head and Black Rock Mountain.

10 ANTI-GHOST TRAILS—map 2

Half-day, day hikes
Unofficial trails with cairns, blazes
High point 2240 m (7350 ft.)
Map 82 O/6 Lake Minnewanka

Main access Hwy. 940 (Forestry Trunk Road) north of Hwy. 1A. Drive 25.4 km to Richards Road junction (sign). Keep right, then in 150 m take the first left (west) onto a gravel road signed "Trapper's Hill Lodges 8." This is the TransAlta Road built by TransAlta Utilities into the forest reserve. It can be further identified by a metal gate and a kiosk.

READ BEFORE YOU GO This road is good to the bridge over Lesueur Creek, then in poor shape with waves of potholes all the way to the top of the big hill. Overall, expect a slow drive.

In detail: Drive the road for 16.6 km to the top of the big hill down to the Ghost River. En route turn right up the hill after the first bridge; keep straight at red marker 15 (Enviros access road to right) and straight where a Sutton Energy well access road turns left. For the final few km you drive through cutblocks. Come to the top of the big hill down to the Ghost River. Turn right into an unsigned parking area.

Also accessible from #9 Indian Springs loop, #11 Black Rock Mountain, #13 Black Rock Meadows.

There is much more to Black Rock Mountain than the trail to the summit. There is its southeast ridge, called the Anti-Ghost by rock climbers, which has a slew of interconnecting trails. A few of the trails are cutline access and exploration roads; most are trails made by climbers, horse riders and dirt bike bikers who have since been turfed out of the Don Getty Wildland Park.

These trails are particularly handy in spring. Not only do they dry out fast, but walking them means you don't have to drive down the big hill or cross the Ghost River—a big consideration. Carry water.

By far the most fascinating aspect of the area is its crazy terrain, which the topo map doesn't even hint at. Not just a straightforward ridge, it harbours hidden passes, pinnacles and boulder gardens, smooth grassy benches in the midst of crags and scree fields, rifts in the ground that start suddenly and go nowhere, and a downward headed gully that runs uphill.

Anti-Ghost from Enviros Ridge. Anti-Ghost crag at centre, the pointy lower nub at right. Anti-Ghost traverse crosses the lower bench. Anti-Ghost Ridge diagonals from lower right to upper left across the face. Motocross Hill is plainly visible as a white scar.

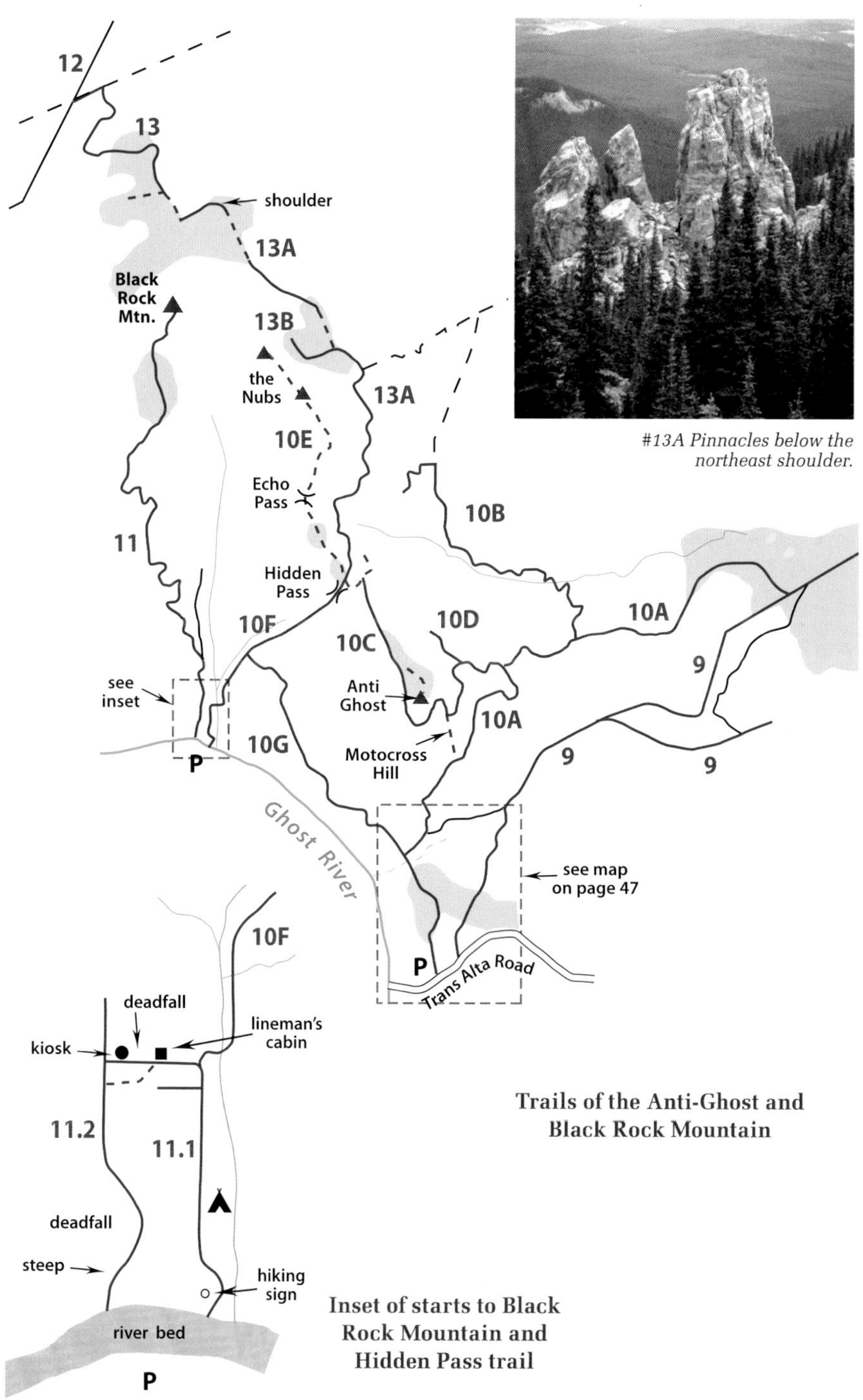

#13A Pinnacles below the northeast shoulder.

Trails of the Anti-Ghost and Black Rock Mountain

Inset of starts to Black Rock Mountain and Hidden Pass trail

The higher bench with dead tree. View over the Ghost River Valley to Orient Point and End Mtn.

10A Anti-Ghost traverse

Half-day, day hike
Unofficial trails
Distance 6.2 km
Height gain SW–NE 206 m (676 ft.)
Height loss SW–NE 220 m (722 ft.)
High point 1760 m (5774 ft.)
Map 82 O/6 Lake Minnewanka

From Main access
Also accessible Via #9 Indian Springs loop in Meadow Creek at 324863.

The trail undulates across the southeast-facing slope of the Anti-Ghost between the Ghost River and Meadow Creek. It's a higher version of Indian Springs loop and can be combined with it. Expect some steep hills getting on and off benches, but also good views in compensation. Used by climbers to access the Anti-Ghost and by hikers to make a loop with Anti-Ghost Ridge, Hidden Pass and West Side trails.

To West Side trail 1.1 km

The easy section is via an undulating track that is difficult to drive on account of sand. Walkers don't bother trying and use horse trail shortcuts that eliminate some hills.

Straight off, a horse trail leaves the far end of the parking area to the right of the track. (ASIDE The track leads past camping areas to a viewpoint for Devils Head. And that's all.) In a few metres keep straight where a horse trail turns off to the left, bound for the Lower Ghost. Your trail traverses a slope, crosses a cutline and joins a sandy track at a Y-junction.

Turn left, climbing through meadow to a T-junction of tracks at 297838 (but which is actually a 5-way when you factor in trails). The track coming in from your right is the driveable one from Indian Springs trail.

Rather than continue ahead on the up–down track, take the first left on the horse trail that shortcuts downhill. Rejoin the track that crosses a meadow, hiccups over a rib, then climbs to Small Hill parking area at 4-way junction 294845. Turn right onto a trail. (Track ahead joins a cutline; trail to left is West Side trail to Hidden Pass trail.)

To Anti-Ghost Ridge junction 2.2 km
The trail traverses hillside to a Y-junction. Keep left. (Trail to right connects with Indian Springs trail.)

Climb slightly, onto a treed bench below a steepening. Zig left, then head up the fall line, going either way at a split, the ever steepening stony trail the hardest work you'll do all day. Top out on a higher bench at a dead tree, a logical place to stop awhile, ostensibly to look at the view across the Ghost River toward Devils Gap and Orient Point.

The trail then undulates below rough, craggy ground to the bottom of the infamous Motocross Hill, gouged out by dirt bikes, the scars visible even on Google Earth. Climbers use this hill as a shortcut to and from the Anti-Ghost cliff. (There's even a climb named Motocross Crack.)

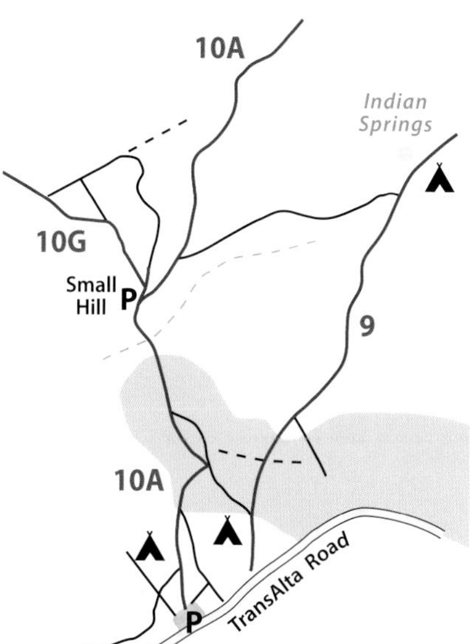

Trails leaving the top of the big hill parking area

Not too far beyond, the trail makes a long ascent on scree into an amphitheatre below a line of crags called Electric Lady Land, where it briefly wends its way between boulders and Castle Pinnacle to the highest point on the trail.

On the far side, the trail descends in short, steep drops to a wide bench at a clearing, then turns sharply left and climbs gradually to T-junction 301859. Turn right. (Trail to left is Anti-Ghost Ridge.)

To #10B junction 920 m
Heading east, the trail descends through pine forest, the going gentle apart from one stony hill. Reach T-junction 309859 with a wide track. Turn right. (Track to left is #10B Boulderfield Viewpoint.)

To Indian Springs trail 2 km
After an initial drop off the bench, the track gradually flattens and straightens, becoming grassy underfoot just before entering a big meadow. Indian Springs trail lies only 400 m to the south as the crow flies, to the left of that small forested hill. If you prefer extra kilometrage to bushwhacking, continue following the track that heads even farther east before it curls south through lovely meadows with pond eyes and joins Indian Springs trail in a grassy dip at 324863.

Looking up Motocross Hill to Anti-Ghost crag.

10B Boulderfield Viewpoint

Day hike from trailhead
Unofficial trail, some white flagging
Distance 3 km from #10A
Height gain 260 m (853 ft.) from #10A
High point 1860 m (6102 ft.)

Access Via #10A at 309859.

A rather pleasant old track, now narrowed to trail, climbs to a viewpoint on the east side of Black Rock Mountain at 295871. Consider biking Indian Springs trail, then hiking the northeast leg of Anti-Ghost traverse to the junction.

To ridge 2.5 km
From the junction a track heads north through pine forest. After a small creek crossing there's a damp section at the edge of willowy meadows where tall grasses have obliterated the trail. Look for white flagging. Then cross a fork of Meadow Creek issuing from the gullies on the east side of Hidden Pass.

Back on dry ground, the track heads west, climbing gradually along the north bank of the creek. After passing below a grassy bank, it leaves the creek and veers right, crossing a parallel creek at 298868. This is the start of a long climb out of the valley bottom to a grassy ridge at 298873 where you meet a newer exploration road come up from the other side.

To viewpoint 470 m
Turn left on the newer exploration road, which follows the ridge crest. After a small rise, it descends, then climbs more determinedly to its abrupt end at the edge of a large boulderfield. The view is southeast across to Anti-Ghost Ridge. I'm not sure what the cairn signifies.

THE NON-OPTION
What happens if at ridgetop 298873 you follow the newer exploration road north? It simply descends in a straight line to a NE–SW cutline, losing most of the height won previously. A copious spring at the halfway point is its most interesting feature.

The cutline to right flattens out in Meadow Creek. The cutline to left makes a beeline for treeline on the eastern slope of Black Rock at 292880—a height gain of 219 m (720 ft.). Low down, one is grateful for a zigging access road, but high up the zig builders gave up, leaving you to hang on by your toenails. There is a far better way to this spot via #13A.

View across boulderfields to Anti-Ghost Ridge.

The summit from the bald top.

10C Anti-Ghost Ridge

Day hike, long-day in combo
Distance 3.2 km
Height gain S–N 267 m (876 ft.) from #10A
Height loss S–N 134 m (440 ft.)
High point 1987 m (6520 ft.)

Access Via #10A at 301859.

A scenic but rather roundabout route when combined with #10A that takes you to the top of the Anti-Ghost and along the ridge to Hidden Pass. Combine with F and G to make an 11 km loop. I strongly recommend anticlockwise for the views. However, in reverse a shortcut of dubious merit is available down Motocross Hill.

SOUTH TO NORTH

To east viewpoint junction 300 m

Start from Anti-Ghost traverse at junction 301859.

If approaching from the south, turn left (northwest) and uphill through small pines. The trail steepens to a split in a glade. On the better trail veer left and slightly downhill. Shortly, the trail turns right and starts a gradual climb through trees to the right of a boulder slope. (NOTE Just after the split comes in from the right in an open area, a faint 60-metre-long trail heading left shortcuts through trees to 298858. It you want to miss out the next three hills and the side trip #10D, this is well worth considering.)

If sticking to the main trail, climb a short, steep, stony hill, then turn sharp left at T-junction 299859. (Trail ahead leads to SIDE TRIP #10D East Viewpoint. The junction is not obvious.)

To Motocross Hill junction 500 m

After the sharp bend, climb a less steep hill, traverse left and, losing all height recently gained, descend to the not obvious 3-way junction at 298858 with the 60 metre shortcut.

Here the trail turns right and climbs steeply onto a terrace above a crag. Moving away from the edge, you next come to the junction with Motocross Hill trail and turn right.

Anti-Ghost Ridge to Hidden Pass 2.4 km Flog up a short hill to a T-junction immediately below Anti-Ghost cliff. Turn left. (Climber's access trail straight on leads to the Bluebell Crack area of the cliff.)

Enjoy a lovely bit of undulating trail that ends up between a pinnacle and the northwest corner of the cliff—an impressive place as you can see by the photo on the next page.

Turn the corner, the trail now running along the west flank of the ridge through lightly treed meadows, eventually gaining the bald top north of the highest point.

To reach the summit above Anti-Ghost cliff, detour right and up a steep, shaley trail to the summit area. There and back is 500 m.

Return to the bald top, and heading north, descend a stony hill. The trail takes you through trees and meadows to a second top, then on down more rocky ground into trees and another meadow. Continue descending to a T-junction near a small col. Here the trail to Hidden Pass turns left.

But first you have to visit the last top. So turn right at the T-junction and follow the trail onto a rocky nubbin, a delightful place to eat lunch in shelter from the wind. From its top look down east to the Finger Boulders. (To reach them, walk north along the ridge a way, then descend easy-angled scree and rubble.)

Return to the T-junction and keep straight. Descend gradually into Hidden Pass, which is long and sinuous with a grassy floor.

GOING FARTHER

For Hidden Pass and West Side trails just stay on the trail, which morphs into Hidden Pass trail and heads south. For East Side traverse, walk to the right through Hidden Pass. Scramblers have another option: the Black Rock Nubs, which are really the culmination of the southeast ridge of Black Rock. See #10E.

SIDE TRIP

10D East Viewpoint

Distance 920 m return to #10C
Height gain ~20 m (~66 ft.)
High point ~1798 (~5900 ft.)

A side trail to a grassy terrace on the east side of Blackrock Mountain at 296861.

Start from junction 299859 at the top of the steep, stony hill.

Keep straight and continue climbing onto a grassy ridge supporting the outside edge of a terrace. To left the east slope of the Anti-Ghost is a mess of crags and screes. Follow the ridge to the north end of the terrace at 296861, where you are treated to a view of Black Rock Mountain, the lower Nub and Meadow Creek. Nearer in, you can spot the track leading to Boulderfield Viewpoint.

Looking toward Black Rock Mountain and the lower Nub.

#10C The trail at the northwest corner.

#10E The twisted pinnacle at Echo Pass.

#10E View from the top of the lower nub of Anti-Ghost Ridge. Note the narrowish bit of ridge before the summit.

Looking north to the higher nub.

10E Black Rock Nubs

Day, long-day scramble
Distance 2 km from Hidden Pass
Height gain 387 m (1270 ft.) from pass
High point 2240 m (7350 ft.)

Access At Hidden Pass via #10F.

Attaining two pointy little summits on the southeast ridge of Black Rock at 287880 and 284884 ups the difficulty. Apart from there being no trail, there are steep slopes, scree and route-finding problems. Still, this is by far the easiest of four routes I have used to reach this very attractive area.

Start from Hidden Pass, gained most easily from #10F, but also accessible from ##10C and 10G.

To Echo Pass via the ridge 790 m
Climb out of the pass onto the north side ridge. This is best done by walking a short way through the pass in a northerly direction, then taking a faint trail climbing up and right through a few rocks into trees on the ridge crest. Turn right and walk a broad ridge with meadows to its far end, which drops off into Echo Pass. The drop-off is beset by crags on three sides, so you have to descend one side or the other well before then and contour in. Hemmed in by steep slopes at 287873 it produces good echoes. Note the twisted pinnacle.

To Nubs 1.21 km
With the help of game trails, climb out of the pass to the north via a grassy gully between trees and a rocky ridge to its right. When the angle eases, head right to a meadow atop the rock ridge. This is the shoulder. Rising above you in scree and slabs is the lower Nub (2210 m, 7250 ft.).

Walk right to the foot of the southeast ridge. Climb rubble up the right side of the ridge where the going is easy, only taking to the ridge crest when forced to by a line of spectacular cliffs. A narrow slabby bit just below the summit cairn is shown on the picture on the previous page.

Stroll down the other side to a sloping plateau out of which rears the higher nub. A direct ascent appears challenging, a buttress on its right side looking as if it's about to break away at any given moment. Traverse a bit, then head up scree.

Descent
Return the same way. When you get to the low point between the two tops it's worth heading down right onto a conspicuous outlier supported on three sides by cliffs. From there view Black Rock's south cirque and a great rounded arch over a canyon. Somewhere in its blackness there must be a waterfall?

NOTE "Traversing" from the outlier to Echo Pass involves unavoidable height loss and height gain to avoid crags, so just head back up.

10F Hidden Pass

Half-day hike
Distance 1.9 km
Height gain 314 m (1030 ft.)
High point 1884 m (6180 ft.)

Access Via #11.1 Black Rock Mountain, the side creek start. See inset map on page 45.

A steep forest trail follows alongside a creek with running water to the pass at 290867. It gives the shortest access to Black Rock Nubs, the eastern traverse to Black Rock Meadows and the Finger Boulders. Most obviously, the upper part of the trail can be used in combo with Anti-Ghost traverse, Anti-Ghost Ridge and West Side trail to make an 11 km loop.

To West Side trail 840 m

You've reached the hiking sign and are walking the bench to the left of the side creek past excellent camping spots. Opposite the last trail climbing the bank to the lineman's cabin, cross the creek and walk up the right bank. After crossing a tiny tributary and just before a larger one with water, turn right. Almost straightaway you're into a series of steep climbs interspersed with relief sections. After the third climb, you meet West Side trail in a flurry of red flagging at the T-junction at ~281860. Go straight. (West Side trail to right leads to Main access.)

To Hidden Pass 1.1 km

A lovely stretch alongside a lively creek brings you to one of its sources at a spring gushing out of a steep bank. A calcareous flat below the spring is a place to find butterworts.

At the foot of the bank the trail splits. Zig right up the bank to the draw above. Follow the draw — keep right at splits to avoid unnecessary uphills — that opens out into a long pass between stony ridges on both sides. The floor is flat and grassy, with shale.

GOING FARTHER

To Anti-Ghost Ridge, Finger Boulders

As soon as you enter the pass, keep right on the main trail that climbs gradually onto the north end of Anti-Ghost Ridge. Turn right if heading south. Turn left for Finger Boulders, passing over a rocky

Hidden Pass, looking west.

Finger Boulders.

A pleasant section of West Side trail.

top and along the ridgeline a way before descending scree on the right side to the line of boulders.

To Eastern traverse
Walk to the north end of the pass. Don't descend a trail heading into trees. Otherwise you'll be lost in the rifts forever; it's a hugely complex area down there. Your fainter trail starts to the left. Keep straight (flagging) and onto a ridge. Then read #13A backwards.

10G West Side trail

Half-day hike, long-day in combo
Distance 2.3 km
Height gain N–S ~12 m (~40 ft.)
Height loss N–S ~76 m (~250 ft.)

Access Via #10F to #10A.

A useful connecting trail between Hidden Pass trail and the main access enables you to complete a loop over Anti-Ghost Ridge. Regrettably, this trail has a Jekyll and Hyde personality.

FROM NORTH
Start from Hidden Pass trail at T-junction 281860.

Heading SSE, traverse forested hillside. A right turn leads into two steep downhills. Another pleasant traverse through trees below crags ends when you emerge from cool forest into the bright glare of rocks. At this point you are very close to the Ghost River and expecting an easy ending to the trail. But no. You must endure a long, steep and stony climb. On reaching the top, all is forgiven as you enjoy a view of Phantom Crag from a grassy bench and revel in a sandy trail.

At a junction keep right. Keep right again and surf a sandy ditch to 4-way junction 294845 (Small Hill parking area). For main access keep right on the track, reversing the first section of Anti-Ghost traverse for 1.1 km.

11 BLACK ROCK MOUNTAIN—map 2

Black Rock from the Ghost River. Route more or less follows the left skyline.

Day hike
Official trail with signs
Distance 4.8 km from trailhead; 15.6 km return from top of big hill
Height gain 892 m (2928 ft.)
High point 2462 m (8078 ft.)
Map 82 O/6 Lake Minnewanka

Access Hwy. 940 (Forestry Trunk Road) north of Hwy. 1A. Drive 25.4 km to Richards Road junction (sign). Keep right, then in 150 m take the first left (west) onto a gravel road signed "Trapper's Hill Lodges 8." This is the TransAlta Road built by TransAlta Utilities into the forest reserve. It can be further identified by a metal gate and a kiosk.

READ BEFORE YOU GO This road is good to the bridge over Lesueur Creek, then in poor shape with waves of potholes to the top of the big hill. After that the going is reasonable—*once* you get the big hill and the river crossing behind you. In summer and fall the Ghost River is usually dry. DON'T try crossing it during runoff. Even a little water can turn seemingly hard cobbles into quicksand. Overall, expect a slow drive.

In detail: Drive the road for 16.6 km to the top of the big hill down to the Ghost River. En route turn right up the hill after the first bridge; keep straight at red marker 15 (Enviros access road to right) and straight where a Sutton Energy well access road turns left. For the final few km you drive through cutblocks. Come to the top of the big hill down to the Ghost River.

Descending/ascending the big hill with its loose stones can be negotiated by cars with high clearance, 4 wheel drive and determined drivers. If unsure about driving any farther, use the big hill parking area on the right side and continue on foot or by bike for another 3 km.

At the bottom of the hill is a T-junction. Which way to the crossing? Spring floods are constantly undermining the east bank, and the route changes almost yearly. As of fall 2012 you go straight down a shaley ramp and follow tire tracks across the wide, stony bed. At the far side turn right, then climb up left onto the levee by the side of a groyne. A big cairn marks the spot for the return.

On the levee road turn right. At junction marker 31 turn left on the better road that joins the levee road farther on at marker 33. Go left. After this it's easy going on dryas flats to marker 37, where you turn right. Drive the side road for 300 m to Black Rock Mountain trailhead at marker 32.

Big and solitary, girdled by cliffs and topped by an historic lookout, Black Rock's an attractive-looking mountain that was lookout man Jack Carter's favourite. Understandably: there is nothing boring about the old pack trail to its summit, which takes a daring line up the south slope of the mountain, causing you at many points to wonder where it can possibly go next. Its slippery shales and scree may not suit everyone and there's a hint of exposure near the summit. Overall, though, the trail's still in fair shape after 84 years.

Also the access to #10F Hidden Pass trail and sundry frozen waterfalls at the head of the side creek.

CAMPING NOTE A lot of people camp at the trailhead. If you need water there are excellent flat camping spots on the bench above the side creek. See Start 1.

HISTORY NOTE The trail was built in 1928. I'm not sure what possessed the Canadian Forest Service to choose such an intimidating-looking mountain for a lookout, because they had a lot of trouble finding a route to the summit, let alone one that could be navigated by pack horses. From Aura ranger station it was a three-day trip to supply the "towerman" and this was one of a few reasons why in 1950 Black Rock was closed, to be shortly superseded by Mockingbird, which could be driven by pickup. Around this time, an exploration road (continuation of access road between markers 37 and 32) was pushed a way up the south slope on top of the trail.

GHOSTLY NOTE Noted landscape painter Roland Gissing associated the mountain Black Rock with something sinister. He may be right. In 1998 a J. Dawson, hiking alone, heard "vocalizations" and found seven 16-inch-long footprints. Luckily the chance of spotting a Sasquatch are much less than that of spotting Brangelina on the trail, so why worry?

To the kiosk 370 m

Walk across the stony creekbed of the Ghost River. Usually it is dry. Now what? Spring floods continually erode the far bank and strong winds gusting down-valley fell the trees on the slope above it. This means the start to the trail changes every few years. As of 2013 there are two starts. See the inset map on page 45.

1. Side creek start Aim for the hiking sign to the left of a side creek. A trail winds up the bank to the sign, then runs along a flat bench on the left side of the side creek. Here are excellent camping spots. The problem is getting up the steep bank behind the bench onto Black Rock Mountain trail proper. The vertical dirt chutes made by campers are unappealing. Walk farther along the bench to where easier trails climb the bank to the ruins of the lineman's cabin. The route between the cabin and the kiosk on the old exploration road is blocked by big fallen trees, which must be circumvented to the left.

2. Direct start Start farther to the left of the hiking sign where a "trail" climbs a stony gully to the banktop. The trail continues above the steep bank overlooking the side creek, passing through some easy deadfall onto the main trail (exploration road). Follow it up to the kiosk, where you can have a good laugh reading the register.

To the summit 4.4 km

With every expectation of an "excellent trip," continue up the steepening exploration road to a junction. Turn left onto the lookout trail.

The trail makes a long sweep to the left, then winds pleasantly up to treeline meadows. This section ends with a steep, shaley hill, followed by a traverse left to gain the broad south ridge. Head up the ridge in last trees. Scattered all around are small whitish-coloured pinnacles. "Polar Bear," right by the trail, is the most popular on which to strike a pose for a pic.

Black Rock Mountain. The traverse before the draw.

You are now heading straight for the massive cliffs girdling the mountain. On screes below the cliff the pack trail has disintegrated, which is a huge pity. Instead of several easy-angled zigs as of yore, the present trail makes only two, which are far too steep for the eroded nature of the slope.

The defences can be breached at only one spot and judging by the photos of men spread-eagled on precipices, the trail builders had some trouble finding it. You traverse left below the cliff on a good built-up section of scree trail, until, it seems, some desperate manoeuvre must be made to get higher. Suddenly a break appears in the cliff and the trail sweeps up into a draw offering wonderful views back to Mt. Aylmer. It's an intriguing place. Who can resist squeezing into slits in the cliffs and throwing rocks into fissures to see how deep they are.

After a grassy flat with large cairn, a badly eroded section of trail climbs rusty-coloured shales onto—a plateau, surely the mountain's most surprising feature. Having found a way through Cathedral Formation cliffs you have entered the new world of the Stephen Formation shales and associated fossils. The plateau is several grassy football fields laid end to end, isolated by cliffs on all sides and harbouring a few less-common alpines like *Townsendia* and dwarf harebell. To the west, Devils Head Mountain sticks up like a thumb above the similar tableland of Bastion Ridge.

The summit is still a long way off. At one time you were guided by a line of tripods carrying the telephone wire, which dropped dizzily down the cliff to the trees. Nowadays you follow a line of cairns.

Arrive at the base of the final rise, a tapering scree ridge. The steep trails are shortcuts, not the main trail. Go this way if you want, but why struggle up or down this mess when you don't have to? I strongly recommend using the original pack trail, which starts much farther to the left at cairns and whose long zigs make the going effortless and enjoyable.

Walking the plateau. Ahead is the final ridge up to the summit, showing the shortcuts. Photo Bob Spirko

Crossing the narrow rock ridge.

High up, the ridge tapers alarmingly, the distance between the sunny southern cliffs and the gloomy northern precipices lessening to a half-dozen steps in either direction. This is where the pack horses stopped.

Clamber up rock steps to the crux for nervous walkers — a two-metre-wide rock ridge that can be crossed in a couple of minutes to a geocache. Easy, yes, but watch your step if the wind is blasting.

A few metres of easy ground leads to a flat summit and in the centre, tethered by wires, the 12-foot-square lookout. In an effort to preserve the building, the sides were shingled in 1996 by the Friends of the Eastern Slopes in cooperation with the Alberta Land & Forest Service. As you hunker down inside to eat your lunch, you wish the FOESA had replaced the windows and door as well (it's drafty in there), but it's kinda fun reading messages covering every square inch of the walls and ceiling. Some might call it graffiti.

You come away thinking that lookouts were tough in those days, living alone in a such a cramped building on top of a high mountain that attracts clouds. The sparsity of good viewing days was another reason why Black Rock was abandoned in favour of the much less exciting Mockingbird. But on a fine day what a view!

The lookout, sporting new shingles.

12 GHOST RIVER TO WAIPAROUS CREEK via Johnson Lakes — maps 3, 2

Half-day hike to Johnson Lakes, long-day hike, backpack
Unofficial trails, river and creek crossings
Distance 14.9 km
Height gain S–N 268 m (880 ft.)
Height loss S–N 174 m (570 ft.)
High point 1807 m (5930 ft.)
Map 82 O/6 Lake Minnewanka

South access Hwy. 940 (Forestry Trunk Road) north of Hwy. 1A. Drive 25.4 km to Richards Road junction (sign). Keep right, then in 150 m take the first left (west) onto a gravel road signed "Trapper's Hill Lodges 8." This is the TransAlta Road built by TransAlta Utilities into the forest reserve. It can be further identified by a metal gate and a kiosk.

First Johnson Lake, below Bastion Ridge.

READ BEFORE YOU GO This road is good to the bridge over Lesueur Creek, then in poor shape with waves of potholes to the top of the big hill. After that the going is reasonable—ONCE you get the big hill and the river crossing behind you. In summer and fall the Ghost River is usually dry. DON'T try crossing it during runoff. Even a little water can turn seemingly hard cobbles into quicksand. Luckily, if you get stuck there are plenty of weekend warriors around to haul you out. Overall, expect a slow drive.

In detail: Drive the road for 16.6 km to the top of the big hill down to the Ghost River. En route turn right up the hill after the first bridge; keep straight at red marker 15 (Enviros access road to right) and straight where a Sutton Energy well access road turns left. For the final few km you drive through cutblocks. Come to the top of the big hill down to the Ghost River.

Descending/ascending the big hill with its loose stones can be negotiated by cars with high clearance, 4 wheel drive and determined drivers. If unsure about driving any farther, use the big hill parking area on the right side and continue on foot or by bike for another 6.3 km.

At the bottom of the hill is a T-junction. Which way to the crossing? Spring floods are constantly undermining the east bank, and the route changes almost yearly. As of fall 2012 you go straight down a shaley ramp and follow tire tracks across the wide, stony bed. At the far side turn right, then climb up left onto the levee by the side of a groyne. A big cairn marks the spot for the return.

On the levee road turn right. At junction marker 31, turn left on the better road that joins the levee road farther on at marker 33. Go left. After this it's an easy, flat drive up-valley on dryas flats. Pass marker 37, which indicates the side road to Black Rock Mountain trailhead.

Continue and cross a bridge over the diversion canal where the Ghost River pours into a drain bound for Lake Minnewanka. Directly after, keep right. (Road to left leads to

Johnson Creek trail south of Johnson Canyon. Black Rock Mountain in the background.

campsites.) A short distance on, go straight at a split on a ruler-straight road. (Road to right passes campsites near the river.) After the split comes back in from the right, cross a stony creekbed that is often dry. At the next junction, turn right and park on gravel flats near the edge of the Ghost River.

CAMPING NOTE You can camp anywhere along the road past Lesueur Creek Bridge.
North access Via #3 Waiparous Creek. Leave the trail at the NE–SW cutline immediately west of the first creek crossing.

The tracks connecting the Ghost to the Waiparous via Johnson Creek run parallel to a tremendous line of cliffs, where the mountains of the Ghost end in abrupt and spectacular fashion. The walking is easy with occasional steep hills and several creek crossings. Most times, this trail is used to access Johnson Lakes or the fabulous Johnson Canyon (#14).

RIVER NOTE Because the route depends on water levels, try from mid-summer on.

FUTURE TRAIL NOTE Because the route between Johnson Lakes and Johnson Canyon goes all around the boonies, the Ghost Watershed Alliance Society is trying to get a more direct trail built. Right now the route is flagged. See #12A.

SOUTH TO NORTH

To Johnson Lakes 2.9 km

Wade the Ghost to the north bank and pick up a trail heading rightward to the cutline cum access road, which starts above the overhanging riverbank.

After a flat the cutline road ascends the valley between Black Rock Mountain and Bastion Wall, which is the long line of cliffs to your left. A deep gash necessitates a detour up the left bank. At the top of a steep hill you cross the Alberta Wildland Park boundary where mature spruce have been felled across the road to deter OHVs.

One more steep, stony hill and then the angle eases right off, the rise a gradual one to the watershed between the Ghost and Johnson drainages. (En route a cairn signifies a climber's access trail to the cliffs.) A slight descent brings you to the first Johnson Lake, a shallow body of water reflecting the magnificent cliffs of Bastion Wall. The cutline road runs along the right (east) side of the lake to the second lake, where it turns right. The second lake has a reedy surround, meaning anyone fishing for brookies and cutthroat should pack waders, even haul in an inflatable.

To Black Rock Meadows turnoff 2.1 km
Enclosed by trees, the cutline road soon heads back left and crosses the feeder stream for the second lake. After the dip, it sets northeast, taking you far away from where you are supposed to be going. This is a long, rolling stretch that en route crosses a tributary of Johnson Creek.

When Black Rock Mountain is behind you (you can't see it), start a long descent, at 270905 crossing an ENE–SSW cutline. Keep straight. (For #13 Black Rock Meadows trail turn right.) A little farther on, a blaze on the right side indicates the northerly start to #13, used by outfitters.

To Johnson Canyon 5.3 km
Keep descending. Where the road turns right at the bottom of the hill, go straight with the cutline into a boggy meadow. Cross the meadow. On the far side intersect a stony track and turn left at 274911. Finally the rejuvenated hiker heads for the mountains.

The track degenerates to grass briefly, then picks up again as you pass a pond reflecting the amazing line of cliffs—all of it Bastion Wall—extending north and south as far as the eye can see and at the back of a bowl, the waterfall Sorcerer. Above the cliffs is Bastion Ridge traversed by #16.

Descend to the tributary crossed earlier and cross it a second time. A stint through pines ends in a steep, shaley downhill to meadows about Johnson Creek. Cross the creek. It's a boisterous little stream that is crossed another six times in the space of half a kilometre.

On the northeast bank, the trail climbs to a traverse line above the creek. Keep right at a junction. (The trail descending the bank criss-crosses the creek and climbs back in later.) Climb higher on the west slope of a hill to vantage points revealing the splendid isolation of Black Rock Mountain. Up next is the white shale traverse that is definitely skimpy and probably the reason for the creekside detour. (There is also a bypass trail higher up the slope in the vegetation.) After the detour comes back up, you pass the wide stony creekbed

Devils Head Meadow under Devils Head. Bastion Ridge to left.

of Johnson Canyon seen down below you, heading west. If going that way, some backpackers shortcut down the bank. Continue along the banktop above a small tributary to a meadow. Keep straight at a junction at ~243917. (The trail to left that crosses the tributary is the conventional route into Johnson Canyon.)

To Devils Head Meadow 1.9 km

Shortly, the grassy avenue you're following opens into Devils Head Meadow, the tributary's birthplace, the watershed between Johnson Creek and the Waiparous, where horses run free under the saturnine eye of Devils Head.

The main trail crosses the tributary and heads along the left (west) edge of the meadow. Pass the mouth of a NE–SW cutline, which offers yet another route into Johnson Canyon.

The trail continues along a ridge of firm ground between a bright-green fen and the tributary trickling lazily out of a pond, then dekes behind a copse into the northern half of the meadow, which drains to Waiparous Creek. Continue to follow the left edge to an intersection with an exploration road that doubles as an OHV trail. Turn left. (For the curious, the road to right ends shortly on the east side of the meadow at a viewpoint with marker 133. Regrettably, there is nothing to stop OHVers from playing merry hell in the fragile meadow.)

To Waiparous Creek 2.7 km

The exploration road/OHV trail climbs through pines to your day's high point, then swings right and downhill not too far away from the valley running east from Castle Rock. Here's a chance to explore a new canyon. I never say no.

Ultimately the road levels and meets a NE–SW cutline at a T-junction. Turn right and walk down to the Waiparous Creek exploration road. For Hwy. 940 turn right. The ford is just metres away.

Now read #3 Waiparous Creek.

FUTURE OPTION

12A GWAS Shortcut

Distance 4 km

When this trail comes into common use, it will reduce the distance by nearly 3 km and take a more direct and pleasant line, cutting out cutlines and 7 creek crossings. Right now it is flagged and sorta followable with faint trails here and there.

It starts from between the two Johnson Lakes at 256891 and follows the west shore of the smaller lake a short way before climbing up and away in a northeasterly direction. En route to Johnson Creek it crosses the stony bed of Sorcerer Creek, passes within earshot of a big spring, climbs over a ridge and skirts the edge of a few meadows. It emerges on Johnson Creek's stony bed at 243915, where you're in position to turn left up Johnson Canyon. Otherwise, turn right and on approaching the tributary turn left on a trail that leads back to the main trail at ~243917.

Checking the GPS while walking the shortcut under Bastion Wall.

13 BLACK ROCK MEADOWS—map 2

Day hike from trailhead
Unofficial trail
Distance 1.5 km from #12; 6.5 km from trailhead
Height gain 241 m (790 ft.) from #12
High point 1957 m (6420 ft.)
Map 82 O/6 Lake Minnewanka

Best access Via #12 Ghost River to Waiparous Creek on the NE–SE cutline at its intersection with an ENE–SSW cutline at 270905. **Also accessible** from the terminus of #10C and #10F at Hidden Pass.

An enjoyable outfitter's trail leads to extensive meadows on the northeast corner of Black Rock Mountain. The meadows are more tundra-y than flowery, but offer a fabulous view along the length of Bastion Wall and of Devils Head and Castle Rock rising up above it. The sketch map on page 45 shows the route. NOTE Expect breaks in the trail on open ground where the horses have spread out.

Turn right onto the ENE–SSW cutline and follow it to 273903, where a horse trail heads right into mossy spruce forest.

It's a gradual climb with lots of traversing to a bench that is followed around onto west-facing slopes. At the end of the bench, two short consecutive uphills lead to the base of an open ridge at ~270898 — your first viewpoint.

Here the trail turns sharp left (east) and follows the right side of the ridge, then after a short climb in trees, the ridgeline itself, which is wide and billowy, a mix of grass, stones and dryas. Keep going to a small cairn at the top. Ahead are the meadows and looming over them the precipitous northeast face of Black Rock.

Turn right (south). Descend slightly at the edge of trees, then climb a short, steep rocky slope onto a sloping bench. For the best views head right to its far end overlooking a gully at 274897.

NOTE if returning via Johnson Lakes, bushwhackers can shortcut down easy hillside with a little deadfall from ~270898 onto the cutline.

Black Rock Mountain from the meadows. The northeast shoulder is out of sight to the left.

GOING FARTHER

13A Eastern traverse

Long-day hike from trailhead, backpack
Unofficial trails, route, some flagging
Distance 4.6 km from meadows
Height gain N–S 110 m (360 ft.)
Height loss N–S 177 m (580 ft.)
High point 2057 m (6750 ft.)

This route connects the meadows to the Anti-Ghost trails at Hidden Pass via a route along the east side of Black Rock and the Nubs. Because the terrain is complex and trails intermittent, careful route finding is a must. For the experienced hiker who can handle this kind of thing the route is incredibly rewarding.

From Hidden Pass you can choose from three trails back to a trailhead. See ##10C, F and G. Whichever, you'll need two vehicles or bikes.

NORTH TO SOUTH

To Northeast shoulder 730 m
From where you first gained the sloping bench, continue straight and up a broad, open ridge that is treed on the left side. About two-thirds up, watch for yellow flagging indicating the start of a trail traversing left through trees, then on scree below a small crag to the next ridge over. Arriving on a flat platform above rocky ground, do not turn uphill. Your trail descends the far side into a treed hollow, then climbs diagonally across a grassy slope to gain the northeast corner below a prominent free-standing crag. Look behind it and down the east slope a way to ghostly grey pinnacles poking up out of the forest.

To top of cutline 1.8 km
Head SSE down a grassy draw. When it fades out, step left slightly and continue down a lower draw to a flattening.

Go right around a knoll and descend slightly on game trail that traverses a short stretch of steep forested hillside to a bench. From a clump of rocks a slightly rising dell leads onto the bench proper.

The going is easy along the bench in open forest below scree slopes. When the terrain changes to grass, pass a fissure and intersect a track. This is the continuation of the cutline sum access road risen up from Meadow Creek. Turn left on the track. (Track to right is SIDE TRIP #13B.)

Keeping left, undulate along the track to the top of the NE–SW cutline at 292882. Keep right on a narrow trail.

The free-standing crag on the northeast shoulder.

The grassy draw you walk down from the northeast shoulder. Black Rock Nubs at top right.

To Hidden Pass 2.1 km

This final section wends its way among a mess of other trails through a confusing area of look-alike rift valleys and ridges compressed between Echo Pass, Hidden Pass and a high wall of moraine. The secret is to keep high.

Initially all is straightforward as you follow the trail into the rock garden, winding around between boulders. The trail climbs out of it into forest below a scree slope and reaches a high point.

The trail then descends, soon plunging into one of those rifts. Leave the rift IMMEDIATELY and head right, past two pools and down a short, steep hill into a meadow. The trail curves right and down. Within a very short distance, keep straight three times, neither climbing onto a grassy top to left, nor heading right up the lower slope of the Nubs. Cross a dip. Shortly after, again keep straight. (Trail to left along a grassy ridge likely joins the myriad of trails in the forest below the rifts.)

The next section has no trail. Just follow flagging along a slightly rising bench. Watch for where the route turns left at flagging down a steep, open bank to flagging marking the continuation of the trail. Climb onto a ridge and follow it. The trail descends briefly into the rift to your right (fainter trail to right leads to Echo Pass) then continues along the ridge that eventually irons out flat. At flagging, the trail ends. Just continue ahead, climbing a little into the north end of Hidden Pass where you can pick up a trail come in from the left off Anti-Ghost Ridge.

SIDE TRIP

13B High Viewpoint

Unofficial trail
Distance 590 m from cutline
Height gain 150 m (492 ft.) from cutline

A shaley platform below the screes and cliffs of Black Rock Nubs at 286884 gives a fine view of the northeast shoulder area and the Meadow Creek flatlands.

Start from the top of the cutline at 292882, or from where you intersect the track when doing the N–S traverse. Heading northeast, the track climbs gently through open terrain of grass and rock with scattered small trees, then steepens for the final approach up scree. Flower mats carpet the shale.

Looking south from the viewpoint to the lower nub.

14 JOHNSON CANYON—map 3

Johnson Canyon, looking east.

Backpack
Unofficial trail, route, creek crossing
Distance 3.5 km from #12 to campsite; 12.5 km from trailhead
Height gain 137 m (450 ft.) via approach no. 1
High point 1905 m (6250 ft.) at campsite
Map 82 O/6 Lake Minnewanka

Access Via #12 Ghost River to Waiparous Creek. There are two accesses, depending on which direction you are coming from.

The quintessential Ghost is epitomized in the spectacular valley north of Devils Head: canyons, cliffs, waterfalls, mountains. I count it as one of my favourite destinations, which I've visited as early as the May long weekend, exulting in sunshine and dry rock while our friends were suffering the traditional whiteout on the Columbia Icefield.

TWO APPROACHES

1. From the Ghost River end 3.5 km
The usual way in. After the scree traverse, turn second left on a track that crosses a tributary and runs alongside it to the flat, stony bed of Johnson Canyon. Turn right. Walk easily up the creekbed on an intermittent trail. Usually there is no water at this point.

2. From the Waiparous end 2.7 km
Use the NE–SW cutline. Near its end watch for where a forest trail cuts across to Johnson Canyon at a cairn. Turn right.

Entering a canyon is always thrilling and here there are sights to make you forget your blistered heels (eh, Norm?}: a montage of vertical and overhanging walls culminating in the big daddy of them all, the Devils Head.

About halfway along, the trail turns left into the first side canyon to the south. A meadow with running stream makes an idyllic camp spot (~219910) backdropped by a string of cascades tumbling down a gully from the basin above. Ice climbers call them Venus Falls.

#14B Looking back down Johnson Canyon from the slope leading to Lord of the Ghost Ridge.

EXPLORING FARTHER

14A Bastion Ridge north

Half-day scramble
Unofficial bit trails, route, creek crossings
Distance 1.5 km to summit
Height gain 500 m (1640 ft.)
High point 2405 m (7890 ft.)

The route, which features a bit of easy scrambling, follows the side valley from the campsite onto Bastion Ridge—a fabulous viewpoint for Devils Head. To continue on to the Ghost River see #16 Bastion Ridge.

From the campsite follow the trail across the creek and along the east bank to the foot of Venus Falls, which is a series of cascades. Recross the creek and ascend a scrambly trail rising along the west bank. Recross the creek below the highest fall, then scramble some more into a grassy basin.

The headwall below the Bastion/Devils Head col is guarded by a double-tiered rockband low down. No need to go that way. Keeping left of some trees, make for a straightforward slope left of the rockbands that gains the west ridge of Bastion about halfway up. Turn left and walk up to the white, shaley summit, at 225901.

14B Lord of the Ghost Ridge

Day hike
Route
Distance 4 km
Height gain 610 m (2000 ft.)
High point 2515 m (8250 ft.)

A more strenuous climb onto the northwest ridge of Devils Head. You end up below the south face of the mountain, from where experienced scramblers can connect with Malamute Valley and Devils Head Valley. (See ##15B and 15A.) Expect steepish slopes and scree but no actual scrambling.

NAMING NOTE The ridge holds a mystery. On one smooth facet of rock facing north look for the words "To the memory of Guy Gibson. Lord of the Ghost.

#14A Looking up Venus Falls. The route follows a scrambly trail up the right bank.

#14A Devils Head from summit 225901 at the north end of Bastion Ridge.

18-- Ghost River Valley." Despite being printed in bright yellow paint, the words are hard to decipher after all these years and whoever wrote them remains incognito. What's known since the last edition of this book is that Gibson's ashes were *not* scattered on this fabulous ridge.

Guy Gibson, who preceded Tolkien, really *was* known as "Lord of the Ghost" after he returned from the First World War to live in Benchlands on Hwy. 940. He was a skilled axeman who built over 1000 log cabins. His own cabin down by the Ghost River had door hinges made from roots that hooked into one another, and his bedspread was his favourite horse with tail and mane intact.

Continue up Johnson Canyon (tip of Castle Rock poking up ahead), then follow the valley as it turns to the south and opens up. Devils Head comes back into view, from this side shaped like a stegosaurus. Not too far around the bend, near a waterfall, climb the hillside to the right, choosing the grassy rib to the left of the one topped with pinnacles. Behind your back Johnson Canyon grows in magnificence with every rest stop. After 350 vertical m (1150 ft.) of hard work you reach the northwest ridge and get to look into Malamute Valley and across to Poltergeist Peak, which at 2970 m is the highest in the area.

Travel in the northerly direction toward Castle Rock appears stymied by those pinnacles, so head southeast toward Devils Head along a wide grassy ridge with rocky outcrops and purple saxifrage. Keep a look out for Gibson's rock.

Where the ridge rises near the end, a game trail appears and takes you up some scree to the left and through a number of little rockbands to the base of Devils Head. Don't stop here. The trail continues, traversing the steep scree of the west flank to the south face, where you get to look up the normal climber's route to the summit. Just as interesting is the view down to "gargoyle garden" in the saddle to the southeast.

Devils Head from Lord of the Ghost Ridge.

15 GHOST RIVER TO AYLMER PASS—maps 3, 4

Typical view of the valley near Malamute Valley. Through the V is Mount Aylmer.

Backpack
Unofficial trails, many river and creek crossings
Distance 21 km from trailhead
Height gain 664 m (2180 ft.)
High point 2280 m (7480 ft.)
Map 82 O/6 Lake Minnewanka

Access Hwy. 940 (Forestry Trunk Road) north of Hwy. 1A. Drive 25.4 km to Richards Road junction (sign). Keep right, then in 150 m take the first left (west) onto a gravel road signed "Trapper's Hill Lodges 8." This is the TransAlta Road built by TransAlta Utilities into the forest reserve. It can be further identified by a metal gate and a kiosk.

READ BEFORE YOU GO This road is good to the bridge over Lesueur Creek, then in poor shape with washboard and waves of potholes to the top of the big hill. After that the going is reasonable—ONCE you get the big hill and the creekbed crossing behind you. In summer and fall the Ghost River is usually dry. DON'T try crossing it during runoff. Even a little water can turn seemingly hard cobbles into quicksand. Luckily, if you get stuck there are plenty of weekend warriors around to haul you out. Overall, expect a slow drive.

In detail: Drive the road for 16.6 km to the top of the big hill down to the Ghost River. En route turn rightward up the hill after the first bridge; keep straight at red marker 15 (Enviros access road to right) and straight where a Sutton Energy well access road turns left. For the final few km you drive through cutblocks. Come to the top of the big hill down to the Ghost River.

Descending/ascending the big hill with its loose stones can be negotiated by cars with high clearance, 4 wheel drive and determined drivers. If unsure about driving any farther, use the big hill parking area on the right side and continue on foot or by bike for another 6.3 km.

At the bottom of the hill is a T-junction. Which way to the crossing? Spring floods are constantly undermining the east bank, and the route changes almost yearly. As of fall 2012 you go straight down a shaley ramp and follow tire tracks across the wide, stony bed. At the far side turn right, then climb up left onto the levee by the side of a groyne. A big cairn marks the spot for the return.

On the levee road turn right. At junction marker 31, turn left on the better road that joins the levee road farther on at marker 33. Go left. After this it's an easy drive up-valley on dryas flats. Pass marker 37, which is the turnoff to Black Rock Mountain trailhead.

Continue by the side of a berm and cross a bridge over the diversion canal where the Ghost River pours into a drain bound for Lake Minnewanka. Directly after, keep right. (Road to left leads to campsites.) A short distance on, go straight at a split on a ruler-straight road. (Road to right passes campsites near the river.) After the split comes back in from the right, cross a stony creekbed that is often dry. At the next junction keep left and park on gravel flats near the edge of the Ghost River at marker 39.

CAMPING NOTE You can camp anywhere along the road past Lesueur Creek bridge. BYOW in case.

This is two-thirds of a backpack following the Ghost River and Spectral Creek to Aylmer Pass and out to Lake Minnewanka Road via Lake Minnewanka shoreline trail. You need two vehicles and many extra hours both before and after the trip to switch vehicles. This horrible logistical problem can be avoided by making the backpack a three- to four-day trip by returning to your starting point via Lake Minnewanka shoreline trail and Devils Gap. Then, of course, you would park the vehicle at the top of the big hill down to the Ghost River. The downside to all this is that you have to walk an extra 6.3 km right at the start.

The route to the alpine meadows about the pass, while neither difficult nor particularly strenuous, retains an aura of untouched wilderness despite its old roads and cutlines. Numerous river crossings and grizzlies makes it unsuitable for nervous novice backpackers.

A word on river crossings. For the 15 km of the Ghost River section the old road (track) crosses back and forth 12 times. Except at runoff and after rain this is not a problem, more of a nuisance. While you can cut down the number of fords to four by the judicious use of game trails, this is not always time saving. Carry Tevas.

REGULATORY NOTE Because of numerous run-ins with grizzlies on the Banff National Park side, you are required to travel in tight groups of at least 4 people from Jul 15–Sep 30. This applies to Aylmer Pass trail, the lookout trail and the trail along Lake Minnewanka. At such times Lm8 campground at the junction of Aylmer Pass and Lake Minnewanka trails is closed. The other 5 campgrounds along Minnewanka to the east stay open. See *Canadian Rockies Trail Guide* and *Backcountry Banff*.

Despite all that, though, most day hikers and backpackers don't cross over into Banff Park, but have fun exploring the Ghost's many side valleys. See OPTION ##15A through F.

The start from marker 39

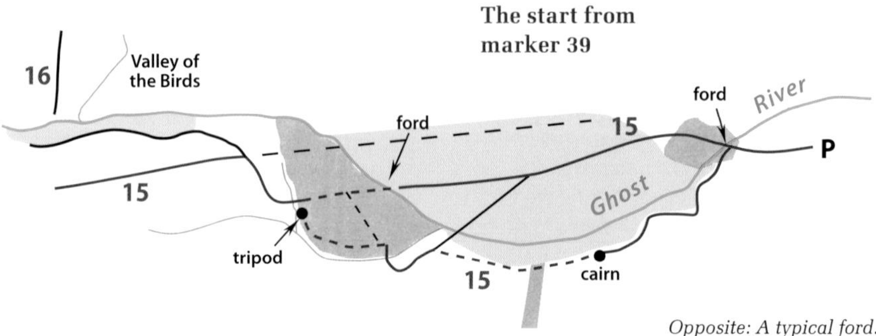

Opposite: A typical ford.

To Bastion Ridge turnoff 1.1 km
Ford the Ghost River. On the north bank the track splits. Use the right-hand fork, which leads to ford no. 2. Walk cobbles to where the track resumes on the far side of a wee creek. This place is marked by a tripod with a sign about bull trout.

(NOTE The first two crossings can be avoided by an undulating trail along the south bank. After a large cairn, make your way to a track come in from the left fork crossing. Turn left and follow the track to a spring creek crossing. On the far bank it's easiest to just follow the right bank of the creek to the tripod where you join the regular route.)

In a few metres the track turns right and joins an E–W cutline at 4-way 421867. Turn left. (Grassy track ahead parallels the cutline past camping areas. If headed for Bastion Ridge, follow it to the Ghost River.)

To Malamute Valley 2.5 km
The cutline is like a dirt road, long and straight. Turn third right (just before it ends) to crossing no. 3.

On the far bank turn left. Heading west, cross the stones of Devils Head Valley. See OPTION #15A.

Continue on below Sunshine Wall to crossing no. 4 at the mouth of Valley of the Sun. A long straight with a few cobbles in the middle leads to crossing no. 5. Keep right in trees, the next big side creek you cross being Claw Creek at 198867. This is where OPTION #15B takes off to the right. Round about here is the last view you'll have of Devils Head, which for the first half of the route has played peekaboo above a succession of walls and box canyons. You are about to enter the Ghost River Wilderness.

To Spectral Creek 10.6 km
Between here and the big bend the track crosses the river four times. Crossings 6 through 9 can be successfully avoided by using game trails along the north bank. Pass the southern outliers of Poltergeist Peak to your right. The isolated peak to the left is called Pakakos, a Peace Indian word meaning "spirit of the flying skeleton." Amazingly, this name was the winning entry in a geographical naming contest for elementary schools to celebrate the Year of the Child in 1979! Though dwarfed in altitude by all the peaks around it, it boasts its share of cliffs. (The ascent from the back is easy, yet people still try and climb it from the front or the sides and fail.) The valley immediately right of it is start no. 1 to OPTION #15C, the so-called Paradise trail to Lake Minnewanka. It can be accessed from the track's second foray along the south bank.

Round the bend and head northwest. The next two creek crossings, 10 and 11, can be eliminated by staying on the northeast bank. However, if making for start no. 2 to OPTION #15C, you have to cross the creek on the track.

On the northeast bank the grass grows unusually long and green below trees charred in the 1970 fire. All through this section be on the lookout for grizzlies excavating the riverbank for yummy hedysarum roots. The mountains on either side have fallen back and finally you pass Mt. Aylmer, which has been in view for many hours.

After another long straight, ford the Ghost at crossing no. 12, upstream of the confluence with Spectral Creek. Fifteen

Above: Looking down the south fork of Spectral Creek to Brock's Ridge (left) and Apparition Mountain (centre). Photo Mike Potter

Below: Aylmer Pass below Mount Aylmer. Photo Heinz Unger

minutes walking through spruce forest brings you to an important junction of tracks at 112898. Go left. (Track to right is OPTION #15E.)

Spectral Creek to Aylmer Pass 6.9 km
I'm not overly fond of the next section up Spectral Creek, which is marked incorrectly on both the topo map and the Ghost River Wilderness pamphlet. The cutline — for this is what you follow to the forks — intersects all the windings of the creek, about 10 in all, and sometimes *is* the creek. A dense spruce forest with deadfall puts paid to any idea of detours. Not only that, you never know what's lurking behind the willow bushes lining the creek. It's a highway for grizzlies moving down into the Ghost River from

Waterfalls in the south fork of Spectral Creek.

Stoney Creek where all the baddies have been banished.

Where fallen trees have blocked a long stretch along the north bank, use a blazed trail on the right that is probably a remnant of the original pack trail. Not long after this, the cutline fords the river one last time, then ends in undergrowth at the river's edge. In between these two points, and well marked by a cairn and flagging, the trail to Aylmer Pass takes off between two blazed trees.

Heading up the south fork, your new trail rises effortlessly out of dark, spooky forest to treeline, then cuts across a scree slope giving views of Apparition Mountain. At the mouth of the pass, grassy benches on either side of waterfalls provide one or two sheltered tent sites.

As you'll discover, Aylmer Pass is long, narrow and endless, a rolling carpet of tough bearberry, juniper and heather on which the passage of many feet has made little impression. Odds are that somewhere along it you are likely to be mobbed by Aylmer's famous bighorn sheep, a gregarious bunch who are not after your lunch, but want a lick of your sweaty skin. A Banff National Park boundary sign identifies the pass proper under Mt. Aylmer.

OPTIONS

Apart from the main loop over Aylmer Pass, there are a great many other options to choose from, some requiring camps, while others can be done in one day from the trailhead. Bastion Ridge is written up separately as #16.

15A Devils Head Valley

Day hike from trailhead 39
Route, intermittent trails
Distance 2.2 km from Ghost River trail
Height gain 186 m (610 ft.)
High point 1829 m (6000 ft.)

Access At creekbed crossing 228869.

This valley (the second one on the north side) is accessible to the forks at 223886. Go for the bathing pool and a spectacular view of Devils Head seen through a canyon. The going is easy apart from one unpleasant scree scrabble to get around a step in the creekbed.

Used as one of three climber's approach routes to Devils Head, this one follows the ridge west of the valley through the gargoyles.

Leave the main Ghost River trail where it crosses the mouth of the creek after river crossing no. 3.

A trail on the treed left bank deposits you in stony creekbed at a left-hand bend. Using bit trails, follow the windings of the bed below cliffs to the crux—a 5 m high waterfall step and pool.

Scrabble up left-side scree on a "trail," at two small trees traversing right across the top of a crag with slight exposure. Descend more easily back to the creekbed, taking the higher trail at a split to avoid avalanche debris.

(SCRAMBLER'S NOTE This scree slope is the climber's access route to Devils Head. While Devils Head is beyond the scope of most scramblers (class 5 climbing), you can have fun exploring the incredible "gargoyle garden" of the upper ridge, which my geologist friend says are erosional features, their tops rounded off by snow and rain. How to get there: as you climb scree, wend slightly left onto grass and continue up to the base of a big cliff. Walk left below the cliff and where the cliff gives out, scramble up right to gain the ridgetop. Follow the ridge, circumventing two impasses on the left side.)

But back to the valley: continue easily as before to a series of potholes, which are turned on the right side. Either stay low and traverse ledges or take the high-line trail across scree to a cairn and then descend. A short distance on, a small cascade falls into a circular pool 2 m deep. Just beyond is the forks.

The right fork soon ends at a black seep; the left fork is an impenetrable canyon. Framed between its vertical walls is Devils Head. It's possible to wander up the ridge between the two forks without too much trouble, then traverse left into the creekbed between canyons.

The bath.

Left fork canyon and Devils Head.

15B Malamute Valley

Backpack, long-day hike from trailhead
Route, intermittent trails
Distance 3.8 km from Ghost River trail
Height gain 229 m (750 ft.)
High point 1920 m (6300 ft.)

Access At Claw Creek crossing at 198867 just beyond river crossing no. 5.

The second-longest valley on the north side of the Ghost, also known as Claw Creek, is enclosed by Poltergeist Peak to the west and Castle Rock at its head. The walking is generally fast and easy, but to do the valley justice you need to camp somewhere en route.

It's the climber's western approach route to Devils Head.

NAMING NOTE Ice climbers call it Malamute Valley "in honour of all northern dogs that love to go on skiing and climbing trips." In keeping with this sentiment, the dozen and more ice climbs have names like Werewolf Waltz and Taiga Trot.

To the lower forks 2.7 km
Walk up the wide, flat valley on stones. Water (Claw Creek) will appear at some point. A cairn on the right bank indicates a trail leading right to a firepit and campsite ringed safari-style by branches. Farther on, utilize left-bank dryas flats dotted with small spruce.

Accompanying you on the left is the long southeast ridge of Poltergeist Peak, characterized by a wavy line of buttresses separated by gullies wherein lie the ice climbs, the features repeating themselves in ever more spectacular fashion all the way to the upper forks.

Arrive at the lower forks. The forested slope to the right just before the confluence is the route onto the ridge to the east, from where climbers access Devils Head. Look for a cairn in a shallow drainage. I haven't tried it, but likely hiker/scramblers could connect up with #14B Lord of the Ghost Ridge.

The north fork 1.1 km
Turn right (north). Initially the going is easy alongside potholes, pools and small cataracts. At a narrowing either scramble or paddle. The valley floor then widens somewhat and winds below high walls dripping with seeps (Runt's Runnel, Muzzle Melody etc.). Shortly, after the ground underfoot becomes bouldery, come to a not obvious fork. The main fork turns left, climbing at a steeper gradient toward the cliffs of Castle Rock. The fork to right ends very soon at a waterfall called Chilcoot Passage, because ice climbers must first climb it to get to Taiga Trot, Idle Incisor and Werewolf Waltz.

Hiker below Chilcoot Passage.

#15D Looking down on Paradise Pass. In the background to right is the Ghost River valley.

15C Paradise Pass

Backpack, paddle 'n' hike from south access to pass
Route, intermittent trail, blazes
Distance 7.9 km to lake
Height gain S–N ~335 m (~1100 ft.)
Height loss S–N 640 m (2100 ft.)
High point 2118 m (6950 ft.)

North access Ghost River trail in two places: no. 1 at ~133867; no. 2 at 145861.
South access Lake Minnewanka trail between Inglismaldie and Costigan backcountry campgrounds at ~150803.

The dots on the Ghost River Wilderness Area brochure lure you to the low point on the long ridge connecting Mts. Costigan and Aylmer at 156815 and on down to Lake Minnewanka. The old outfitter's trail is spotty, hardly used anymore, so follow blazes as best you can through deadfall and strings of wet meadows. Some call this trail "Purgatory."

If you just want to visit the pass and do a spot of ridgewalking, start from the Lake Minnewanka end. There is no good trail from this direction either and it's steep.

To the pass: 6 km via 1, 4.9 km via 2
Two starts:
1. Ford the Ghost River at crossing no. 10 and from ~133867 head southeast through a wide gap to the head of no. 2's creek.

2. At the bend, ford the Ghost River at crossing no. 8. Then, at 145861 shortcut, go up a messy creekbed immediately west of Pakakos Mountain.

Continuing southeast, pass behind the south ridge of Pakakos, which offers an easy ascent up grass and scree. Cross a saddle to a boggy open area and turn up right toward the boundary ridge. About 30 m (100 ft.) below the ridge is an excellent spring from where a good game trail leads up to the pass. Three tiny stones mark the Banff National Park boundary. The view of Lake Minnewanka is limited. For a better view see SIDE TRIP #15D.

To Lake Minnewanka 1.9 km
Making straight for Lake Minnewanka is not a good idea; there are crags. So from the pass veer down right through burned trees, then turn left through meadows with trees to a lip overlooking a flat, forested basin.

Descend steep grass to right of a line of crags into the basin. Pick up a trail in trees heading leftish, then down the fall line to the left of a gully. This bit is flagged. Below a steep step is a junction.

I didn't investigate the left-hand trail. The right-hand one has very steep, twisty sections and crosses the gully near the bottom of the slope. Descending the semi-open slope between the two trails would work just as well. At a rockband, deke around to the left and continue down moderating grass to Lake Minnewanka trail, aiming for 150803.

SIDE TRIP

15D Minnewanka Viewpoint

Game trails, route
Distance 1.2 km to viewpoint
Height gain ~305+ m (~1000+ ft.)
High point ~2423+ m (~7950+ ft.)

From the pass walk east along a grassy ridge. Avoid a shaley orange bump by traversing on trail to a higher gap in the ridge behind it. Climb grass and stones to a flattening, which is a fabulous viewpoint, not just for the lake but also looking north past Pakakos up the Ghost River Valley.

You can continue up rubble to a red scree ridge. Near the top a game trail traverses the left side to a col. I went no farther, but it appears you can continue.

15E Upper Ghost and Spirit Creek

Day hikes from a camp
Unofficial trails, routes

Access The junction above the Ghost River/Spectral Creek confluence at 112898.

1. Upper Ghost 8.5+ km

Leave the main trail at the west bank junction above the Ghost/Spectral confluence. Keep right and head straight back to the Ghost River. Although a game trail can be traced along the west bank of the Ghost to a point just north of Spirit Creek, most backpackers elect to use the NW–SE cutline, river crossings and all, which takes you more or less all the way to the meadows below Mt. Oliver, where you can continue on to the head of the valley and search for four tarns under East Psychic Peak. Only one is marked on the topo map.

2. Spirit Creek 6.6+ km

Leave the main trail at the west bank junction above the Ghost/Spectral confluence. Keep right and head straight back to the Ghost River. Follow the NW–SE cutline heading north with its many river crossings. At 2.8 km, branch right at a Y-junction onto a NE–SE cutline. This junction lies nearly one kilometre south of the confluence at ~103923.

Climb steep cutline. About the high point, keep left twice and drop to Spirit Creek. The cutline crosses the creek twice, then fades away on the east bank. Continue easily through forest to a large area of meadow around the forks. Attractions include a canyon (below the forks), intriguing rock scenery and a chance to wander up the ridge between the forks for a fabulous view back down the valley to Mt. Aylmer. Overlooking the head of the main fork is Mt. Davidson, perhaps more easily scrambled up from the Waiparous Creek side via its south basin.

15F Spectral Wanderings

Day hike from a camp
Unofficial trails, routes
Distance 15 km loop
Height gain 853 m (2800 ft.)
High point 2576 m (8450 ft.) on ridge

Access Upper south fork of Spectral Creek.

Spend an extra day wandering the various headwaters of Spectral Creek—wonderful walking country if you love meadows.

Don't start from the heavily forested forks (I've never been able to find the trail marked on the Ghost River Wilderness pamphlet anyway). Rather, start slightly upstream of the aforementioned waterfalls and find the good game trail on the west bank leading around into the head of the southwest fork, another good camping spot. In early summer a tarn is edged with alpine buttercups, greening and blooming as the snowbanks melt.

The pass to the north at 057885 is an easy walk up grass, and while up there who could resist wandering along Brock's Ridge (also known as Chocolate Ridge) to a cairn and viewpoint around the 2576 m (8450 ft.) contour, where you can look *down* on Aylmer Pass and Spectral Lakes.

Return to the pass. Drop right into the west fork and nip across to the gap at 050902, the grizzly route into and out of Stoney Creek. (See the *Canadian Rockies Trail Guide* and *Backcountry Banff* for routes from the other side.)

Next, head down the west fork, and at treeline contour left into the north fork, where blue-tinted Spectral Lakes are slung between Apparition and Revenant Mountains. This barren spot must be one of the spookiest places in the Ghost. According to Webster, "revenant" means "one that returns after death."

Return the same way to the west fork, and on the south bank find the sheep trail that traverses around the northeast end of Brock's Ridge at treeline into the south fork. From the point where you cross the south fork it's a relatively easy climb up to the Aylmer Pass trail. Turn right.

If camped near the waterfalls, height gain for all points visited is nearly 900 m (3000 ft.) This ain't no rest day.

The more attractive lower Spectral Lake. Photo Mike Potter

16 BASTION RIDGE—map 3

Devils Head from the cairn where you first gain the ridge.

Day hike, backpack
Unofficial trail with blazes and cairns, route, river crossings
Distance 5.7 km from parking area 39; 7.2 km to Johnson Canyon
Height gain S–N 878 m (2880 ft.)
Height loss S–N 79 m (260 ft.)
High point 2414 m (7920 ft.)
Map 82 O/6 Lake Minnewanka

South access Via #15 Ghost River at 4-way junction 421867.

Between the Ghost River and Johnson Creek lies a most beautiful ridge with side ridges winging out above one of the most stunning cliffs in the Ghost: Bastion Wall. While the ridge itself is walker friendly, being wide and rounded, the side slopes are most definitely not. Don't expect to bail out anywhere along its length. You'll see what I mean by perusing the ridge from Black Rock Mountain.

Use it as a day hike from marker 39 to *the* ultimate viewpoint for Devils Head and Black Rock Mountain. Make time for side trips to view two of the greatest ice climbs in the Ghost: Hydrophobia and The Sorcerer, both black seeps by full summer. Backpackers can take advantage of rough trails at both ends to traverse from the Ghost to Johnson Canyon, and make a loop with ##12 and 14. The ultimate high level trip would be a circuit of Devils Head via ##14B and 15B.

To Valley of the Birds 310 m

Read the first three paragraphs of #15.

At 4-way junction 421867 continue straight on a grassy track. Hop off it at its nearest approach to the Ghost River and wade across to the north bank. A trail starts just left of Valley of the Birds.

To the ridge 1.5 km

Climb a forest strip between two blocks of scree. Then head right to a crag and up a very steep slope of hard-packed shale with the odd tree to hang on to. Or not. To avoid the shale completely, climb the vegetated slope left of the left-most scree block, then on easy terrain traverse right to regain the trail. This is where the trail *should* be!

The worst climb of the day done with, enjoy an easy walk through forest, following blazes. After the trail turns left, it twists a little more steeply uphill to treeline. Here it turns right and makes a rising traverse up easy-angled scree to a large cairn. From here pick your way up scree to another large cairn on the crest of a south ridge—the first terrific viewpoint for Devils Head. Walk out left to the end of the ridge for peeks into the Ghost River Valley. Looking across Devils Head Valley you can pick out the climber's access route to Devils Head.

The ridge 2.8 km

Turn right and climb over two rocky knobs to top 233879. Here the trail ends. Come into sight is the main axis of the ridge and the ridge connecting with it.

First, descend to an orange shale col. On the up again, bypass crags via a snip-

Descending from top 233879 to the orange shale col. Across the skyline is the main axis of the ridge.

Looking back along the ridge from the northernmost top to top 233879.

pet of trail on the left side to some grass. Then climb two risers of scree. At the top, walk left under a small rockband, around it, then along the top of it onto the main axis at about top 234892. This is where SIDE TRIP no. 1 heads right (southeast) along the main axis.

Turn left. A little farther along, SIDE TRIP no. 2 turns off to the right down an east ridge.

From here a steeper pull gains you what is likely the high point. Continue to the northernmost top at 225901, its white shales dazzling in sunlight. SIDE TRIP no. 3 is the ridge extending to the northeast.

From this viewpoint, Devils Head is at its most stunning. Explorer H.W. Seton Karr said it resembled the Matterhorn with the top broken off. Hardly. More appropriately, the Stoney Nakoda call it Devils Nose or Devils Thumb. Wrote Seton Karr in 1887: "It was said that when the summit of The Devil's Head should fall... the country would pass from the possession of the Stony Indians into that of the white man."

Return the same way. En route, don't be lured into the Valley of the Birds with its promise of an easy way down. If carrying on into Johnson Canyon, read #14A.

SIDE TRIPS

Explore side ridges overlooking Bastion Wall for some incredible views. You'll be hard-pressed to do all three in one day.

1. At 234892 where you first gain the main axis, turn right heading ESE over two tops. From the second one, a short descent to the north will reveal The Sorcerer. Going farther—heading south to top 247879 means losing considerable height. However, all along this stretch are terrific views of Black Rock Mountain and Johnson Lakes. Add 4.4 km return.

2. At 234892 turn right (east) and descend a grassy ridge with one rocky step. A short climb gains you top 241897, where, with a bit of manoeuvring you view Hydrophobia and look down into Johnson Creek where you can see route #12 edging along the northeast bank. Add 2.6 km return.

3. From the final white top descend in a northeasterly direction, then up to top 229907 on the point overlooking Johnson Canyon. Add 1.6 km return.

Side trip no. 2. Looking back over Bastion Ridge to Devils Head.

17 DEVILS GAP TO LAKE MINNEWANKA—maps 2, 3

Sand near Third Ghost Lake.

Day, long-day hike
Unofficial trails
Distance 6 km from boundary
Height gain 15 m (50 ft.)
Height loss 37 m (120 ft.)
High point 1530 m (5020 ft.)
Maps 82 O/6 Lake Minnewanka, 82 O/3 Canmore

Access Hwy. 940 (Forestry Trunk Road) north of Hwy. 1A. Drive 25.4 km to Richards Road junction (sign). Keep right, then in 150 m take the first left (west) onto a gravel road signed "Trapper's Hill Lodges 8." This is the TransAlta Road built by TransAlta Utilities into the forest reserve. It can be further identified by a metal gate and a kiosk.

READ BEFORE YOU GO This road is good to the bridge over Lesueur Creek, then in poor shape with waves of potholes to the top of the big hill. After that the going is reasonable—ONCE you get the big hill and the river crossing behind you. In summer and fall the Ghost River is usually dry. DON'T try crossing it during runoff. Even a little water can turn seemingly hard cobbles into quicksand. Luckily, if you get stuck there are plenty of weekend warriors around to haul you out. Overall, expect a slow drive.

In detail: Turn right up the hill after the first bridge; keep straight at red marker 15 (Enviros access road to right) and straight where a Sutton Energy well access road turns left. For the final few km you drive through cutblocks. Come to the top of the big hill down to the Ghost River at 16.6 km.

Descending/ascending the big hill with its loose stones can be negotiated by vehicles with high clearance, 4 wheel drive and determined drivers. If unsure about driving any farther, use the big hill parking area on the right side and continue on foot or by bike for another 3.4 km.

At the bottom of the hill is a T-junction. Which way to the crossing? Spring floods are constantly undermining the east bank, and the route changes almost yearly. As of fall 2012 you go straight down a shaley ramp and follow tire tracks across the wide, stony bed. At the far side turn right, then climb up left onto the levee by the side of a groyne. A big cairn marks the spot for the return.

Turn left. Turn next right off the levee and follow a flat, stony draw, passing below the levee's steep ending, which is no longer navigable. At a split, keep left on the lower road and onto a smaller levee. After turning west, the split comes in from the right and you come to marker 25 at a 4-way.

Go straight. (River Road to left heads south down the Ghost River flats. The road in the angle between your road and River Road is another way in to the Banff Park boundary, but is only available before June and after mid-September when no one is home at the Ghost River Rediscovery Camp.)

Your road drops off the levee and winds about cobble flats to the right of a high, curving berm. Ignore two side roads heading left through the berm and a road heading right toward the Ghost River diversion. Round the end of the berm to a popular camping area near the diversion creek. Here turn left and drive alongside the Banff Park boundary to a parking area with kiosk at marker 27. (The road to left is the alternative way in from marker no. 25.) See the sketch map below.

This is an easy walk between the Ghost River and Lake Minnewanka via the spectacular Devils Gap, which oozes with historical significance. If you want to reach the lake, hurry past the sand dunes and intriguing side canyons, which should be left for another day. For a half-day, combine it with the dune route to Third Ghost Lake.

To get in the appropriate mood for this ghostly hike, pick a dull, brooding day in late fall when the wind is rattling the dried-up leaves on the poplars and the mountains seem withdrawn from life, waiting patiently shoulder to shoulder for the first snowfall. Personally, I prefer a fine summer day for lolling about in the sand.

TRAIL NOTE Apart from the two routes described to Third Ghost Lake, there is also a trail that starts from the camping area. Initially it follows the left bank of the diversion, but it gets very vague later on.

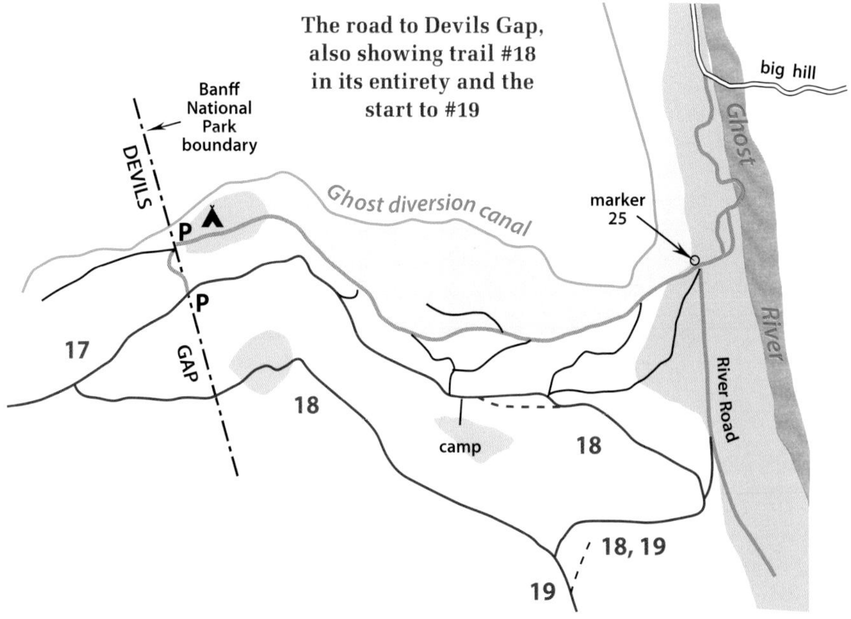

HISTORY NOTE Over 100 years ago Devils Gap was the major thoroughfare to Canmore and Banff (had they existed at the time) from Morley.

Conversely, the gap also brought marauding Kootenai Indians from British Columbia into the Prairies to hunt buffalo. Fierce battles with the Blackfoot, who eventually drove the Kootenai back into the mountains, and frequent skirmishes between warring factions of the Plains Indians are the basis of a legend which tells of a ghost seen going up and down the Ghost River, picking up the skulls of the dead who had been killed by the Cree. In another legend, the restless ghost of a Blackfoot warrior who drowned in the river (considered an ignominious way to die) is seen only after sundown, riding a white horse up and down the river in search of Stoneys. It's said he's seated facing backwards on the horse and brandishes a spear. Actually, it's well documented that there are many Indian graves along the riverbank. According to Sir James Hector, the woods atop Deadman Hill in the angle between the Ghost and the Bow rivers were one vast burial ground.

The RCMP post at Devils Gap in the early 1970s. It was later burned down.

To Third Ghost Lake 1.3 km

Continue west, following the straight, stony track to the LEFT of the kiosk as you read it or the smooth dirt trail twining about it. (As you cross over the boundary, smile for hidden cameras set up to catch errant OHVers.) In 510 m, at 272825, a narrow trail heading left is #18 Devils Gap Viewpoint loop.

In another 310 m come to Y-junction 269824. Choose from two ongoing routes which can be joined to make a loop.

1. Main trail

Wend left on a trail into the trees. A small cairn to left indicates the climber's trail to Planters Valley (#17A). A short distance on, a trail to right reaches Third Ghost Lake in minutes.

The trail then climbs into a scree traverse offering a view across the valley of Spectre Crag (farther to its left the eye is caught by a waterfall blowing in the wind like a lacy curtain), and of Third Ghost Lake, which is also called First Ghost Lake, depending on which direction you are coming from. Above you looms an overhanging cliff, a mini El Capitan look-alike that is still unclimbed.

A scree trail descending to the lake is the way onto or off route no. 2.

2. Dunes

Keep straight on the track heading downhill to a stony draw with seasonal water and follow it out to Third Ghost Lake. Alternatively, cross the draw and explore a dune area more appropriate to Saudi Arabia. Peaks covered in snow and the sound of waterfalls thundering down side canyons dispel the illusion, but it's lots of fun while it lasts.

The wind blasting through the gap has scattered sand all through the forest, and as you'll see, it all emanates from Third Ghost Lake, which is a desert come fall.

Head along the southwest shore. There are two ways to regain the main trail: the short trail through the trees and the one up the scree slope farther along.

To Lake Minnewanka 4.7 km

Unlike what is shown on the topo map, the trail then climbs over the 1500 m contour line and crosses the mouth of a spectacular canyon known as Hoodoo Hall. See #17B.

Between here and the south shore of Second Ghost Lake, cliffs on either side of the gap reach their greatest height. It's awe-inspiring on squally days when mists lift and part momentarily to reveal tantalizing outlines of ridges nearly 1000 metres overhead. In 1884 George Dawson called it a singular valley after observing the "towering cliffs."

The trail divides at an unmarked junction midway between Second and First Ghost Lakes, an important intersection comparable 200 years ago to the Hwy. 93 interchange on the Trans-Canada Hwy. Go straight.

(The trail to right fords the channel and becomes the shoreline trail along Lake Minnewanka — Narrows backcountry campground lies 5 km distant. Sir George Simpson, governor-in-chief of the Hudson's Bay Company, passed this way between the 1st and 3rd of August 1841 on the start of his world tour.)

Third Ghost Lake when dry.

Third Ghost Lake with water. View from the southeast shore of Spectre Crag and West Phantom Crag.

But back to the junction. Keep straight on the historic Carrot Creek trail, which edges along the south bank of First Ghost Lake, the route taken just a few weeks later by James Sinclair's party. Their guide was the great Cree Maskepetoon of future North Kananaskis Pass fame, who was so miffed at Simpson for not letting him guide that he disregarded instructions to go via Athabasca Pass and took a willing Sinclair over the *southern* route to Oregon via Whitemans Gap above Canmore.

In 2 km reach Minnewanka Reservoir. Before the two dams were built in 1912 and 1941, the surface of the lake was lower by 28 m and didn't exist at all in this place. It's had as many names as water levels: Devils Lake, Cannibal's Lake (M'ne'-sto in Stoney), Long lake (Ki'-noo-ki'-mow in Cree) and Wild Cat or Peechee Lake after Simpson's guide Alexis Piché, whose Cree name was Lynx or Wildcat. Finally in 1888 it was officially designated Lake Minnewanka, "Lake of the Water Spirit" or "Where the Spirits Dwell" (Minnee-wah-kah), and the name Peechee was transferred to the mountain facing you across the water.

OPTIONS

17A Planters Valley

Distance 2.4 km from #17
Height gain 320 m (1050 ft.)
High point 1829 m (6000 ft.)

Planters is a major rock and ice climbing valley with nutty route names. Endure rough rockhopping up its creekbed. Higher up you'll find water.

Turn left at the cairn onto a narrower trail that delivers you into the stony creekbed of Planters Valley. Follow the bed past cairns, in mid-valley passing between West Planters Wall on the right and East Planters Wall on the left. The narrows occurs at a left-hand bend, the pool easily bypassed by taking to scree on the left side.

Easier walking between high rock walls ends at a small but impenetrable canyon of whitewater—the obvious dead end for walkers. A small fall tumbles down the cliff on the left.

Looking down Planters valley from near the narrows.

Looking back down the main valley.

17B Hoodoo Hall

Distance 3.1 km from #17
Height gain 268+ m (880+ ft.)

An easy walk past hoodoos into a claustrophobic side canyon.

Some 800 m west of Third Ghost Lake the trail crosses a creekbed at 251813. This is Hoodoo Hall, as ice climbers call it, a wide, flat, stony valley enclosed between vertical walls. Stream-hop your way past the hoodoos on the right bank to the forks at 254800. The left-hand fork is a narrow slit sneakily disguised by a few trees and easily missed.

Whereas the right-hand fork is regular canyon, the left-hand fork is so narrow, and the walls so high, it remains locked in perpetual shade. Speaking in whispers—it's that awe-inspiring—you wind past such features as the yellow wall and 50-metre-high Green Angel waterfall, the entertainment lasting for about a kilometre before the cleft opens out into remnant forest below Orient Point.

One of the hoodoos.

#17B Looking back down the left-hand fork of Hoodoo Hall from where it opens out.

18 DEVILS GAP VIEWPOINT LOOP—map 2

View of the gap and Third Ghost Lake.

Half-day hike
Unofficial trails
Distance 5.6 km loop
Height gain/loss 91 m (300 ft.)
High point 1600 m (5250 ft.)
Map 82 O/6 Lake Minnewanka

Access Via #17 Devils Gap to Lake Minnewanka at the Banff National Park boundary. **Also accessible** from #19 Devils Gap to South Ghost.

The highlight is the view of Devils Gap from a grassy hilltop. See sketch map on page 85.

To the viewpoint 1.3 km
Follow the straight, stony track to the LEFT of the kiosk as you read it or the smooth dirt trail twining about it. In 510 m, at 272825, turn left onto a narrow trail heading back left.

The trail climbs the hillside, crosses a NW–SE cutline (Banff Park boundary) and climbs some more to a grassy hilltop at 279823. Look back for the view of Devils Gap. Thunder God Buttress can be seen rising to the summit of Mt. Costigan, with Costigan's Boil poking up just to its right. Lining the north side of the pass is Phantom Crag, a rock-climbing mecca.

The loop 4.3 km
Continue climbing up a small ridge with patches of meadow, the trail rocky, then descend slightly into pine forest about T-junction ~291815. Turn left. (Trail ahead leads to Trails End Camp.)

Descend a small valley to the flats of the Ghost, and keeping left, curve around to the left, for a brief while following a cutline through spruce forest out to the disused access road (track) to the Banff Park boundary. Turn left or initially use the horse trail to the left.

As you follow the track to the kiosk, pass various side trails, some heading across to the access road and others accessing the Ghost River Rediscovery Camp, which offers "outdoor and cultural programs based on aboriginal traditions."

19 DEVILS GAP TO SOUTH GHOST—maps 2, 5

Half-day one way
Unofficial trails
Distance 6.9 km
Height gain/loss 55 m (180 ft.)
High point 1579 m (5180 ft.)
Maps 82 O/6 Lake Minnewanka, 82 O/3 Canmore

North access Devils Gap. Drive the access road to the 4-way junction with marker 25. Take the first left and drive 900 m along the River Road to Y-junction ~294820. Park.
South access Hussey's Cabin at the mouth of the South Ghost Valley at ~313777.
Also accessible from #18 Devils Gap Viewpoint loop at ~291815, the west terminus of #20 Lower South Ghost, the east terminus of #22 the South Ghost and the northern terminus of #26 Yamnuska to South Ghost.

This route connects Devils Gap to the South Ghost at Hussey's Cabin. Hussey's Cabin is a hub where many trails meet: the Lower South Ghost to the east, the South Ghost to the west and the Yamnuska to South Ghost to the south, and, of course, this one from the north.

While you can get there by following the track through the Ghost River Valley and then the old road, this route is a little more aesthetic, a good half of it undulating along through forest on a trail. It also provides water en route.

The south end of the route accesses #21 Hussey's Hill.

HISTORY NOTE Hussey's Cabin was built in 1929 by Jim and Bill Brewster for Fred Hussey, who invested capital in the "Brewster Brothers" in 1904 and later became president of the Brewster Trading & Brewster Transfer. It was used for several years as a hunting cabin, then abandoned to local hunters until some time in 1977 or 1978 when it was burnt down by the Forest Service. Using this as a bargaining point, the Brewster/Stanton family erected the present-day cabins and cookhouse on the same site as the cabin to succour their guests on overnight pack trips from the Kananaskis Guest Ranch. The area is still referred to as Hussey's Cabin.

The side creek you cross. Looking up to Orient Point and the notch.

To track 312796, 4.3 km
Leave the River Road and veer to the right onto a trail which leads in short order to a T-junction. Keep left and climb up a small valley to T-junction ~291815. Turn left. (Trail to right is #18.)

Continue climbing (ignoring minor trails to left) to Trails End Camp, also spelled "Trials End Camp"—I am still trying to decide if this is a spelling error—run by the Lazy H Trail Company as a British Army adventure training camp. The Lazy H also runs Trapper's Hill Cabins on the TransAlta Road and it's from here that the Brits ride in on horseback.

The camp is serviced by a track from the River Road. You, however, use a trail running parallel to its right. Cross a cutline to a trail junction above a side creek, turn right and cross the creek, which has copious running water emanating from the bowl below The Big Drip ice climb. The view upstream is of Orient Point and the notch out of which rises The Peanut, a "totem-straight pinnacle," best seen from the camp or from marker 25 with binoculars.

On the opposite bank the main trail turns left and heads downstream a way before turning back right. Keep right and meander along to 4-way 312796 with old roads (tracks) in a meadow. Go straight. (The track to left, washed out in a few places, descends a shallow valley to the Ghost River flats and is no longer driveable by the average vehicle. Track to right is #21 to Hussey's Hill.)

To Hussey's Cabin 2.6 km

Your track heads south, a horse trail winding about it. At a meadow on the right side, use the horse trail crossing the grass. Straightaway, pass a longitudinal meadow stretching out to the left. (A rough track along it offers a shortcut to #20 Lower South Ghost.) Stay on the better track, which soon reaches a Y-junction on the bank of the South Ghost. Turn right. (Trail to left is #20 Lower South Ghost.)

Stay on the road. A side track rising up the right bank leads to Hussey's Cabin. Between this junction and the drift fence are camping spots below the bank on the right side. A spring provides water.

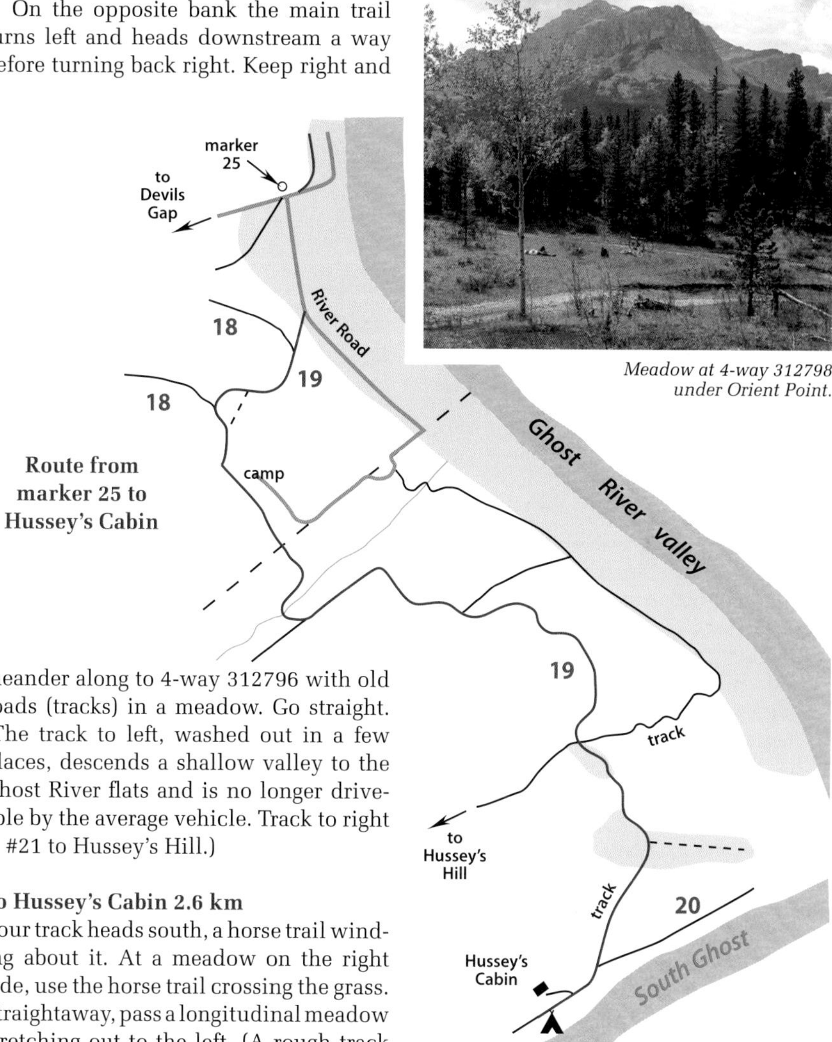

Meadow at 4-way 312798 under Orient Point.

20 LOWER SOUTH GHOST—maps 1, 2, 5

The South Ghost from the trail on the banktop.

Half-day hike one way
Unofficial trail, river & creek crossings
Distance 11.1 km
Height gain 168 m (550 ft.)
Height loss 67 m (220 ft.)
High point 1570 m (5150 ft.)
Maps 82 O/6 Lake Minnewanka, 82 O/3 Canmore

Access Hwy. 940 (Forestry Trunk Road) north of Hwy. 1A. Drive 25.4 km to Richards Road junction (sign). Keep right, then in 150 m take the first left (west) onto a gravel road signed "Trapper's Hill Lodges 8." This is the TransAlta Road built by TransAlta Utilities into the forest reserve. It can be further identified by a metal gate and a kiosk.

READ BEFORE YOU GO This road is good to the bridge over Lesueur Creek, then in poor shape with waves of potholes. Expect a slow drive.

In more detail: Turn to the right up the hill after the first bridge over Lesueur Creek. In 7.2 km from the gate, at an intersecting cutline, turn left and drive to the top of the steep slope down to the Ghost River Valley. Park.

Also accessible from #22 The South Ghost at Hussey's Cabin, from #19 Devils Gap to South Ghost, #8 The Lower Ghost, #26 Yamnuska to the South Ghost.

This route follows the South Ghost River from its confluence with the Ghost to Hussey's Cabin (cabins owned by the Brewster family) at the mountain entrance. We used to slog along the stony South Ghost river bed, but in the last decade a good horse trail has developed on the ridge between the two rivers and takes you all the way. The going is fast, uncomplicated and enjoyable. But first you have to get to the start of it, and this involves a fair bit of wading.

RIVER NOTE The Ghost River changes its course regularly in this area. New side channels fill with water and others dry up. What you see now in 2013 is different from what it was in 2001 and what it will be in the future.

To start of trail 900 m

Immediately below the parking area a stony cutline swoops down the steep slope. Forget it and walk farther east along the banktop. At 382817 take a trail that traverses in to intersect the slightly less vertiginous cutline access road. Turn right and descend the rest of the hill.

Shortly, after the cutline comes in from the right, the road veers west along the banktop of the Ghost River. Where it descends to the river, transfer to Beaver Ponds trail, which continues along the banktop. (The Ghost River at the old road crossing is nowadays far too dangerous a fording place.) Carry on to 379812, which lies just before a pronounced dip in the trail.

River crossing 780 m

Turn left and descend the bank on steep trail to the creek flowing out of beaver ponds. Wade or use the dam if it is still intact. Head across flats sprinkled with small spruce to the Ghost River and walk upstream. Cross a new watery channel. Then cross the Ghost to the east bank, using a recently formed island as the stepping stone. If this doesn't work, head even farther upstream to where the valley track crosses the river at ~380808.

If on the latter course, follow the valley track downstream close to the east bank. Before it disappears under water, turn right onto a trail which intersects the resurrected track farther to the east. There are two routes onto the ridge.

1. Longer way. Turn right and follow the track to the South Ghost creekbed. Walk up the right side of the bed, picking up a trail at ~383808 heading into the forest toward the ridge.

2. Shortcut. From the trail (just before it intersects the track), turn right and walk a grassy avenue (cutline right-of-way?) between pines. This way you're sure to intersect route 1 at the trail. Turn right.

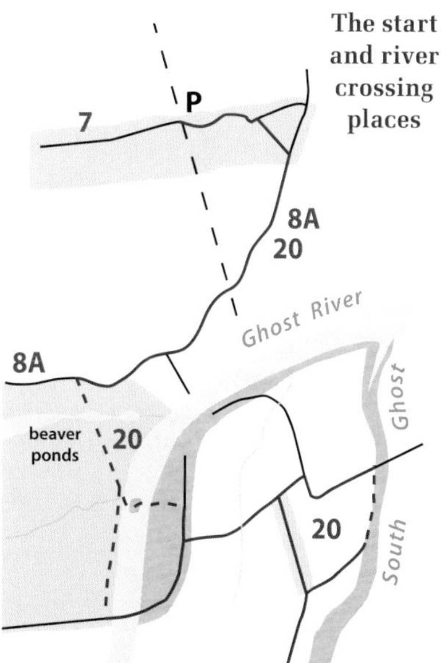

The start and river crossing places

Lower South Ghost 9.4 km

Climb steep zigs onto the wooded ridge. The wet and hilly section behind you, enjoy a long, easy amble along the high northwest bank of the South Ghost. Stretches of open forest alternate with headlands allowing views of silvery channels and Front Range mountains. Spring water is available in a dip.

About halfway along, the trail joins a track risen from the valley. Cross a NW–SE cutline, then a gate in a drift fence. Shortly after this, the track heads inland to a junction near the edge of a long, narrow meadow. Turn left on a trail. (The track continues through the meadow to join #19.)

The trail winds back to the riverbank (here much lower) and follows it to a T-junction with the gravel road used by #19. Keep straight and stay on the road. A track rising up the bank to right leads to Hussey's Cabin at ~313777. Between this last junction and the drift fence are camping spots below the bank on the right side. A spring provides water.

Looking back to Lesueur Ridge.

21 HUSSEY'S HILL (The Viewpoint)—map 5

Looking down the descent ridge from the summit toward the Ghost and the South Ghost.

Half to short day from Hussey's Cabin
Unofficial trails
Distance 7.7 km loop from cabin
Height gain/loss 366 m (1200 ft.)
High point 1935 m (6350 ft.)
Map 82 O/3 Canmore

North access Via #19 Devils Gap to South Ghost at 4-way track junction 313794.
South access Via Hussey's Cabin.

Behind Hussey's Cabin rises Hussey's Hill, also called The Viewpoint, a grassy outlier of Orient Point at 296782. An exploration road cum horse trail leads up one side and down the other, making available a very scenic loop when combined with #19 for anyone camped near Hussey's Cabin. Go anticlockwise for the surprise view.

ANTICLOCKWISE FROM NORTH

To the summit 5.4 km

If camped at Hussey's Cabin, walk north on #19's old road for 2.6 km to the 4-way junction at 312796. Here leave #19 and turn left onto a track.

The track heads southwest toward the hill, which appears dwarfed below the cliffs of Orient Point. Not too far along, use a horse trail to right to avoid a stony section. Rejoin the track and start a sometimes steep, twisty climb to the top of a small ridge. At a T-junction veer right on a trail. (Track to left traverses to the south ridge, so missing out the summit.)

Climb into meadows below the gap between the hill and Orient Point. At a Y-junction turn left (trail to right goes through the gap) and walk up to the summit. What an amazing view of the Ghost rivers! And who could guess there would be so much grass on the lower southeast slopes of the mountain. With luck you'll catch a glimpse of the wildies that call this verdant oasis home.

Down to Hussey's Cabin 2.3 km

The trail carries on down the "front" south ridge, dropping steeply past the junction with the traversing track at 301780. In front are views of End Mountain and of a long, green meadow closer in. Low down the ridge, the trail drops into the aspens of a small valley on the right side, ultimately travelling through the long meadow you saw. Here another trail joins in from the right and is possibly the one from the col that has circumvented the ridges.

In aspen forest the trail upgrades to track and heads very gradually downhill to Hussey's Cabin. Just past the fence, turn right to join the main South Ghost trail (track).

#21 In the long meadow, looking back at Orient Point and grassy Hussey's Hill at middle right.

#22 Looking east from the track in the South Ghost valley.

22 THE SOUTH GHOST—maps 5, 6

Looking west from Saddle Creek.

Backpack
Unofficial trails
Distance 13.8 km to South Ghost Pass
Height gain 640 m (2100 ft.)
High point 2210 m (7250 ft.) pass, lake
Map 82 O/3 Canmore

East access Via ##19, 20, 26 at Hussey's Cabin.
South access Via #32 Exshaw Creek.

The South Ghost is perhaps the most magnificent of all the major Ghost valleys with its great unclimbed cliffs and extensive meadows. There's even a couple of lakes.

Along its length runs a track, then a trail, which takes you to South Ghost Pass, where options exist for experienced backpackers to join the Carrot Creek trail or to trudge over the tops to Cougar Creek. You can peel off long before that over Exshaw High Col into Exshaw Creek or poke around several interesting side valleys and ridges on the north side.

HYDROLOGY NOTE The most important thing to know about the South Ghost River itself is that there IS no river. The country is like a sieve, the water generally surfacing in only two spots: a stretch of about 500 m in the meadows below Stenton Lake, and about 2.5 km lower down, in the vicinity of Guinn's camp, where it reappears. R.G. McConnell was right on when he wrote in his famous report of 1886: "In the latter part of summer, the circuit of the group might be made without crossing a single running stream." (You wonder how such a small, intermittent stream has cut such a large valley 1000–1200 metres in depth and almost 2 kilometres wide in places.) Interestingly, TransAlta believes the name "Ghost" came about because the rivers "ghost," i.e., appear and disappear at different points along their courses! Luckily for backpackers, some of the side creeks have copious, year-round water.

BEAR WARNING Be aware that problem bears removed from Banff to Carrot Creek travel over the pass into the South Ghost. In the late 1990s one such collared grizzly caused panic at sheep hunters' camps up and down the valley as it blithely barged through electric fences to get at the food. Shades of the movie *The Ghost and the Darkness*: the bruin was often never seen, but nevertheless sent panicked hunters fleeing to their OHVs in the middle of the night to "get the hell out of there." We were camped at Guinn's Camp at the time, but never had a problem and I've never heard of any incidents with backpackers, either before or since. If this worries you, travel in a group of 4 or more and eat freeze-dried.

EAST TO WEST

To Guinn's Camp 10.6 km

From Hussey's Cabin head west along the track though a gate in a drift fence. This stretch of track soon ends in stony river bed at two cairns. Follow imprints on stones to a vegetated island where the track picks up and crosses a stony channel back to the north bank. At this point (~299763) is a campsite next to a side creek with water. Look up to the right to the freestanding arch on a ridge of rotten teeth descending toward the valley.

Continue along the north bank, crossing two stony side creeks. The third is Saddle Creek, a much longer, two-pronged valley dividing Orient Point and Saddle Peak. To right, a small 700-ft.-high cliff is a dead ringer for Yamnuska.

Between here and the end of the gravel flats, the cliffs are at their most awesome, some rising sheer from the riverbed. The track does a stint on the left (south) bank, then returns to the north bank at two side creeks close together. Pass a hunting camp below a remarkable piece of rock bristling with roofs.

A long stretch through trees ends at the bend near where a side creek comes in from Exshaw Pass (the valley you DON'T take). Here the valley undergoes a charac-

A challenging cliff with roofs untouched by climbers. Around the corner is a big east-facing wall and a line of cliffs heading up a side valley.

The tower on the southeast ridge of Saddle Peak.

SIDE TRIP

22A North Side Valley

Unofficial trail, then route
Distance 3.4 km to col
Height gain 128+ m (420+ ft.)

Heading into the valley. Photo Alf Skrastins

The valley north of Guinn's Camp is worthy of a day's exploration.

Two trails starting from either side of the camping area zig up the north bank, then unite for the final climb to banktop meadows—a viewpoint for Exshaw High Col and the meadows about South Ghost Pass. The trail heads west, then traverses above the side creek onto a bench. Contour across and into the right fork. Sans trail, climb to the col at the valley head, then climb the red scree ridge on its right to a minor top on the south end of Saddle Peak for the view of Lake Minnewanka.

Heading for Stenton Lake. The South Ghost trail traverses from right to left at treeline to South Ghost Pass at top left. Photo Alf Skrastins

ter change, the stony flats replaced by a V-shaped valley of meadow and spruce. The track pays a brief visit to the left bank, then continues along the north bank to its end at a campsite (no water that I could see).

A good trail carries on, straightaway climbing to get above a mini-canyon. Descend to valley bottom and cross and recross the South Ghost to Guinn's Camp, located on the north bank at 227728. Constructed by Alvin Guinn of Guinn's Pass fame (note the words "Rafter 6" carved into the table), it has recently been "enhanced" with a pit biffy and food lockers. There is copious water at this point.

The outfitter's camp is an ideal base for exploration. The trail to Exshaw High Col (#32A) crosses the South Ghost upstream of the side creek. In the opposite direction two trails starting from either side of the camp climb into the side valley to the north. See SIDE TRIP #22A. And of course, the meadows of South Ghost Pass and a couple of lakes lie not too far ahead.

To South Ghost Pass 3.2 km

So far, the route has been flat and easy up what pilots call a "sucker canyon" because it lulls you into thinking there's an easy way through, only suddenly the ground is rising faster than a light aircraft can climb and the canyon's too narrow to turn round in. Sadly, this area was the site of a fatal crash in 1994.

And for the hiker this is where the hard work begins. From the camp the trail crosses the river twice in quick succession, the bed again dry when you cross the north tributary. Here the trail gains height up the west bank of the tributary, then settles into a sometimes steeply rising traverse above the upper canyon of the South Ghost. Levelling off at treeline, it follows the contours of the mountain around a buttress, dips into a shallow cirque, and finally dissipates behind a clump of spruce trees. Cross an intervening hillside into a narrow defile that is South Ghost Pass on the Banff Park boundary at 198724.

To Stenton Lake 1.5 km from the trail

Before reaching the defile, descend left into the head of the South Ghost, a checkerboard of meadows and spruce thickets rising gradually to a lake officially named in 1987 after James "Ernie" Stenton, a Banff Park warden who in 1946 artificially crossed a male brook trout with a female lake trout to produce a "splake."

Camping just below the lake on flat ground near a small waterfall — source of the distant water music heard from the trail — places you in a good position to cross over into Cougar Creek and reach Canmore the next evening before the bars close.

GOING FARTHER

22B to Carrot Creek trail

Route, then trail
Distance ~14.9 km to #17
Height gain 137 m (450 ft.)
Height loss 823 m (2700 ft.)

Access South Ghost Pass.

One option is to join historic Carrot Creek trail and connect with #17 Devils Gap to Lake Minnewanka. Overall, a not very interesting hike, nearly all through forest with bushwhacking. NOTE Walking the Carrot Creek trail to Hwy. 1 with its 25 creek crossings is discouraged because of wildlife concerns (though the trail is not legally closed).

From the pass descend the steep-walled drainage (east fork of Carrot Creek) to ~163728. Bushwhack north to intersect the Carrot Creek trail. At this point old campsite Ca9 lies about 1 km downstream.

Turn right and climb to Carrot Creek Pass at 1905 m (6250 ft.). Descend the steep north slope alongside a creek, criss-crossing it numerous times en route to Lake Minnewanka's south shore. Turn right and walk an undulating trail past campsite Lm31 to the terminus of #17.

22C to Cougar Creek

Scramble route, game trail
Distance 3.6 km from Stenton Lake
Height gain 488 m (1600 ft.)
Height loss 183 m (600 ft.)
High point 2637 m (8650 ft.)

A highly recommended route over the ridgetops to the Carrot/Cougar Col at 186691, from where you can descend #70C into Cougar Creek. Expect scree and one short section of steep rubble.

First you have to get onto the big grass hill at 192713 on the boundary ridge, either from South Ghost Pass or from Stenton Lake. This is a fabulous viewpoint in its own right, looking northwest over Carrot Creek to the cliffs of Mt. Peechee.

Turn south and walk over a grassy rise with cairn. Down below you on the left is a tarn and ahead the next section of ridge. Getting a few butterflies? The upcoming step with chossy cliff bands certainly intimidates. Fortunately, it's one of those places that looks harder than it is, and with your nose to the rock you discover the sheep have trodden out such huge indentations in the brown rubble that a veritable staircase exists up the right-hand edge where the going is firmer. Sheep have no aspirations on summits and from the flat shoulder above the step, the trail traverses the west slope of peak 200693 to the col at 197693. Look down vertiginous red scree into the head of Cougar Creek.

Still the trail continues, climbing those red screes toward, then passing just to the right of, the highest summit of the day, at 195691. It's easy enough to walk up to the top for an outstanding view taking in Lake Minnewanka, Mt. Aylmer, The Three Sisters and, yes, Mt. Assiniboine.

Back on the trail, descend to a saddle between the summit and a lower top to the south and turn right along a ridge heading northwesterly down to the Carrot/Cougar col. Turn left and descend into the lovely basin below Mt. Charles Stewart, a welcome return to the feel of soft grass underfoot and the resinous scents of pine wafting up from the valley below.

The boundary ridge above Stenton Lake. Photo Alf Skrastins

Bottom: On col 198692, looking up to the highest summit. Photo Alf Skrastins

Top: Plodding up the ridge. Photo Alf Skrastins

Now read route #70C to Carrot/Cougar Col, then #70 Cougar Creek.

NOTE Between June 1 and August 31 these meadows are a helicopter landing spot for tourists who are fed a picnic, go for hikes "choice of three led by highly trained guides," and get married. Because it's a designated protected area for sheep between June 1 and August 31, no camping is allowed for sweaty backpackers who must carry on down into Cougar Creek. "Let them camp on stones" would appear to be the motto

BAD WEATHER ALTERNATIVE

This is another way to Carrot/Cougar Col without going over the tops. It's 340 m shorter. But because it dips into the head of Carrot Creek's south fork, there is a price to pay: an added height loss of 85 m (280 ft.) and height gain of 58 m (190 ft.)

At 195710 descend WSW off the boundary ridge via a shallow drainage. Keep alert for a sheep trail that veers left along a bench below a scree slope. When the bench gives out, descend at the edge of scree into valley head trees. From here ascend to the col to the right of steep, craggy ground, using a broad ridge initially, then a reasonable slope angling up left.

23 BOW VALLEY PROVINCIAL PARK north—map 5

#23E Many Springs. Not so long ago there was no lake, just a creek running through the basin into the Bow River. Dams made by beavers gradually raised the water level to what you see today. Probably it is cyclical. Photo Tanya Koob

Official interpretive trails with signs
High point 1326 m (4350 ft.)
Map 82 O/3 Canmore

Access Hwy. 1X, reached from Hwy. 1 (Trans-Canada Hwy.) at interchange 114. In a few metres is a 4-way junction. Right leads to Willow Rock Campground and Flowing Water interpretive trail. Left (Bow Valley Park Road) leads to Bow Valley Campground and all of the other trails.

Access 1 Turn right into Willow Rock Campground. Park near the showers building.

Access 2 Turn left. In only a short distance from Hwy. 1X, turn right into a parking lot in front of the park office.

Access 3 Turn left, and 3.5 km from Hwy. 1X turn left into Middle Lake parking lot.

Access 4 Turn left, and 3.7 km from Hwy. 1X you'll come to a road junction. Turn right and follow the road into Bow Valley Campground. Park at the amphitheatre.

Access 5 Turn left. Then, 3.7 km from Hwy. 1X, at a road junction, turn left and follow the road to its end at Whitefish day-use area.

Access 6 Turn left. Then, at a road junction 3.7 km from Hwy. 1X, turn left and follow road for 2 km to Many Springs parking lot.

Access 7 Turn left. At 3.7 km from Hwy. 1X you'll come to a road junction. Turn left and follow the road for 1.4 km to Elk Flats Group Camp and day-use area.

ACCESS NOTE The park road is closed mid-Oct to mid-May at the T-junction beyond Middle Lake parking lot. At such times use a bike.

This refers to the section of park north of Hwy. 1 and overlapping Hwy. 1X that was created pre K Country, in 1959. While the terrain appears flat from the highway, it is not, and trails, though easy, are bumpy and twisty as they weave through a varied landscape including riversides and lakeshores in a kaleidoscope of dry meadow and forest. Because they lie in a snow shadow area and are hit with strong chinook winds, they can be hiked pretty well all year round. Nevertheless, do go in summer when the flowers are at their best. Around late June the western wood lilies and orchids are an amazing sight.

FACILITIES Two campgrounds: Willow Rock (open Apr–Nov) and Bow Valley (open May 1 to the first week in Oct). Bow Valley has an amphitheatre for interpretive programs and a small store located at the check-in. Elk Flats Group Campground and day-use area (open May 1 to the first week in Oct) has a shelter and playground. Day-use areas are located at Whitefish and Middle Lake. The park office doubles as an information centre whenever anyone is in residence.

EVENTS NOTE Each year, Parks Day is celebrated in BVPP in late July. Watch the K Country website for the exact date and location.

GEOLOGY NOTE The parks's irregular terrain is the result of stagnant ice left stranded here and there during the retreat of the last ice age. When the ice melted it left behind features like kames, eskers, crevasse fillings and kettle lakes. End (recessional) moraines, on the other hand, are deposits of rubble pushed ahead by the ice, then left behind when the ice paused during its retreat.

23A Flowing Water loop

Hour walk
Distance 1.8 km; 1.3 km from campground loop road between sites 87 and 89.

From access 1.

An interesting and varied walk taking in the Kananaskis River, a grassy ridge, and wetlands with beaver ponds. Birders should look for warblers and flycatchers (including ovenbirds) in the willows of the swamp and rarities like the tail-wagging eastern phoebe on Douglas fir branches overhanging the river.

Start from the hiking sign on the campground loop road opposite the showers building. The trail heads through forest to the far end of the loop road and crosses it between sites 87 and 89.

A short distance on is a T-junction. Go straight. (Left is the return route.)

Walk the bank above the Kananaskis River between wolf willow bushes. Steps down to the river allow a closer look at butterworts and big prairie gentians growing on calcareous flats. The red colour in the little creeks you cross results from actual

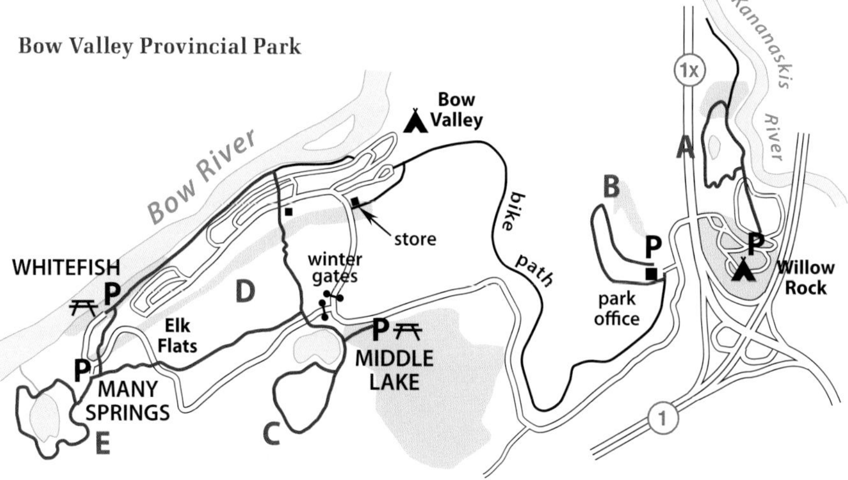

#23A Flowing Water. Kananaskis River from the bench.

flakes of iron carried there in a dissolved state by water seeping from the swamp on your left. All along this section are drippy banks that morph into curtains of ice in the winter.

After entering meadow, climb steps onto a ridge with bench—a satisfying viewpoint looking upriver to the mountain gateway. (NOTE Trail ahead at the top of the steps continues to follow the riverbank across a powerline right-of-way and ultimately down and across CPR tracks into a big parking lot used by river rafters. This parking lot is accessed from the Seebe road before the bridge.)

The interpretive trail veers left along the ridgetop a way, then descends into woodland between Hwy. 1X and the swamp. After pausing at a viewing platform above a series of beaver ponds, cross the swamp on boardwalk back to the T-junction.

Turn right to regain the campground loop road.

23B Montane

Hour walk
Distance 1.5 km loop

From access 2.

The shortest of the interpretive trails is known for its meadows.

Head around the right side of the park office where the trail takes off through an aspen grove into a big meadow with creamy camas lilies. Pass under powerlines. After more meadow the trail climbs onto an esker with a grand view of McConnell Ridge. Leah's memorial bench reads "Remember me as you pass by."

Walk the winding crest a way, then drop off the left side into Douglas fir forest. Pass a fallen fir giant en route to the powerline right-of-way. From here the trail wanders through mixed forest back to the parking lot.

#23B Montane. Walking the esker.

#23C Middle Lake. Photo Tanya Koob

23C Middle Lake

Hour walk
Distance 2.2 km

From access 3.

While most of the loop takes place in forest, the meadows 'twixt parking lot and lake are a flower hot spot.

From the parking lot the trail descends flower meadows (western wood lilies in June) to Middle Lake, en route detouring to the interpretive exhibit. At the T-junction on the east shore turn left onto Middle Lake interpretive trail. (Trail to right is Moraine.)

This rather pretty lake, backdropped by the Three Sisters and fringed with reeds, is the place to see diving ducks like buffleheads and goldeneyes after their arrival in April.

At the next junction keep left and walk clockwise around the loop. The loop is forested with aspen, spruce and remnant Douglas fir (stumps) logged at the turn of the 20th century for James Walker's sawmill at Kananaskis, which provided lumber for the new railway. Circle back to the south shore of the lake, through aspens clawed by black bears. From benches you can enjoy views of Yamnuska.

Back at the T-junction, turn left and return to the T-junction with Moraine.

23D Moraine/Elk Flats loop

Half-day walk
Distance 5.5 km loop
Height gain ~30 m (~100 ft.)

From access 3. Also accesses 4, 5, 6, 7.

It makes sense to join the four remaining trails—Moraine, Bow River, Whitefish and Elk Flats—and make a longer loop that can be walked in either direction. Many Springs can also be added into the mix.

ANTICLOCKWISE

Moraine 1.2 km

From the parking lot the trail descends flower meadows to Middle Lake. Turn right. (To left is Middle Lake interpretive trail.) Walk around the north shore past a bench to the park road. Cross the road to the left of the winter gate. At the T-junction go straight on Moraine. (To left is Elk Flats trail.)

The trail climbs onto a moraine and follows the crest past benches and interpretive signs. Wind-beaten spruce lining the trail have a distinct lean to the east, telling you this ridge gets the full force of winds blowing through the gap.

All too soon the trail drops off the end, winding through sheltered hollows and crossing a powerline right-of-way into Bow Valley Campground. To your right is the amphitheatre.

The trail continues straight, crossing three campground roads. (If you head to the right on the first you'll come to the amphitheatre parking lot—access 5—and the campground entrance.)

Bow River trail 1.6 km

At a T-junction of trails on the bank of the Bow River, turn left. (Trail to right follows the riverbank past benches to A loop.) Your trail follows the riverbank within sight of campsites in C and E loops. Throughout are views over the water to Yamnuska, Door Jamb Mountain and limestone quarries. Look for beautiful blue columbines by the side of the trail.

At the west end, just before the trail reaches Whitefish day-use area parking lot in a meadow (access 5), turn left onto Whitefish trail, the connector to Many Springs parking lot.

Whitefish trail 400 m

Almost straightaway the trail heads up a bank into the trees. It crosses the powerline right-of-way encountered earlier, then the park road to the left of the access road into Many Springs parking lot (access 6). At a T-junction turn left. (A right turn leads into the parking lot.)

Elk Flats trail 1.9 km

The trail climbs and in 400 m crosses the park road opposite Elk Flats group camp and day-use area (access 7).

#23D Typical view along Elk Flats trail.

I really like this next section of trail, which meanders from one meadow to another, each one carpeted in a patchwork of kinnikinnick and juniper. Look back for views of McConnell Ridge, Mt. McGillivray and Pigeon Mountain. The terrain becomes more undulating as you near the T-junction with Moraine (you can spot Middle Lake from one high point). Here, turn right.

Back to parking lot 400 m
Cross the park road. The trail heads for the north shore of Middle Lake at a bench, then turns left, following the shore around to a T-junction with Middle Lake trail. Turn left and climb the hill back to the parking lot.

#23D Moraine trail.

23E Many Springs

Half-day walk with stops
Distance 1.9 km

From access 6.

The trail circles a lake fed by underground springs. Orchids, birds and beavers are the main attraction. The beautifully written interpretive signs along the way are works of fiction, so don't go running to the Glenbow to find out who this early traveller was. The pic is of Jean Habel, who was never here.

Keeping alert for elephants as per the sign at the trailhead, head down a wide track to a T-junction where the trail loops around the basin holding the springs—or rather the new and expanding Many Springs Lake courtesy of beaver construction. Turn right onto a narrower trail.

The trail cuts across to the power line right-of-way, turns left and follows it down to beaver ponds at the lake's egress. Cross the bridge between dams to interpretive signs overlooking a channel of the Bow River and many beaver houses.

The trail heads inland, crosses the powerline right-of-way, then makes its way to the west shore of the lake. Here, boardwalk crosses flats slowly being inundated by the expanding lake. Is the sign still visible? The one barely above water asking you to keep to the trail? Arrive at the far end platform, where you look down on springs bubbling up from the ground. This is a great viewpoint for Yamnuska.

23E Interpretive sign gradually being inundated.

From here the trail climbs out of the basin onto the wide track that takes you back to the parking lot.

24 KANANASKIS DAM TO HORSESHOE CANYON—map 5

Bow River at the bluffs.

Half-day, short-day hikes
Unofficial trails
Distance 3.4 km to canyon
Height gain ~36 m (~120 ft.)
High point 1295 m (4250 ft.)
Map 82 O/3 Canmore

Access Hwy. 1X. Just north of the bridge over the Bow River, opposite the entrance to Kananaskis Guest Ranch, turn east onto a dirt road and park just before the bend.

Enjoy a scenic walk alongside the Bow River from Kananaskis Dam to Horseshoe Canyon through TransAlta reserve land. Most people just go as far as Horseshoe Dam, where there is a handy picnic table. A good trail for spring, but better in summer when you can watch raftloads of tourists navigate the class IV rapids at Horseshoe Canyon. Birdwatching for ospreys and bald eagles is great all year round. NOTE Connecting with Nakoda Lodge for brunch is no longer an option; it is now a medical facility.

WARNING Wandering the toe of the dams is dangerous owing to sudden fluctuations in water levels. Signs ask you to stay away.

MOVIE HISTORY Many movies have been made in the vicinity, from 1954's *River of No Return* to 2003's *Open Range*. See GOING FARTHER.

RECENT HISTORY NOTE As someone once stated, the Bow River has a most unnatural hydrology. Before man started eyeing this particular stretch of river for hydroelectric power, photos show it was a stunning place with cardium sandstone cliffs anchoring two remarkable waterfalls: Kananaskis Falls that thundered over four drops and the graceful Horseshoe Falls that like miniature Niagaras fell a total of 70 ft. over two U-shaped ledges.

Horseshoe Dam, built at the head of Horseshoe Canyon, was the very first dam to be built on the Bow River in 1911. Kananaskis Dam was started soon after in 1913. The hamlet of Seebe housed employees and featured a store, cafe, one-room school and ice rink. In 2004 the hamlet was closed down and the land reverted to the Stoney Nakoda (Moondance

Land Company), who are quoted as saying that "the Horseshoe Lands will be developed with upscale housing for artists and writers with room for big-box retail like Canadian Tire or Walmart."

To the bluffs 1.7 km
From the parking area continue on the same line on a narrow trail in the trees. Just after crossing a bridge, keep straight and climb a hill. In a meadow turn right down a hill to the Bow River. The trail and variations follow the open bank above crumbly shale cliffs, passing two islands separated by a river-wide ledge rapid. Re-enter trees, then climb uphill to a faint Y-junction at the edge of a large meadow.

Keep right across the meadow and under a powerline, soon enjoying a lovely bit of river scenery at rocky bluffs sprinkled with Douglas firs. The cross on the far bank is in memory of Brad Sheer.

To Horseshoe Falls Dam 1.7 km
After a trail comes in from the left, enter trees and descend under another powerline. The trail then follows the river around a bend and up the bank. At the top turn right. Walk the banktop, ultimately turning left through a small meadow to join a track. (This track comes in from Hwy. 1X and is possibly a section of the old Bow Fort Trail.)

Turn right on the track that rounds the top of a small deep gully. Just after, there is a choice of routes.

1. Stay on the track and enter a big meadow above Horseshoe Dam's forebay. Keep right and down, aiming for a picnic area in aspens above a deeply incised side creek. Unfortunately the biffy is toppled over and the picnic tables look set to collapse on wonky legs.

2. Immediately turn right on a side trail that descends by the side of the gully to the lower meadow and cuts across the bench to a "picnic area."

Descend a grey shale path to the left of some barbed wire fencing into the side creek. Cross and climb one of the trails up the other side into an even bigger meadow. Go right, following the bank around to a new picnic table. From it a trail leads to overlooks for Horseshoe Falls Dam and Horseshoe Canyon downstream.

Kananaskis Dam to Bow Fort Trail via Horseshoe Dam

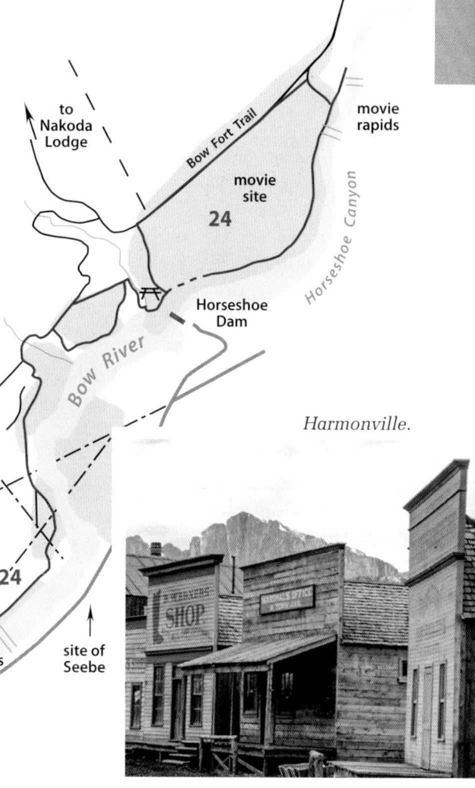

Harmonville.

Bow Fort Trail, looking west to the mountains, the same terrific view seen by early explorers.

As you head north, converging on Bow Fort Trail, the meadow tapers. Down right the river is narrowing, broken here and there by class IV rapids (double ledge, figure 8) run by rafting companies who also offer clients cliff jumping for the same price. The rapids were featured as the *River of No Return* in the 1954 movie of the same name starring Marilyn Monroe and Robert Mitchum. Fast forward to the exciting part near the end where the Indians are chasing the raft along this cliff top.

Bow Fort Trail 2.2 km
When you hit Bow Fort Trail, which is a track, it's time to turn around. Go left and head southeast, following the very same wagon trail used by all the early explorers of the Canadian West, starting with David Thompson in 1800, who commented on the beautiful meadows hereabouts. Farther on, the track was upgraded to handle all the paraphernalia of a movie set.

Just before meeting the deeply incised side creek, the track turns right. Leave it here and turn left, following a trail back to the crossing place.

GOING FARTHER LOOP

Horseshoe Canyon 2.1 km
Continue along the edge. Circumvent a line of crags to the left and pick up a good trail that follows the top of the canyon wall. The big flat to the left was where Harmonville was erected for the movie *Open Range*, starring Kevin Costner and Robert Duvall. I'm told that also in this area you'll find a linear row of prehistoric cairns, marking in all likelihood a bison drive lane to the canyon edge.

Movie rapids in early spring.

25 YAMNUSKA—map 5

#25A At the first viewpoint below Yamnuska. Photo Alf Skrastins

Half-day, day hikes
Map 82 O/3 Canmore

Access Hwy. 1A (Bow Valley Trail). At 2.1 km east of Hwy. 1X, turn left (north) onto the quarry road. Take the next left into a large parking lot (opened in 1999) with biffy, picnic tables and kiosk. The quarry road is gated beyond the parking lot.

These three hikes centre on the mountain of Yamnuska — over 50 years ago the birthplace of rock climbing in the Canadian Rockies. A, C and D follow on one from the other, each becoming progressively more strenuous. Raven's End (A) is merely the start to bigger and better things. NOTE The traverse of Yamnuska, recently made safer by means of a bolted chain on the exposed traverse, is described in Alan Kane's *Scrambles in the Canadian Rockies*.

NAMING NOTE The mountain's official name is Mt. Laurie, after John Laurie, who was a teacher at Morley and an advocate of aboriginal rights. But everyone calls it Yamnuska or the Yam, a derivation from its Stoney name, *Iyamnathka*, meaning "Wall of Stone."

GEOLOGY NOTE The Yam is the poster mountain for the McConnell Thrust Fault, where older rocks have been pushed up over younger ones. The actual line, representing an age difference of 420 million years, is easily seen between the grey cliff of Cambrian Eldon formation and the brownish Cretaceous Belly River Formation of sandstones and silts below it. The latter is quarried by Lafarge for its high-grade silica content needed in the manufacture of cement and is the reason why the whole area is closed down periodically for blasting.

GAME FARM NOTE On your way in to the parking lot, there was once a road to the right accessing Wildlife Unlimited, a game farm (now ruin) that ran between the late 1960s and 1978, the idea being to "provide captive wolves, cougars, bears and other beasts that could be photographed and filmed for a fee." It was rumoured the beasts included a tiger that had escaped and was roaming the forests of the Yam. For a while, this "news" certainly had us all in jitters!

BOOK & MOVIE HISTORY The Yam is the scenario for Ben Gadd's novel *Raven's End* and the star of the book *The Yam: 50 Years of Climbing on Yamnuska*, by Ben, Chic Scott and Dave Dornian. In Steve di Maio's novel *Suicide Wall* the exciting climax takes place on the great wall. The TV movie *The Legend of the Ruby Silver* was filmed in the quarry.

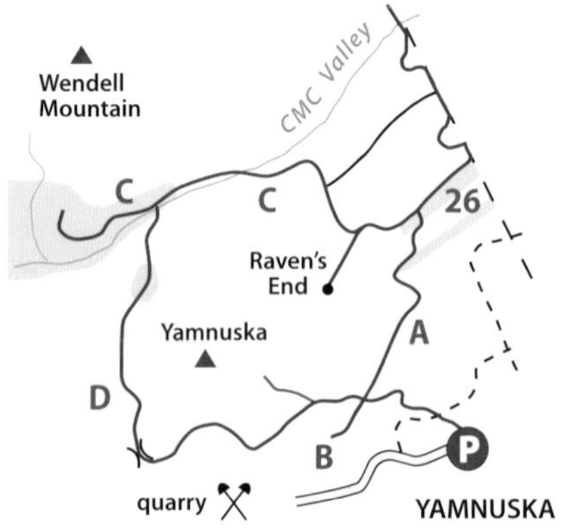

25A Raven's End

Half-day, short-day hike
Official trail, cairns, paint marks
Distance 2.6 km to second viewpoint; 3.6 km to cliff
Height gain 460 m (1510 ft.) to cliff base
High point 1829 m (6000 ft.) at cliff base

This popular trail takes you to a superlative viewpoint, then on up onto the east ridge where #25C takes off, then even higher up the ridge to the base of the great cliff called Raven's End. The first section is the ideal early-season hike. Snow may lie deep on the Front Ranges to the west, but here the blooming of the prairie crocus in the meadows and the drumming of the grouse in the woods tell you that spring has arrived at Yamnuska. NOTE Since the third edition of this book a new trail has been built that misses out the quarry.

Parking lot to climber's trail 820 m
The trail starts from the kiosk, and after running parallel to the quarry road for a short distance, crosses it to a climber's registration box. From here it meanders through flowery aspen forest, in a dip at 430 m crossing a grassy track. (Track to right accesses a NW–SE cutline, a route a few scramblers take to the east ridge.)

Just after passing Stoney prayer flags, climb to a gap in the sandstone escarp-

SIDE TRIP

25B Practice Cliffs

Distance 1.2 km from trailhead

Highly recommended for a short stroll from the parking lot. Not only is there a great view of the Bow Valley, there are alpines growing among the slabs at the cliff edge.

At 4-way junction 332653 turn left and follow a trail along the top of sandstone cliffs for 370 m, gradually descending to a rickety-looking fence high above the quarry. Cracks in the ground hereabouts are a bit worrying, so stay well back.

The trail and Raven's End. Photo Bob Spirko

ment. Here's where I wish for another zig; the grade is ultra-slippery when wet. At the top is 4-way junction 332653. Turn right. (Straight on is the climber's access route to the Yam and #25D. The smaller trail to left is SIDE TRIP #25B.)

To CMC Valley junction 2.3 km

The trail follows the escarpment edge, soon turning inland to join the original trail from the quarry. A creek crossing (usually dry) signals the start of the climb to the east ridge. This is not at all onerous. After the initial left-hand bend just follow the well-worn trail nearest the creek. At about half height it traverses right onto a shaley bench above outcrops, the first of two fabulous viewpoints for the Yam in profile and the Bow Valley. Who would have thought there were so many lakes sprinkled about the forest? Another easier climb through aspens leads into a higher traverse. Keep right and follow the bench to junction 331665, marked on the ground by an arrow fashioned out of rocks (the old cairn). It's here where many half-day trippers decide to stay put and enjoy the views. If carrying on to Raven's End and CMC Valley turn left. (The trail continuing along the bench is #26 to the South Ghost.)

Within a short distance veer left (west), keep straight, then right and up a steep little hill onto the broad east ridge of the Yam, reached at T-junction 329663 with cairn. Keep left. (The right-hand fork is #25C to CMC Valley.)

To Raven's End 520 m

The trail winds about a few trees up the ridge toward the great cliff. To its right is Mt. Doom, divided from the Yam by a deep gash called Windy Gap. At the base of the cliffs where a climber's access trail joins in from the left, the trail downgrades to the scrambler's route up the Yam.

If you have read *Raven's End*, you will never again regard this place — the meeting of the east ridge with the great cliff — in quite the same way as before. In our imaginations it is now the scenario for "the Flap," or meeting place of ravens, some of whom are really — oops! better not give the story away. In reality, this is a good place to spot the "wildies" as opposed to the "townies."

25C CMC Valley

Day hike
Unofficial trails, creek crossings
Distance ~3.5 km from east ridge; ~6.6 km from trailhead
Height gain 543 m (1780 ft.)
Height loss 174 m (570 ft.)
High point 175 m (5750 ft.)

CMC Valley, a quiet cul-de-sac at the back of the Yam (previously called Logger's Valley), can only be approached from the east ridge of Yam unless you happen to have Stoney Nakoda connections.

Also the scrambler's access to Wendell Mountain.

CMC stands for Calgary Mountain Club, which for many years had a hut down near the creek. Called the Archie Simpson Memorial Hut, it was an old logger's cabin rebuilt and used by the CMC during the time of first ascents in the valley. For weeks at a time it was lived in by colourful characters like Billy Davidson, who is possibly the inspiration behind the rather scary fireside story *The Man of the Mountain who lived in this valley behind Yam* as told at Camp Chief Hector. After 25 years of service the hut was razed to the ground in June 1995.

To CMC Valley 1.5 km

At the cairned junction on the east ridge, go straight. Almost straightaway is a view across CMC Valley to Wendell Mountain and its fantastic array of cliffs. Start the descent of the north flank through pines, then spruce, to a T-junction with a logging road (infiltrated by alder) that has traversed the hillside from the boundary fence. Note cabin ruins on the right side.

Continue straight down the fall line to valley bottom, the stony, trenched trail bearing more than a passing resemblance to a streambed. In fact, all the water coursing down the north flank pools on the terrace above the creek and it's here where the trail divides and becomes nebulous on soggy ground. The drier trail goes right, then left around a rectangle of grey ash—the residue of Archie Simpson's Memorial Hut. Now, you either descend the bank below

25C Mt. Doom and Yamnuska from CMC Valley. At far right is the Goat/Yam col.

the hut site to the south fork and paddle across, or follow a gradually descending trail upstream, en route noting a tree of considerable girth bridging the creek. (This trail on the southeast bank continues past the tree and camping areas to a side creek.) Either way, on the northwest bank pick up a good trail (née logging road) and turn left.

To turnoff for #25D, ~920 m

The trail follows every bend of the creek upstream into Tolkien country. Rising above the trail are sun-baked meadows and cliffs named Bilbo Buttress, Frodo's Buttress and Isengard Pillar, all this in sharp contrast to the soggy forest of the south slope and the shadowy cliffs of Mount Doom. Occasional washouts require small detours, the last one on scree. After a short stint through willows, come to ~314668 where #25D takes off across the creek at a pool.

To viewpoint 1.1 km

Leaving 314668, the trail climbs onto open slopes and traverses above a large beaver pond. Coming into view ahead are mountains encircling the end of the valley: Goat Mountain on the left, "Hassel Castle" (The Hunchback) and "Morrowmount," named after Pat Morrow, who was the second Canadian up Everest. Looking left you can pick out #25D's route to the Yam/Goat col up the side valley to the right of Yam and check out the trails on the final scree approach.

Above some trees the trail dips, then climbs onto a grassy rib above a side valley. A very much fainter trail carries on into the forest of the valley head. I have never followed this, preferring to climb the rib to a levelling at ~306667, a heavenly spot looking up the side valley to the great cliffs of Ephel Dúath—the Mountains of Shadow. This is also the taking-off point for East Wendell by its south ridge, rated an easy scramble by Andrew Nugara (see *More Scrambles in the Canadian Rockies*).

The cliffs of Wendell Mountain from CMC Valley, Wakonda Buttress at left.

Ephel Dúath from the viewpoint.

Goat/Yam col, looking up the descent route off the Yam.

25D The Round of Yam

Day scramble
Unofficial & official trails, route, creek crossing
Distance 10.7 km complete loop
Height gain from CMC Valley 366 m (1200 ft.)
Height gain/loss from trailhead 802 m (2630 ft.)
Highpoint at col 1996 m (6550 ft.)

Following on from #25C, #25D makes a complete circuit of Yamnuska, returning via the Goat/Yam col. It is the next-best trip after the traverse of the Yam because it includes the greatest scree run in the Rockies.

While you are following trails most the way, I've rated this a scramble because it calls for familiarity with steep scree slopes. Rock fall is a definite hazard.

CMC Valley to Goat/Yam col 2 km

Leave CMC Valley trail at 314666, just before the trail climbs. Cross the creek. A trail on the open south bank heads directly toward the side valley to the right of Yam. Where it becomes faint, climb slightly through a few trees and into a very large, damp meadow. Keeping near the right-hand edge of the meadow, cross to the far side trees. Look for a tree with yellow flagging, where the trail continues.

For a long way the trail up the side valley is very good, the going flat through trees. After passing scree slopes below Mt. Doom, the trail winds up to the right in tall trees, then back left to open moraines. Either follow the faint trail in a grassy draw to the right of the moraines or walk the moraine top. Either way, come to the stony creekbed of a side gully.

Cross the creekbed and walk up the right bank into a large, steep meadow. The next bit is complicated by the sheer number of game trails leaving the meadow for the final climb up scree to the col. They interconnect high up, so it's no big deal which one you start out on. However, if you want to get onto the main trail straight away, you have to climb high up the meadow, then angle right below a belt of small, skirted spruce onto the highest game trail of all, which makes a rising traverse below intermittent crags to the col's low point.

Lying in the orange shale zone, the col is wide and marked by a cairn. To your left the Yam rises in a mess of rubble and slabs down which winds the descent trail off the Yam. Going up this way is an easy scramble of 244 m (800 ft.), but not very appealing. Alternatively, you can wander west along a grassy, treed ridge toward Goat Mountain and look along Goat Wall.

Descent 1.3 km

A well-worn, slippery trail heads south down easy-angled orange shales. It veers rightwards to the edge of trees, then back left and into the scree traverse below the great cliff. The going is easy, with one thin section. Cross a large area of rockfall—your nearest approach to the cliff base—then enter a second scree slope. While you can continue the traverse below the cliff to inspect the McConnell Thrust Fault and return via the climber's access route or go right through to Raven's End, I don't recommend it unless you're wearing a helmet. The chance of getting hit by rocks dislodged by climbers is quite good. And it's definitely *not* the place to tote the baby!

This second scree slope, streaky white with numerous scree runs is your way off the mountain. Pick any run and in minutes surf in excess of 200 vertical m (650 ft.) down to the end of a trail built in 2001. Pick it up at ~321650.

Back to the parking lot 1.9 km

The trail heads left across treed hillside, the easy going interrupted by a glitch at the midpoint. This is a down climb with footholds chopped out of a muddy bank to access a small gully below a waterfall step. The water is ice cold nectar.

Arriving at the junction with the climber's ascent trail, turn right and descend rather steeply (en route passing a descent trail from the east end of the cliff) to a 4-way junction with the old track from the quarry. Go straight. In a minute come to the 4-way junction met with on your way up. Again go straight and return the same way you came.

The traverse below the cliff.

Looking up at the scree runs.

26 YAMNUSKA TO SOUTH GHOST—map 5

Looking back down the draw from Association Pass. Association Hill to left.

Long-day hikes, backpack
Unofficial trails, creek crossings, blazes, flagging
Distance 18 km from trailhead
Height gain S–N 1006 m (3300 ft.)
Height loss S–N 759 m (2490 ft.)
High point 1920 m (6300 ft.)
Map 82 O/3 Canmore

South access Via #25A Yamnuska Raven's End at T-junction 331665.
North access Old Hussey's Cabin on the South Ghost. Via #22 South Ghost, #20 Lower South Ghost, #19 Devils Gap to the South Ghost.

This moderately strenuous route connects the Bow Valley at Yamnuska to the South Ghost at Hussey's Cabin. Besides offering another way into the Ghost, it is also a leg of a 3-day backpack taking in Exshaw Creek and the South Ghost.

Some 20% of the route is a mix of old exploration roads, and 80% is new horse trail forged by the guides at Kananaskis Ranch Resort. Once you've escaped from Old Fort Creek, an incredibly scenic section of route runs high across the eastern slopes of Association Peak and End Mountain, en route crossing two small passes. Going in the N–S direction, the climb onto the east ridge of the Yam late in the day is brutal.

Day trippers can explore the head of Old Fort Creek and climb Association Hill. For scramblers, it brings Association Peak and End Mountain within range of a very long day trip.

ACCESS NOTE Some scramblers shun Raven's End trail at the start in favour of the direct route up the southeast face via a cutline close to the Stoney Reserve boundary. The cutline has steep sections, and after it ends at 335662 you're left to make your own way up successive steps to the Yam's east ridge northeast of junction 331665. The distance it saves is only 300–400 m depending on start.

SOUTH TO NORTH

East Ridge to CMC Valley 1.5 km

Start out on #25A. Leave it at T-junction 331665 at 2.6 km. Instead of turning left for Raven's End, continue straight ahead.

The trail traverses, rising slightly in trees to gain the east ridge to the right of a disintegrating corral. A few metres beyond is the reservation boundary fence at 333669. Turn left and start the 189 vertical m (620 ft.) muddy descent of the north face into CMC Valley. Initially you use a firebreak alongside the fence. Not far down you have the option of making two zigs to the left. Cross a logging road. (The alder-infiltrated road to left joins with #25C; the road to right passes through a gate into the reserve.) Continue on down via the fence trail, ultimately heading left at a split, which cuts out some of the muddy slithering. Reach CMC Valley trail (grassed logging road) at ~327677.

The next section, to Old Fort Creek at the start of the climb to Association Col, has two routes, each taking about 1 hour.

1. Old roads to Old Fort Creek 2.9 km
This route follows old roads in the valley bottoms along the Stoney Reserve boundary. While there is no height gain, the roads have washouts, so expect creek crossings and messy diversions.

Turn right and follow the grassed logging road downstream. At first the going is easy (keep high at a split). Not far after a steep downhill, you hit the first of numerous washouts. Keep right at the first one, after which you cross back and forth 3 times, finally ending up on the left bank. At ~336690 is a T-junction with another old road come in across CMC Valley creek from the reserve. At this point you are close to the confluence with Old Fort Creek opposite sandstone bluffs. Turn left, now heading up Old Fort Creek.

Shortly the road crosses the creek. After a long stretch on the right (east) bank, it crosses and recrosses another 4 times, but you don't have to. Bypass trails are available on the east bank.

At ~329697 come to the T-junction with route no. 2. Keep right.

2. Horse trail to Old Fort Creek 2.9 km
The direct route over the forested northeast ridge of Wendell Mountain is via a hilly horse trail built in 2001. While you can't lose the trail, look for blazes and flagging indicating the better route at splits. Expect two creek crossings.

Straight off, cross CMC Valley creek. The trail climbs a steep bank to splits a quarter of the way up. Go any way you fancy, at the top of the bank heading

Association Peak from between the two passes, showing scrambler's route up the peak.

rightish. The trail wanders through dry forest, gradually winding uphill to its high point. From here, it's nearly all downhill on a wetter, muddier trail. Edge around a willowy meadow back into forest and descend to the right bank of Old Fort Creek. Parallel the creek a way, then at splits drop to a flat next to the creekbed. Just beyond a spring is a camping and picnic area.

Continue on through a meadow, watching for where the trail crosses Old Fort Creek to the north bank. At the north bank T-junction turn right (east). (The trail to left heads west to gravel flats below the upper fork. It also accesses the canyon on the west side of Association Peak.)

Nor far downstream you meet route no. 1 at aT-junction at ~329697. Turn left.

To Association Pass 2.6 km

This refers to the gap between Association Peak and its eastern outlier, which is known as Association Hill.

After leaving Old Fort Creek, the trail enters a draw, wandering through pines and aspens and out onto the lower grassy southwest slopes of Association Hill, where it climbs ever more steeply with zigs. Near the top, traverse left through willow bushes to gain the pass at an exploration road (track) at 318719. Turn right.

NOTE if walking this route in the opposite direction, do not make the mistake of continuing to follow the track down across the east flank of Association Peak. It ends cold turkey.

To End Mountain Pass 3.3 km

For a brief distance the road traverses the fairly open east slope of Association Peak. Scramblers bound for its summit should step off here. (See the photo on page 121.)

The road then turns right and descends the right bank of a creek issuing from the little northeast cirque. Cross the creek to a T-junction. Turn left. (Road to right leads to Brokenleg Lake.) Climb alongside the creek, then swing right around a grassy rib and up the other side of it back into the traverse line. For a much longer stretch you pass below a long line of cliffs and pinnacles running between Association Peak and End Mountain.

Nearing the second pass, turn right down a hill to a T-junction with another road. Turn left and in a minute or two reach the pass at 319741. This is where you leave the roads and turn left onto a trail in the trees. (The road to right winds onto the small grassy outlier to the east of the pass and ends.)

To the South Ghost 5.1 km

A convoluted descent on horse trail and cutlines. See the sketch map on page 123.

In spruce forest, climb, traverse, then descend steeply. Wend left to an open hilltop offering first views across the South Ghost Valley to Saddle Peak. This is also the southern terminus of a N–S cutline you will be meeting later on.

Another steep pitch brings you to the right bank of a side creek not marked on the topo map despite copious running water. More or less follow the creek downhill. Low down, the trail crosses the creek, follows the left bank briefly, then cuts away left to a T-junction with an E–W cutline at ~310760 on top of a rib.

Turn right (east) and descend the cutline. Watch for where the trail turns off to the left and heads northeast to the N–S cutline reached at ~317760. Turn left on the cutline.

Recross the creek and continue to follow the cutline through pines. Again, watch for where the trail leaves the left side, descending steeply to the stony flats of the South Ghost Valley bottom just to the right of the side creek. (NOTE If going in the opposite direction, this side creek makes a good trail marker.)

Cross the side creek on the flats. On the far side the trail resumes to the left of a fence, soon intersecting the South Ghost exploration road. Turn right (east), passing through a gate in the fence. In a few metres, a grassy track to left is the route to Hussey's Cabin and Hussey's Hill. Below the bank on the left you'll find camping spots and a spring.

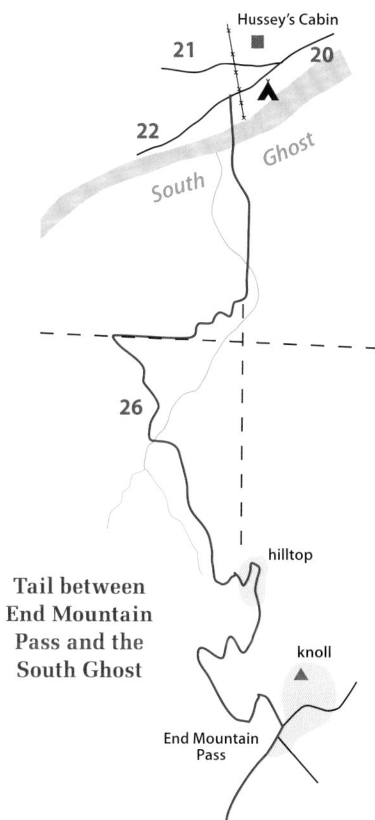

OPTION

26A Association Hill

Unofficial trail, route
Distance from pass 1.1 km; from trailhead 21.6 km return
Height gain from pass 76 m (250 ft.)
High point 1960 m (6430 ft.)

Standing apart from the Front Ranges at 327712 is a big hill with grassy south- and west-facing slopes. It's a fine viewpoint that can be reached in one long day.

Start from Association Pass where the trail from Old Fort Creek meets the old road. Your fainter trail heads right (southeast) in the angle between them.

Simply follow the northwest ridge, on grass initially and then through small spruce to a lower top. After a slight dip, walk an increasingly stony crest to a small summit cairn.

The view is of the Bow Valley through to Black Rock Mountain, in between taking in Yam, the peaks at the head of Old Fort Creek, Association Peak, End Mountain and End Mountain Pass.

On descent you can knock off 2 km by descending directly to the draw. Apart from having to circumvent a few crags below the summit, the going is easy.

View from Association Hill of Association Peak (left) and End Mountain, showing the ascent ridge from Association Pass.

27 YAMNUSKA NATURAL AREA—map 5

Below Yamnuska.

Half-day, day hikes
Unofficial trails
Map 82 O/3 Canmore

Access Hwy. 1A (Bow Valley Trail):
1. At 2.1 km east of Hwy. 1X turn left (north) onto the quarry road. Take the first left into the large Yamnuska parking lot with biffy, picnic tables and kiosk. Serves the northern sector.
2. At 510 m east of Hwy. 1X park at the side of the hwy. at a gate in the fence. Gives access to Moraine loop, the Great Swamp and the golf course.
3. Old borrow pit entrance 540 m west of Hwy. 1X. There's room for 3 vehicles in front of a gate. Gives the fastest access to the central lakes and Moraine loop. NOTE In early spring the meadow of the normal route is waterlogged; in winter it's a huge sheet of ice that extends into the aspens. At such times use the borrow pit route.
4. At 3.2 km west of Hwy. 1X turn left into a parking lot below the hwy. Good access to Moraine loop alongside the Francis Cooke Class III Regional Landfill.

Yamnuska Natural Area—now a little piece of Bow Valley Wildland Park—is a unique mosaic of dry meadows, forests, kettle lakes, springs, sinks, moraines, eskers, kames, depressions and drumlins—all of it centred about the Great Swamp. Besides being geologically fascinating, it's a bird place (loons nest on Loon Lake) and a flower place, particularly on the calcareous shores of lakes and swamps, where you'll find orchids and beautiful fringed gentians. And looming over everything are the great walls of Yamnuska and Goat Mountain, "the inaccessible Steep..." as described by David Thompson on November 30, 1800.

A fence with only one gate in it divides the area into two unequal parts: the small northern sector and the much larger southern sector. Trails are easy and usually walkable all year round. Carry water.

I have described three loops, but you can mix it up as you please, e.g., making side trips your objective or combining B and E loops to make an all-day walk. For

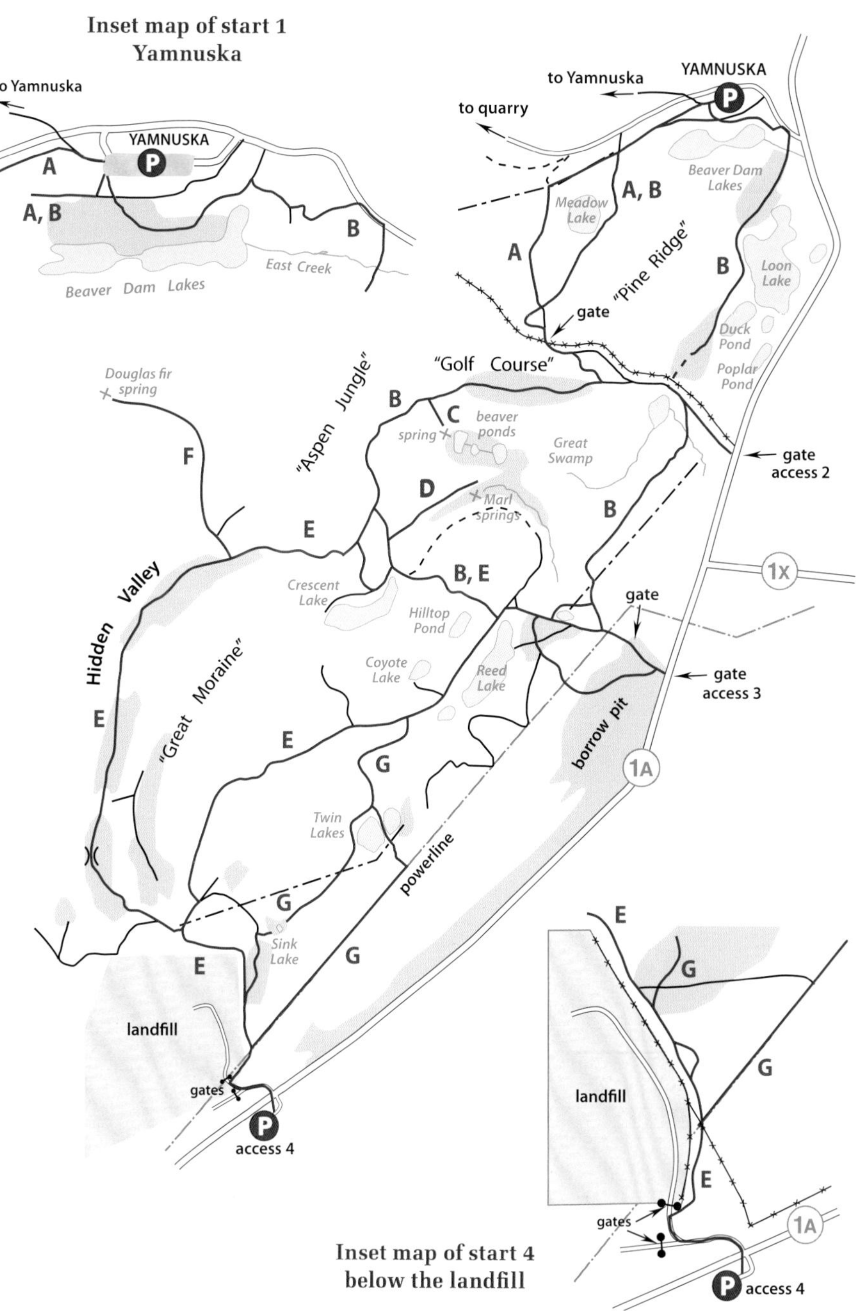
Yamnuska Natural Area
Inset map of start 1
Yamnuska
to Yamnuska
YAMNUSKA
A
A, B
B
East Creek
Beaver Dam Lakes
to Yamnuska
YAMNUSKA
to quarry
Beaver Dam Lakes
Meadow Lake
A, B
A
"Pine Ridge"
B
Loon Lake
gate
Duck Pond
Poplar Pond
"Golf Course"
Douglas fir spring
"Aspen Jungle"
B
C
spring
beaver ponds
Great Swamp
gate
access 2
F
D
Marl springs
B
E
B, E
1X
Hidden Valley
Crescent Lake
gate
Hilltop Pond
"Great Moraine"
Coyote Lake
Reed Lake
gate
access 3
E
E
borrow pit
G
1A
Twin Lakes
powerline
G
Sink Lake
G
E
landfill
gates
access 4
E
G
G
landfill
E
gates
1A
access 4
Inset map of start 4
below the landfill

the free-roamer there are dozens of game trails to wander about on.

ACCESS NOTE Accesses 1 and 4 are the recommended starting points because they have parking lots. Access 3 is also popular. Bring garbage bags if starting from access 4 near the landfill (which offers online tours). Access 4 is also the rock climber's access to Goat Mountain.

NAMING NOTE Names on sketch map come from *Yamnuska: Introductory studies of a natural area with proposals for its protection and use* (1974).

27A Meadow Lake loop

Half-day walk
Distance 2.8 km
Height gain/loss ~12 m (~40 ft.)

From access 1.

A northern circuit on good trails to a lake amid aspen woodlands.

CLOCKWISE

Start from the kiosk. A trail heads out to meadows overlooking Beaver Dam Lakes, which vary over the years between one and two lakes and many little ponds. Turn right on a grassy track and follow it to an intersection with a nice grassy cutline. Turn left and walk the cutline to a 4-way junction with a gravel road. Turn left onto the road, which undulates along to a meadow on the east shore of Meadow Lake. Calm waters mirror the bright green of aspens and the great cliff of Yamnuska. The road ends here.

A good trail carries on, climbing below a ridge, then descending a dell to 4-way junction 332641. (Trails ahead and to left lead to the gate in the fence separating the two sectors. See #27B.)

Turn right. The trail meanders through aspens, ultimately climbing to the cutline you left earlier. Turn right. Follow it back across the gravel road, then keep straight all the way in to the parking lot.

Aspen return from Meadow Lake.

27B Aspen Jungle loop

Short-day loop
Distance 8.4 km
Height gain/loss ~39 m (~130 ft.)

From access 1.

Also accessible from access 2. Beyond the gate, walk the trail alongside the fence to where a trail comes in from the left at 338636.
Also accessible from access 3. Beyond the gate, keep straight on the grassy track to the right of the fence and through another gate. Keeping left, cross the powerline right-of-way. At the Y-junction immediately after, either veer right if headed for Loon Lake or keep straight for Reed Lake and through a meadow where trails join in from right and left. At the northern tip of Reed Lake go left at a second Y-junction to gain the west shore.

When conditions are wet or icy, turn left after the first gate through a gap in the fence and walk around the right side of a borrow pit. Look for a gap in the trees to the right where a good track develops and takes you out to the powerline right-of-way. Cross. On reaching the meadow, the track narrows to trail and joins the usual track just before the second Y-junction.

#27B Walking the "Golf Course." Ahead is Loder Peak, with Goat Mountain at right.

A circuit carrying on from #27A that takes in the "Golf Course," the "Aspen Jungle" and another 5 lakes. Trails vary from good to faint in the latter part of the jungle. It's not called the jungle for nothing!

ANTICLOCKWISE

To Reed Lake 4.4 km

Start from the kiosk. Follow #27A to 4-way junction 332641 beyond Meadow Lake.

Go straight. The trail enters meadows, then turns sharp left and climbs slightly to a T-junction. Turn right through a gate in the fence.

Turn left on the fenceline trail, then turn next right down a hill. On meeting another trail, turn right (trail to left joins the fenceline trail) and walk a long, flat meadow called the "Golf Course." Gradually you enter the "Aspen Jungle." The trail is obvious to 326637 (small meadow on the left side) where SIDE TRIP #27C turns left.

After the next small meadow the trail becomes increasingly hard to follow in the jungle but reasserts itself just before T-junction 324632. Turn left. (Trail ahead joins Great Moraine loop.)

The trail dips into a small valley, then climbs onto a ridge from where it descends diagonally right to the north corner of Crescent Lake. En route a side trail to left at 324630 is SIDE TRIP #27D Marl Springs.

Keep straight at the T-junction with the shoreline trail and climb over a low ridge to Hilltop Pond and on down much more steeply to a track on the west shore of Reed Lake.

SIDE TRIP

27C Beaver ponds

Distance ~200 m

This trail is the easiest way to access beaver ponds watered by springs.

At 326637 turn left into the meadow, where you pick up a trail heading down into trees past some artfully arranged leg bones to a T-junction at the edge of the aspens. Go right a bit, then step out into the open, where springs rising out of stony ground amalgamate into a creek feeding the first, deepest beaver pond. Beyond are many more ponds in a surround of soggy grasses, the water draining northeast into the Great Swamp. A trail on terra firma to the right connects with Marl Springs.

SIDE TRIP

27D Marl Springs

Distance 660 m one way

Several springs emerge below a bank and run as one creek through the old drainage channel of Crescent Lake (soggy fen with ancient beaver dams) before flowing south out of the Great Swamp into the meadow northwest of Reed Lake and disappearing down a muddy sinkhole. The water runs fast all winter and is largely responsible for the huge ice sheet that spreads across the meadow and adjoining forest crossed by access 3.

The trail leaves #27B at 324630 and heads northeast across a dry bank above the channel. Entering trees, it crosses a trail and descends to a side valley filled with grass and aspens. Cross and climb up the far open bank using one of several trails. At the top turn right and continue to follow the banktop sans trail until you see a trail diagonalling down the bank to the springs at 329634. Look for tufa deposits and green and pink algae.

Loon Lake and beaver canal.

Fringed gentian.

Trailhead via Loon Lake ~4 km
Turn left. At the north end of the lake veer right and keep right at the Y-junction. (Track ahead and left is another route to Marl Springs but it involves crossing the soggy fen.)

There are two ways on:

1. The foolproof way is to continue on track until just before the powerline right-of-way and then turn left onto a narrower track. In a meadow it crosses the trail used by route no. 2 just metres before joining a really good track coming in from across the powerline. Turn left.

2. The first trail to the left is shorter but can be muddy. It intersects route no. 1 in the meadow. Turn left, then left again.

After crossing a cutline the track turns sharp right, heading north through a few trees into another meadow, where it ends. Pick up a trail at the far end of the meadow and enter a pleasant forest of pines and aspens, the main trail always obvious among many forks because it has tread. Dip to cross a creek emanating from the Great Swamp, then carry on in much the same sort of way to the fenceline trail, which you hit at split 338636. Turn left. (Trail to right leads to access 2.)

Follow the fence. At a bigger split near a beaver pond, keep right by the fence. Enter a big area of meadow. There being no gate, shimmy between strands of barbed wire into the meadow heading north. A trail develops when you enter trees (flagging) and runs parallel to Duck Lake, which lies on your right. If you have time, search the area between this lake and Poplar Pond for tipi rings.

The trail continues through more open country to the north end of Loon Lake, the largest lake in the area, where you'll find signs of recent beaver activity. Continue north, through a small meadow, then across East Creek joining Loon Lake to Beaver Dam Lakes. Continue to the access road for access 1. Turn left. In a few metres turn left onto a trail alongside an old road. Round the berm onto another trail and turn right. Keep left and head left into meadows above Beaver Dam Lakes. Take any trail to the right. They all lead back to the parking lot.

27E Great Moraine loop

Short-day hike +
Distance 8.6 km from access 4
Height gain/loss ~109 m (~360 ft.)
High point 1417 m (4650 ft.) at col

From access 4.

Also accessible from access 3. Read #27B access for directions to Reed Lake.

The most popular circuit loops around the Great Moraine on good trails. Takes in Hidden Valley and Crescent Lake, in addition to offering side trips and a return option via Twin Lakes.

#27E The pass between Loder Peak and the "Great Moraine," Goat Mountain to left.

In the HiddenValley, getting directions to the big fir.

CLOCKWISE

To loop 1.1 km

From the parking area, cross Hwy. 1A and follow the access road to Francis Cooke Class III Regional Landfill. (Ribbon cut and champagne sipped in June 2001.) Keep right at a road junction. Just before the landfill gate, turn right onto a trail that cuts across to a wooden section of fence you can step over. On the far side, turn left and cross the powerline right-of-way. Keep left by the chainlink fence and down a hill. Continue along the east boundary of the landfill, which is sited in the windiest part of the Bow Valley. On good garbage-flying days, unidentifiable junk and plastic sheets go sailing over the fence and are caught, floating like ghosts, on spiky tree branches. Three times a year the forest gets a cleanup by Boy Scouts and inmates.

After another downhill, the fence trail climbs gradually to the northeast corner, then undulates along the northern perimeter. The trail levels and you come to a T-junction. Go straight. (If headed for Reed Lake turn right on a track, then keep right.)

SIDE TRIP

27F Big Douglas Fir

Distance 690 m
Height gain 100 m (328 ft.)

A varying trail leads to a spring on the lower slopes of Goat Mountain at 312633.

From 315629 a faint trail heads in a northwesterly direction to the left of a dry, stony creekbed. At a junction climb up left onto a bit of a ridge with Douglas firs. Continue ahead through aspens and poplars, wending a bit right, then up a wide ditch to the spring at 312633. Below are two small muddy pools, and far above them hang hunters' tree stands, where cheaters can wait in comfort for thirsty deer to come to the pools.

Up on the east bank between the two pools is the big Douglas fir, one of several biggies on the hillside.

Left: the trail alongside the landfill before cleanup.

Crescent Lake, showing the trail and Yamnuska.

At a second T-junction turn left. Then, in metres, join a wide, stony track. Veer right.

Hidden Valley trail 3 km

The track heads north and uphill, bound for the pass between Loder Peak and the "Great Moraine." At T-junction 314613 keep straight on a good trail. (The track heading left is the climber's access to Kid Goat.)

Continue climbing to a low pass between Loder Peak and the "Great Moraine." (From here, bit trails climbing onto the moraine crest are worth taking for the view.) Descend through a few trees into Hidden Valley, wide and grassy and lined with willows. Yamnuska has come into sight ahead. At 315629, near the demarcation with trees, a faint trail to left is SIDE TRIP #27F, Big Douglas Fir.

Enter trees, at the last descending stony ground to T-junction 323630. Turn right. (Trail straight on leads to Aspen Jungle.)

To Reed Lake 1.1 km

Not too far along, the stony trail descends to the northwest shore of Crescent Lake and follows it around to the left to the northern tip. On meeting trail #27B, at a T-junction, turn right. The trail climbs over a low ridge to Hilltop Pond and on down more steeply to Moraine loop (track) on the west shore of Reed Lake. Turn right.

To Twin Lakes turnoff 620 m

After leaving Reed Lake behind, the track plies between a series of eskers and sinks to the left—one occupied by a small pond—and slopes rising up to the right. At 326622 is a 5-way of sorts. The track is obvious. (Rising trail to right accesses the west end of Coyote Lake. The route to Twin Lakes follows the grassy draw ahead. See OPTIONAL RETURN #27G.)

Completing the loop 2.8 km

Then follows a long uneventful stretch where trees crowd in: aspens, spruce and pine. More-open country signals the approach to the landfill. At a bend 316613 a trail to left is a route to Sink Lake.

A little farther on veer left to reach the trail alongside the landfill fence. Turn left and return the same way you came.

OPTIONAL RETURN

27G via Twin Lakes

Distance to #27E: 2 km via powerline; 1.8 km via Sink Lake

A more scenic return requiring some navigational know-how.

At 5-way 326622, go straight through a grassy draw to a small meadow, then climb up left onto a drumlin and head right. Descend off the end to a T-junction and turn left. The trail runs through a dell between ridges, ultimately descending to the isthmus between the two lakes.

From here there are two ways to reach access 4.

1. The easiest route is to cross the isthmus between the lakes on a faint trail. Your trail soon morphs into a track leading to the powerline right-of-way at dip 326616. (In reverse, this is the surefire way to the lakes.) Turn right and simply follow the undulating track back to the landfill fence.

2. This route is complicated by a surfeit of game trails going every which way. I fully expect you to become confused. If all else fails, use the map screen on your GPS to navigate to Sink Lake.

Turn right and on trail walk the northwest shore of the larger lake and a little bit of the west shore. Heading off right, climb slightly to a NE–SW cutline that year by year is becoming harder to detect. Rather than walk the cutline, which has deadfall problems, turn off left onto a trail that makes a beeline for Sink Lake. The route varies between clear and faint, crosses a better trail at a right angle, and on the final downhill approach picks up a good trail coming in from the cutline.

The sink is usually seen as a large, soggy grass basin enclosing a minuscule pond in the middle. What is it about this place? Every time I visit I find a new scattering of deer bones.

There are various ways out of it, including one reasonable trail onto Great Moraine loop at 316613. To reach access 4 with the least amount of hassle, cross the flat, grassy floor of the sink. At the far west end, pick up a trail, initially flagged, that climbs diagonally left through aspens onto an open ridge of juniper and kinnikinnick. The trail continues a way, then fades out within sight of the landfill fence. Continue in the same direction. The trail picks up as it climbs slightly to an old track and crosses it, continuing on to reach the fence trail at the bottom of the first descent at 318610. Turn left and return the same way you came.

Twin Lakes from the northeast.

28 JURA CREEK—maps 5, 7

Jura Creek's celebrated false fault. Exshaw Formation on the left, Palliser Formation on the right.

Half-day, day hike
Unofficial trails & route, many creek crossings
Distance ~3.5 km to fault
Height gain 216 m (710 ft.)
High point 1524 m (5000 ft.)
Map 82 O/3 Canmore

Access Hwy. 1A (Bow Valley Trail).
Usual Parking lot Just west of the entrance to Graymont's Exshaw plant, turn south into a small parking lot at 303591.
Powerline Just east of the entrance to Graymont's Exshaw plant at 304594 turn north onto a track that leads in a few metres to a parking area with picnic tables on a powerline right-of-way.
Also accessible from #30 Exshaw to Jura Creek.

A popular hike with a hint of scrambling up a geologically interesting valley. The false fault is the usual objective. Canyoneers may not get that far: on a hot day there are lots of baths to dip into. Non-scramblers can avoid the lower canyon by using bypass trails.

It is also the scrambler's route to #29 Loder Peak and Morrowmount.

PARKING NOTE Such is Jura Creek's growing popularity, with commercial groups arriving by bus, that the MD of Bighorn is considering building a proper parking lot on the north side of the highway.

The powerline access is also the scrambler's access for Door Jamb Mountain.

BOULDERING NOTE The lower canyon is a popular bouldering area described in *Bouldering in the Canadian Rockies*, by Marcus Norman.

NAMING NOTE The creek's name should really be Devon or Carbon, or Paleo. When named in 1913 it was thought the

The lower canyon. Photo Derek Ryder

prominent black shale outcrop at the "false fault" was of Jurassic age in the Mesozoic. It was later proved to be late Devonian and early Carboniferous/Mississippian in the Paleozoic Era. So what if the geologists were out by 200 million years.

To the lower canyon

The two starts join a little way in.

1. Usual access 740 m Walk east along the highway to Graymont's entrance. Opposite, on the north side of the highway, a trail climbs the bank and heads north, crossing a powerline to a 4-way junction. Go straight on a track.

2. Powerline access 920 m Heading west, follow the track to the right of the powerline right-of-way. Keep straight where the powerline road joins in. At a 4-way junction turn right onto a track. (Trail to left is access 1.)

Travel a wide alluvial fan. On reaching the right (east) bank of Jura Creek's stony creekbed, the track narrows to trail. Just before the mouth of the lower canyon where the valley pinches in between Door Jamb and Exshaw Mountain, turn second left down the bank to the creekbed.

Trails around the lower canyon

Jura Creek
high-water trail
lower canyon
30A
28

Lower canyon

There are three ways forward:

1. Lower Palliser Canyon 720 m Anyone with a shred of curiosity will take a look at the canyon route, even if you decide to retreat when confronted with deep pools crossed by skinny logs. Locals call the pools the "Indian Baths." A little way beyond the canyon end, the lower bypass trail comes in from the left at 298598.

2. Lower bypass trail 700 m My preference for when water levels are low.

Follow the trail up onto the left-hand bank and into forest at a cairn. In a few metres turn right off the main trail onto a slightly narrower trail. Keep left twice and climb a short, steep hill. Descend, keeping left and pass below a crag. Reach the stony creekbed at 298598.

Follow the stony creekbed, criss-crossing the creek to 296601, where the upper bypass trail comes in from the left. On the treed flat is a camping area.

Orthocone cephalopod fossils.

3. Upper bypass trail 580 m Use only when there is a lot of water in the creek.

Follow the trail up the left-hand bank into forest at a cairn. Keep left and climb a steep hill to a junction. Turn right. (Note that the trail to left is a much gentler way up from #30A.)

Continue climbing to a high point. A slightly descending traverse ends in two very steep hills plunging to a camping area at creekbed level at 296601.

To the false fault 2 km

Follow the winding, stony creekbed. When the bed veers right, a trail is on the right bank. When it veers left the trail is on the left bank. And so on.

Come to where rusty-coloured cliffs meet grey slabs in a V. Walk through some boulders to the bottom of the V, which looks like a fault, but is not. On the left the black shales of the Exshaw formations rest "disconformably" on smooth, waterworn, pale-grey slabs of Palliser Formation on the right. At the contact, geologists have found bone fragments of extinct armoured fish that grew as long as 10 m called arthrodires. About 1 m above is a layer of ash from Mt. Mazama.

Scramble up the slabs. Surprising to me, the creek glides from bathtub to bathtub down the slabs to your right and not down the V where you'd expect the water to be. As you go keep an eye out for orthocone cephalopod fossils.

The deeper potholes of the upper Palliser canyon are avoided by a steep little trail on the left bank. Everything flattens out at the confluence 289617. If carrying on, keep left. (Side valley to right is #29 up Loder Peak.)

GOING FARTHER

Upper valley 4.8 km

After the dramatics of the canyons, it's back to flat, wide, stony creekbed all the way to the valley head. On the right, slabby summits alternate with stony avalanche tongues swallowing up balsam poplars. To the left, Exshaw Ridge is a six-decker sandwich of cliffs and forest. The orange peak at the far end on the right is Morrowmount, an easy scree ascent from this direction with a long approach walk of 16.5 km return. From its summit you get an extraordinary view of "Hassel Castle" the hunchback.

Looking up upper Jura Creek towards Morrowmount. Hassel Castle at centre. Photo Bob Spirko

29 LODER PEAK—map 7

Day scramble
Distance ~1.9 km from Jura Creek
Height gain 564 m (1850 ft.) from #28
High point 2088 m (6850 ft.)
Map 82 O/3 Canmore

Access Via #28 Jura Creek at 289617.

This is the easier route up Loder Peak from the Jura Creek side. Experienced scramblers could combine it with the more difficult scramble up the south ridge via Door Jamb to make a loop. While gaining the col between Loder Peak and Goat Mountain is a straightforward trudge, it's worth making the extra effort to win Loder Peak for a superior view and the satisfaction of summiting a named peak.

NAMING NOTE After Edwin Loder who incorporated the Loder Lime Company in 1905.

HISTORY NOTE Door Jamb Mountain, really the lower summit of Loder Peak, is most likely the mountain David Thompson of the North West Company climbed with Gabriel Dumond and Duncan McGillivray on Sunday, November 30, 1800. They had rejected the "inaccessible steep" (Yamnuska) in favour of something more "practicable." How far they climbed—possibly they reached Loder Peak—no one knows. I can just imagine Thompson, his long black hair cut square across his eyebrows blowing in the wind from under his hat pulled down tight, cursing the rock in his Welsh accent, but writing later: "... where the rock was solid, it was extremely rough and full of small sharp points like an enormous rasp. This enabled us to mount places very steep, as the footing was good and sure, but it cut our shoes, socks etc., all to pieces in a trice." I'm curious as to what the etc. was, but I can imagine the trio hobbling back to their horses with their behinds shredded to ribbons and some poor woman faced with a mammoth repair job.

Loder Peak from Exshaw Ridge, showing the route.

To the col

At 289617 turn right up the side valley to the east. A trail on the right side takes you into the narrows, leaving you to stumble another kilometre up stony creekbed to a side gully on the right at 296619. If you inadvertently pass the ascent gully you'll fetch up against a rock step in a small canyon.

Climb the moderately inclined gully, which is easy with a few scrambly bits. Higher up, the going is better on the left slope. At the start of grass and slabs, the gully forks. Stay left or start up the left fork, then cut across to the right fork above its first awkward step. Both forks can be followed up to the col at 303617 between Goat Mountain to your left and Loder Peak (rising another 70 vertical m) to your right. Your reward is a vertiginous view into the Bow Valley with not a mountain in sight.

Loder Peak

Head rightward over two humps and up scree to the slanting rockband guarding the summit. Hard-core scramblers tackle the band at the left edge above the abyss—a difficult 2-tier 6 m high scramble for which I recommend the security of a rope.

The summit from the col. The upper band is tackled out of the photo to the right.

Descending the upper band the easy way.
Photo Rachel Oggy

If this route doesn't appeal, follow the rockband down to the right and scrabble up a weakness waymarked by a cairn. See the pic above. The trouble is, the farther right you go the steeper and more rubbishy the slope is above the rockband. Plod up this slope below a higher rockband. After the band peters out the going gets easier to the summit. From two cairns you look northeast for a fabulous view of Yamnuska.

DESCENT NOTE Look south down the connecting ridge to Door Jamb Mountain—a moderate scramble from Hwy. 1A that lures you with a game trail, then confounds you with crags. Only take this route if you are familiar with the route. A direct descent down the west face to Jura Creek also appears attractive. In 2000 a scrambler tried this route, got cliffed out and had to be slung off the mountain. Returning the same way is the safest option.

30 EXSHAW TO JURA CREEK—map 7

One hour to half-day hikes +
Map 82 O/3 Canmore

Access Hwy. 1A at the hamlet of Exshaw. On the west side of the bridge over Exshaw Creek turn north onto Mt. Allen Drive and follow it to a parking lot on the right side at the left-hand bend.
Also accessible from #28 Jura Creek.

From Exshaw, Bear trail accesses the old road along the west bank of Jura Creek to the lower canyon. (This road is gated at Hwy. 1A, but you wouldn't want to walk the lower part of it anyway—it's just a garbage tip.)

There is a second, more scenic route beneath the powerlines used by mountain bikers. The two trails connect before Jura Creek, thus making possible a pleasant après lunch loop of 2.6 km.

Western wood lily meadows on Powerline trail.

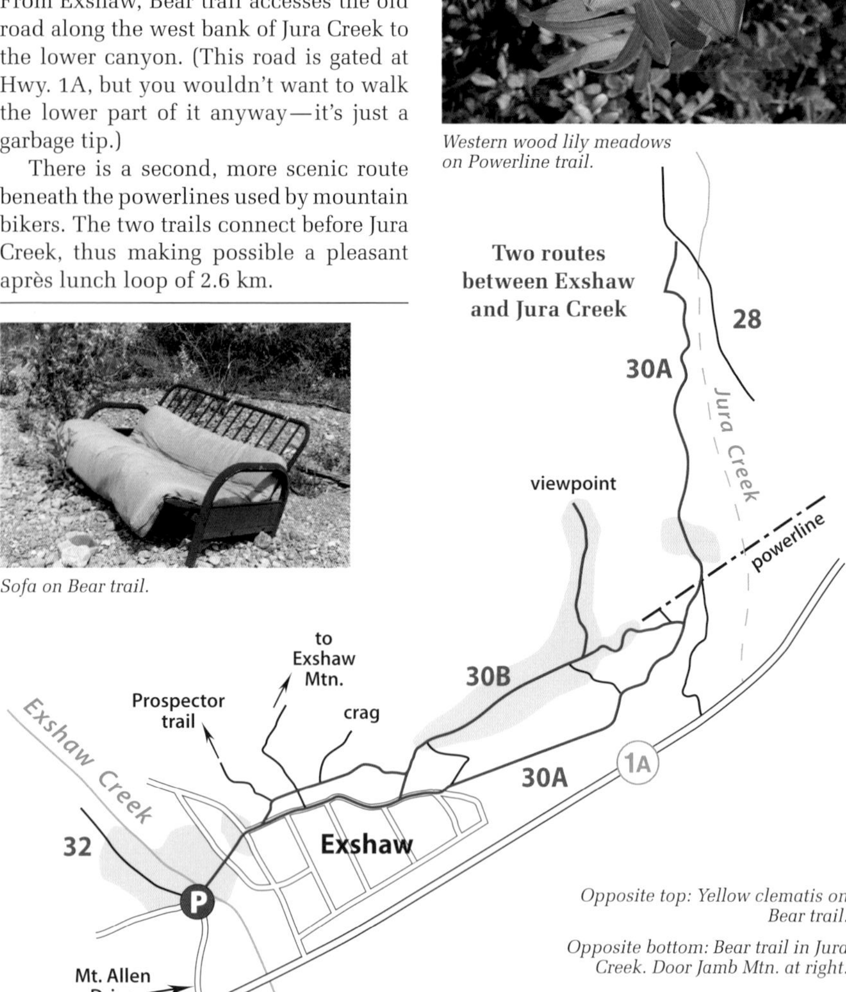

Sofa on Bear trail.

Opposite top: Yellow clematis on Bear trail.

Opposite bottom: Bear trail in Jura Creek. Door Jamb Mtn. at right.

30A Bear trail

Distance to lower canyon 2.3 km
Height gain to canyon 46 m (150 ft.)

A flat, easy route mainly on tracks. Black bears are often seen in the forest close to Exshaw, hence the local name for the trail. Can be biked.

WEST TO EAST

To Powerline trail 1.4 km

Cross the footbridge over Exshaw Creek. Go straight on a trail that crosses a paved lane en route to Windridge Road. Cross and walk an unnamed gravel road at the foot of Exshaw Mountain. Just before the fourth road to the right, which is Pigeon Mountain Drive, turn left onto a track, which is Bear trail.

Head ENE through forest, disregarding a side trail to left. On entering Jura Creek's alluvial flat, the track becomes increasingly stony and winds a bit. Keep right. (Side track to left climbs up to the Powerline trail.) Reach a former channel of Jura Creek and turn left, following ruts imprinted in stones. The Powerline trail comes in from the left at 298588 opposite a comfortable sofa.

To the lower canyon 910 m

Continue on stones until you intersect the west bank road (now track) at the powerlines. Turn left. The track gives fast, easy walking below the craggy east face of Exshaw Mountain. The final section is again on stones closer to Jura Creek, the track ultimately curving left into trees to its end at a firepit.

For the lower canyon and lower bypass trail, do not enter the trees, but instead continue straight, to intersect #28 where it crosses the creek below the canyon. For the upper bypass trail, just after the track enters the trees, turn right on a good trail that climbs easily to a T-junction with the upper bypass trail. Keep left.

30B Powerline trail

Distance 1.2 km to trailhead
Height gain 15 m (50 ft.)

A rolling trail used by mountain bikers that traverses the lower slope of Exshaw Mountain. For views, it's best walked east to west in combination with Bear trail—you don't really notice the powerlines and odd power pole. In early summer, western wood lilies brighten the meadows.

EAST TO WEST

So you're in the old channel of Jura Creek sitting on the sofa. If looping with Bear trail, head left up a track, in a minute or two turning off left onto a trail that climbs to the powerlines. Heading west, undulate along the trail a bit, then keep straight at a staggered 4-way junction.

(The track to right climbs steeply up the hillside to a viewpoint on the southeast face of Exshaw Mountain—a fabulous place from which to view Heart Mountain Horseshoe—see the photo on page 178. There's a faint trail carrying on up the mountain, which is steepening and getting craggy. I didn't follow it very far. The staggered track to left descends to Bear trail.)

Climb to a T-junction and go straight. (Trail to left descends past a bird nesting box to Bear trail.) Descend to a T-junction. This time veer right. (The trail ahead descends rather steeply to the gravel road.)

Your trail traverses above the gravel road. The first side trail to right with a ladder is a climber's access trail. The second trail to right with a blank sign is the route up Exshaw Mountain. At both junctions you can also cut through to the gravel road. Next up is the Junkyard. Here, go left onto the gravel road and turn right. In a few minutes cross paved Windridge Road onto a trail that crosses a narrow paved lane en route to the footbridge over Exshaw Creek and the parking lot.

#30B Heading west on Powerline trail.

31 EXSHAW MOUNTAIN—map 7

Route of ascent follows facing ridge above the tiers of cliffs.

Unofficial trails, mostly route
Distance 1.9 km to summit
Height gain 472 m (1550 ft.)
High point 1783 m (5850 ft.)
Map 82 O/3 Canmore

Access Hwy. 1A at the hamlet of Exshaw. On the west side of the bridge over Exshaw Creek turn north onto Mt. Allen Drive and follow it to a parking lot on the right side at the left-hand bend.

Exshaw Mountain is shaped rather like a Christmas pudding, in no way attractive, but countering that is its close proximity above Exshaw. One imagines the locals, after a hard day's work manufacturing cement, climbing up there every evening for a breath of fresh air before turning in. They call it Cougar Mountain.

The route follows an open, steepish ramp above rockbands offering great views. But strangely there is no good trail to the top, just bits and pieces. There is the option of making a loop with #31 and/or #32 back to Exshaw.

To the start 360 m
From the parking lot cross the footbridge over Exshaw Creek. Go straight on a trail that crosses a narrow paved lane to Windridge Drive. Cross and walk along an unnamed gravel road below the mountain. Shortly before Fortress Mountain Way, turn left on a trail into the bush. At a T-junction a few metres in, turn right. In a few metres more, turn left up a steep trail marked by a blank sign.

To summit 1.5 km
The trail climbs diagonally left up a grassy slope. Where it eases off and enters bushes leave it and head to the right up a ramp above a diagonal rockband. Remnant trails wind up steep, stony hillside, avoiding slabs and picking up grassy patches. A big cairn signals the end of the steep bit.

From the parking lot to the open slopes

33
Prospector
to Exshaw Mtn.
31
Windridge Drive
Exshaw Creek
Exshaw
32
P
1A
Mt. Allen Drive

After the angle eases, keep leftish to avoid getting on the down side of a rockband, and climb a second ramp to the second cairn. Then follow the edge of the rock band, two small scree rises with trails preceding a third cairn. This marks the end of the ramps and the best viewpoint of the cement plant, Exshaw and Lac des Arcs.

At the third cairn a trail turns left and climbs onto the summit ridge, which offers intermittent views of McConnell Point and Heart Mountain between and above the trees. Follow a grassy strip above the northern drop-off to a small cairn, and through more trees to the summit—a small glade with two cairns. At least it's sheltered from the wind.

Return the same way and enjoy the views.

Looking down on Exshaw and Lac des Arcs.

OPTIONAL LOOP

31A via Exshaw Col

Route, unofficial trails
Distance ~3.5 km

This route descends to the col between Exshaw Mountain and Exshaw Ridge, then descends the west slope to pick up either the Exshaw Creek trail or Prospector trail that twines around it. Both return you to your starting point. While nowhere near as steep as the ascent route, the route requires route-finding savvy while bushwhacking. See the sketch map on page 153.

To col 285602, 1 km

The 122 m (400 ft.) descent of the northwest ridge is not quite as straightforward as it looks on the map. After crossing a glade with slab, a short descending trail starting to the right of a cairn leads to a semi-open flat section. NOTE Be very careful at the bottom of the descent to wend left and not continue with the flow of the terrain down a rib on the east side of the ridge.

The summit cairn.

At the end of the flat section the ridge rises to an overlook above crags with a good view of Exshaw Ridge. Turn it on the right-side trail and descend easily to the complexities of the col, which consists of numerous parallel ridgelets. You need to hit the low point on the westernmost ridgelet at 286600. (Possibly you can reach the same place by turning the crag on the left side.)

To #32 or #33, ~2.5 km

At the low point there's a gap in the west-side rockband and from it a trail descends some scree, soon turning left into the trees of the west slope. After a short, steep descent the trail peters out on easy ground. Bushwhack downhill, crossing a multitude of traversing game trails, possibly following them a bit to the left before continuing downwards. Just have faith that at some point you are going to hit either Exshaw Creek trail (preferably near the junction with lower Prospector at 282594) or, if you've been bearing a little more to the left, lower Prospector trail. Both trails are well used and obvious.

Now turn to route ##32 and 33 on how to get back to Exshaw.

GOING FARTHER

31B to Exshaw Ridge

Unofficial trail & route
Distance ~700 m
Height gain ~213 m (~700 ft.)

Connecting with the south end of #34 Exshaw Ridge is fairly straightforward.

Follow #31A to Exshaw Col.

From 285602 a game trail heads north, following the westernmost ridgelet, which is semi-open and gradually rising.

The ridgelet morphs into the south ridge, which is not as steep as it looks. While the trail is intermittent, the going is straightforward through trees, with some scree and avoidable pieces of rock. Higher up, the ridge narrows, with a cliff band down the right side.

At the top of the rise you can join the trail up the southwest spur by heading left onto the west flank.

#31A View from the overlook of Exshaw Col area. Shows also the westernmost ridgelet, which is semi-open and rises to become the south ridge of Exshaw Ridge climbed by #31B.

#31 The trail on the west bank below Mount Fable. Photo Alf Skrastins

32 EXSHAW CREEK TO EXSHAW PASS—maps 7, 6

The upper valley below the Mythic Towers.

Long-day hike
Official hamlet trails, then unofficial trail & route, creek crossings
Distance 12.6 km to pass
Height gain 948 m (3110 ft.)
High point 2210 m (7250 ft.) at pass
Map 82 O/3 Canmore

Access Hwy. 1A at the hamlet of Exshaw. On the west side of the bridge over Exshaw Creek turn north onto Mt. Allen Drive and follow it to a parking lot on the right side at the left-hand bend. NOTE Parking on Mt. Lorette Drive is prohibited.

The long walk up scenic Exshaw Creek to Exshaw Pass and back will wear your legs down to stumps. Luckily, the going is generally easy, with one steep hill at the end. Except at runoff, creek crossings are no big deal: low down you can rock hop or use rustic bridges built yearly. Higher up you will be pushed to find any water at all.

Most people just go to Fable Creek and back. The other alternative is to combine the lower trail with #33 Prospector trail, which twines around it. For backpackers, Exshaw Pass is the gateway to the upper South Ghost; for scramblers, it is the access to Mt. Fable and Exshaw Ridge.

WARNING The upper valley and valleys leading into the South Ghost are grizzly hot spots.

IMPORTANT TRAIL NOTE Since the last edition there have been two changes to the start to this trail. First, the building of a trailhead on Mt. Allen Drive has diverted out-of-towners away from Mt. Lorette Drive where we used to park. To encourage us further, a trail was built along the big berm to connect with the old trail from the Knowlerville bridge.

And so it remained until April 2013, when Lafarge permanently closed the trail beyond Knowlerville junction. This is a trail that's been used by locals and visitors alike for a hundred years—courtesy of Lafarge. Not many people realize that the company's leasehold extends another kilometre beyond the dam and that at some point way in the future all of the treed ridge on the west side of Exshaw Creek will be quarry. But back to the present. The danger of people being felled like skittles from boulders rolling onto the trail after blasting was deemed too great and it was considered better to close the trail now and with Lafarge's assistance build a permanent trail along the east bank, once the various factions come to some agreement. For now, people must use the existing east-bank trail, which does some unnecessary climbing before descending to the creek far north of the dam. On the bright side, it misses out three creek crossings.

The new start is shown on the sketch map on page 153.

HISTORY NOTE The first part of the valley is a history of Exshaw's municipal water system. From the early 1900s water to Lafarge's cement plant and the company houses came from a concrete dam built in 1907. Up until April 2013 you could walk alongside wooden flumes and a more modern pipeline to the dam aka waterfall. Nowadays most of the dam is buried under rocks. More recently a water treatment plant was built on the east side of the creek, and this you will see as you pass by.

The remains of the dam in 2011. The route no longer runs past this feature onto pebble beds.

The Knowlerville footbridge over Exshaw Creek replaces the one swept away by the great floods of June 2005. A bridge of one kind or another has been here since the old days when it joined the northern part of the village, called Knowlerville, to the main part of the hamlet, which was on the west bank. After demolition of west-bank houses to make way for the expansion of the cement plant in 1973, the only original building left standing was St. Bernard's Catholic church, built in 1907. Take a look by simply following the road around from the parking lot.

Big Berm trail 500 m

From the parking lot, head northwest, following Big Berm trail up a steep hill onto the big grassy berm separating Exshaw Creek from the cement plant. Follow it along to a T-junction. Turn right and cross Exshaw Creek on the Knowlerville foot bridge to Mt. Lorette Drive. (Original trail ahead is closed.)

To Exshaw Ridge turnoff 1.5 km

Immediately turn left on a narrow trail that runs between the creek and the water treatment plant access road. Reach the powerline access road above the plant and turn left up a hill. At the top, turn right onto a trail. (The road ahead climbs a grassy rib to the right of the power poles, then descends to the trail at 4-way junction 282591.) Your route dekes through a dell to the 4-way. Go straight and climb a steepening hill to the 4-way with lower and middle Prospector trail at 282594. Go straight.

The gradient eases and you walk a draw below a slabby bank. At T-junction 280599 with occasional cairn go straight. (Exshaw Ridge trails turns off to the right.)

To Exhaw Creek 1.3 km

Continue straight, past 4-way junction 278600 with middle and upper Prospector trail into Blair Witch Woods, a creepy place in the rainy dusk of a late fall day. Come to—no, not a house (that's located higher up the slope and back a bit in the middle of the woods. Or rather, *was* located; it is now collapsed)—but to a Y-junction at 275607. Turn left. (Right is upper Prospector.)

Descend a winding hill to Exshaw Creek valley, where the good trail ends. On the flats, cross a spring-fed creek and veer rightish across scuffed ground, aiming to hit the original Exshaw Creek trail at ~273607, which is just before original creek crossing no. 4. Turn right. For anyone walking the trail in the opposite direction, the small cairn marking this exceedingly important junction is easily missed.

To Fable Creek 1.9 km

In a few metres ford the creek to the left bank. Pass a stony side creek, then a camping area on the left side. Cross to and fro another two times, the three creek crossings coming in close succession. Then follows a long stretch along the left bank which sees you to the wide mouth of Fable Creek at 264623. The large cairn indicates the climber's access to shapely Mount Fable that has been framed between the banks for the last kilometre. It was named in 1947 by the first ascent party after the would-be first ascent party got lost in the bush and returned to tell a tall tale. I believe the reaction was "Oh, yeah?"

To Exshaw Pass 7.4 km

Under the cliffs of Fable's east buttress, cross Exshaw Creek for the 4th time. A long forested stretch on the right bank passes a side creek to right at 260637. Slopes to left and right of it are the ways on and off Exshaw Ridge.

The forest trail ends shortly and you head for a cairn in a waterless creekbed. Ahead is your first view of the pass. It's here where the valley widens into dryas

The trail beyond Exshaw Ridge turnoff.

Closing in on the pass. The trail heads for the right-hand gap.

flats that bake in the midday sun. You're either walking the stones of the creekbed or using snippets of trail on one side or the other. Pass "Mythic Creek" to your left, and an unnamed tower (which only looks tower-like from this angle—Bob and Dinah found a relatively easy route up from Mythic Creek), then the more technical "Mythic Tower" and "Epic Tower"—together known as the Mythic Towers—that were first traversed by Kananaskis guru John Martin.

Marking the western portal of the pass, is "Mt. Townsend," a name suggested by the Bivouac.com naming committee, not after Pete of *The Who*, but after Group Captain Peter Townsend, "the first true love of Princess Margaret." Appropriately, Princess Margaret Mountain is separated from Townsend by miles of mountains and valleys.

At the side creek to right at 250673 the trail reasserts itself on the right (east) side of the valley. It runs through the middle of a flat meadow, then traverses between creekbed willows and grassy sidehills where grizzlies are busy digging for hedysarum roots. If you're thirsting for water by this point, there is nearly always a waterhole at the foot of the final slope.

As you will see, Exshaw Pass is actually two gaps separated by a grassy hill. The trail aims for the lower right-hand gap (the pass proper), attained by plodding up 122 vertical m (400 vertical ft.) of steep grass. On top is a flat meadow. It's worth dragging yourself up the hill in the middle for a stupendous view back down Exshaw Creek, which looks endlessly long.

GOING FARTHER

32A to the South Ghost

Route and unofficial trails
Distance 4.4 km
Height gain to col 122 m (400 ft.)
Height loss 479 m (1570 ft.)
High point at col 2331 m (7650 ft.)

To Exshaw High Col 1.2 km

The V-shaped valley on the other, north side of the pass is not the best way into the South Ghost. It has no water and there is no trail as far as I can tell. You have to climb higher to Exshaw High Col at 238700 on the north ridge of "Townsend."

Route selection needs care. Do not make a beeline from Exshaw Pass. Unseen are steep slopes. It's best to climb over the hill to the left-hand gap, then up through trees to the open slopes. From here there is an obvious traverse line along a grassy bench to the col.

The col is a heavenly place of grass that turns bright orange in fall. To right, a long ridge laced with scree is a definite

Looking back down Exshaw Creek from the pass.

Looking up to Exshaw High Col from the bench.

come-on—if one only had time. Ahead is a view looking down your descent valley to the mountains of the South Ghost. The bend in the valley at 235707 where you pick up the trail is obvious.

To Guinn's Camp 3.2 km

Descend very steep grass to the flat valley floor of a small tributary. Follow the creekbed, then a grassy avenue between trees to its right. Near the left-hand bend at 236704 a game trail climbs onto the grassy right bank and enters forest. (NOTE Should you elect to follow the tributary to the main side valley like we did once to avoid tagging along behind a grizz walking the trail, know that the valley "goes" fairly easily and has the bonus of water.)

The amazing trail, though, is much the better route and takes you all the way down the valley via a gradually descending forested bench between the creek and open slopes.

Nearing South Ghost Valley, it descends and crosses the creek near the confluence, then crosses the South Ghost to Guinn's Camp at 227728.

The descent trail down the valley to Guinn's Camp. Photo Alf Skrastins

33 PROSPECTOR—map 7

Unofficial trails
Distance 5 km of trails
High point 1560 m (5118 ft.)
Map 82 O/3 Canmore

Access Via #32 Exshaw Creek.

This trail made by mountain bikers, which is also fun to walk, can be amalgamated with Exshaw Creek trail to make loops. It naturally falls into three different parts. Doing a figure 8 with the upper and middle sections is the obvious choice. The lower section takes you back down to Exshaw. See the sketch map on page 153.

FROM Y-JUNCTION 275607

Upper section 2.2 km

Heading northwest, it follows a rarely used hunting trail, gradually climbing to a T-junction on the bank of a side creek. Turn right and wind uphill to the trail's high point.

The return to 4-way junction 278600 is mainly downhill, the odd sharp bend and steep little downhill alternating with flats. A few technical features make their appearance as you near the junction.

Lower section near the viewpoints.

Middle section 1.3 km

From 4-way junction 278600 the trail heads onto Weader Ridge and makes two big loops. The jump off the end can be circumvented by Girls Out to its left. After the runout the trail continues to snake around the forest, in the process crossing a black pool creek and climbing onto another small ridge on its way down to 4-way junction 282594.

Weader Ridge in the middle section.

Lower section 1.5 km

The well-signed trail leaves 4-way junction 282594 and traverses slightly downhill to a dell, then across the semi-open west face of Exshaw Mountain. (Just beyond the dell you cross a less defined up–

down trail, the down part ending at the 4-way junction 282591 on Exshaw Creek trail.) At picturesque trees is a viewpoint for the Lafarge cement plant.

On open, slabby ground start the descent, keeping left at a split on the blue circle route. Below is a terrace with a closer view of the cement plant, Exshaw and Heart Mountain. Walk down slabs.

So far this has been a great trail to hike. That all changes when you come to the fan technical feature. Below it, in a bushy gully, the trail morphs into a luge run with banked corners winding into the Junkyard. Should a biker come zooming down behind you, it's curtains for you both. Naturally, this is a big concern and I would like to suggest that before the luge run you traverse left on a faint trail to pick up Exshaw Mountain trail.

Arriving in the Junkyard, a flat area of technical features, head out right to a gravel road. (The continuing trail passes below the start to Exshaw Mountain, ultimately connecting with the Powerline trail to Jura Creek.)

Turn right on the gravel road. In a few minutes cross paved Windridge Road. A trail cuts across to a paved lane. Cross and continue on trail to the footbridge over Exshaw Creek to the parking lot.

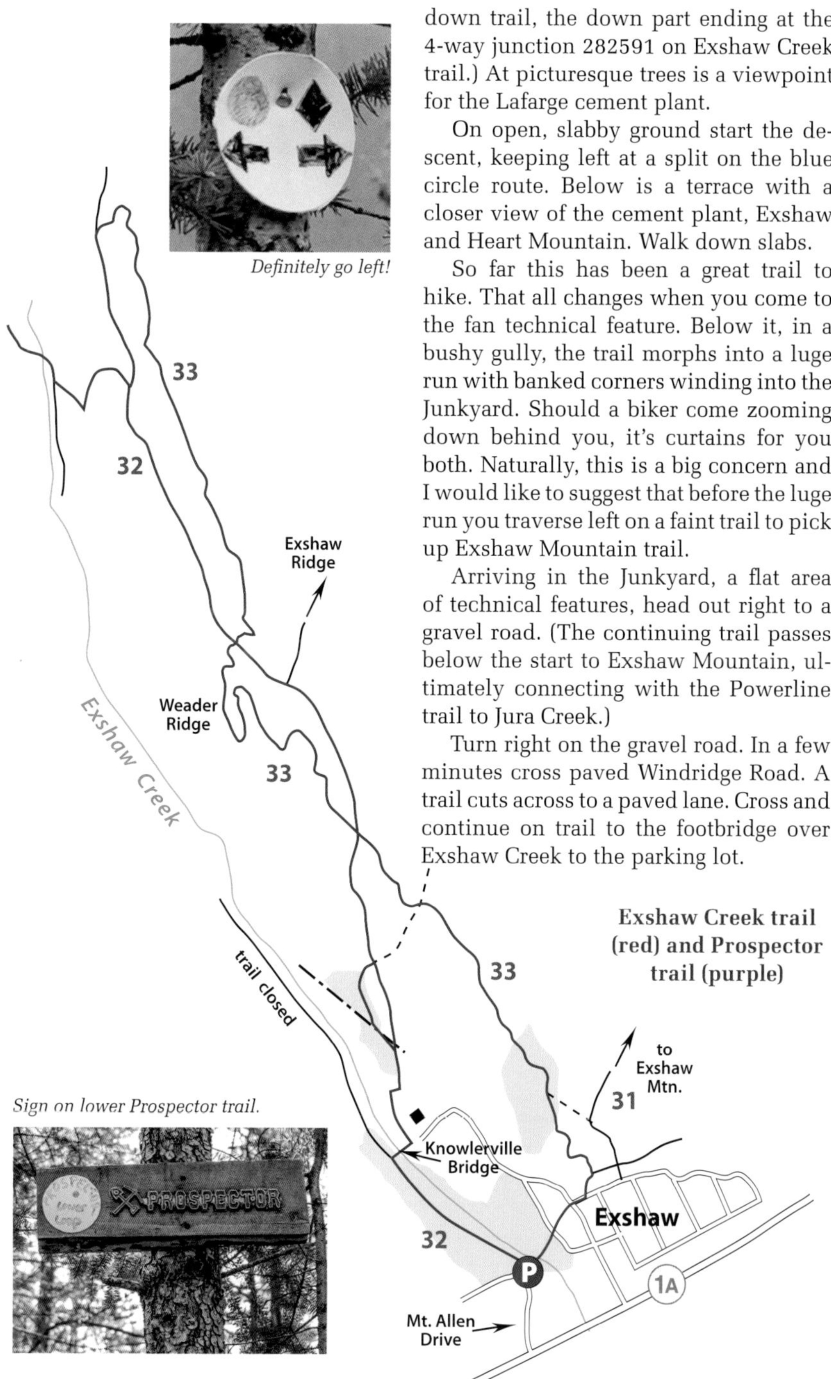

Definitely go left!

Exshaw Creek trail (red) and Prospector trail (purple)

Sign on lower Prospector trail.

34 EXSHAW RIDGE—maps 7, 6

Looking across Exshaw Creek to the Mythic Towers. Photo Alf Skrastins

Day, long-day scramble
Unofficial trail & route
Distance 6.2 km to 6/7 col;
13.5 km loop with Exshaw Creek
Height gain S–N 722 m (2370 ft.)
Height loss S–N 579 m (1900 ft.)
High point 2088+ m (6850+ ft.)
Map 82 O/3 Canmore

South access #32 Exshaw Creek at 280599.
North access #32 Exshaw Creek at ~260637.

The south end of the ridge between Exshaw and Jura creeks is ideal for ridge-walkers hankering for great views. While scrambling can be avoided (unless snow lies on the eastern flank), this is not a route for novices: the going is rough and time-consuming over numerous tops, and there is some bushwhacking to do on the descent.

Most people make a loop with Exshaw Creek trail. Clockwise or anticlockwise, it doesn't matter. I describe it counter-clockwise, starting from the south end, so as to get the hard work over early in the day. There is the option of including Exshaw Mountain at the beginning, which is a bit like eating a hot dog before feasting on prawn vindaloo.

SOUTH TO NORTH

To first summit 1.6 km

Follow Exshaw Creek trail to T-junction at 280599. Turn right on the much smaller trail that aims not for the col between the ridge and Exshaw Mountain as one might expect, but turns left below it at some flagging and makes a beeline up a southwest spur to the summit ridge—480 vertical m (1500 vertical ft.) of climbing in one go. At first the going is easy through trees with occasional cairns to keep you on the right track. But after diagonalling left across a patch of orange scree, the trail zooms straight up the fall line, a muscle-aching plod on dusty grey shale.

The summit ridge is gained near the junction with the south ridge at ~284609. (If reversing the route, aim for Pigeon Mountain.)

The trail turns left here and is well defined as it follows west-side meadows below the ridge crest. Reach top no. 1 in the trees at 284612.

The Ridge ~2.6 km

On trail, descend to a flat section of narrow ridge. Either follow the trail on the right side below a rockband or just as easily walk the ridge crest above slabs falling down the west slope. A gentle rise leads to top no. 2.

The steep descent to the 2/3 col can be complicated by snow on the east flank. Unable to use the trail on the right side, your only alternative is to scramble down the rocky ridge crest. From the col stroll up through trees and meadow to top no. 3.

Top no. 3 signals a definite change in character with the widespread appearance of grass and a widening of the crest. As you pass easily over tops 4 and 5 to 6 there are new views to be enjoyed: all the way up Exshaw Creek to Exshaw Pass, which "*looks bloody miles away*," and across to Mythic Towers and Mt. Fable, a prominent peak accessible to advanced scramblers. On the other side of the ridge across Jura Creek rises an equally fascinating line of peaks: "Morrowmount," "Hassel Castle" (the Hunchback), then Goat Mountain and mere bumps along the ridge, Loder Peak and Door Jamb Mountain.

The 6/7 col is where most people call it a day.

Going farther

Hiker-scramblers can carry on quite happily over several more tops, bearing in mind that the day trip is becoming a long-day trip. The ultimate top is 269657, which requires you to leave the crest for the scree of the west flank. After this the ridge becomes a lot more serious.

Descent to Exshaw Creek 600 m

There is no one route. Most people descend the west slope on one side or the other of the side creek developing below 6/7 col: steepish grass giving way to steepish open forest that gradually moderates as you near Exshaw Creek Valley. Hit Exshaw Creek trail somewhere between side creek 260637 and the dryas flats.

Right: Looking back at top no. 1 from top no. 2.

Below: The ridge beyond 6/7 col. In the background at far right is Hassel Castle.

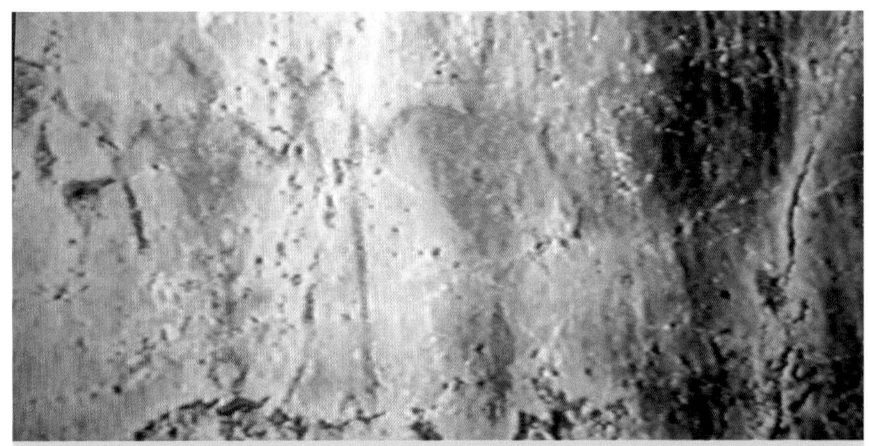

35 GROTTO CANYON—maps 8, 6

Computer-enhanced images of the pictographs, by James Henderson.

Day hike
Official trail, route, signs, creek crossings
Distance from official start 1.5 km
Height gain 128 m (420 ft.)
High point 1433 m (4700 ft.) end canyon
Map 82 O/3 Canmore

Access Hwy. 1A (Bow Valley Trail) in two places.

1. Longer, official Grotto Pond day-use area. Park on the right side a little way in. On summer weekends the lots fill up quickly.

2. Shorter, unofficial Turn north onto the road signed "Baymag Plant 2." Go straight at a junction onto a gravel road and park at the intersecting powerline right-of-way just before Enviro Enterprises quarry (currently being reclaimed).

Shorter still? Some people drive the powerline access road to left and park where the trail turns right off the access road. There is room for 4 cars.

Grotto Canyon is the epitome of inspiring rock scenery with the added bonus of Indian rock paintings. The going is easy along the creekbed, and consequently the trail attracts huge numbers of people ranging from first-time walkers to musicians to dancers to rock climbers and their entourages, which always include dogs. If you're bothered by crowds you'll find peace in the 90% of valley beyond the first canyon.

A word on water levels. Normally the creek idles along and is easily crossed on rocks. During flash floods, however, it becomes a raging torrent and has been known to trap people behind the canyon. In winter the canyon floor is a popular ice walk.

This is the scrambler's start to Gap Peak's south ridge route.

ACCESS NOTE Since the last edition the climber's off-road parking lot 1.2 km west of Grotto Pond on the north side of the highway has been blocked off by the MD at the bequest of truckers barrelling along the highway.

PICTOGRAPHS NOTE Archeologist Marty Magne believes the rock paintings were painted 500–1,300 years ago by the Hopi, who live 2,000 miles to the south in Arizona. According to the old stories, some Hopi travelled north to the land of snow and ice and tried settling for a while. On the other hand, the Stoney Nakoda believe the images were painted by Stoneys who had travelled south to Hopi land. But it cannot be denied that the flute player

In the canyon.

(a Hopi spiritual leader) at bottom left, is typical of Hopi art. Playing a flute was supposed to warm up the earth so crops could be planted, but it obviously didn't work here. Look also for a line of human figures, a moose kill (the animal believed chased up the canyon) and a line of what looks like deer. Enhanced computerized images by James Henderson have inspired designer Simon Wroot and you can now buy "ancient image bracelets" using images from Grotto. Back in 1970 they also inspired poet Andrew Suknaski to write a poem called "Tracings."

Access 1 to access 2, 500 m
Starting at the trail sign, a narrow, stony trail follows the powerline right-of-way. In 140 m Steve Canyon trail turns off to the right. Following the hiking sign, continue on the right-of-way and cross Steve Canyon creek, which has done a thorough job of washing out the trail. At 340 m another trail heads rightward to Steve Canyon. Descend slightly to Enviro Enterprises quarry access road, which is access 2. In sight ahead and within hearing is the huge Baymag plant 2, the world's largest and most technologically advanced MgO fusing facility.

The Canyon 1 km
Cross the quarry road and continue ahead on the powerline access road. When muddy, use a bypass trail to right. Just as the noise from plant 2 becomes deafening, turn right onto a trail with hiking sign. At the junction is a small parking area.

The trail reaches Grotto Creek near a memorial bench. In the spring of 2012 a flash flood churned up the stones at the canyon entrance and steepened the banks, making the usual access into the creekbed difficult. Bypass the impasse via a new 2012 section of trail that traverses the hillside to the right. (En route, a side trail takes off up a ridge to The Uncharted Sea (a sport climbing slab) and Gap Peak via the south ridge.)

Back in the creekbed, you follow snippets of trail on one side or the other deeper into the canyon. All the way along, entertainment is provided by sport climbers attempting routes with names like *Nubile Sheep and Velcro Gloves*. Big Hemingway Wall on the left was the vertical platform for Springboard Dance Company's performance of *Corvidae* in August 2001.

Two-thirds of the way along on the left the eagle-eyed will discern faint, red ochre

Cliffs of till beyond the canyon.

marks across a smooth slab about two metres up from the ground. These are the pictographs. See the photo on page 156.

Around the next bend the canyon opens out slightly into an amphitheatre at the forks where the official trail ends. In about 1990 and at a time of day when most climbers are only thinking of getting out of bed, the cantata *Stones*, the first phase of The Canyon Shadows Project with music by Robert Rosen and words by poet Peter Christensen made its debut at this unlikely spot. It was snowing at the time and all the performers wore ponchos.

You'll notice that most of the water in Grotto Creek comes from a waterfall in the right-hand cleft. A huge chockstone precludes all but the most determined explorer from going any farther in that direction, so you turn left below what in winter are *His and Hers* ice climbs and thread a hitherto unseen passage below Illusion Rock where walls on either side reach their greatest height. It also marks the end of the canyon.

The rest of the canyon 2.8+ km

After the theatrical doings of the canyon, the valley opens out into dryas mats and forest. The cliffs are still there, but mostly farther away and higher up, part of Grotto Mountain's precipitous east face. A trail carries on, crossing and recrossing the creek right up to 234617. Points of interest: straight off on the left is a large buttress of pale orange till eroding into hoodoos, the first of many incipient hoodoos and by far the most bizarre with its prominent cave. A little farther on is Garden Rock and Armadillo Buttress and another 15 minutes walk beyond Armadillo you'll see Grotto Slabs on the right.

The upper half of the valley offers the same stony creekbed, the odd incipient hoodoo and one small canyon, plus a rare backward view of Grotto Mountain embattled with cliffs.

#35A The right (east) bank trail up Steve Canyon.

OPTION

35A Steve Canyon

Half-day
Unofficial trails
Distance 950 m loop

Access Via #35 Grotto Canyon trail.

The valley east of Grotto Creek sees many hikers on sunny weekends and is conveniently located close to both parking lots. By summer the creek is usually dry.

From access 1. Turn right onto the Steve Canyon trail, which leads in a few minutes to the creekbed below the canyon.

From access 2. Turn right on the powerline access road. At the top of a small hill, turn left onto a trail that leads in a few minutes to the creekbed below the canyon.

There's a trail up the left west bank and a better one up the right (east) bank that has two scrambly starts. The two trails can be linked above the lower canyon to make a loop. Or continue exploring higher up the creekbed. Most people just like to follow the floor of the lower canyon and return the same way. At runoff there is a small waterfall.

NOTE The right (east) bank trail splits higher up. Most casual wanderers take the lower trail. The upper one takes off up a ridge and leads in about an hour to a steep diagonal cliff called The Sanctuary.

36 BOW VALLEY PROVINCIAL PARK SOUTH—map 7

Whale Lake and Yates Mountain from the northeast shore.

Half-day, short-day, day hikes, bike 'n' hike
Unofficial trails, junction markers
Map 82 O/3 Canmore

1. Official access Hwy. 1 (Trans-Canada Hwy.). At interchange 114A with Hwy. 1X, follow signs to Rafter Six Ranch Resort. At the 3-way junction go straight into a parking lot edged with rocks. This is also the trailhead for Stoney trail (see Volume 1). There are no identifying signs other than a hard to spot hiking sign.
2. Rafter 6 Ranch Resort access Hwy. 1 (Trans-Canada Hwy.). At interchange 114A with Hwy. 1X, follow signs to Rafter Six Ranch Resort. At the 3-way junction turn left and drive to the ranch parking lot.
Also accessible from Stoney trail (see Volume 1).

South of Hwy. 1 is a lesser known section of Bow Valley Provincial Park. It actually extends as a long narrow strip all the way down the Kananaskis Valley between Hwy. 40 and the powerline right-of-way to Lorette Creek. The part I am describing is enclosed by the highway. Camp Chief Hector, Rafter Six Ranch Resort and the NW–SE section of Stoney trail. It is accessed from Hwy. 1, whereas other trails farther south in the park are accessed from Hwy. 40.

The long distance Stoney trail (see Volume 1) is a wide track that serves as the backbone for a network of hiking cum equestrian trails, none of which are official K Country trails but are nevertheless well used by orienteers, runners, ranch guests and the kids from Camp Chief Hector.

Most junctions are numbered with small brown markers fixed to trees, so unobtrusive they are sometimes hard to spot. Using these waymarks (the numbering system is entirely random, by the way), you can have fun devising your own loops or follow the suggestions outlined below. I do my best to keep you off the boring Stoney trail and Powerline trail.

On the topo map the terrain looks flat. But because this is knob and kettle country, the trails are a lot more undulating than you might think, climbing over drumlins and ridges, diving into shallow depressions and following high riverbanks. In four words: perfect for spring training.

ACCESS NOTE re the official access: At one time you could drive through Scouts Field to Soapy Smith parking lot central to the trails. Now you are required to walk in on a gravelly track (Stoney trail) for 1.7 km. I suggest biking this bit.

While there is unrestricted access between Rafter 6 land and the park (just keep the gates shut), the same is not true for Camp Chief Hector, run by the YMCA. As per the "No Entry" signs on fences and gateways, the public are discouraged from using their parking lots and trails. This means that Yates Route to Prairie View trail touted in the 3rd edition and now renamed Lookout trail is out of bounds.

FACILITIES NOTE There are group campgrounds at Owl and Grouse. You can also camp at Rafter Six—tables and primitive biffies provided, but bring your own water.

I've always found the folks at Rafter Six to be hospitable. However, if you are going to use their parking lot, it's simple courtesy to spend a bit of money in the lodge, at the very least having a beer in the bar. Better still, arrange walks around their Sunday brunches, lunches or evening meals, which are available to non-guests. The ranch is open year round for drinks and lunch. Book ahead at 403-673-3622 for evening meals and brunches, the latter usually starting up in mid-May.

While there, visit the gift shop, museum and Teton the white buffalo.

BOULDERING NOTE Bonsai Rocks are described in *Bouldering in the Canadian Rockies*, by Marcus Norman.

MOVIE NOTE Marilyn Monroe was here briefly during the filming of the 1954 movie *River of No Return*. A cabin (exterior shots only) was built near the shore of Whale Lake and was still around to be photographed in the 1980s. Other movies filmed here include *Grizzly Adams*, *Wilderness Family*, *Wolf Boy*, *Across the Great Divide* and *How the West Was Won*.

On the cutline between markers 15 and 1.

HISTORY NOTE As you will read on plaques near access 1, the big meadow called Scouts Field was the site of Canadian and World Scout Jamborees in 1981, '83 and '93. At those times the whole meadow was filled with tents and flapping flags. Running through the meadow is Stoney trail, the original Hwy. 40 built in 1934, which ran between the Bow Valley and POW camp #130 under Mt. Baldy. You can still see remnants of the road bridge across the Kananaskis River at Broken Bridges picnic area.

In the late 1800s Col. James Walker ran his horses on land east of the big meadow where he built a shack. A half diamond over 6 (rafter 6) was his brand. The next land owner was old-time trapper Soapy Smith and his young wife Eva, who ran a guiding business, but it wasn't until Eva and Alvin Guinn (of Guinn's Pass) took over in 1929 that Rafter Six Guest Ranch really got going. A small lodge (now the Mad Trapper dining room) was built and cabins replaced tents. Illahe was where artist and climber Belmore Browne and his family spent their summers within sight of Belmore Browne Peak.

The ranch changed hands in 1976 "on a handshake." Present owners Stan and Gloria Cowley expanded the place even further into what you see today—the latest addition being a ropes course and zipline. It is interesting to note that back in the snowy 1980s, the Cowleys touted the horse trails in the future Bow Valley Provincial Park as ski trails and produced two trail maps.

The ranch has been up for sale since 2012, but until it once again changes ownership, I'm told it's business as usual.

36A Rafter Six trails

Hour strolls

Short and easy après meal strolls along the Kananaskis River that can be combined. While access is through Rafter Six land, the trails themselves lie in snippets of Bow Valley Provincial Park.

FROM ACCESS 2

From the parking lot head left on a road in front of the lodge. Pass various corrals, barns and the museum and descend a hill past the chalets. Then turn right onto a gated track. At the first junction you have a choice of routes

1. Riverbank trail 1.1 km one way

Go left on a track. Out of the trees keep left (trail to right leads to a bridge site over a channel) and follow the track alongside the Kananaskis River, past the cowboy cutout and picnic area to its end at teepees. Return the same way.

2. Flats trail 860 m one way to river

Go straight on a track. At the next junction keep left on a track and cross an intermittent channel of the river. Looking right, you can spot a bridge over a pool. Go straight (trail to left ends at a bridge site), then bend right onto a figure 8 of gravel tracks. From the far end a trail makes a beeline for the river's edge.

On return you can check out the bridge, which can be accessed by faint trail from the figure 8. On the far side a track leaves the shed and returns you to the track you started out on. Keep left.

#36A.2 The bridge over the pool.

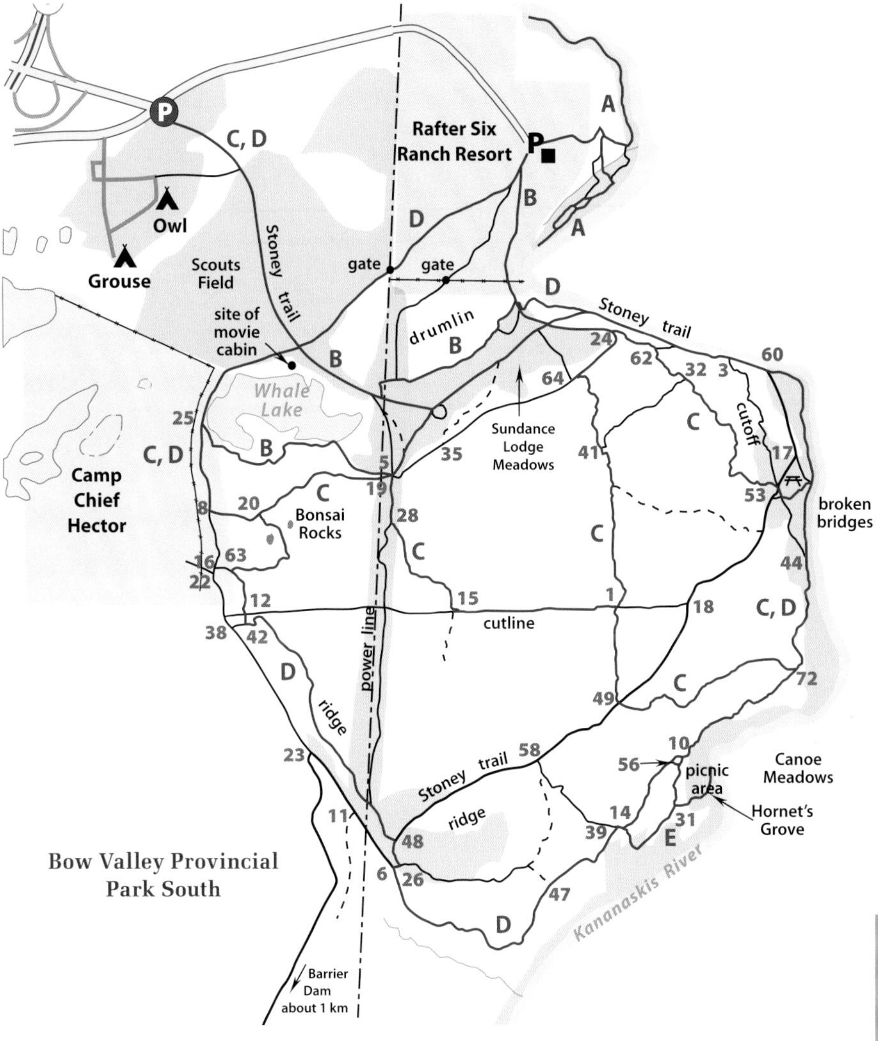

Bow Valley Provincial Park South

The movie cabin at Whale Lake.

Rafter Six Ranch Resort.

36B Drumlin & Whale Lake

Half-day hikes
Distance 5 km
Height gain 30 m (100 ft.)
High point 1347 m (4420 ft.)

A longer walk, taking in a country church, a drumlin, a lake and sundance lodges. The loop can also be picked up from access 1.

FROM ACCESS 2, ANTICLOCKWISE

Drumlin

The route starts from the right side of the lodge as you face it. Follow a track under a gate into the camping meadow. Keep left of the helicopter circle, then right of the church. (It's worth making a detour to the church for a look-see.)

In trees the track climbs up over a drumlin and through an open gate. A little down the other side is a 4-way junction with a narrower trail. Turn right.

The trail traverses the south-facing slope of the drumlin through Douglas firs, occasional openings letting in views of the Diamond X face of Yates Mountain. Cross under the first powerline. (Trail to right following the right-of-way returns to the camping meadow via the forested north slope of the drumlin.)

Cross under a second powerline and descend left to Sundance Lodge Meadow where you intersect Stoney trail, at this point a gravelly track grassing over. Turn right.

Around Whale Lake

Stoney trail veers around the west side of the drumlin to a 4-way junction with small cairn. Turn left (Straight on leads to access 1. Right leads to access 2.)

Before continuing, Marilyn Monroe enthusiasts may want to delve into the aspens between the junction and Whale Lake. At ~372593 you'll find a few burnt wood fragments with nails attached, all that's left of the movie cabin.

Aging Sundance lodge.

Head along the south edge of Scouts Field to a green power box, then turn up left, following the trail alongside the boundary fence with Camp Chief Hector. En route is a view of shallow Whale Lake enclosed by grasses. Unofficially named many years ago for its whale shape, it is also called Buffalo Bill Lake by the folks at Camp Chief Hector.

At junction marker 25 opposite a "No Entry" sign on the fence, turn left onto a faint trail in grass. Gaining clarity, it snakes along a grassy rib, heads inland through some trees, then returns to the south shore from where you can make forays to the lake. Another stint through trees brings you to 6-way junction 375588 on the grassy powerline right-of-way (markers 19 and 5). Go second left on a track.

Sundance Lodge meadow

Keep right and reach the old Soapy Smith trailhead on Stoney trail. Turn right and walk the length of Sundance Lodge Meadow (also known as Sundance Circle Prairie). En route visit the sundance lodge with interpretive sign "*Ti-jurabi-chubi,*" which has almost completely succumbed to the elements. Then detour next right to visit two more sundance lodges in slightly better shape with a few pieces of cloth still attached. At the edge of the trees is a sweat lodge.

Return to Stoney trail and cross it. Other trails join in from right and left as you climb up over the drumlin to the camping meadow you started out on.

36C Broken Bridges loop

Short-day hike
Distance 11.3 km from access 1; 8.2 km from access 2
Height gain ~61 m (~200 ft.)

A more strenuous loop with occasional steep hills takes in the original Hwy. 40 bridge site over the Kananaskis River and the banktop above Shaugnessy Canyon. Return routes give very pleasant walking through open forest. NOTE Starts and finishes vary depending on access.

CLOCKWISE

1. From access 1, 2.2 km

Heading southeast, follow Stoney trail across Scouts Field to a 4-way below the drumlin. Go straight here, curving left under the powerlines and past old Soapy Smith trailhead into Sundance Lodge Meadow, a strip of grass between the drumlin and the forested slope to the right. Keep straight (northeast) to meadow's end at 4-way 382594 just before Stoney trail descends into forest. Turn right on a trail identified by a boulder etched with names and initials.

2. From access 2, 820 m

From the right side of the lodge as you face it, follow a track under a gate into the camping meadow. Keep left of the helicopter circle, then right of the church. In trees the track climbs up over a drumlin and down to a 4-way junction at the northeast end of Sundance Lodge Meadow. Cross Stoney trail, heading straight on a trail identified by a boulder etched with names and initials.

To bridge site 1.5 km

The trail runs between the meadow and the forested bank dropping to the Kananaskis River. On entering trees keep straight past junction marker 24. Climb a little to junction marker 62 and keep right.

The following climb onto a ridge at junction marker 32 is the start of serious undulations, the trail plying up and down ridgelets and across intervening dells. Finally it turns left and descends to junction marker 53 in a meadow where you intersect the Cutoff trail to the right of a pipe sticking out of the ground. It will have occurred to you that you could have got to this point more easily by using the Cutoff trail from junction marker 3 on Stoney trail.

Turn right and in seconds reach Stoney trail—at this point a trail crossing grass. Cross it, and keeping left, descend through a few trees, then between the corral and the biffy into Broken Bridges picnic area. Located in a meadow above the Kananaskis River it features many picnic tables and a firepit.

The old Hwy. 40 bridge in 2012.

The grassy track coming in from the left is the original Hwy. 40. Follow it down the bank to the bridge over the Kananaskis River. The stringers have gone now, but the abutments, protected by metal gabions, still stand firm.

To Stoney trail 3.2 km
Crossing the old highway on the river side of the picnic area is the Riverbank trail. Pick it up heading south. All is straightforward to junction marker 44. Keep left here and start a long, sometimes steep climb through aspen forest onto the upper banktop. Just before reaching your objective is a significant dip.

For a brief time enjoy the view, because at junction marker 72 you turn right (inland), the trail wending its way along a ridge between sinks and valleys on both sides. Reach Stoney trail at a borrow pit at junction marker 15.

Return to access 2, 2.7 km
Cross Stoney trail and continue on trail through an open forest of pine and aspen. Cross an E–W cutline at junction marker 1. The trail undulates slightly to junction marker 41 (trail to right connects with marker 32), then drops into a spruce-filled valley with deadfall. Walk over the lip of the valley and down a high, forested bank to a good E–W trail at junction marker 64. Turn right. Shortly, join the trail you started out on at junction marker 24. Turn left and return the same way.

Return to access 1, 4.4 km
Cross Stoney trail and continue on trail through an open forest of pine and aspen. On reaching an E–W cutline at junction marker 1, turn left and follow the cutline trail to the west. At junction marker 15 turn right, off the cutline, and wind down to the powerline trail at junction marker 28.

Turn right and descend very much more steeply to the 6-way in a meadow at junction markers 5 and 19 at 375588.

Turn first left on a track that takes you past junction marker 20 to junction marker 8 at the boundary fence with Camp Chief Hector. Turn right. A narrower trail, slightly undulating, follows the fenceline through meadows and light trees, ultimately descending to Scouts Field at a green powerbox. Turn right and follow the trail to the 4-way on Stoney trail.

Turn left on Stoney trail to return to the parking lot.

Between marker 72 and Stoney trail.

#36D Riverbank loop. High above the Kananaskis River, looking towards Mount Baldy and the mountains of the Kananaskis Valley.

36D Riverbank loop

Short day hike
Distance 11.1+ km from access 1; 9.9+ km from access 2
Height gain ~85 m (~280 ft.)
High point 1417 m (4650 ft.)

The longest loop follows the scenic west bank of Shaugnessy Canyon with an option of descending to the Kananaskis River for a closer look at kayakers and rafters. Return along a ridge and down past Bonsai Rocks to Scouts Field. NOTE there are separate start and finish descriptions depending on your access.

CLOCKWISE

1. From access 1, 2.4 km
Heading southeast, follow Stoney trail across Scouts Field to a 4-way below the drumlin. Go straight here, curving left under the powerlines and past old Soapy Smith trailhead into Sundance Lodge Meadow between the drumlin and the forested slope to the right. Keep straight (northeast) ignoring various trails to left and right to meadow's end. Here Stoney trail descends through forest to the Kananaskis River. At the bottom of the hill the trail from access 2 joins in from the left. Keep right on Stoney trail, which for a period of its history was called the River Road.

2. From access 2, 1 km
From the right side of the lodge as you face it, follow a track under a gate into the camping meadow. Keep left of the helicopter circle, then right of the church. In trees the track climbs up over a drumlin. Before reaching Sundance Lodge Meadow, turn left at a 4-way onto a narrow trail. The trail winds downhill onto the flats of the Kananaskis River, then heads right to join Stoney trail, which is a track. Turn left.

To Broken Bridges picnic area 1.6 km
Follow Stoney trail alongside the Kananaskis River and below a steep, forested bank. Pass junctions markers 46 and 3. At the next, unnumbered junction keep straight on another track. (At this point Stoney trail curves to the right.)

The track soon narrows to trail and enters meadows alongside the river. Continue to follow the trail around a river bend and slightly uphill into a meadow at Broken Bridges picnic area.

Riverbank section 3.1 km
Several trails lead out of this area. Your trail continues to follow the riverbank heading south. All is straightforward to junction marker 44. Keep left here and start a long, sometimes steep climb through aspen forest onto the upper banktop. Just before reaching your objective is a significant dip. Keep left at junction marker 72.

The trail continues above a steep bank falling to Shaugnessy Canyon—a really enjoyable stretch with views down to the slalom course. At junction marker 10 keep right on a trail that wades through forest to junction marker 14. The alternative is SIDE TRIP #36E.

At junction marker 14 keep right, then left at junction marker 39. (Trail to right widens into a track leading to Stoney trail at junction marker 58.)

Enjoy another scenic section along the banktop, with views across the Kananaskis Valley of Horton Hill, Mt. Baldy and the Fisher Range. After one final viewpoint for Widowmaker rapid, the trail curves right along the top of a side valley to junction marker 6 on Stoney trail. Turn right.

(NOTE Stoney trail ahead leads to junction marker 23, where it turns sharp left bound for Barrier Lake. Should you go straight here on Camp Chief Hector trail you would eventually descend past junction markers 38 and 16 to junction marker 8, where you could pick up the route from the escarpment.)

SIDE TRIP

36E Kananaskis River

Distance 790 m
Height loss/gain ~46 m (~150 ft.)

A side trip to the slalom course, where you can watch kayakers and rafters in breathtaking close-up. You descend the bank on one trail and return via another. Expect steep hills on both trails.

Down
At junction marker 10 turn left, keep left at marker 56 and in two steep zigs descend the bank. Where the ground levels, keep left at what is possibly junction marker 31, then left at the next junction. Emerge in a small meadow with aspens called Hornets Grove—a popular picnic area. From here the usual trail down the riverbank has been blocked by deadfall. So, on a fainter trail walk farther to the left from the meadow and find a steep, muddy bank.

Reach the river halfway between Cartwheel Corner and Green Tongue rapid. The shore is pebbled and features berms and slalom gates. Even the riverbed itself has been refashioned at this point.

Up
Return to junction marker 31. Turn left here and traverse to another junction. Keep straight on a grassy trail morphing into a wide, stony track that climbs steeply up the sandy bank in two zigs to junction marker 14. Go left to junction marker 39.

Bonsai Rocks.

Escarpment 1.2 km

Climb past junction marker 26 to junction marker 48 at the high point of Stoney trail. Turn left onto the powerline access road.

Climb to the high point of the powerline right-of-way, which is another fine viewpoint. Cross the right-of-way and follow a very nice trail that alternates between the escarpment top and inland forest, at the end descending on the edge of the slope to a 4-way junction with the E–W cutline at a survey marker and Alberta Provincial Park boundary sign.

Go straight down a hill. (Trail to left leads past junction marker 42 to Camp Chief Hector trail at marker 38.) In a very short distance come to junction marker 12.

Bonsai Rocks 1.7 km

Veer right down a very steep hill, gradually levelling off to junction marker 63. Turn right.

The trail traverses to Bonsai Rocks, a line of cardium chert pebble conglomerate boulders, partially coated in moss, that offer climbers 33 bouldering problems. The trail curves left between them, then keeps heading left to junction marker 20. Turn left on a track. Reach junction marker 8 at the boundary fence with Camp Chief Hector.

Turn right. A narrower trail, slightly undulating, follows the fenceline through meadows and light trees, ultimately descending to Scouts Field at a green powerbox. En route is a view of Whale Lake enclosed by grasses. Turn right and follow the trail to the 4-way on Stoney trail.

Return to access 1, 1.1 km

Turn left on Stoney trail to return to the parking lot.

Return to access 2, 1.3 km

Cross Stoney trail, following a trail that runs through meadow below the forested north slope of the drumlin. A gate in the fence accesses Rafter Six land. Arriving in the camping meadow, keep left of the helicopter circle and descend to Rafter Six parking lot in front of the lodge.

37 QUAITE VALLEY TO JEWELL PASS—map 7

Quaite Valley trail near the campground, with Yates Mountain in the background.

Day hike, bike 'n' hike
Official trail with signposts and TCT markers
Distance 6.8 km via official start; 4.2 km via unofficial start
Height gain 326 m (1070 ft.)
High point 1630 m (5350 ft.)
Map 82 O/3 Canmore

Access Hwy. 1 (Trans-Canada Hwy.) in two places.
Official access At Lac des Arcs interchange 105 follow signs to Heart Creek parking lot.
Popular access From the eastbound lane of the hwy. opposite the Loder Peak sign, pull off the road at the entrance to Quaite Creek logging road. This is ~2.7 km east of the Lac des Arcs overpass. A gate prevents vehicle travel up the road.
Also accessible from Prairie View and Jewell Pass trails (see Volume 1).

This track (old logging road) is popular with mountain bikers and youth groups headed for a backcountry campground not too far from civilization. For walkers, Jewell Pass is a boring objective best combined with Prairie View trail and Razor's Edge to make a scenic loop or as access to McConnell Point. NOTE The upper section of track holds the snow well into late spring.

ACCESS NOTE The official access is part of the Trans Canada Trail. Most people use the popular start.

FACILITIES Quaite Valley backcountry campground in the meadow.

NAMING NOTE In the one and only meadow, Jack Quaite ran a sawmill for purposes of experimentation with "overmatured Engelmann spruce, white spruce and alpine fir." Incredibly, the federal government's Forest Experiment Station in the Kananaskis Valley reached over Jewell Pass into this valley.

There are two starts:

1. Official 2.9 km
From the kiosk follow a trail up and around a forested ridge to powerlines, then descend a long hill to Heart Creek bridge. On the east bank is a 5-way junction.

Go straight up a short hill, then keep right, heading east alongside the highway. Apart from traffic noise, this is a surprisingly pleasant section through aspen forest. You pass a pond, duck under the powerline, then cross the bridge over Acéphale Creek (taking-off place for #40 Acéphale Waterfall; return place from #41 Heart Mountain Circuit). Recross the powerline right-of-way, then cross Quaite Creek to the logging road on the east bank. Turn right. (The popular start lies 260 m to the left.)

2. Popular 260 m

Follow the logging road (track). About 260 m beyond the gate the official trail joins in from the right across Quaite Creek. Keep ahead on the old road.

To Quaite Creek campground 1.8 km

Head up the narrow valley, the track nicely gravelled for trainee backpackers, squashed between the creek and steep slopes of McConnell Point dappled with snow-white slabs of Palliser limestone.

After 1.4 km the valley opens into a meadow (cutblock) where the sawmill used to be. Ahead rises the shapely high point of McConnell Ridge—Yates Mountain—crowned by Barrier Lake Lookout. Here the road crosses the creek via culvert into the environs of Quaite Valley campground, which is located across the meadow in the trees. Keep right at T-junctions with trails leading to campsites, food lockers, a biffy and picnic tables.

To Jewell Pass 2.1 km

Shortly after entering trees, come to a fork in the logging road at 324573. Both forks converge on Jewell Pass like pincers, but the left-hand one is longer and growing bushes. So take the official, right-hand fork that crosses Quaite Creek and climbs moderately steeply through forest to a levelling out just before a 4-way junction with signpost. Go straight (left-hand logging road to left, loop road to right) and in seconds come to the 3-way signposted junction with trails Prairie View (left) and Jewell Pass (straight). This marks the pass, which lies entirely in trees. In the area of the loop road Bud Jewell had a lease to log Douglas firs still standing after a fire.

Showing how the Quaite Valley, Razor's Edge and McConnell Point trails interconnect

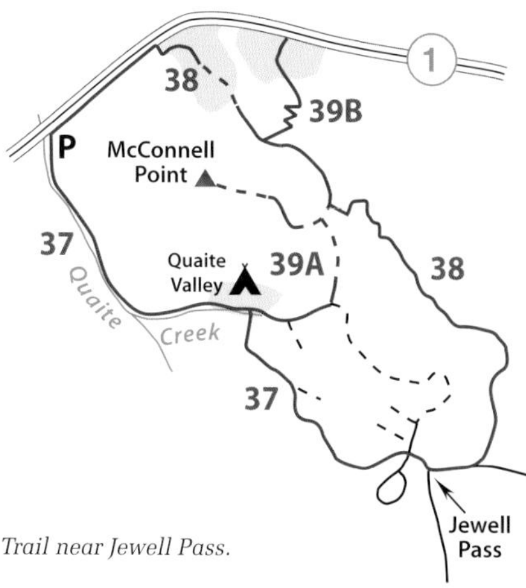

Trail near Jewell Pass.

38 RAZOR'S EDGE—map 7

Looking southeast along McConnell Ridge to Yates Mountain.

Half-day, day hike in combo
Official trail with cairns and flagging
Distance 5.9 km
Height gain SE–NW 106 m (350 ft.)
Height loss SE–NW 435 m (1439 ft.)
High point 1722 m (5650 ft.)
Map 82 O/3 Canmore

Access Via #37 (access 2) at Jewell Pass.

An unofficial hiking trail along a scenic section of McConnell Ridge is about to become an official DHS mountain bike trail. Bikers always ride it in a SE–NW direction. Hikers can go either way if doing the highly recommended 10.1 km loop with Quaite Valley trail, but if you want to save the best views until last, go the same way as the bikers.

TRAIL NOTE As of spring 2013, the final section of trail closing the loop between the open ridge and Quaite Creek has not been built. It is expected to emerge on Quaite Valley trail opposite the trail from Heart Creek parking lot.

Trail between Jewell Pass and McConnell Ridge.

NAMING NOTE "Like the sharp edge of a razor is that path, so the wise say, hard to tread and difficult to cross."—*Katha Upanishad*

FROM SE TO NW

From Jewell Pass take Prairie View trail. In 500 m, at about 339563, turn left.

Razor's Edge traverses the west slope of Yates Mountain, climbing gradually through pine forest onto McConnell Ridge, reached in a small meadow.

Turn left and descend to a gap. Climb the far side and amble along the lightly treed ridge to the day's high point at a cairn. The following gradual downhill, featuring lots of drop-down slabs, ends in a small flat meadow bounded on the far side by a big, straight-walled outcrop. Climb up shale behind the outcrop onto a lovely area of grassy troughs slung between smaller outcroppings. Watch carefully for where the trail goes over a slab to the left (cairn) and down a steep slope to a woody col at 328581. You have to find this col. Not so easy when the lay of the land does its best to take you elsewhere, aided and abetted by the view opening up to the northeast.

Ascend trees into a dry, shaley meadow with cairns. A second meadow signals the taking-off point for McConnell Point from #39B.

Enter cool, mossy forest. A steep, twisty downhill leads onto a bow-shaped bench that spans the entire east face of McConnell Point. Going down you enjoy views above cliffs of the Bow Valley, mainly Camp Chief Hector lease land about Chilver Lake. At the lowest point, in a patch of aspen and poplars, a trail to right at ~323585 is Headwall trail, #39B. Climb up the far side to the top of a northwest ridge.

This open ridge descends all the way to Hwy. 1, grassy promontories alternating with slabby steps offering everything the DHS biker desires. The rest of us, to avoid getting clobbered, must find safer ways around the drop-offs. While route finding, stop often to admire stunning views of the Bow Valley and its mountains.

While waiting for the last bit of trail to be built, drop off the end onto the Trans-Canada Hwy. Well, not quite. Because of a rock cut at this point, you must traverse left above it and descend a shaley draw. Turn left and walk the ditch for 1 km back to your starting point.

View from the open ridge across the Bow Valley to Grotto Mountain, Exshaw Mountain, Exshaw Ridge and Graymont's Exshaw plant.

39 McCONNELL POINT—map 7

Day hikes
Official & unofficial trails, route
High point 1752 m (5750 ft.)
Map 82 O/3 Canmore

This remarkably fine viewpoint is the northwestern outlier of McConnell Ridge that overlooks the Trans-Canada Hwy. For years, hikers have threaded a way up the steep west ridge between slabs. Nowadays it's more usual to ascend the point from Quaite Valley via route A, an intermittent trail made by campers looking for something more interesting than Jewell Pass. Route B offers a shorter way up from the north side. It makes use of Razor's Edge trail but shares the same finish as A. Either way, be prepared for some steep, rough ground.

NOT described is the direct "trail" up the south face from campsite #5. It takes a very steep line through the trees and is discontinuous. Two words sum it up: Not enjoyable.

39A from Quaite Creek

Distance 5.4 km from trailhead
Height gain 448 m (1470 ft.)

Access #37 Quaite Valley to Jewell Pass.

The easiest ascent route via the east ridge.

To East Ridge 1.4 km
Follow Quaite Valley trail to the campground. At the logging road junction just beyond, take the less travelled, left-hand (east) fork. The old road wends left and climbs. Near the apex of the hill at 329576 is a cairn with a pole.

Turn left up a trail that starts well with faded flagging and old blazes. Higher up it fades on more open ground. By just continuing uphill you are sure to hit Razor's edge at some point, but it's better to aim for 326581 just below the east ridge of the point, remembering that the climbing is always at a comfortable angle.

Near the summit of McConnell Point, looking southeast to Yates Mountain and Jewell Pass.

To summit 890 m
Turn left and tackle the steep east ridge, initially threading through a line of crags to a cairn, then climbing a twisty trail in scree. Finish along a flattish crest of grass, rocks, juniper and pines contorted by wind. Look back over dark-forested Jewell Pass to the mountains of the Kananaskis. As you near the summit the industrial portion of the Bow Valley comes into view, with a jumble of familiar mountains to the north and west.

Just down the west slope from the summit is a wooden shed that at first glance looks like an outhouse, partially tied down and laden with rocks inside to keep it from blowing away. It's used for storing electrical equipment for various antennas.

#39B On the second bench.

39B via Headwall trail

Distance 2.7 km from hwy.
Height gain 408 m (1340 ft.)

Access Hwy. 1 (Trans Canada Hwy.) eastbound lane. Park off road at 326591. To your right are four boulders.

Headwall trail takes a very steep line up a forested east slope between cliffs. Look for orange flagging. NOTE This trail lies at the northwest corner of land leased by Camp Chief Hector. The staff ask that you stick to the trail and don't go wandering about without permission.

To Razor's Edge 1.1 km
Walk past the four boulders to the obvious boulder pile where you pick up a trail. Turn left and follow the banktop above a short-lived valley, keeping right at a Y-junction and traversing. Cross a flat area of aspens, then climb through pines onto open ground encircling an aspen-filled sink. Cut across to junction marker 67 (small brown marker on a pine tree) at 326587.

Turn right and follow Headwall trail through an aspen dell, then steeply up a weakness between crags. Turn left and walk a grassy bench, dropping off the end to a T-junction. Turn right, then up left onto a second bench, this one slabby. At the far end, the trail heads into the trees, shortly curving right into a diagonal climb. When you turn up the fall line you're starting a steep, twisty climb to the low point of the bow-shaped bench. Blazes guide you onto Razor's Edge trail, reached at ~823585 in aspen poplar forest.

To #39A, 660 m
Turn left and follow Razor's Edge uphill onto McConnell Ridge. On or about 327581 turn off right, into the forest. Descend slightly to 326581, where you join #39A below the steep east ridge. Now read the last paragraph.

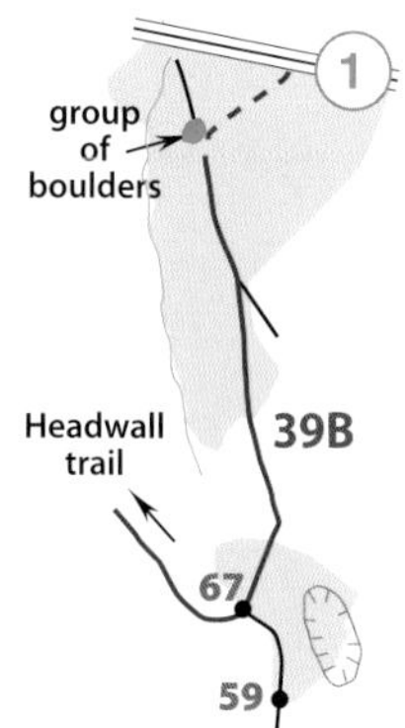

The start to Headwall trail

40 ACÉPHALE WATERFALL—map 7

Half-day hike
Unofficial trail
Distance 1.3 km from hwy.
Height gain ~130 m (~426 ft.)
High point 1440 m (4724 ft.)
Map 82 O/3 Canmore

Access Via #37, Quaite Valley trail official start near Acéphale Creek crossing 305578.
Climbers access Hwy. 1 (Trans-Canada Hwy.). From the eastbound lane park off road 1.2 km east of Heart Creek at a yellow road sign with arrow at 304578. A trail can be seen climbing the bank.

This is a trail used by sport climbers to access a crag named Acéphale, which provides some of the hardest climbs in the Canadian Rockies if not in all of Canada. The hiker's objective is not the crag (just getting to the bottom involves hauling yourself up chains), but a small waterfall at a step in the creekbed below, a quiet refreshing spot on a hot day.

NAMING NOTE For the philosophically inclined, "Acéphale" was both a journal and a French secret society existing between 1936 and 1939. Guided by Georges Bataille, the group participated in secret rites dedicated to certain basic social values such as risk. They "promoted a mythology with man as the pivot between extreme celestial and terrestrial forces, and Acéphalic man as its significant hero." In keeping, the hardest climb on the crag at #14B is called "Existence Mundane."

To Quaite Valley trail
Follow the trail up the bank to the stony bed of Acéphale Creek, cross it and walk the right bank to intercept Quaite Valley trail just right of the bridge over the creek. All this takes about 5 minutes.

To waterfall
A trail heads up the right bank of the creek, crosses to the left bank and reaches a powerline. Turn left. After about 40 m the trail heads right, into the forest. The trail returns to the left bank of the creek (here usually running), then turns away to a Y-junction where you go right. (To left is Heart Mountain loop.)

The trail follows a draw (keep right), then again returns to the creek and traverses a steep bank. Eventually you drop to creek level, where the forest is dark and mossy. Shortly after the valley turns slightly right (a gleam of white can be seen through the trees), turn right at a junction and arrive at your objective. About 10 m high, Acéphale waterfall spills down a rocky niche into a pool.

Opposite top: #41 The ascent ridge face on, showing the crux where you climb onto the upper ridge.

Opposite bottom: #41 Hikers on the ridge between Heart Mtn. and Grant MacEwan Peak in the background. Photo Alf Skrastins

Left: Acéphale waterfall.

crux

The ascent route follows the right-hand ridge onto Heart Mountain at right, then undulates along to Grant MacEwan Peak at centre. The route then follows the ridge to the left-hand summit, then drops down the ridge facing onto Quaite Creek trail.

41 HEART MOUNTAIN CIRCUIT—map 7

Day scramble
Official trail to first top with red markers and arrows, then unofficial trail
Circuit distance 9.6 km from Heart Creek; 11.1 km from official trailhead
Height gain/loss circuit 911 m (2990 ft.)
High point 2157 m (7080 ft.)
Map 82 O/3 Canmore

Access Hwy. 1 (Trans-Canada Hwy.).
Official access At Lac des Arcs interchange 105 follow signs to Heart Creek parking lot.
Popular access From the eastbound lane of the hwy. Park off-road just beyond the guardrail east of Heart Creek.

Heart Mountain is good fun, a popular scramble that comes into condition early in the season. The northeast ascent ridge is one of those places where experience decides how high you should climb. Some people quit halfway and have a sit-down in view of the cement plant, some reach the first summit, but many go on to complete the highly recommended circuit with Quaite Valley trail. This involves a ridge-walk over the highest summit and a rocky descent ridge, but nowhere are there difficulties comparable to those of the ascent.

NAMING NOTES Heart Mountain is named after the summit syncline in the shape of a heart.

Grant MacEwan Peak, the highest summit on the traverse, honours an Alberta lieutenant governor, popular Calgary mayor and prolific author of western history (among other things) through the labours of David Wasserman and the Grant MacEwan Outdoors Club. Though overshadowed by higher, more spectacular mountains, this was the summit chosen to bear MacEwan's name because "any reasonably fit or agile person can reach the top," something that Grant—a man of the people—would surely have approved of. After government employees twice vetoed a small commemorative plaque on the site, the name of the peak and the date of the official naming was painted onto the summit canister.

Getting to the start

1. Official access From the kiosk follow a trail up and around a forested ridge to powerlines, then descend a long hill to Heart Creek bridge. On the east bank is a 5-way junction. Turn second right onto a trail with a yellow warning sign.

2. Popular access A trail starting between

The crux starts with an overhang.

rocks leads to the powerline right-of-way. Turn right and continue to a T-junction with #37 Quaite Valley trail. Turn right down a hill to the 5-way junction on the left bank of Heart Creek. Turn second left onto a trail with a yellow warning sign.

To Heart Mountain 2.7 km

After climbing an initial step, the trail is easy for a way. Then comes a long rise up scree and broken rock where it's best to use the zigzag trail cutting back and forth across the up–down routes. Come to a flat. Above is a rock step, which accomplished scramblers tackle head on, not too far above cliffs plummeting into Heart Creek. Most people traverse left below the slabs into trees and follow a gently rising trail to regain the crest.

Continue on one of several trails to an unavoidable step. Scramble up the obvious diagonal crack, at the top continuing up left until another easy crack presents itself on the right.

The trail then follows an easy stretch of ridge to a large sloping scree ledge below a vertical rock step—the crux, where you must transfer from the lower ridge to the upper ridge. Though only about 5 m high, it's harder than it looks and even harder going down. Red markers indicate the usual route that requires a high step up left to get started. At the top is a small cairn for descenders. However, if you can't reverse the crux, you're stuck with going all the way around the loop! (NOTE Some consider a diagonal left to right crack to its left the easier way up.)

Escaping the yellow gully.
Photo Cal Damen, courtesy Rob Laird.

The upper ridge, easy at first, rears up into steeper slabs that climbers like Tony greet with enthusiasm. The easy way follows the trail into the security of the yellow scree gully to the left of the slabs. Where the gully steepens, head right at a red marker to a small tree on the gully's right-hand edge and step around a corner onto easy ground above all difficulties. From here it's a simple uphill walk to the first summit. After the drama of the ascent it seems strange to be greeted by meadows, trees and ground squirrels after your trailmix.

To Grant MacEwan Peak 1.5 km
The route continues over minor humps, then suddenly narrows to a stony ramp with slabs on both sides—a suitably impressive approach to the highest summit of the day at 318550 where three ridges meet. This is Grant MacEwan Peak, which has a register in the small cairn and a view of Barrier Lake. This is where scramblers bound for "the Twin Towers" take off along the south ridge.

Looking back at Grant MacEwan Peak from top 322554.

To top 323558, 1 km
Now heading northeast, the trail descends broad grassy slopes to a col, then zigs up scree to top 322554 (large cairn and even better view of Barrier Lake). Traverse a delectable ridge to a farther top at 323558 marking the culmination of another northwest ridge—your descent route.

Descent to Quaite Valley trail 2.9 km
Contrary to its scary appearance from the summit ridge and the Trans-Canada, this northwest ridge is straightforward and apart from the initial slope, set at a much gentler angle than the ascent route.

The trail down it makes a few lazy turns on scree, then descends a scree ramp to the right of the rocky ridge crest. (Should you be going uphill, stick to the ridge.)

Emerge on a broad section of ridge with grass and scree, flat areas with trail alternating with easy scramble steps. On entering trees, the route continues in much the same sort of way as before with many more scramble steps and one twisty scree descent on the left side of the ridge. The surprise is that immediately after the steps have ended and you're into mature mossy forest you encounter this huge drop right across the ridge, which the trail takes cold turkey. Slither down.

After this the trail gradually moderates in reverse proportion to increasing noise from traffic on Hwy. 1. Here and there are views of Quaite Creek and McConnell Point. Low down, below all hills, keep right at a Y-junction. (Trail to left leads to the Acéphale waterfall and climbing area.) In a few minutes more you're walking the banktop above Acéphale Creek, which provides ice-cold water!

Continue on trail to a powerline right-of-way. Turn left. Before reaching the by now dry bed of the creek, the trail turns right, then crosses the bed to the far bank, where a few metres farther on it intersects Quaite Valley trail at 305578. Turn left.

Follow Quaite Valley trail for 1.5 km to the 5-way junction you started out from.

View back from top 323558 to top 322554. Kananaskis Valley to the left.

Looking down the descent ridge. Photo Alf Skrastins

42 HEART CREEK interpretive trail—map 7

Half-day hike
Official trail with bridges
Distance 2.2 km via access 1
Height gain 64 m (210 ft.)
Height loss 24 m (80 ft.)
High point 1660 m (5446 ft.)
Map 82 O/3 Canmore

Access Hwy. 1 (Trans-Canada Hwy.).
Official access Hwy. 1 (Trans-Canada Hwy.). At Lac des Arcs interchange 105 follow signs to Heart Creek parking lot.
Popular access From the eastbound lane of the hwy. Park off-road just beyond the guardrail at Heart Creek.

The interpretive section through the canyon is easy, replete with bridges, interpretive signs and sport climbers. To go farther up this dead-end valley is a culture shock for anyone not used to rough forest trails.

ACCESS NOTE In the past, everyone parked off-road where the creek crosses the highway. To stop this, a long guardrail was erected and people were encouraged to walk an extra 520 m from the official Heart Creek parking lot, which meant an unwelcome uphill climb on the return. In the last few years, people are once again parking off road at the east end of the guardrail.

Access 1 to Heart Creek 770 m

From the kiosk follow the trail up and around a forested ridge to powerlines, then descend a long hill to Heart Creek bridge. On the east bank is a 5-way junction just metres away from the Trans-Canada Hwy. Turn first right.

Access 2 to Heart Creek 250 m

A trail starting between rocks leads to the powerline right-of-way with sign "Pets Must Be on a Leash." Turn right and continue to a T-junction with #37 Quaite Valley trail. Turn right down a hill to the 5-way junction on the left bank of Heart Creek. Turn second left.

View from the 7th bridge.

Interpretive trail 1.4 km

Crossing and recrossing the stream seven times on bridges, you wind between high rock gates introducing each new twist of the canyon floor. Up left are a higher tier of cliffs below Heart Mountain.

The trail comes to a full stop below a vertical step in the creekbed. Within earshot is a waterfall hidden by a twist in the canyon wall, a grand sight available to the determined person willing to paddle.

GOING FARTHER

42A Upper Valley

Unofficial trails, creek crossings
Distance ~1.7 km
Extra height gain ~122 m (~400 ft.)
High point 1524 m (5000 ft.)

A playground for adventurous hikers.

Rock step

There are ways up each side of the creek. Both are steep.

1. Left easier (east side) Hop across the creek to the left of the rock step. Not to be confused with a muddy rake below the ascending cliff line is the forest trail farther to the left that takes you to the top of a little ridge. At a T-junction turn left, then take the second trail to right that drops back to valley bottom above an impasse, en route passing a wondrous spot where half of Heart Creek wells up in a very large spring. On reaching Heart Creek, cross to the better trail on the west bank.

2. Right harder (west side) Just before the end of the interpretive trail, turn right up a side valley on a trail. Shortly it turns left and you grovel up hard-packed shale to a high point, then make a gradual descent into Heart Creek above the canyon. Viewing the waterfall is possible but perilous in the extreme because it entails hanging on to trees on the canyon rim. I've warned you, so don't sue me if you kill yourself.

Back at creek level the trail crosses the creek four times on logs. Route 1 joins in opposite the spring.

Upper valley

Follow the west bank trail past a tributary to where the valley briefly turns left. At this point it's worth detouring along the shingle bed to a small waterfall emerging from a stunning set of potholes.

Back on the trail, you climb into trees Go either way at a split, then keep going straight over a bit of a ridge and down to the creek above the potholes. Tramped by Boy Scouts in 1983, the trail remains fairly clear to a camping spot used during the 15th World Jamboree. Thereafter it deteriorates, alternating between banks to the bathtubs, then carrying on in much the same way below Grant MacEwan Peak and the twin towers to the side creek ~314537, after which it fades away in dense forest.

The waterfall from route 2.

The bathtubs.

43 BOW LINK TRAIL—maps 7, 8

Half-day hike
Official trail with TCT signs
Distance 7.6 km
Height gain E–W 91 m (300 ft.)
High point ~1417 m (~4650 ft.)
Map 82 O/3 Canmore

Access Hwy. 1 (Trans-Canada Hwy.).
East At Lac des Arcs interchange 105 drive to Heart Creek parking lot.
West At Dead Man's Flats interchange 98, follow signs to Banff Gate Mountain Resort. Park at the side of George Biggy Sr. Road just after leaving the interchange.
Intermediate Hwy. 1 eastbound. At 3.5 km east of Dead Man's Flats interchange 98 turn right into the McGillivray Creek parking lot. On foot follow a grassy track out of the parking lot. Keep straight at the first junction and pass between large rocks to a second T-junction with interpretive sign. Bow Link trail is straight and right. See map on page 189.
Also accessible from #45 McGillivray Creek.

This section of the Trans Canada Trail, which opened with much fanfare on October 18, 1997, runs between Heart Creek parking lot and George Biggy Sr. Road at Dead Man's Flats. It incorporates bits of old roads and even a section of Lawrence Grassi's forgotten trail between Bragg Creek hostel and Canmore. Though running parallel to Hwy. 1 and within sound of traffic, it is unexpectedly hilly and has many interesting things to look at on the way.

EAST TO WEST

To intermediate access 3.7 km

The trail leaves the west side of the parking lot and straightaway crosses a dry creekbed (See OPTION #43B to McGillivray Arch) to a T-junction with an old road.

Turn left on the road and climb over a hill to a T-junction. Keep left. On your right is a borrow pit. Very shortly turn left onto a trail that follows the tree edge across another dry creekbed to a T-junction with a second old road come up from the borrow pit. Turn left. The road climbs uphill to a 4-way junction. Turn right. (The roads straight and left are SIDE TRIP #43A.)

At the top of the long hill on the side ridge.

Descend a hill to a T-junction and turn right. (Straight leads to Lac des Arcs climbing school cabin.) At the next T-junction close above the highway, turn left. Cross a trail (the access trail from the highway to the cabin) and pass an interpretive sign about bighorn sheep. Just before the road ends at a power pole, turn left onto a descending trail. A little way down, on the right side, a faint trail leads to the southeast shore of McGillivray Pond.

At the Y-junction following go straight (trail to left is another route to the cabin).

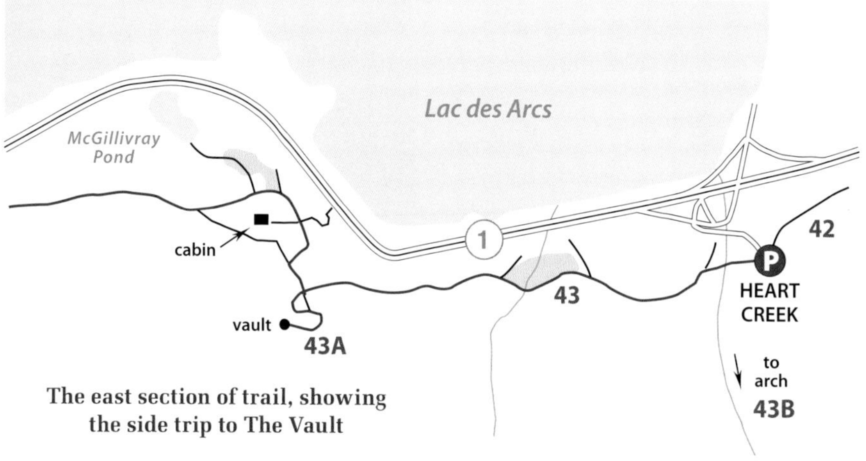

The east section of trail, showing the side trip to The Vault

To avoid the cliffy west shoreline of McGillivray Pond, the route follows a section of Grassi's trail up a longish hill onto a side ridge. Pass through a fence. On the right is a viewpoint for Grotto Mountain. Descend two slabby areas on your way back down to highway level. In the aspens meet up with another lot of old roads (tracks) at a T-junction. (Turn to the sketch map on page 189.) At an interpretive sign turn left onto a track signed "Pigeon Mountain Natural Area." (The track ahead leads to McGillivray Creek parking area, the intermediate access.)

To west access 3.9 km
The track follows the forest edge to the left of the Boneyard, where road kill is disposed of. Where the track turns left, continue ahead on a trail into trees harbouring at last visit a bench and the usual lawn chairs. Enjoy a flat stretch through creaky old spruce forest, said to be one of the easternmost stands of white spruce. Cross the dry bed of McGillivray Creek.

Suddenly you smell sulphur, which emanates from a warm 10 degree sulphur pool a little way in to your left. Around the springs grow highbush cranberry and the rare (for Alberta) moss *Fissidens grandifrons*. Getting there requires a bit of bushwhacking.

SIDE TRIP

43A The Vault

Unofficial roads
Distance 330 m

At the 4-way continue straight up the winding road to the "cave" mouth at the bottom of McGillivray Slabs. It's about 61 m deep and 3 m high, with a long side passage off to the left near the end.

The vault was tunnelled out by Rocky Mountain Vaults & Archives in 1969 at the height of the Cold War. In the event of a nuclear attack it was seen as a secure place in which to store important documents and artwork.

Cross the outflow on a Japanese-style bridge. The bridge ushers in an undulating traverse of craggy, mossy hillside requiring three sets of steps. Cross a deep creek on a bridge and continue in the same sort of way down to highway level. Ponds on the right are fed by a sizable spring.

A stint alongside the highway (so close you can pick up garbage thrown from car windows) is followed by a walk across a field between a wildlife underpass on your right and a shooting range on your left owned by the Kananaskis Gun Club. Follow power poles to George Biggy Sr. Road where the trail ends.

To continue to Canmore en trail see #52 Quebexican.

NOTE Wildlife fences mean that humans on a long-distance jaunt along the Trans Canada Trail to Canmore can no longer run across Hwy. 1 to the hamlet of Dead Man's Flats for a bite to eat. Now we must use the overpass, which has neither sidewalk nor shoulder.

Steps on the craggy, mossy traverse.

The arch from above.

OPTION

43B McGillivray Arch

Half-day scramble
Unofficial trail
Distance 750 m
Height gain ~213 m (~700 ft.)
High point ~1554 m (~5100 ft.)

A short, steep trail to an arch on the lower northeast ridge of Mt. McGillivray. If you don't fancy the hike up, look for it from the Trans-Canada west of Heart Creek.

Shortly after leaving Heart Creek parking lot you come to a dry, stony creekbed. Turn left and follow the bed to where it steepens, then transfer to a trail on the forested left bank.

The trail follows the left rim of the deepening canyon, climbing onto successive ribs slanting down right. The third and final steps are the highest, with a little easy scrambling. Arrive at a T-junction on a ridge overlooking a side gully bridged by the fat rock arch. To get below it, follow a trail down the ridge, then contour left.

44 LAC DES ARCS waterfowl viewing trail—map 8

One hour walk
Official trail with interpretive signs
Distance 1.7 km return
Map 82 O/3 Canmore

Access Hwy. 1 (Trans-Canada Hwy.) westbound. At 10.7 km west of Hwy. 1X at Interchange 114, park on the right side of the hwy. at a widening.

A short stroll along the south shore of Lac des Arcs past hides and interpretive signs. Bring binoculars.

NAMING NOTE The name of this very shallow lake dates back to 1858 and refers to the widening at this point of the Bow River's meanderings. Until recently, dropping water levels in winter revealed sand bars that blasted sand on west winds through the gap toward the community of Lac des Arcs and Bow Valley Provincial Park. To counteract this, a dike was built in 1998 to keep the water levels up.

BIRDING NOTE The lake is well known as a staging area for waterfowl during the spring and fall migrations. The sight of tundra and trumpeter swans in their hundreds is amazing, even in early spring before the ice totally melts on the lake and coyotes are abroad looking for an easy meal.

Just out of your vehicle, look for a clump of white birch trees, which are much less common than their look-alikes the aspens. Moving on, walk west alongside the highway before heading right, into the trees. At a T-junction walk straight to a point with picnic table with a view across the water of Lafarge Canada's cement plant. Farther to the right are McConnell Point, Yates Mountain and Heart Mountain. Close in is a tiny island, equipped with picnic table and at times a territorial flag.

Back at the T-junction turn right and amble through forest to the south shore, en route passing three blinds with interpretive signs and benches. Opposite the third blind keep straight. (Trail to left leads out to the highway.)

A short uphill is followed by steps down to two more blinds marking the end of the trail above small bays divided by rocky promontories. The view here is of Grotto Mountain and the mountains about Canmore.

Looking across Lac des Arcs to the cement plant, McConnell Point, Yates Mountain and Heart Mountain.

The McGillivray Creek chockstone.

45 McGILLIVRAY CREEK—maps 8, 7

Half-day, day hike
Unofficial trails & route
Distance to chockstone ~2.1 km; to Skogan Pass trail 7.1 km
Height gain to chockstone 152 m (500 ft.); to Skogan Pass trail 649 m (2130 ft.)
High point 1966 m (6450 ft.)
Map 82 O/3 Canmore

Access Hwy. 1 (Trans-Canada Hwy.) eastbound. At 3.5 km east of Dead Man's Flats interchange 98 turn right into unsigned McGillivray Creek parking area.
Also accessible from #43 Bow Link trail and from #46 Skogan Pass.

The geologically interesting McGillivray Creek is a valley for adventurers. The recommended half-day destination is the celebrated McGillivray chockstone, reached via an adequate trail, then a walk up the bed of the canyon.

Going farther over the McGillivray/Pigeon watershed and returning via the Skogan Pass trail is a 13.2 km all-day trip requiring vehicles at both ends. To visit this less travelled valley be prepared to endure a mishmash of boulders, bush and avalanche debris, your progress aided by intermittent game trails. McGillivray is a creek that dries up, so bring water just in case.

To McGillivray Creek trail ~400 m
A grassy track leaves the parking lot. Keep straight at the first junction and pass between large rocks to a second T-junction with interpretive sign. Turn right onto Bow Link trail, a track at this point.

Where the track heads left, continue ahead on Bow Link trail. Turn off it to the left just beyond the Trans Canada Trail post at a small cairn.

To the chockstone ~1.7 km
In a short distance the trail becomes a cutline heading straight for McGillivray Creek. En route the track you just left comes in from the left.

DO NOT attempt to follow the creekbed. The lower canyon was and still is, as far as I know, an obstacle course strung with ropes, slings and notched logs, that was best left to students of the Lac des Arcs Climbing School. The penalty for failing the course (as we did) is an impromptu bath in a pothole.

Stick with the much improved trail that heads left along the banktop, gradually climbing to the steep foot of Mt. McGillivray's north ridge. Here it turns right into a traverse line that is rarely level. A couple of steep downhills precede the short, twisty drop-off to the creekbed (keep left near the bottom), that is reached above the final knotted rope of the obstacle course.

Head up the bed of the canyon between high rock walls. After about 20 minutes of walking you're standing under a huge diamond-shaped chockstone, neatly slotted between the walls and pointing downward like the dagger of doom in an Indiana Jones movie.

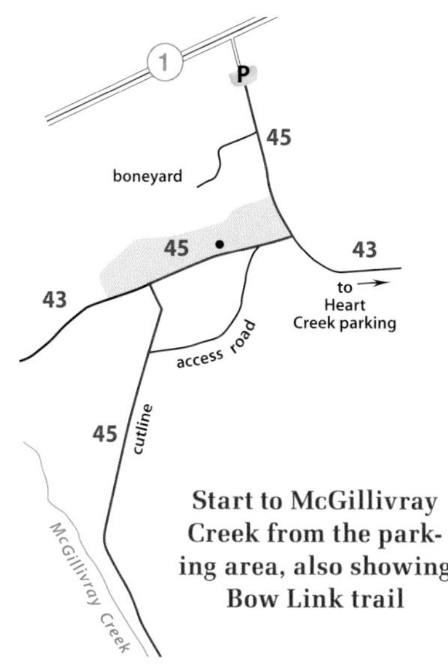

Start to McGillivray Creek from the parking area, also showing Bow Link trail

Above the chockstone. Photo Alf Skrastins

In the rockpile. Photo Alf Skrastins

GOING FARTHER

To Skogan Pass trail 5 km

The climb out of the canyon is up large boulders, facilitated by bits of trail on the right side. Above, a side valley comes in from the right and the main valley turns left. For a short while the going is easier, with a view ahead between trees of the huge rockpile slid off the west face of McGillivray. Something to look forward to. But first there is some avalanche debris to deal with. Then, to avoid the upcoming mini-canyon, follow a game trail starting from grass a little way up the avalanche slope on the right. The trail rises easily through mossy old forest to reach the rocks.

Pick a line left of centre for your clamber up and across the rockpile. The trail is vague but can be picked up on the far side where it descends into forest. A long stretch of flat forest with many trails leading onward returns you to the stony creekbed at a narrows. The going is then easy apart from one steep detour up the right bank to avoid a second round of avalanche debris.

At 278531 leave the main valley, which is veering to the east. Turn rightish up a draw shown as a dashed blue line on the topo map. As you climb toward the watershed with Pigeon Creek the trail improves, the forest opening up with a few flowery glades. At a steepening is a spring and above that the flat watershed meadow with casual camping sites used by hunters and Boy Scouts. It's a lovely spot, bisected by a trail that heads right onto the open slopes of Pigeon's lower summit and left onto an alluring west ridge curving toward the highest summit of the area (at 2662 m, even higher than Mt. McGillivray), which Andrew Nugara calls Skogan Peak. He describes the ascent from Mt. Lorette. Who knows whether it goes from this side?

From the watershed, your trail descends a short distance to Skogan Pass trail reached at 276519. At the junction the trail divides with a blazed tree in between.

46 SKOGAN PASS from the north—map 8

Long-day hike
Official trail
Distance 8.6 km
Height gain 670 m (2200 ft.)
High point 2073 m (6800 ft.)
Maps 82 O/3 Canmore, 82 J/14 Spray Lakes Reservoir

Access Hwy. 1 (Trans-Canada Hwy.). At Dead Man's Flats interchange 98 follow signs to Banff Gate Mountain Resort. Drive up George Biggy Sr. Road past Thunderstone Quarry to a T-junction at road's end. Turn right into Skogan Pass trailhead (biffy, kiosk, interpretive signs). The trail is the continuation of the dirt road.
Also accessible from #45 McGillivray Creek.

This is the northern section of the Skogan Pass trail that connects Dead Man Flat with Ribbon Creek. (See Volume 1 for the southern section.) It's a mundane walk on a powerline access road. But there is no accounting for people's tastes. I did talk to someone whose idea of a good walk WAS to follow a powerline right-of-way. I have to admit, though, that it sports one great viewpoint. Livening it up is the chance of meeting a grizzly during buffaloberry season. To reduce encounters, the right-of-way has been bulldozed of all bushes.

Generally, only mountain bikers go right through to Ribbon Creek. Most hikers use the powerline to access Pigeon Mountain.

CLOSURE NOTE A few years ago, mountain bikers built a single track trail called "A Taste of Class" upslope of and running parallel to the access road. Hikers were also looking forward to using it, but were disappointed when the trail was decommissioned in 2011 by the powers that be, citing "it was constructed in a preservation zone and without prior approval." A sign asks for your cooperation. However, all is not lost: keep an ear and eye open for the future extension of Highline trail to Skogan Pass.

Walking the powerline. Photo Gord Dobson

HISTORY & NAMING NOTE Just over a hundred years ago, Pigeon Pass, as it was called then, was a quiet, undisturbed place crossed by an Indian trail shown on George Dawson's map of 1886. Likely it was the same trail, by then called the Kananaskis Pack Trail, that was widened in 1936 by the Forest Service to carry the telephone line linking Dead Man Flat ranger cabin to Boundary ranger cabin near the mouth of Ribbon Creek. Henceforth it was known as the Canmore Boundary Telephone Line trail over Deadman Pass. Since then, the trail on the north side has been largely obliterated by the powerline right-of-way and its access road. Just a small portion of trail remains, near the summit.

Strangely, none of the old pass names stuck and it was left to Don Gardner, who was reconnoitering the Ribbon Creek ski trails in 1972, to name it "Skogan," a name that has since come into general use. Translated from the Norwegian, it means a magic forest with elves and trolls.

If the Canmore and Bow Valley Chamber of Commerce had had its way a number of years back, a four-lane highway would now be sweeping across Skogan Pass from the south end of Canmore to Nakiska and Kananaskis Village.

To Pigeon Mountain trail 4.6 km
Continue along the dirt road and at the 4-way junction with the powerline right-of-way turn left up its access road.

After the first hill, the road heads left into forest and climbs steadily past three tracks connecting to the right-of-way. Interestingly, the tiny side creek you cross after the gate is a monster rift by the time it reaches the right-of-way, and is the reason for this foray. Keep next right (grassy track ahead) and on rejoining the right-of-way, turn left.

After a flat stretch, the uphill plod continues under powerlines aiming for the skyline, which looks very far away. En route, the road dekes briefly into the forest to cross a side creek with bridge remains, and the grassy track joins in from the left.

Game trails you can rely on to make sensible decisions, but powerline right-of-ways by their very nature do illogical things, as you'll find out at the 4.1 km mark when you finally reach that skyline, which is NOT Skogan Pass.

On the brink of a great dip, the access road turns left (cairn, arrow) and winds uphill, coming in 800 m to a junction with a "Living with Wildlife" sign at 263520. Stay on the road. (Trail to left is Pigeon Mountain trail.)

To McGillivray Creek turnoff 1.5 km
Not long after, the road turns right into the meadow traverse, which is the route's one great viewpoint. Take a break in long grasses and enjoy a vista taking in the Bow Valley, the Three Sisters in profile and Collembola's north face and ridge in awe-inspiring close-up.

Back in the forest, you pass two geologically interesting slumps on the uphill slope, then the trail into McGillivray Creek at a small blaze at 276519.

To Skogan Pass 2.5 km
The road descends slightly. To the left is Skogan Pass proper, the low point in the watershed between Pigeon Creek and Lorette Creek. Here the old telephone trail cuts across to join the road on the south side of the pass, thereby avoiding extraneous climbing. Either follow it or stay on the road as it climbs to its high point, a vague spot in the pines determined solely by the downhill inclination of the road in front of you. From here I recommend a five-minute detour to the summit power pole, where every great view is ruined by powerlines. Sorry, Ruthie.

The steep east face of Mount Collembola from the viewpoint.

47 PIGEON MOUNTAIN—map 8

The summit cairn, looking back along the summit ridge to "Skogan Peak."

Day hike
Unofficial trail
Distance 2.8 km from Skogan Pass trail; 7.4 km from trailhead
Height gain 535 m (1755 ft.) from Skogan Pass trail; 992 m (3255 ft.) from trailhead
High point 2394 m (7855 ft.)
Map 82 O/3 Canmore

Access Via #46 Skogan Pass from the north at 263520.

Pigeon is an easy climb from the west, almost entirely through meadow. And the view from the summit of the Bow Valley is exceptional. NOTE The trail is closed Dec 1–Jun 15 during lambing season.

NAMING NOTE Pic des Pigeons was named by the Palliser Expedition of 1858 for a flock of pigeons—or, more likely, birds that looked like pigeons.

HISTORY NOTES The view is so outstanding, the summit was once slated for a teahouse by Bob Johnson of Canadian Rockies Touring, who later built half a teahouse on Lady Macdonald. The aim was to put a gondola up the steep north face, which was already adorned with CBC and CFCN towers. The idea was perhaps not as far-fetched as the short-lived Pigeon Mountain Ski Area that sprang up on the lower northwest slopes between 1962 and 1974. Despite local skepticism, it proved quite popular (who can forget the Poma?), but when the lean snow years came to pass it folded. Ten years on, lack of snow didn't stop it from being touted it as an Olympic venue. Today, the very nice ski lodge is the base for a slew of time-share cabins built up and down the ski hills that are growing trees very fast.

Even stranger is what happened on the mountain in 2002 during the G8 Summit in the Kananaskis Valley. According to X, who was in a position to see what was going on, the meadows near the summit were designated a military security zone and patrolled by armoured vehicles equipped with surface-to-air missiles.

Follow the Skogan Pass trail for 4.6 km to waypoint 263520. At a left-hand bend marked with a "Living with Wildlife" sign, turn left onto Pigeon Mountain trail.

The well-trodden trail ascends through trees into long-grass meadows, then climbs more steeply to the top of a triangular-shaped grass spur. From here it settles into a upward rolling traverse along a bench below the craggy west face of the lower summit. Arrive at the saddle between the two tops.

Turn left. After a short, rocky descent it's an easy stroll up the southeast ridge, initially on grass laced with scree, then totally on scree to the summit cairn.

While the mountain views are spectacular in every direction (you can pick out the crux on Collembola and the route up Wind Ridge), it pays to walk a little farther along the summit ridge to where it drops off. Now you get a bird's-eye view of the Bow Valley towards Canmore, allowing you to check on construction and count golf courses.

Descent

In the last edition I touted a direct descent to the old ski hill that reduces the kilometrage by a whopping 4.4 km. While zeroing in on Banff Gate Resort is not a problem with a GPS, some people let me know they had a really horrible time in the bush. So until there is a trail (fat chance), return the same way.

OPTIONAL RETURN

47A Lower summit

Distance add 2.3 km
Height gain add 61 m (200 ft.)
High point 2332 m (7650 ft.)

Return to the col between the two summits. Go straight on a trail that ascends up right on ruddy-coloured screes, picking its way between little rockbands to the lower summit. Once topped by a wooden cross, it now sports a solar-powered telemetry station.

Walk down the grassy southeast ridge to the pass between Pigeon and McGillivray creeks, en route enjoying a front-row view of Mt. McGillivray and the line of unnamed peaks stretching to Mt. Lorette. Andrew calls the highest "Skogan Peak."

At the pass pick up trail #45 and follow it down to the right to the powerline access road, which is Skogan Pass trail. Turn right and follow it back to the trailhead. Alternatively, head a little right as you near the pass and join the powerline access road directly.

Returning down the trail below the lower summit. Photo Alf Skrastins

48 MOUNT ALLAN FROM THE NORTH—map 8

Near the start of the north ridge, looking up to the Black Band. The peaks of Mount Lougheed to right. Photo Bob Truman

Long-day hike
Official trail with cairns, red markers on trees and posts
Distance 11.1 km to summit
Height gain 1441 m (4729 ft.)
Height loss 24 m (80 ft.)
High point 2819 m (9249 ft.)
Maps 82 O/3 Canmore, 82 J/14 Spray Lakes Reservoir

Access Hwy. 1 (Trans-Canada Hwy). At Dead Man's Flats interchange 98 follow signs to Banff Gate Mountain Resort. Drive up George Biggy Sr. Road past Thunderstone Quarry to a T-junction at road's end. Turn right into Skogan Pass trailhead (biffy, kiosk, interpretive signs). The trail is the continuation of the dirt road.

The complete traverse of the Centennial trail over Mt. Allan from Dead Man Flat to Ribbon Creek (or vice versa) is one of the most wonderful ridgewalks in the Canadian Rockies, a very long day indeed, requiring two vehicles but with the bonus of cafes and pubs at both ends. Take plenty of water for the in-between bit.

Most people, though, go up one side and return the same way, which is why you'll have to turn to Volume 1 for info on the more popular southern half. (See "Mount Allan via Centennial Ridge.") The northern half is a tad more strenuous and calls for an early start if you wish to make the summit and back before dark. Start even earlier if making a loop with Collembola. The part that does your knees in—especially on the descent—is the coal exploration road to treeline. After that it's a thoroughly enjoyable ridgewalk with one scramble step and mild exposure at the Black Band traverse, which gets tricky when snow-covered early or late in the season.

A less strenuous option for flower buffs is Jubilee Tarns in the cirque between Allan and Collembola.

REGULATORY NOTE The route is closed Dec 1–Jun 21 for spring lambing.

TRAIL HISTORY NOTE The start has reverted to that of the second edition, following for the main part the original route up the coal exploration road from Dead Man Flat up the north ridge of Collembola.

When the Patrician Land Corporation owned land in Wind Valley, a spate of "No Trespassing" signs sprang up everywhere, forcing K Country planners to look for another route to the K Country boundary. The only option open to them went steeply up Skogan Pass trail, steeply down to Pigeon Creek, along the Pigeon Creek exploration road, then steeply up onto the ridge of Collembola. Understandably, that height loss in the middle proved mighty unpopular and the trail was little used. So hikers were extremely happy to get their original route back after a land swap. Not that people love walking the coal exploration road; it's more something to be endured en route to the good stuff above treeline where the Rocky Mountain Ramblers scratched out their fabulous trail in the late 1960s.

To Pigeon Creek 820 m
From the parking lot the dirt road takes you out to the powerline right-of-way. (Skogan Pass trail to left.) Cross and wind downhill to Pigeon Creek crossing (bridge). At the T-junction on the west bank turn left. (Road to right accesses the Wind Valley trails.) You have now joined the original route from Dead Man Flat.

To East Wind Pond turnoff 2.5 km
Straightaway is a sign at a fork. Keep left on the better road. The going is slightly uphill, paralleling Pigeon Creek. The grassed-over Pigeon Creek exploration road takes off from the right-hand bend at 235533.

This prominent bend marks the start of a 518 vertical m (1700 vertical ft.) climb up the north ridge of Collembola to road's end at treeline. It is mind-numbing with little to see except lodgepole pines and the odd cheery arnica spotlighted by a ray of sunlight. Best, then, to start an intense discussion with your friends to last an hour or two. There's some relief a third of the way up at the K Country boundary at 239524 (no sign). A number of things happen: just before two stumps, a side road to right is the route to East Wind Pond. Then a faint trail on the left side is route A of the 3rd edition. Just before a second set of three stumps, a more vegetated road to right joins #50. After all this, a hiking sign points to your route ahead.

Traversing the Black Band. Photo Rod Plasman

The scramble to regain the ridge beyond the Black Band. Photo Bob Truman

To Mt. Collembola turnoff 2.7 km

Continue labouring up the other two-thirds of road, which steepens even more after coal dust corner. At a levelling high up, the upper ridge of Collembola comes into view, an exhausting prospect should you be headed that way. A dip, then one final uphill and the road dwindles to trail. Spirits pick up. Shortly the trail turns right and it's here that the route up Collembola turns off at cairn 253503.

To Jubilee Tarns turnoff 1.3 km

The trail traverses the lip of the cirque between Collembola and Allan (cairns and posts). Anyone bound for Jubilee Tarns should turn left after crossing the cirque creek.

To the summit 3.8 km

Zig up a steep, grassy slope onto the north ridge of Allan. Turn left and without much trouble walk up to the foot of the Black Band. To get around this impasse, traverse a grassy ledge on the left (east)

Threading the red pinnacles. Note the post with red marker at bottom left. Photo Bob Truman

The summit from the false summit. Photo Bob Truman

side below the rockband, then scramble up the tail end of it to a cairn with post on the ridge crest.

The easy section following is terminated by a row of red pinnacles straddling the ridgeline and dipping down the western flank. Slip through a gap on the right (west) side and climb a rubble slope back to the ridge. En route, look for *Saxifraga cernua* growing in tiny pockets of soil among the boulders. Plod on to a false summit, where you discover the highest summit is still half a kilometre distant across a slight dip. Rather than follow the sheep trail around it to the right, climb the mountain's final upheaval of orange screes to a cairn, plaque and survey marker.

The summit panorama is severely limited by the great height of Mt. Lougheed to the west and Collembola to the east, both of which have been with you for some time. Nevertheless, another window has opened up to the south disclosing the lovely country about Ribbon Creek's north fork. In the afternoon sun, second Memorial Lake "the emerald" glitters tantalizingly like fizzy crème de menthe.

OPTION

48A Jubilee Tarns

Distance 1.4 km from trail

From the lip of the cirque a faint trail follows the right bank of the cirque creek through fields of dwarf willow and delphiniums (pale blue variants) into the hanging valley between Collembola and Allan. Higher yet, the inner cirque is a labyrinth of small, grassy hills and little ponds, the largest one graced with the name Queen's Tarn. As a destination, Jubilee Tarns are not worth the effort of the long walk in, but the valley itself is lovely, bounded by grassy slopes and seven-star flower gardens on the lower slopes of Collembola.

NOTE From Queen's Tarn you'll notice the north ridge of Mount Allan is easily accessible via a steep grass slope. Should the need arise, this offers an easy escape route off the ridge in a sudden storm. Similarly, a reasonable slope leads to the col between the two Collembolas. Besides acting as an escape route, it offers the non-scrambler a route to the highest summit.

#48A Looking down into the lower cirque from near Jubilee Tarns.

49 MOUNT COLLEMBOLA TRAVERSE—map 8

Climbing the northeast ridge of Mount Allan. Looking back at the two summits of Collembola, showing the mountain's tame side. Photo Bob Spirko

Long-day scramble
Unofficial route & occasional trail
Distance 5 km; trailhead to Mt. Allan, 11 km; circuit with #48, 22.1 km
Height gain to Collembola 1380 m (4530 ft.); to Mt. Allan 1685 m (5529 ft.)
Height loss 268 m (880 ft.)
High point Collembola 2758 m (9050 ft.); Mt. Allan 2819 m (9249 ft.)
Map 82 J/14 Spray Lakes Reservoir

Access Via #48 Mt. Allan from the north at the 6 km mark.

The traverse of the two summits of Mt. Collembola is a demanding ridgewalk, a much more serious undertaking than the traverse of Mt. Allan. Not because the ridge is a knife edge (far from it), but because route finding is occasionally tricky and there's one unavoidable step of exposed scrambling. I recommend traversing north to south. Travelling in the opposite direction means downclimbing the crux—not a good idea if you don't know where the route goes.

Combined with #48, this route is guaranteed to leave you dead on your feet and ready for a holiday at Club Med. Alternatively, without going to the summit of Allan you can hop off into Jubilee Tarns or head down Marmot Basin to Ribbon Creek (see Volume 1) for which you'll need two vehicles.

REGULATORY NOTE The area is closed between Dec 1 and Jun 21.

NAMING NOTE Pronounced Col-EM-bo-la, Collembola is named after snow fleas (order Collembola) mown down in their millions by cross-country skiers at Ribbon Creek. These amazing critters produce antifreeze proteins that keeps them springing around all winter.

NORTH TO SOUTH

To Mt. Collembola 2.5 km

Follow the coal exploration road to its end. Go a little farther up the Mt. Allan trail to where it turns right, then at a cairn transfer to a short-lived trail on the left that takes you to treeline. Ahead lies the hard work of the day, the consistently steep north ridge, bounded on the right by grassy slopes roll-

Looking up at the crux below the north summit. The route gains the prominent notch via the discernible trail, then takes to the steep east face.

ing tamely down to the cirque and on the left by the precipitous east face, furrowed and faulted, ringed with alternating bands of sandstone and shale—all the strata of the Kootenay Formation exposed in one go. High up, a couple of small rockbands are easily managed.

Finally the ridge levels and you look down on Skogan Pass, noticing below you on the east face a tiny tarn on a bench, the result of a slump. To your right, Mt. Allan and its north ridge are eclipsed by the four great peaks of Lougheed.

After a series of gentle rises, the summit of Collembola comes into view, guarded by a diagonal rockband. The nearer you get the more impossible it appears, but the alternative, dropping into the cirque then plodding all the way up the gully between the two summits, is too shameful to consider. There is nothing for it but to take a peek at the east face.

The crux

A trail heads up to the right on scree, then back left on soft shale below the band to a notch on the left-hand skyline. Set foot on the east face. Above is the crux: two tiers of cliffs separated by a wide, grassy ledge.

At the obvious place scramble up the lower tier to the first ledge. Accomplished scramblers can tackle the upper tier via the chimney to the right. Everyone else should walk left a bit, then scramble up to a narrow rock ledge. The move onto the ledge is the hard bit—kindly replace the handholds for others to use. Traverse left along the ledge into a recess. The handholds are firm, and at the narrowest point you can wrap your arms comfortingly behind a large flake. Scrabble up the back of the recess to a large, grassy ledge and walk out right to above the rockband.

Finish up grass and scree to Collembola's highest summit (cairn). Look down on Lower Collembola, which is likewise immune to a frontal approach.

East face crux from the notch. The route goes up the snow to the grassy ledge, left along it, then up and left along a narrower ledge. Photo Roy Millar

Crossing the col to Lower Collembola.

To Lower Collembola 700 m

Descend yellow shale to the col between the two summits. On your right is the easy escape gully into the cirque. Ahead, Lower Collembola is a bizarre sight caused by massive conglomerates from the Blairmore Group sitting atop the Kootenay. Since a frontal approach is out of the question, it requires careful route finding to gain the summit without circling the whole kit and caboodle to the southwest ridge.

So, starting from near the col, traverse the east face under the cliffs until you are lower than the col. At a break, climb a swath of scree (faint trail, cairns) to a broad, sloping bench. Wend left a bit, then at a cairn ascend an easy-angled scree gully, distinguished by an odd-shaped pinnacle on its left wall, to the upper bench. Turn right and traverse until you can break through the dwindling third tier of rock without resorting to scrambling. A cairn marks the exit. The summit is just to the right.

To Mount Allan 1.8 km

All difficulties at an end, stroll down the grassy southwest ridge to the Collembola/Allan col, a height loss of 183 vertical m (600 vertical ft.) From here the escape into Marmot Basin is as described in Volume 1.

Having to regain the height lost plus another 100 m to Allan's summit is more than one would wish for at this stage, especially when the northeast ridge appears steep. Luckily, the going is without difficulty and it's just a matter of putting one foot in front of the other until you reach the cairn for a well-earned collapse.

Climbing Lower Collembola. The scree gully with odd-shaped pinnacle between benches.

50 EAST WIND POND (Connolly Lake)—map 8

Long-day hike, backpack
Unofficial trail & route, creek crossings, flagging to valley head
Distance 6.7 km; 10 km from trailhead
Height gain 832 m (2730 ft.)
Height loss 54 m (180 ft.)
High point 2209 m (7250 ft.) at col
Maps 82 O/3 Canmore, 82 J/14 Spray Lakes Reservoir

Access Via #48 Mt. Allan from the north.

Wind Pond, tucked close under Mt. Lougheed in a hanging valley, is accessed from Wind Creek Valley by old exploration roads and a trail sketched out by the Boy Scouts. Since the last edition the trail has been improved and partially flagged and sees ongoing clearing by X. Unfortunately the flagging and the clearing haven't reached the last bit to the col above the lake. So if route finding and bushwhacking are not your thing, don't bother going.

You need an early start. To goad you on, there are grassy ridges to explore and larches. The alternative to a rush hike is to camp en route, if you can hack carrying camping gear up the Mt. Allan trail.

Other options from the head of the valley is the Allan/Lougheed col and the amazing west face of Mt. Allan featuring 2000 ft. of grass. Consider using the latter as a descent route off Allan to make a loop. Plentiful sparkling water in the creek is a come-on.

HISTORY NOTE Also known as Pothole Lake and Connolly Lake, this tarn was first noted by M.B.B. Crockford and Gordon Scruggs in 1946/7 while investigating the geology of the Ribbon Creek area. Hidden by a fold of the hills from the eye of the ridgewalker on Mt. Allan, the lake remained undetected by the vast majority of hikers (though not by climbers doing the Lougheed traverse) until 1972 when Harry Connolly's much-publicized attempts to reach the lake by snowmobile and on foot were splashed across the pages of the *Calgary Herald*.

East Wind Pond from the col.

Liberal use of the words "impossible" and "impenetrable" was alarming and seemed to put it in the same category as Stanley's forays into darkest Africa, much to Harry's embarrassment. They were not *his* words and he hated the article.

Exploration roads 2.8 km
Follow #48 to the two stumps just before the K Country boundary at 239524. Turn right onto another road (track).

Keep straight a little way in and walk gently downhill into Wind Creek Valley. The road continues along the left (east) bank, the going easy apart from two soggy-mossy wet bits to splosh through. The first occurs just after a junction where the road loops. Keep left here up the mossy hill. (Road to right crosses the creek.)

Cross a cutline, then descend to Wind Creek. Wade or try using the log. The road then follows the right (west) bank to a T-junction with a cutline at 242502. Across the creek is a well-used camping spot.

Turn right with the road and make two uphill zigs. At the second bend, flagging at 240501 denotes the start of the ongoing trail through old forest.

The forest trail.

Trail 2.9 km
So you turn left and follow the flagged trail as it undulates across side hill, the going easy aside from two pesky gullies that must be crossed, the second dip much steeper than one would wish for. After a skimpy traverse of grassy banks, it is back into forest, the trail approaching the creek at many points. After a flat, the trail curves left and ends in a meadow strip by the creek. Unfortunately, this is also the end of the flagging. Ahead are views of Mt. Allan and the impressive northeast face of Mt. Lougheed, which has a tragic connection to Memorial Lakes. For it was here where one of the search planes went down during the 1986 search for Orval Pall and Ken Wolff.

Follow the meadow strip, then a stony strip down by the creek, eventually taking once more to the forest where fainter trails lead to the forest edge.

To the col 800 m
Coming up are over-the-head willow bush and deadfall. Keep close in to the steep right-hand slope and thrutch your way through beaten-down bush. About halfway up, you reach scree where the going gets much easier. Climb the left bank of the shallow gully, wending left on easier ground, then cutting back right to the col at 227476, a mix of scree and flowery meadow.

To the pond 150 m
The pond lies in a hanging valley beyond the col. Take any route down meadows dotted with spruce, fir and larch to the lakeshore. The lake is actually a composite of several deep springs joined one to another like florets, which is not obvious when the lake is full. The upper layer of water seems quite tepid and teems with tiny red freshwater shrimp.

SHORTCUT TO POND ANYONE? 1 km
At ~236485 on the forest trail, turn right up the fall line at the side creek. Where the ground steepens, move away left and climb into the hanging valley with larches. Saves 2 km return.

51 WIND VALLEY TRAILS—map 8

Half-day, day hikes
Official, unofficial trails
Map 82 O/3 Canmore

Access Hwy. 1 (Trans-Canada Hwy.). At Dead Man's Flats interchange 98 follow signs to Banff Gate Mountain Resort. Drive up George Biggy Sr. Road past Thunderstone Quarry to a T-junction at road's end. Turn right into Skogan Pass trailhead (biffy, kiosk, interpretive signs).

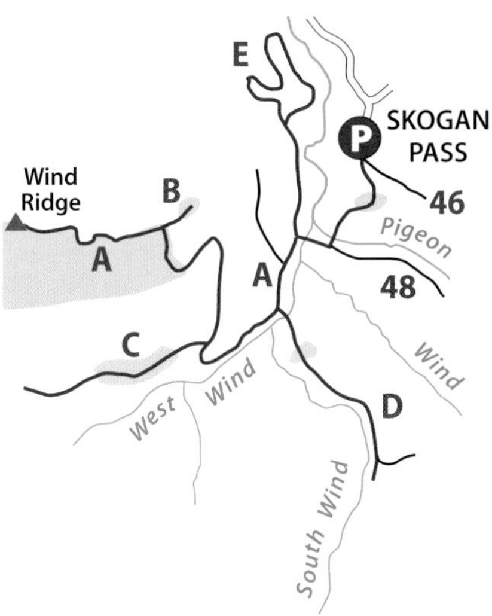

Trails radiating out from Skogan Pass trailhead

From Skogan Pass trailhead in Wind Valley, trails radiate out in all directions, the most popular of which by far is Wind Ridge. Trail ##46, 47, 48, 49 and 50 are described separately.

HISTORY Back in 1924, at the very start of the Spray Hydroelectric Project, Calgary Power seriously considered building a tunnel under what is now West Wind Pass and running a conduit the length of the valley to Dead Man Flat. That fell through when the Whitemans Gap option was decided upon. Then in the years leading up to the 1988 Winter Olympics, a road was proposed along the valley and through a tunnel to access ski areas in the Spray River Valley. That also fell though when Mt. Allan was chosen instead.

Wind Ridge and Wind Valley were not exactly pristine during those times and still aren't, the whole area criss-crossed with coal exploration roads, now reverted to tracks. No mines were developed though the valley is "full of coal." Apparently, Canmore Mines could not justify the expense at a time when the markets were shutting down.

POLITICAL NOTE K Country controls the south end of the valley and the Town of Canmore the north end. But when the mines closed in 1980, it was owned by the Dillingham Corporation, who bought out Canmore Mines and were the first to recognize the potential of tourism. They sold to KGN Developments, who a year later sold to Patrician Land Corporation under Peter Pocklington, then owner of the Edmonton Oilers. He planned a 300 hectare subdivision in the valley called Echo Valley that included a grand hotel with a view of Windtower from every room. Those plans came to naught when the parent company folded and the land was sold to Three Sisters Resorts. After NRCB recommendations that nothing be built in the valley, a land swap was arranged. And in 1995 the valley was designated a Natural Area under the Special Places 2000 initiative, which meant hunting and trapping would likely be allowed "for the management and preservation of the animal and plant life." Today its status has changed once again with its incorporation into Bow Valley Wildland Provincial Park with wildlife corridor, which means no new trails can be built in the area. Hunting is still allowed, so take precautions in the fall months.

Wind Ridge from #51D, showing the route to the summit and the route to Windy Point.

51A Wind Ridge

Official trail to saddle & Windy Point, unofficial to summit
Distance 6.5 km
Height gain 792 m (2600 ft.)
Height loss 24 m (80 ft.)
High point 2170 m (7120 ft.)

From the Trans-Canada, the dark, timbered mass of Wind Ridge doesn't look too interesting. On the other side of the mountain, though, hidden from view, grassy slopes wearing crags like necklaces provide a beautiful route to the summit with one pitch of easy scrambling. B groups and non-scramblers have the option of going to Windy Point.

REGULATORY NOTE The trail to the summit is now open all year. But if you want to drop into Wind Valley from the ridge, it will have to be after June 15.

NAMING NOTE The Stoney Nakoda call it *Ganutha împa*, which means Windy Point.

ENTERTAINMENT NOTE Frank Mills has been here, tootling away on a grand piano. And Pink Floyd filmed their video *Learning to Fly* on its summit.

To Centennial Ridge junction 820 m
From the parking lot the dirt road takes you out to the powerline right-of-way. (Skogan Pass trail to left.) Cross and wind downhill to Pigeon Creek crossing (bridge). At the T-junction on the west bank at 225538 turn right. (To left is #48, the Centennial Ridge trail up Mt. Allan.)

To Spray Falls turnoff 150 m
Shortly, cross Wind Creek on a bridge to gain the main West Wind Valley exploration road at T-junction 224539. Turn left. (Road to right is #51E Spray Falls loop, the road eventually leading to Quebexican and the Trans-Canada Hwy. at Dead Man's Flats.)

To South Wind Hoodoos turnoff 1.2 km
The road stays on the northwest bank of what soon becomes West Wind Creek, winding and undulating slightly through a spruce forest gloomily dark on a cloudy day. In 500 m, after the first uphill, keep straight at junction 223535. (Side road to right leads to the mine haulage road on the other side of Wind Ridge and ultimately to Three Sisters Mountain Village.)

During the next 700 m, the main thoroughfare up the valley is always obvious despite a number of offshoots to right and left. Immediately after an up–down, come to what is actually a 4-way at 221529. Keep straight. (Road to left crossing West Wind Creek on a bridge is #51D to South Wind hoodoos.)

To West Wind Valley turnoff 870 m
Continue in much the same way as before, ignoring all side trails to the left. Suddenly the road turns sharp right. A little way along, a red marker on the left side at 214525 indicates the trail #51C, West Wind Valley.

To saddle 2 km
Stay on the exploration road that in the next kilometre climbs many vertical metres to a 3-way (was 4-way) junction at the top of the hill—just the place for a memorial bench, but you won't find one. It's been a relentless uphill plod through Douglas fir forest.

At a cairn turn left, then climb a little more and with much anticipation traverse out of the trees onto the lush meadows of Wind Ridge's southeast face. Ahead is a breathtaking view of Windtower, best seen in late afternoon light when the sun picks

Right: The crux. Climbing onto the ledge.

Below: Looking towards the final climb onto the summit ridge. Photo Alf Skrastins

Optional descent. Walking along the southwest ridge, the summit in the background. Photo Alf Skrastins

out every rib and gully. It's hard to believe this dramatic summit is an easy walk up the back side via #81.

The track, narrowing to trail, curves right and uphill to gain a saddle on the east ridge—vantage point for Wind Ridge up ahead, Rimwall, West Wind Pass, and behind Windtower, the original Wind Mountain, now peak no. 1 of Mt. Lougheed. Historians would have us believe that while James Hector was busy discovering Kicking Horse Pass for the railway, Eugène Bourgeau climbed Wind Mountain while botanizing. More likely he was running from one new flower to another on the lower grassy slopes of Wind Ridge, having a marvellous time. In damper facets, blue-eyed grass grows in abundance like a blue haze.

At the saddle veer left with the trail. (Go right for OPTION #51B Windy Point.)

To the summit 1.5 km

Rather than follow the crest of the ridge at the demarcation of north slope trees, the main trail stays on the grassy south slope, passing the occasional picturesque Douglas fir leaning into the slope.

A steeper, winding climb between outcrops leads to the foot of a horizontal sandstone rockband, one of many that give the ridge its attractive, castellated appearance. This is the crux scramble. Starting is hard if you can't put your left foot where your left ear is. Get someone to give you a shove, because the rest is easy: the obvious ledge that traverses from left to right back onto grass.

Gain the top of the first step. The ridge is flat for a way, then rises to the summit ridge, the trail winding around outcrops with a selection of alpines my friend would like to take home.

All climbing at an end, walk the summit ridge to the far end cairn and geodetic survey marker. A new view has opened up to the north of Stewart Creek, The Orphan and The Three Sisters.

Most people return the same way.

OPTIONAL DESCENT

To West Wind Valley 2.4 km

A pleasant ridgewalk followed by steep slopes with not much in the way of trails. Doable only after June 15.

Continue southwest along the summit ridge, either scrambling down the rockband below the summit or bypassing it on the right side. Follow the ridge or a game trail below it over a lower top to the col between Wind Ridge and Rimwall where north side trees spill over onto the south slope.

Turn left and descend the steep grass slope to a gully bed about halfway down. Transfer to the grassy ridge to your left (now sans rockbands), aiming to bottom out halfway between the gully and another one to your left.

With luck (sorry, no waypoint) you should find a blazed tree at the tree edge and trail #51C. If you can't find it, aim for the exploration road at 214525.

OPTION

51B to Windy Point

Distance 340 m from the saddle

An alternative objective for the B party.

From the saddle, head right on grass. Where the slope to right steepens, a trail develops at the tree edge and takes you all the way to a survey marker at the east end of the ridge. Known as Windy Point (one of many), it's a great viewpoint for the Bow Valley and Skogan Pass area.

Immediately below you in a forested gully is the birthplace of Marsh Creek. It's a year-round spring that in sub-zero temperatures sends clouds of steam rising above the treetops.

51C West Wind Valley

Half-day hike
Unofficial trail
Distance ~1.9 km from #51A
Height gain 90 m (295 ft.) from #51A
High point 1554 m (5100 ft.)

Access Via #51A at T-junction 214525.

Explore a beautiful valley that is the optional return route from Wind Ridge.

REGULATORY NOTE Beyond the Wind Ridge turnoff the valley is closed Dec 1–Jun 15.

BEAR WARNING Grizzlies are attracted to the fens occupying the other half of the valley, so stick to the trail and carry bear spray.

From the exploration road at 214525, turn left on a trail that leads to the big meadow once lusted over by developers for its million dollar view of Windtower and Wind Ridge. Continue on trail through the meadow and a few trees to a cutline. Follow the cutline to the right, the trail then leading through two glades to open slopes at the foot of Wind Ridge where it peters out at a blazed tree.

Look across to West Wind Pass, which in the preliminary plans for K Country was earmarked for a grade 7 bike path. Seeing what mountain bikers are capable of 35 years on, a DHS trail weaving between rockbands doesn't seem quite so far-fetched!

#51C West Wind Valley, looking towards Mount Lougheed, Windtower and Rimwall. Photo Geoff Williams

51D South Wind hoodoos

Half-day hike
Unofficial trails
Distance 1.7 km; 3.9 km from trailhead
Height gain 237 m (780 ft.)
High point ~1615 m (~5300 ft.)

Access Via #51A at junction 221529.

A moderately strenuous climb on exploration road (track) to capped hoodoos in South Wind Creek.

I first saw a photo of these hoodoos in a 1949 geology bulletin and if it wasn't for Gordon Scruggs I'd still be ignorant of their existence. Actually, if you know where to look, you can pick out the biggest one, called The Obelisk, from Wind Ridge. It certainly puts the "Monolith" in Bremner's Gravel Pit to shame.

REGULATORY NOTE The area appears to be open all year round.

At the junction 1.2 km from the bridge, Turn left onto a grassy exploration road (track), which you're going to be following throughout. It's the one with tread.

Straightaway it crosses West Wind Creek on a bridge. Keep straight and cross a NE–SW cutline. A little farther on, in a large clearing, be sure to look behind you for a fabulous view of Wind Ridge. Farther on, keep right. Proximity to South Wind Creek and a hunter's camp signals the start of a stiff climb up the left bank. In no time at all, the river is far below in a deep V-shaped valley. Cross another NE–SW cutline. Just after the following left-hand bend, a cairn indicates a sketchy hunter's trail into South Wind Creek. In case you're wondering, it doesn't provide a good viewpoint for the hoodoos, but it could be used for other purposes.

The road, still climbing steeply, curves back right. Keep straight, and when the incline moderates, peer over the bank at rows of capped hoodoos aligned like sentries up and down the slope to the creek. Continue climbing up the road to a Y-junction. Go right, on a dead-end track. In just a short distance from the Y-junction descend the mossy slope to a drop-off and hold on to trees. Below you is a second set of hoodoos. If you've hit it right, you'll be stunned by the view of The Obelisk.

The Obelisk.

51E Spray Falls loop

Half-day hike
Unofficial trails
Distance 3.2 km loop from bridge;
5.2 km from trailhead
Height loss/gain 60 m (200 ft.)

Access Via #51A at bridge over Wind Creek.

For anyone looking for the best half-day hike from the trailhead, this is the one. View waterfalls in Pigeon Creek, and the tallest Douglas firs in the valley. While the falls are okay in August, DO GO during spring runoff, when they are spectacular. In 1977 the Canmore Corridor Study identified the falls as a suitable site for interpretive displays, but nothing ever came of it.

REGULATORY NOTE Open all year.

HISTORY NOTE The road you drove up is named for George Biggy Sr., who started Thunderstone Quarries in 1960 and ran it as a family business for 40 years. Nowadays it's owned and operated by Resman Holdings.

To campsites 800 m
At T-junction 224539 just after the bridge, keep right. The exploration road and former route to Mt. Allan from the highway (note the red markers) descends slightly through old forest with moss and mare's tails, then climbs to a powerline right-of-way. Cross, descending slightly to a junction just as you re-enter trees.

Turn right and descend an old road to a 4-way. Go straight on a grassy old road that curves down to the right. At a 4-way veer left (flagging) into a big glade where people have camped. Turn left, passing a recumbent totem and a homemade dreamcatcher hanging from a branch. A little farther on is a teepee made of branches. The trail down Pigeon Creek starts here at flagging.

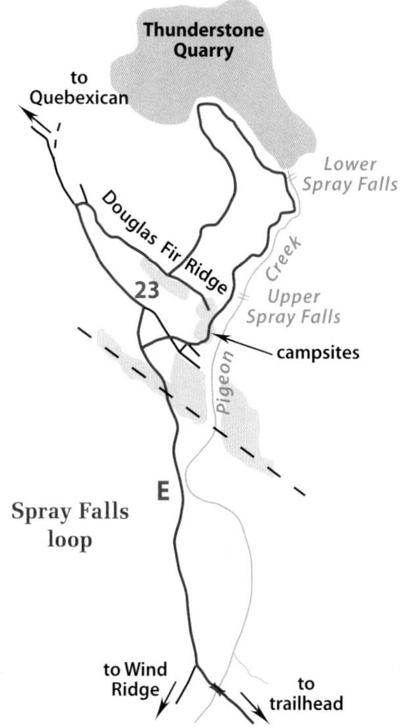

To Lower Spray Falls 600 m
The trail runs along the banktop above picturesque Upper Spray Falls, not long after descending to creekside for a stint past minor falls and chutes. Nearing the brink of the big drop-off, you climb onto a forested bench in great expectations. But if you haven't been following the expansion of Thunderstone Quarry, it comes as a huge shock to find Lower Spray Falls thundering onto the quarry floor, the quarry edge smack dab flush against it. Getting a good full-length view nowadays requires teetering around on the cliff edge (in lieu of a glass-floor observation platform jutting out 30 m).

Douglas Fir ridge 850 m
The trail continues near the edge of the cliffs, then loops back left (flagging), just to the left of a new quarry road.

Roll along through the forest, then climb a steep hill. Veering right, the trail eases off and on reaching a knoll turns left, dropping into a hollow and climbing up out of it onto a small ridge that is open on the far side. Grass and sweet-smelling sage, Douglas firs and an unexpected view of mounts Allan, Lougheed and Windtower make this a natural place for a sit-down.

The faint trail to left descends to camping sites near the teepee from where you can make your way back to the trailhead.

I prefer to go right, the trail undulating along the ridge below tall Douglas firs. Watch for the steep drop-off to left down to the exploration road you started out on at 222658. (The trail ahead gets mired in deadfall.)

Closing the loop 1 km
Turn left. A flat stretch leads to a T-junction at marker 23. Turn right uphill and meet your outgoing route at the Y-junction just before the powerline right-of-way.

#51E Upper Spray Falls.

#51E Lower Spray Falls.

#52 Quebexican between Cairnes Creek and Smith Creek.

52 QUEBEXICAN—map 8

Half-day hike
Unofficial trail
Distance 5.5 km
Height gain 120 m (395 ft.)
Height loss 100 m (328 ft.)
High point 1370 m (4495 ft.)
Map 82 O/3 Canmore

East access Dead Man's Flats, Hwy 1 (Trans-Canada Hwy.). At Dead Man's Flats interchange 98 follow signs to Banff Gate Mountain Resort and Mt. Lougheed viewpoint. On reaching George Biggy Sr. Road, park off road at the intersection with Bow Link trail at 223554.
West access Canmore. Follow Three Sisters Parkway out of town to Three Sisters Mountain Village. At the 4-way intersection with Three Sisters Blvd., go straight on Three Sisters Parkway to a traffic circle. Peel off second right onto Stewart Creek Landing. Drive to where the road turns right and park. Your route is the wide gravel road ahead (old mine haulage road) that is spanned by a chain between concrete blocks.

A trail made and named by mountain bikers connects the Bow Link section of the Trans Canada Trail at Dead Man Flat to Three Sisters Mountain Village from where you can continue on to Canmore via #57 Three Sisters Pathway. It also connects with #53 Stewart Creek to Middle Sister.

It is more interesting than you might suppose as it undulates along the forest strip between the E–W powerline right-of-way and the mine haulage road and Marsh's Mine below Wind Ridge, which was operating well before the railway arrived in 1883.

EAST TO WEST

On a track, head west toward Pigeon Creek crossing, which is avoided by detouring right to cross the culvert near the interchange. On regaining the track, turn right. In a few metres the route splits: hikers should follow route no. 2.

1. Hilly. Go left on a trail that crosses the E–W powerline right-of-way and climbs into dark forest below Thunderstone Quarry. Losing most of the height gain, descend—en route crossing a track—to a second track, which is the original route up Mt. Allan. To your left is a gate with the notice "Private. Three Sisters Resorts." This where route 2 joins in from the right. Cross the track.

2. Flat and easy. Keep right on the track that heads close to the Trans-Canada Hwy., then descend a little to a junction. Keep straight. Just past a gate in the highway fence, your track (now the original start to Mt. Allan) turns left and crosses the E–W right-of-way into the forest. Intersect the trail a little way in. Turn right.

The trail climbs out of range of traffic noise (though you can still hear helicopters thwapping overhead) and crosses a bushy NW–SE power line right-of-way. Back in forest, cross three grassy tracks (old mining roads), Cairnes Creek and Marsh Creek combined in a culvert under the third road, and assorted springs with water. A nice bit of side hill leads to a sunnier forest with bushes. This ends in a long downhill through moss into black bog covered with mare's tails where the trail may be muddy. Cross the usually dry Smith Creek.

In dry forest once again, walk a straight to a man-made ditch, which is crossed lower down on rocks. Turn left and follow the right bank uphill a way. A right turn signals waves of downhills into the bottom of a man-made meadow. From here it's a long, gradual and very pleasant climb to trail's end. Emerge on a gravel road.

Turn left. Thread between boulders onto the old mine haulage road and turn right. A chain across the road signals the end of the haulage road and the start of Stewart Creek Landing.

53 MIDDLE SISTER—map 8

Middle Sister from The Orphan, showing the route.

Long-day scramble, bike 'n' scramble
Unofficial trails, creek crossings, cairns
Distance 8.6 km
Height gain 1414 m (4640 ft.)
High point 2749 m (9020 ft.)
Map 82 O/3 Canmore

Access

1. From Hwy. 1 (Trans-Canada Hwy.). At interchange 93, turn off onto Three Sisters Parkway. At the 4-way intersection turn left onto Three Sisters Parkway (also the road to Stewart Creek golf course) and drive to a traffic circle. Peel off second right onto Stewart Creek Landing. Drive to where the road turns right and park. Your route is the wide gravel road ahead (old mine haulage road) that is spanned by a chain between concrete blocks.

2. From Canmore. Follow Three Sisters Parkway out of town to Three Sisters Mountain Village. At the 4-way intersection with Three Sisters Blvd, go straight on Three Sisters Parkway to a traffic circle. Peel off second right onto Stewart Creek Landing. Drive to where the road turns right and park. Your route is the wide gravel road ahead (old mine haulage road) that is spanned by a chain between concrete blocks. See the sketch map on page 232.

Also accessible via #52 Quebexican.

Middle Sister (also called Second Sister), is the only peak of the Three Sisters accessible to walkers. Seasoned scramblers consider it "boring," meaning easy. Nevertheless, be up at the crack of dawn for this one, which is a very long but surprisingly easy trudge on scree. Neglected no more, thanks to Alan Kane, Middle Sister now sees about a dozen parties on a sunny weekend, so quite a trail has developed, and where there's no trail, there are cairns.

Carry *lots* of water. The water in Stewart Creek dries up around the forks.

ACCESS NOTE Since the third edition the access has changed. Biking is recommended to the end of the roads.

NAMING NOTE Geologist George Dawson is given the credit for naming the Three Sisters in 1886. But really they were named three years before by Albert Rogers, nephew of Major A.B. Rogers of Rogers Pass fame. A snowfall in the night had left a heavy veil of white on the north side "and I said to the boys, Look at the three nuns." He was quite resigned to the name change to "Sisters," saying it was "more Protestant-like, I suppose." Three Nuns, Three Sisters. Whatever, they are definitely *not* known as Faith (Big Sister), Charity (Middle Sister) and Hope (Little Sister) as Wikipedia suggests.

Supposedly the access creek was named after George Stewart, the Dominion land surveyor who became superintendent of Rocky Mountain Park in 1887, although at the time there were more than enough Stewarts in the Canadian Anthracite Coal Company at Canmore to choose from, including directors McLeod, Archibald and John. Walter Riva declares it was named after McLeod. Interestingly, it was Archibald who got everyone drinking water from Canmore Creek in preference to the Bow River, which was contaminated with water pumped out of the mines.

BOOK NOTE Apart from their regular appearance in calendars and picture books, the Sisters can be seen on the covers of a three-part Harlequin Super Romance novel by C.J. Carmichael published in 2002 about the lives of three sisters.

PROTEST NOTE In May 1992 the gravel intake downstream of the flow control structure was the site of an environmentalist camp. They were protesting the diversion of Stewart Creek, which instead of following its natural course into the depths of a mine, was soon to squirt out of sprinklers onto golfing greens.

Road section 2.3 km

Follow the mine haulage road. At a T-junction with boulders go straight, past a water tower. (Road to left is #52.) At the next T-junction veer leftish. (Road to right is signed "Extremely Dangerous Conditions.") Follow the haul road down a hill and up a hill, winding below Stewart Creek golf course to a T-junction. Turn right onto a road with a chain slung across it. A sign reads "Trail to Middle Sister."

It's all uphill to road's end, the road crossed by a number of traversing old roads. The first is actually the former trolley bed, and should you go right here along what is now a service road, you'd end up at tee 16 and a biffy—sorry, restroom—that looks like a regular K Country outhouse until you open the door and go "Wow."

The road ends in a mess of gravel next to Stewart Creek at a flow control structure, waypoint 191652.

Stewart Creek to the forks 1.9 km

Lots of people go wrong here. DO NOT continue along the steep left bank of the creek on an unpleasant dirt trail. It leads only to a small fall in the narrows. DO cross the flow control structure on two planks and climb up a good trail to join the exploration road on the right bank.

Turn left and follow the road through the narrows. The road reverts to trail at a broken concrete dam. A little farther on, follow cairns up the right-hand channel. Shortly after, cross the creek to a really good trail on the left bank that is almost road. Into view ahead comes a spiky peak The Orphan, easily climbed by #79A from the Spray Lakes side.

The Orphan from the easy part of Stewart Creek.

Resting at the top of the gully, which some consider the crux.

At a fork, go either way. Left stays high. Right descends for a stony stint along the creekbed before heading left up the bank to join the higher route. Continue to a third crossing marked with small cairns on both sides.

Now on the right bank, the trail climbs more steeply to the forks at 183536. By this time most of the water is travelling via the underground.

Upper Stewart Creek 2.4 km

The trail continues climbing up the stony right fork. (The left fork, which becomes very bouldery, leads to Boulder Pass.)

A flat, easy stretch precedes the avalanche area. Between here and the upper forks, sections of trail on the left bank alternate with stony flogs up the creekbed. You'll be spellbound by the sight of First Sister girdled in cliffs. To its left, Middle Sister looks equally impregnable and it's sobering to think that before you can even set foot on the mountain you've got to get that long line of cliffs behind you.

Keep right at the upper forks. The going gets rougher, the creekbed reduced to a gully gouged between scree slopes, the bed full of boulders rolled into it. Again use bypass trails and small rock steps. Ultimately the gully bends left and unfolds at a large cairn at the edge of a scree basin.

Middle Sister summit 2 km

Finally you get to set foot on the mountain. Turn right and head up the large scree fan to the left of the great cliffs, a number of vague trails coalescing into one corkscrewing trail, which above the level of the cliffs turns right, onto easy-angled scree slopes—the contour lines on the topo map all a bit wrong at this point. Little ups alternate with long traverses until you hit the draw in the orange rock zone where the slope takes a steeper turn. From the top, walk to the second-lowest col between Big Sister and your objective.

The final slope is a giant helipad slightly tilted to the northwest. The trail hugs the edge of the precipice to the right, where you get your thrills looking across a bizarre array of pinnacles to Little Sister.

At the summit cairn a large chunk of the Bow Valley is revealed, including Canmore and all of Mt. Lawrence Grassi, thus enabling you to sort out the route to Three Sisters Pass from Three Sisters Creek. In the other direction look across to The Orphan and Rimwall. Unfortunately, I'd have to rate the view a 9 because Big Sister hides the mountain that should be in every view, Mt. Assiniboine. The other thing Big Sister hides is approach-

After the scree climb comes the easy scree traverse to the summit at centre. Photo Cole Warawa

ing thunderstorms from the west. At such times it helps to have Steve Rothfels up there with you to advise about weather.

The bad thing about Middle Sister are the sightseeing helicopters that continually whir over the passes to your left and right. The person who had to put up with none of these nuisances, but then he didn't have a trail either, was Mont. B. Morrow, operating officer of the Canmore Mines 1914–26, who on August 12, 1921, was the first person on record to climb Middle Sister. That's him in the metal box.

First Sister from the summit.

Summit cairn, looking back to Third Sister. Photo John Miller

54 THREE SISTERS CREEK—map 9

Half-day, day hike
Official trail with blue posts, then unofficial trail with creek crossings
Distance 1.8 km to fall
Height gain to forks 345 m (1133 ft.)
High point at forks 1615 m (5300 ft.)
Map 82 O/3 Canmore

Access Hwy. 1 (Trans-Canada Hwy.). Heading west, turn off at interchange 93 onto Three Sisters Parkway. At the 4-way intersection go straight up Three Sisters Blvd. The route starts from the end of the road. There is no parking area, so you must turn right onto Hubman Landing and park on the left side.
Also accessible via #55 Highline trail and from #56 Grassi Knob.

Three Sisters Creek is a forested valley between the Three Sisters and Grassi Knob. A new trail and old logging roads offer a fairly easy walk to a small waterfall. Determined hikers can carry on to the forks and beyond. Regardless, it won't be a quiet trip in summer. It lies smack under the helicopter flight path to Assiniboine.

ACCESS NOTE Since the last edition, the first section of route has changed out of all recognition and is now shared with the east end of Highline trail. See the sketch map on page 223.

HISTORY NOTE The valley has been mucked up by humans ever since the loggers first got in about a century ago. Relics of that era and more recent changes brought about by Canmore Mines can be seen at various locations to well past the forks. I've literally stumbled over a cable near the junction with the tributary at 153547.

Highline section 1.1 km

At the head of Three Sisters Blvd, a trail to the right of the gate leads onto a gravelled construction road. In a few metres turn left at a T-junction and walk around another gate. Here the road turns left down a hill, but you keep straight by the side of the wooden fence. There is no marker.

Waterfall at the fault.

The trail follows a treed strip between Stewart Creek golf course on the left and the abandoned Three Sisters Creek golf course on the right, then swings right toward Three Sisters Creek, en route crossing a N–S track. At blue posts, the trail turns sharp left (south) and climbs gradually up valley. Cross an E–W track. At the following intersection with another E–W track go straight on a trail. (Track to right with blue marker is Highline, which crosses Three Sisters Creek on a bridge.)

To the waterfall 700 m

The trail runs alongside long sections of historic water flumes, then crosses Three Sisters Creek via a bridge amid flumes to join the Three Sisters Creek logging road on the right bank. Turn left.

Recross the creek below the breached wall of a reservoir with waterfall to the left bank. Keep straight at Y-junction 165564 (Track to right, identified by a firepit, crosses the creek and zigs up the hillside to the old bench road used by #56A. Currently, the track's a little bushy in places, but the tread is still good.)

Farther along, the wandering creek has ravaged the track. Just make your way up the left side as per the flagging and shortly come to the impasse: a small waterfall marking a major fault where the road collapsed into the creekbed decades ago. Most people stop here.

To the lower forks 1.1 km

With no ladder available, alternatives are a crumbly ledge on the left or the slab on the right, which has a reputation for bloodying the thighs of people who go for a bit of a slide while wearing shorts. You can also use the mossy detour, unattractive though it is, a steep up–down trail above the left-hand cliff.

Above the fall the remnant track continues, shortly crossing to the right bank. Keep left twice and pass two mossy springs and pieces of metal like drums and buckets lying about. Where the track crosses to the left bank (and soon ends), keep straight on a trail.

The trail then crosses and recrosses the creekbed (usually no water at this point) and passes below a cliff to the lower forks at 157554. This occurs where a deeply incised tributary comes in from the right between the Ship's Prow and a similar cliff to its left that is just as dramatic. A few metres upstream on the left bank of the main fork you'll find the ruins of two logger's cabins and the usual mishmash of rusted artifacts.

The old water flumes.

Ruin of cabin at the lower forks.

EXPLORING FARTHER

From a little father up the main creek, a logging road heads up the ridge to the right and splits. The left fork follows the ridge (good views), the right one traverses 'twixt ridge and the incised tributary. Possibly it hooks up with the traversing trail on Grassi Knob's southeast rib.

Beyond this point the main creekbed is easily followed to a brief resurrection of the road and more historical junk. At the upper forks at ~153543, you keep left. A game trail on the west bank develops and circumvents a rock step in the creekbed. When we left it, it was still heading uphill going where?

55 HIGHLINE TRAIL—map 9

One of the few viewpoints on west Highline, looking across the Bow Valley to Grotto Mtn.

Day, half-day hikes
Official trail with blue markers, maps at main junctions
Distance end to end 9.9 km;
loop with West Connector 5.4 km;
loop with East Connector 8.9 km
Height gain/loss ~300 m (~984 ft.)
High point 1580 m (5183 ft.)
Map 82 O/3 Canmore

Access Canmore.
West end access Spray Lakes Road at Quarry Lake parking lot. See also West Connector.
East connector Peaks of Grassi subdivision, at the east end of Wilson Way. Alternatively, park on the east side of Peaks Drive at the intersecting powerline right-of-way. Walk along the powerline access road to a gravel road, turn right and reach the east end of Wilson Way at a gate.
East end access Three Sisters Mountain Village. From Three Sisters Parkway, at the 4-way junction near Hwy. 1, turn right, up Three Sisters Blvd. The route starts from the top of the road. There is no parking area at present, so you must turn right onto Hubman Landing and park on the left side.

Also accessible via #60 Riders of Rohan.

This multi-use trail built by volunteers and used primarily by mountain bikers runs between Quarry Lake and Three Sisters Mountain Village on the forested skirts of Ehgay Nakoda (Ha-Ling Peak and Mt. Lawrence Grassi). Hikers going straight through generally need vehicles at both ends. Right now there is no good way to walk back to Quarry Lake. The only option is to start from Mineside parking lot at Bow River bridge, hike #58 to Quarry Lake, do the Highline, then return via #57 Three Sisters Pathway—which is a lot of kilometrage. Most hikers use the connector trails, which enable you to loop back to your starting point at Quarry Lake quite easily.

For people on foot, it's not a very interesting trail (too much forest, too few viewpoints), but if you want to get fit it's without parallel!

Gives hikers access to #56 Grassi Knob.

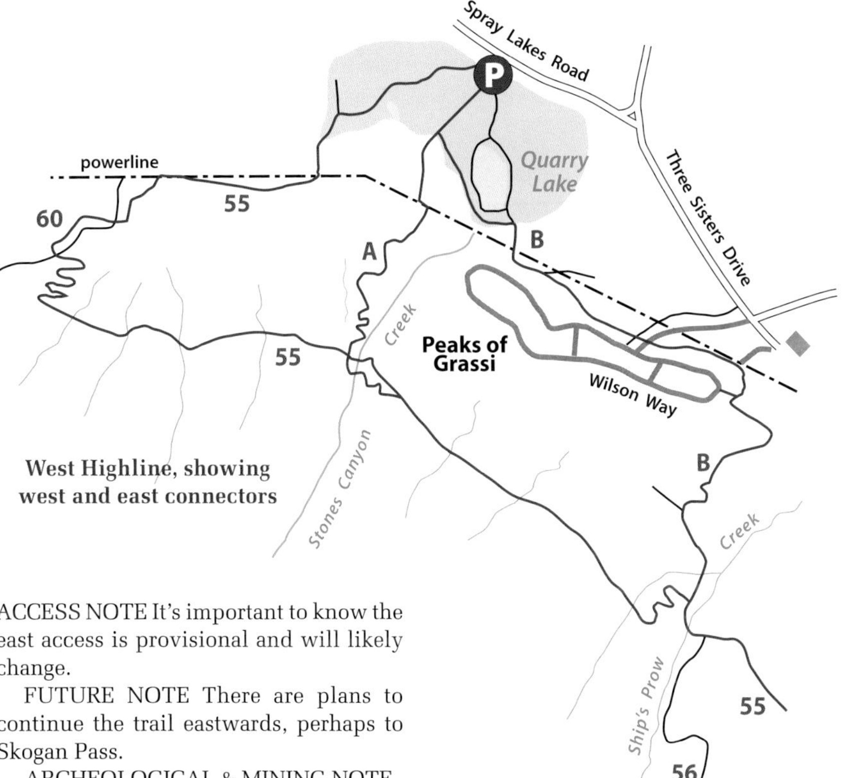

West Highline, showing west and east connectors

ACCESS NOTE It's important to know the east access is provisional and will likely change.

FUTURE NOTE There are plans to continue the trail eastwards, perhaps to Skogan Pass.

ARCHEOLOGICAL & MINING NOTE Nothing can be seen from the trail itself, but higher up in the umpteen gullies you cross, it's another story. About 600 ft. up the first gully is a mining prospect where sources say a little surface gold was extracted. An access trail up the right bank led to cabin ruins and artifacts dating back to late 1800s or early 1900s. Don't all rush at once; the trail is impossible to find.

Farther east, you cross Stones Creek Canyon, which should perhaps be renamed Stone Point or Stone Knife Canyon after the 1974 finding of a stone point about 300 feet below treeline. It was dated at the University of Alberta to be between 2000 and 8000 years old, with 2500 years being the favoured age. Some of the above info comes courtesy of the Calgary Regional Planning Commission's "Findings and Recommendations for the Canmore Corridor" in 1976/7.

It was Bill Baxter, a retired miner, who pointed out to me a spur ridge below Canmore Wall where he found a wheel near galena deposits (occurring bang on a fault line) too small to be worth extracting.

WEST TO EAST

Quarry Lake to powerline 1.3 m

Start at the kiosk at the NW end of the parking lot. On a good, slightly winding track head SE across the grass into a belt of trees. Descend into a big area of meadow. At a 4-way, keep straight and pass to the right of Dog Lake. Climb to a triangle junction on the banktop above Rundle Canal's overflow channel and turn left. Pass through a gate and along the rim of the channel. Keep left (trail to right leads down into the channel at the site of a quarry) and climb to the powerline access road.

Turn right and walk 430 m to the start of the next section at signpost 127594.

Highline trail to Riders of Rohan 770 m
Starting just right of a scree runnel, the trail heads into the forest and winds easily uphill, then traverses right to the lower 4-way junction with Riders of Rohan trail.

Cross R of R and continue zigging uphill to the upper 4-way junction with R of R at 124590. Cross onto the trail with the blue marker.

To west connector 1.6 km
The trail continues to zig uphill, finally heading left and crossing a wide, shallow gully falling from Ha-Ling Peak. This is the first viewpoint for Canmore.

Traverse pine-forested hillside, crossing another three stony gullies, the third deep and rocky. An uphill traverse precedes the junction with West Connector at 135587.

The start above the powerline.

To east connector 2 km
Keep right and cross Stones Creek Canyon, which falls from the gap between Miner's Peak and Mt. Lawrence Grassi. Skiers refer to it as Town Gully or Canmore Gully. After this the trail climbs past two more gullies to its high point, then crosses a third deep gully above a waterfall step. Then follows a winding descent to the junction with East Connector at the side of Ship's Prow Creek at 147678.

To east end access 4.3 km
Keep right uphill and cross the creekbed below slabs. Immediately after, a rough trail climbing the hillside is the start to #56.

Highline climbs across steep hillside with outcrops, then becomes more undulatory to an intersection with the old bench road (now track). Turn right and walk the flat bench. Unseen up above is a high cliff that spans the lower north face of Grassi Knob.

At Y-junction 159568 turn left onto a trail. (The continuing bench road ahead is the start of three routes up and down Grassi Knob via the southeast ridge and rib. See #56A.)

A long, descending traverse with occasional zigs spits you out on the Three Sisters Creek logging road (track) on the west bank of Three Sisters Creek. This is downstream of the dam. Turn left.

Descend a little more, then turn next right onto a W–E track that descends a hill and crosses Three Sisters Creek on a bridge. Climb to a 4-way intersection and turn left. (Track ahead may in time act as a continuation of Highline around Stewart Creek golf course. Trail to right is #54 up Three Sisters Creek.)

Your trail heads downvalley at a very gentle gradient. Cross a second W–E track with red and white flagging. Then keep alert for a sharp right-hand bend. After crossing a N–S track, the trail curves back left between Stewart Creek golf course to right and the abandoned Three Sisters golf course to left. Walk alongside a wooden

Typical view on east Highline. Photo Alf Skrastins

fence to a gravelled construction road come up a hill from the right. Walk around a gate affixed with a yellow and black, diamond-shaped checkerboard sign and in a few metres turn right at a T-junction. Use a trail to the left of the second gate to reach Three Sisters Blvd. at the junction with Hubman Landing.

GOING FARTHER

To Three Sisters Pathway 1.5 km

If you have started from Mineside parking lot, you need to connect with Three Sisters Pathway, which takes you back to your starting point.

Cross Hubman Landing to a walkway with sign. A gravel trail parallels Three Sisters Blvd. to a paved trail. Turn left and head northeast, passing to the right of a playground and disc golf course. Cross Riva Heights (road). Continue by the side of the disc golf course, the paved trail eventually descending by the side of the abandoned Three Sisters golf course to an unmarked T-junction between Three Sisters Creek and Miskow Close. Go straight. (Paved trail to right connects with Miskow Close.)

Go straight on a well-used dirt trail descending by the side of Three Sisters Creek to Three Sisters Pathway, which is paved. It reaches the pathway just southeast of the wide red bridge over the creek.

East Highline, showing connection with Three Sisters Pathway

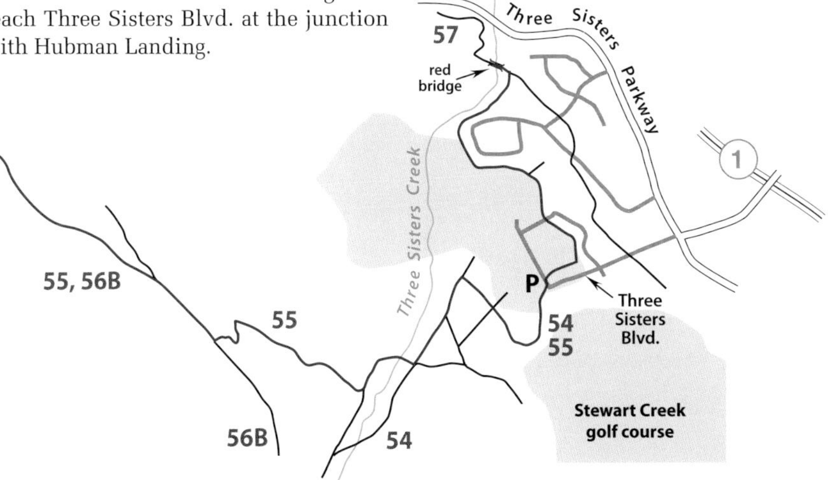

As mentioned, two connector trails can be used to make loops back to Quarry Lake:

55A West connector

Distance 1.7 km
Height loss 133 m (436 ft.)
High point 1520 m (4987 ft.)

A moderately steep, winding trail.

TOP TO BOTTOM

To the powerline 1.1 km
Initially the trail winds down steepish terrain to the left of deeply incised Stones Canyon Creek. The angle eases, the gully shallows out and you turn right and cross its runnel of stones to a junction. Turn left and continue slightly downhill to a junction with a track. Turn left and in a few minutes reach the powerline access road.

To Quarry Lake 620 m
Cross the access road onto a trail that descends into a meadow. Go straight. (Trail to left leads to Dog Lake.) Pass through a belt of trees into the big meadow northwest of Quarry Lake. Keep straight to the kiosk at the SE end of Quarry Lake parking lot.

55B East connector

Distance 3.2 km
Height loss 143 m (469 ft.)
High point 1530 m (5020 ft.)

A much gentler trail than the West connector. After crossing Peaks Drive look for yellow markers on posts. Used as the approach route to Grassi's Knob from Peaks of Grassi subdivision.

TOP TO BOTTOM

To Peaks of Grassi 1.4 km
Descend the left side of a creekbed. Gradually the trail veers left and crosses a bridge over a stony gully. Descend by the side of the gully, then bend left and along to a T-junction with arrows. Turn right. Wind easily down the fall line, en route crossing assorted old trails and roads. Continue down a bank and across a water line, below which the trail turns left and ends at the east end of Wilson Way in the Peaks of Grassi subdivision.

To Quarry Lake 1.8 km
From the east end of Wilson Way, a gated gravel road connects to the Grand Canadian Resort of the Rockies. Follow it just to the powerline right-of-way and turn left onto its access road. Pass through a gate and cross Peaks Drive. On hitting the paved commuter trail turn left, then right onto the powerline access road continued. Plod below the houses of Lawrence Grassi Way to the left of the power poles. You are now on the yellow route.

At 140591 turn right, following yellow trail to the kiosk at the south end of Quarry Lake Park. Keep left at the inverted Y-junction and walk out to a T-junction in view of the lake. Turn left and follow yellow trail around the west side of the lake to an intersection with #55A. Turn right and in minutes reach the kiosk at the SE end of Quarry Lake parking lot.

Bridge on East connector.

56 GRASSI KNOB—map 9

The Three Sisters, just one of the magnificent views from the top.

Day hike
Unofficial trail
Distance 2.9 km to top from trailhead; 9.2 km loop
Height gain 768 m (2520 ft.) from trailhead
High point 2158 m (7080 ft.)
Map 82 O/3 Canmore

Access Canmore, at Peaks of Grassi. Park at the east end of Wilson Way. Alternatively, park on the east side of Peaks Drive at the intersecting powerline right-of-way, then walk along the powerline access road to a gravel road, turn right and reach the east end of Wilson Way at a gate.

Grassi Knob at 149563 is the triangular, forested hill on the north side of Mt. Lawrence Grassi below the Ship's Prow. The open summit is a truly exceptional viewpoint for the Bow Valley, reason enough for a primitive trail to be built up its north ridge by Trailminders. It's a steep grind that the Canmore Nordic Ski Club do in 1 hour as training. Most of us take much longer. Watch for yellow flagging and blazes. NOTE This is the ONLY route up the knob with a trail all the way to the top. See also OPTIONAL DESCENT LOOP for routes using the southeast ridges.

NAMING NOTE In response to the demotion of the name Mt. Lawrence Grassi for the whole massif above Canmore when the name Ehagay Nakoda (The Last Nakoda) was established in 1998, 11 Trailminders under Doug Campbell tramped up the ridge on August 23, 1998, and "proclaimed the little summit as Grassi Knob," in an effort to keep Grassi's name up there somewhere. Doug wrote: "Let it be recorded in the *Canmore Leader* that an informal, repeat informal, designation now exists, witnessed atop the rock by 11 witnesses whose names are available."

I don't think they need have worried. Mt. Lawrence Grassi is still the official name for the highest summit.

East Highline connector 1.4 km
The trail starts at the east end of Wilson Way to the right of the gated gravel road, Straight off it heads into the forest and begins a gentle, winding climb, crossing a water line and assorted old roads and trails en route to a T-junction with arrows. Turn left.

The trail wends diagonally left to a stony gully, climbing up the right side of it and eventually crossing it on a bridge. Head across to Ship's Prow Creek and likewise climb up the right bank to the T-junction with Highline trail. Keep left.

Cross Ship's Prow Creek. In 10 paces Grassi Knob trail turns off to the right at 147578. There is no flagging or cairn. (NOTE This is not the steep trail starting a little farther along Highline, which climbs through the lower cliff bands of the north ridge. This was Trailminders' first attempt at pushing a trail up the ridge—they called it the climber's trail—and the reason why Brian Carter devised a much easier route up the creekbed onto the first knoll.)

Scrambling up Ship's Prow Creek.

Ship's Prow Creek to summit 1.5 km
Climb the steep trail to the immediate left of the creek, at the top stepping down (slightly dicey move above eroding bank) into the creekbed above two slabby steps. Head up the left side of the bed. Pass a log cache and a huge boulder, then behind the boulder make for the right side of the bed. Scramble easy slabs which are icy early and late in the season. The next two impasses, a short vertical rock step and a much higher step, are turned in one swoop by a bypass trail on the left.

Back in the creekbed for only a very short distance, keep your eyes peeled for yellow flagging. This marks the spot where the trail leaves the creekbed for good, climbing steeply up the left bank.

The angle eases and you make a rising traverse, keeping straight, to the top of "first knoll," which is the start of the north ridge proper. Down below are the cliff bands.

Looking down the north ridge from near the summit.

At yellow flagging turn right and climb straight up the forested north ridge with nary a zig. The going is steep, with one relief section called the "second knoll." Near the top is open ground. Head up the right side of some scree, then traverse left below the summit knob onto the southeast ridge, which is followed to the top.

You need panorama mode on your camera or iPhone, because the view is absolutely stunning in all directions. The Three Sisters, of course. Then the Ship's Prow, a 450 m high buttress first climbed in 1965 by Lloyd MacKay and Chic Scott. Next peak along is Mt. Lawrence Grassi, which from this vantage point discloses a scrambler's route from the head of Ship's Prow Creek onto the ridge just south of the summit.

In the other direction, a large chunk of the Bow Valley is visible from Cascade Mountain in the north to McConnell Point in the southeast, the valley bounded on the east by all the familiar peaks of the Fairholme Range. Down below is Canmore and the Stewart Creek golf course. Interestingly, the 5th hole is called Ship's Prow, an appropriate name given that Chic in his youth represented Alberta in the Canadian Junior Golf Championships.

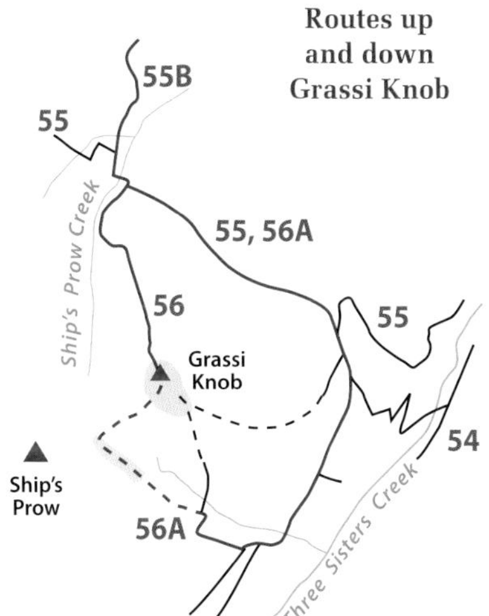

Return the same way or try OPTIONAL RETURN LOOP #56A, which prolongs the views but has trickier route finding.

OPTIONAL RETURN LOOP

56A via the southeast rib

Route, unofficial trails blazed and flagged, then official trails with blue posts
Distance 4.8 km to Ship's Prow Creek; 6.3 km to trailhead

Making a loop is made easy by trails connecting with the old bench road. You can either use Highline trail to get back to your starting point or peel off down to Three Sisters Creek if you have a second car parked in Three Sisters Mountain Village.

But first you have to descend the southeast rib, which is sans trail in its upper part. The following description of the start is based on talks with Gary Hunt, who is responsible for the blazes.

There are actually three routes that hikers and climbers accessing the Ship's Prow use between the old bench road above Three Sisters Creek and the summit, but this (route 1) is the one that works best in the downhill direction. Because of route-finding problems, the other two, which both follow the southeast ridge, are much better used as ascent routes. Route 2 follows the southeast rib trails, then switches to the southeast ridge. Route 3 leaves the old bench road and climbs onto the southeast ridge from the north.

I was not surprised to learn that Grassi Knob aficionados from Canmore actually prefer these three routes over the north ridge trail: the gradients are less steep and the south-facing terrain is more open. All that's needed is a trail!

Anyone wandering this piece of hillside but not wanting to climb to the knob can explore a maze of grassed-over logging roads and hunter's trails.

Top: Summit view of Ship's Prow. #56A continues to the next bump, then turns left down the rib.

Bottom: The old bench road and stove.

Southeast rib 1.6 km
From the top walk the connecting ridge toward the Ship's Prow, ascending about 35 vertical m onto the first bump. Then descend the southeast rib to your left. The upper part is open with views; lower down, the trees crowd in and it's here where you should look for Gary's blazes.

1. It doesn't matter if you don't find them, because at some point you'll hit an obvious trail that traverses the rib from side to side. Turn left. (The trail to right contours to the banktop above the incised tributary at the forks in Three Sisters Creek, then descends steep rubble into it.) Follow the good trail downhill to T-junction 158558 above the gully separating rib and ridge. At this important junction the trail is marked with white flagging. Turn right.

2. If you arrive on the east side of the rib at a flattening, you'll pick up a narrow trail with blazes and occasional red flagging. This is route 2 up the southeast ridge—155558 being the crucial spot where it descends into the gully and crosses it. Continue down the rib on the blazed trail to the banktop and on down to important T-junction 158558, where you meet route no. 1. Go straight.

Return 3.2 km
Slither down an even steeper slope to another T-junction, which again is marked with white flagging. Go straight. (The narrower trail to right climbs diagonally across the slope and on reaching easier ground joins a network of old logging roads, some stretching up to the traversing trail and higher.)

The trail descends a little less steeply, then turns left and plummets to the floor of the gully. Traverse out below a small crag to the start of the old bench road, which resembles a wide trail.

The road makes a gradual descent along the bench, en route passing a side trail to right that leads to a ruined hunter's cabin. At T-junction 161565 keep left on the road. (The 700 m long "road" to right, badly obscured at the entrance by bushes, zigs down the hillside to Three Sisters Creek above the dam and is another way off via #54.)

Pass a rusty old stove. Just after, a vegetating logging road heading left is route 1 onto the southeast ridge.

A blowdown area precedes the T-junction with Highline trail at 159568. Continue straight on the bench road, then transfer left onto a trail which undulates mostly in the downhill direction across the north face of the knob back to Ship's Prow Creek.

57 THREE SISTERS PATHWAY—maps 9, 8

Day hike/s, bike 'n' hike
Official trail with red markers, bridges, signposts, benches
Distance 6.8 km
Height gain 50 m (164 ft.) W–E
High point 1340 m (4396 ft.) at east access
Map 82 O/3 Canmore

West access Canmore's Mineside parking lot, located on the southeast side of the bridge over the Bow River.
East access Three Sisters Mountain Village at Stewart Creek Landing pavilion.
Other access points: Three Sisters Parkway at 168581 and via connector trails from Homesteads and Prospect subdivisions.
Also accessible via #55 Highline trail, east end via connector trail.

Though part of the Trans Canada Trail, this section between Canmore and Three Sisters Mountain Village is most often used for short walks, there and back bike rides, and as access to/from other trails. It's a mix of gravel and pavement, built mainly for bikers of all ilks as can be seen by the long, sweeping zigs up the hills. And while walkers out for a stroll don't seem to mind pushing the pavement, pushing 14 km of it is a bit much. With this in mind, I have diverted from the main trail as much as possible so walkers can tread much pleasanter ground and visit a few historic sites along the way. These variations are coloured blue in the text.

REFRESHMENT NOTE The Market Bistro in Three Sisters Mountain Village at 75 Dyrgas Gate is open 9–9 Tue to Sat, 9–6 Sun. French chef Anthony offers breakfast, lunches, light dinners, ice creams and drinks.

HISTORY NOTE The first half of the trail is more or less on the line of the CPR railway track to No. 2 coal mine. When the mine opened, a new settlement of company houses was built en route called Prospect, none of which survive today, the last occupant leaving the road that is now called Prospects Heights about 1990.

The big "meadow" is the site of No. 2 mine, that operated with a cycle of declines and revivals from 1903 to July 13, 1979—a Friday. The main entry lies at the foot of the slope below the lamp house where miners bound for mines farther east picked up a lamp and a brass disc with their number on it before boarding the trolley. The trolley line is still followable until it gets lost in Three Sisters Mountain Resort and the Stewart Creek golf course. (It can be picked up again east of Stewart Creek.) The only other remnant left is locomotive no. 4 that ran along the CPR line. It now resides in Heritage Park in Calgary.

To see what this area once looked like visit the Canmore Museum and Geoscience Centre.

Chinook sculpture on the banks of the Bow.

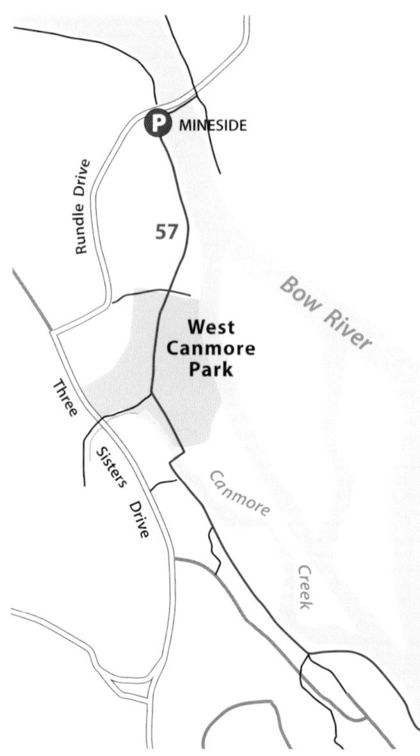

CANMORE TO THREE SISTERS MOUNTAIN VILLAGE

To lamp house 2.2 km

From the far end of the parking lot walk through to the gravel trail alongside the Bow River and turn right. Pass the TCT pavilion and the Chinook Sculpture representing "wind in all its facets." Turn away from the river, and after a straight, cross a paved service road into West Canmore Park, a big flat, grassy area. On your left is a playground and biffy—the only one en route. At a T-junction keep left. (Trail to right is the yellow-marked trail to Quarry Lake.)

Pass interpretive signs, then cross the bridge over Canmore Creek and climb a hill into the site of old Prospect, en route ignoring side trails to the right. As you descend, the trail morphs into a wide, straight track that used to be the CPR line to No. 2 mine. At a 4-way, turn left on a narrower trail down a hill. (The stepped trail to right leads into the Homesteads; the wide track ahead accesses Prospect Court.)

The trail runs alongside the Bow River past benches. Disregard the first side trail to right. The second side trail to right occurs at a left-hand bend at the demarcation with pavement. Turn right up this trail. (The paved trail continues near the edge of the Bow, crossing a big meadow that is waste from No. 2 mine. You will join it at the far end of the meadow.)

The lamp house has seen better days.

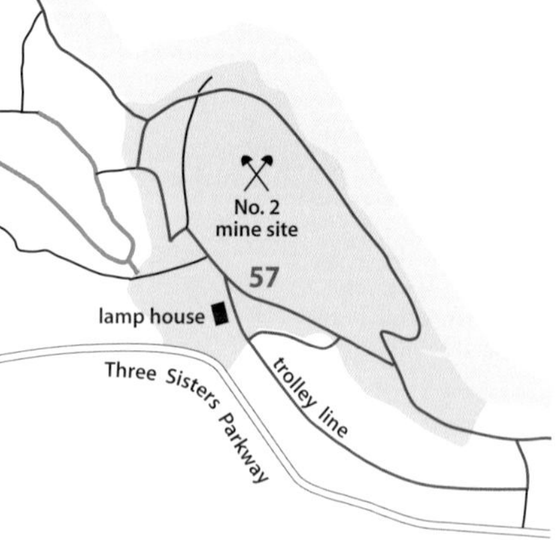

Trail between Mineside trailhead and No. 2 mine site. Three Sisters Pathway is red; variations are purple.

The trail leads to Van Horne (road). Turn left to road's end, then continue on gravelled service road to a gate. Beyond the gate, the service road heads left and a trail heads right, into the meadow. Follow the trail across the meadow below a steep hill. In mining days, trucks would dump coal from the strip mines down a steel chute from the top of the hill to the washery building below.

Climb a small hill to the lamp house at 154590, the site once strewn with boots and gloves. Shamefully, this important historic building is in dire need of saving, barely standing on its last legs, the railing beset by small trees and the inside filled with graffiti.

Loop

Walk out to the edge of the bank and look down on the meadow that was once dotted with small buildings: a coke oven, compressor plant, power house and electricity transformer. From here head right on a trail that descends to the meadow by the side of a filled-in portal tastefully decorated with a coal cart and indecipherable metal objects picked up from elsewhere. Walk out to the paved trail. Just beyond is a man-made pond where sulphurous waters poured out of No. 2 mine into the Bow River. Still does, I gather.

Return to the portal and keep right on the trail below the bank. Come to No. 2 mine entry, now closed a little way in with a locked gate. A trail to its right leads back up the hill to the lamp house.

Trolley line.

Bow River

Three Sisters Parkway

Riverside trail

Cairns on the Bow

57

Riverside trail section

Gerry Stephenson and group at No. 2 mine entry.

Riverside trail 2.2 km
Walk beyond the lamp house under coal spoil, then turn right into a cut that was quarried for the trolley line. In places, you can still spot the wooden cross ties and discarded rails in the bush. Follow the cut, then the built-up railbed to an intersecting gravel track at a boulder. Turn left down the track and join the official route, which is paved at a T-junction. Turn right

Shortly, the path starts long, sweeping zigs down to the river. At the first bend, you can miss them all out by turning right onto a dirt trail that descends through trees. On joining the path. Turn right. A forest walk by the side of a channel of the Bow brings you to a major T-junction with two seats and a bike lock-up at 163586.

Go left on Riverside trail, which is all gravel. (Trail to right is paved and runs between the parkway and Cairns on the Bow to join Riverside at the road crossing.)

Lovely Riverside crosses a bridge, then winds alongside the channel. Keep left at a junction, then head inland and cross a bridge before heading to the Bow River. The very pleasant riverside section ends when you climb long zigs past benches up to the parkway. Cross the road.

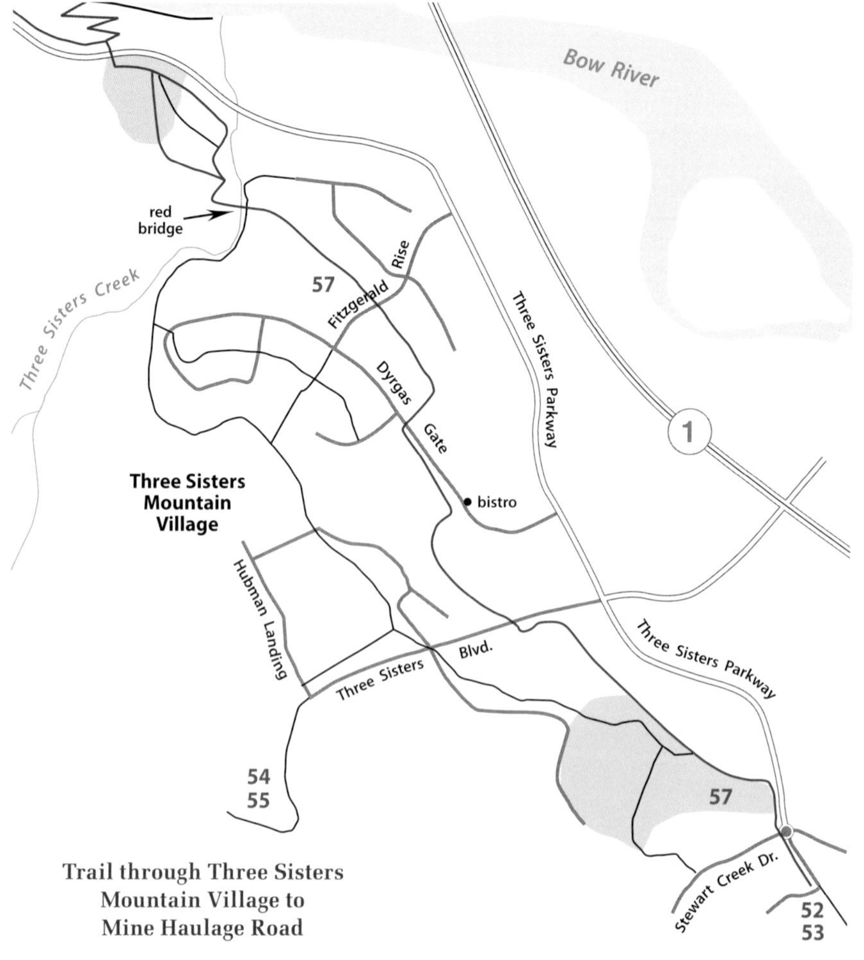

Trail through Three Sisters Mountain Village to Mine Haulage Road

Bottom: The red bridge over Three Sisters Creek.
Top: Riverside trail.

Three Sisters Mountain Village 2.4 km
The paved trail heads left. In a few metres turn first right onto a dirt trail that climbs meadow, then heads left through forest to join the paved trail at a bend. (Meanwhile, the paved trail dips, then climbs up by the side of Three Sisters Creek, en route picking up the two forest shortcuts.) The trail turns left and crosses a wide red bridge over Three Sisters Creek.

NOTE Dirt trail immediately right is a route to Highline's east access.

After a long, paved straight, cross Fitzgerald Rise. Another paved straight curls up to Dyrgas Gate. Cross the road and turn left on a paved trail paralleling Dyrgas Gate. Where the trail turns right, detour to the bistro just a few metres down the road on the other side.

Back on the trail, bypass a fenced-in subsidence, then head left to Three Sisters Blvd. Cross. Another long, paved straight leads to a T-junction with another trail in an open area. Turn left, descending past an unfinished interpretive loop to the traffic circle at the east end of Three Sisters Parkway. The trail crosses Stewart Creek Drive and runs alongside Stewart Creek Landing to a pavilion.

For Quebexican continue ahead on the haul road, which is spanned by a chain strung between concrete blocks.

58 QUARRY LAKE via Canmore Creek—map 9

Quarry Lake.

Day hike/s, bike 'n' hike
Official with yellow markers, signposts
Distance 2 km one way
Height gain 61 m (200 ft.)
High point 1387 m (4550 ft.)
Map 82 O/3 Canmore

Access Canmore.
1. Mineside parking lot, located on the southeast side of the bridge over the Bow River.
2. Spray Lakes Road at Quarry Lake parking lot.
Also accessible via #55 Highline trail, #57 Three Sisters Pathway.

An interesting walk from the heart of Canmore following Canmore Creek and its waterfalls to Quarry Lake Park where you can picnic, swim, and fish for grayling.

MINING NOTE Lots of mining history on this trail. You walk through No. 1 mine site on your way to Canmore Falls. The coal in Canmore Creek was first noted in 1884 by William McCardell and Frank McCabe (who first found the hot springs at Banff, the springboard for Banff National Park). It soon came under control of the Canadian Anthracite Company, who operated No. 1 mine from 1887 to 1916.

Quarry Lake was once a strip mine gouged out to a depth of 120 feet. When it came time to reclaim the mine, Gerry Stephenson, Canmore Mines's chief engineer and an avid fisherman, envisaged turning it into a fishing hole, so it was backfilled to a depth of 80 feet and the outlet sealed with a clay plug. To learn more, take Gerry's History of Mining tour organized by the Canmore museum.

On the optional return you pass the site of No. 4B mine, a relative latecomer to the Canmore mining scene, worked from 1969–72, though some say it was 1972–74. Regardless, it was very short-lived. On July 11 and 12, 1996, the public had the opportunity to tour the mine before the entrance was filled in.

MOVIE NOTE The 1999 movie *Mystery Alaska*, starring Russell Crowe, was filmed at Quarry Lake Park. The town of Mystery sprang up in the dog park area, the 53 buildings erected from plywood and plastic augmented by real buildings scheduled for demolition brought up from Canmore. Locals were conscripted for crowd scenes at the hockey rink and plied with endless hot chocolate during the freezingly cold days of filming.

To West Canmore Park 500 m
From the far end of the parking lot walk through to the gravel trail alongside the Bow River and turn right. After passing the TCT pavilion and the Chinook Sculpture the trail turns away from the river and after a straight crosses a paved service road into West Canmore Park, a big flat, grassy area. On your left is a playground and biffy. At a T-junction turn right onto the yellow trail. (Trail ahead is Three Sisters Pathway.)

Canmore Creek to Quarry Lake 1.5 km
Walk by the side of Canmore Creek to Three Sisters Drive. Cross and walk up Rummel Place to a gate. Beyond the gate the road becomes Olympic Drive. Pick up a trail on the left side of the road above Canmore Creek and its beaver dams. You can make out the line of a railbed below.

Turn left onto Prendergast Place. Beyond the houses, the trail enters the narrows that was once crammed with the buildings of No. 1 mine. Smell H_2S? Look left across to the creek to where a waterfall pours out of the main portal, which is now filled in. Back then, it was reached via a trestle bridge. On your right are the ruins of the hoist house. As you can see, the area all around is a mess of mine tailings, filled-in entrances and subsidences half hidden by new tree growth.

Keep straight at a T-junction. Descend steps in coal detritus to Canmore Creek at lower Canmore falls.

Return to the T-junction. Turn left and climb 60 steps, at the top wending left to seats and a signpost at a viewpoint. (En route trails to right lead to a sandstone quarry.) From the viewpoint you can't quite see the upper falls; you must descend the ridge toward the creek.

Traverse hillside to a T-junction close to Spray Lakes Road. Go left. (Trail to right leads to the Canmore Nordic Centre.) Pass above the Canmore Creek culvert. Down below was the site of a small dam, bits of concrete retention walls still in evidence.

Near Spray Lakes Road is a junction with a dirt trail. Go right. (Trail to left

Lower (top) and upper Canmore Falls.

During filming of Mystery Alaska, *Quarry Lake Park was filled with pseudo buildings like this courthouse.*

Remains of hoist house at No. 1 mine.

Trail to Quarry Lake (red) and optional return (purple)

MINESIDE
Rundle Drive
58
Bow
West Canmore Park
Olympic Drive
No. 1 mine site
Spray Lakes Road
Quarry Lake Park
Quarry Lake
Three Sisters Drive
Prospect
River
Carey
Heights
Morris
McNeill
58
No. 4B mine site
Walker
No. 2 mine site
Three Sisters Parkway

runs along the banktop between the road and Canmore Creek, eventually dropping to Three Sisters Drive. En route are more relics of No. 1 mine, including a fan house.) Cross the road immediately opposite the entrance to Quarry Lake Park.

Quarry Lake Park

A large number of trails criss-cross the park, some joining with Grassi Sulphur Spring loop, and others with the Highline trail. A loop taking in Dog Lake and an interpretive sign is just one possibility. If you feel like an invigorating swim or a picnic, head to Quarry Lake. The trail starts from the far left-hand corner of the parking lot and is paved. On reaching the north beach (picnic tables, biffy), the trail splits and circles the lake to the south beach (picnic tables).

OPTIONAL RETURN 4 km

A pleasant mix of dirt, paved and gravelled trails, at times following yellow and red markers through the Homesteads and Prospect neighbourhoods.

To 4B mine site

Approach Quarry Lake's south beach via the east (left-hand) trail. At the 3-way at the beach, head straight to a 4-way. Turn left across grass. Then keep right and descend into trees. At a 4-way in a glade, turn right. A pleasing narrow trail follows a strip of meadow to a T-junction with an old road (track). Turn right. Ignoring all manner of side trails, follow the track through forest to a paved commuter trail near Peaks Drive. Turn left. Keep straight on the paved trail to its intersection with Three Sisters Drive opposite Walker (road).

Cross the road. The paved trail continues to the right, soon curving left into a small park with playground. The rocks in the centre and hereabouts mark an air shaft and fan house for No. 4B mine. Continue to Walker. Cross a private road entrance and continue straight ahead on Walker. The open area to right marks the site of No. 4B mine at 149591.

To Mineside parking lot

Just before the road dead-ends, turn off right on a trail that crosses the open area to a T-junction. Turn left. (Trail to right is a super-scenic trail following spoil terraces to the end of Morris (road), where a coal trail carries on down the grassed hill to the vicinity of the lamp house. Use it to take in No. 2 mine, then return via Three Sisters Pathway. See #57.)

Descend to Morris opposite a crag. Cross to the walkway sign and continue downhill. At the next two T-junctions keep left. (Both trails to right descend to Prospect Heights (road). Descend two tiers of steps and pass under a crag. Then climb slightly to a T-junction. Keep right. (Yellow trail ahead climbs steps to McNeill (road) opposite Carey (road).)

Wend slightly uphill through forest to Prospect Heights (road). Cross and descend to Three Sisters Pathway at the 4-way above the Bow River. Turn left onto a wide gravel track with red markers.

Follow this main trail above Canmore Creek, eventually crossing the creek via a bridge into West Canmore Park. At the red/yellow T-junction beyond the interpretive signs you meet your outgoing route.

Go straight and return the same way to Mineside parking lot.

Entrance to No. 4B mine before being filled in.

#58 return. The two tiers of steps between Morris and Prospect Heights.

#58 return. The trail above Prospect.

#59A Man-made caves in the cliffs.

59 GRASSI SULPHUR SPRING LOOP—map 9

Half-day hike
Unofficial trail
Distance 4.2 km
Height loss/gain 40 m (130 ft.)
Map 82 O/3 Canmore

Access Canmore, Spray Lakes Road. Just beyond Quarry Lake entrance and opposite Rundleview Drive, turn left onto a track. Drive to a parking area just before a gate.
Also accessible from Quarry Park.

A short, forested loop between Rundle Forebay and Quarry Lake Park takes in a sulphur spring and the middle reaches of Canmore Creek.

HISTORY In part this loop follows Lawrence Grassi's 1921 trail to Grassi Lakes, which has since been severed by the Rundle Forebay. Back then, the spring was a resting place with bench on the way up to the lakes. Grassi also shored up the sides of the pool below the spring for therapeutic bathing, but before it could be opened to the public, it was condemned by the local health officials, who declared it unsanitary.

SPRING NOTE This is a really slow-running spring that maintains its temperature between 6 and 12 degrees all year round. Because the sulphur content is low, only the most acute noses will get a whiff of the H_2S.

To the spring 940 m

Walk the track beyond the gate. Keep straight, cross under a powerline, then keep right at Y-junction 135600. (The track to left is the return route.)

In 100 m turn left onto a trail. (If you want, you can continue following the track to its junction with the trail. The spring is directly below you at 128601.) The trail through the woods, though, is much the pleasanter option.

At the second junction to the right, at 131600 (pile of wood on the left side), detour to the spring via a narrower trail opened up by Trailminders. It leads directly to the pool below the spring.

Grassi's Spring and pool.

To the overflow channel 1.6 km

Backtrack to the last junction, 131600, and turn right.

Another forest stint leads to the crossing of the tiny spring creek via a plank. Turn right on the far side and climb a hill. At the next Y-junction keep left and meander along to regain the track just below the forebay. Turn left

As you walk, listen for Canmore Creek bursting out of a culvert down below you to your left. The open area beyond it with pond is a borrow pit.

Come to a faint junction where the stony track climbs up to the right onto the bank of the forebay. Go straight and cross grass to the prominent yellow warning sign above the forebay's overflow channel.

Between the spring and the dike.

Canmore Creek, below the dam.

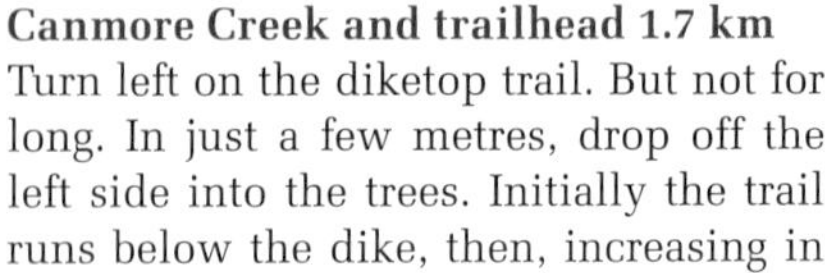

Canmore Creek and trailhead 1.7 km Turn left on the diketop trail. But not for long. In just a few metres, drop off the left side into the trees. Initially the trail runs below the dike, then, increasing in width, it veers off left in great big windings featuring an array of cleverly constructed technical features for bikers. Only the see-saw and swing bridge are hiker friendly. Just after the latter, at T-junction 131597,

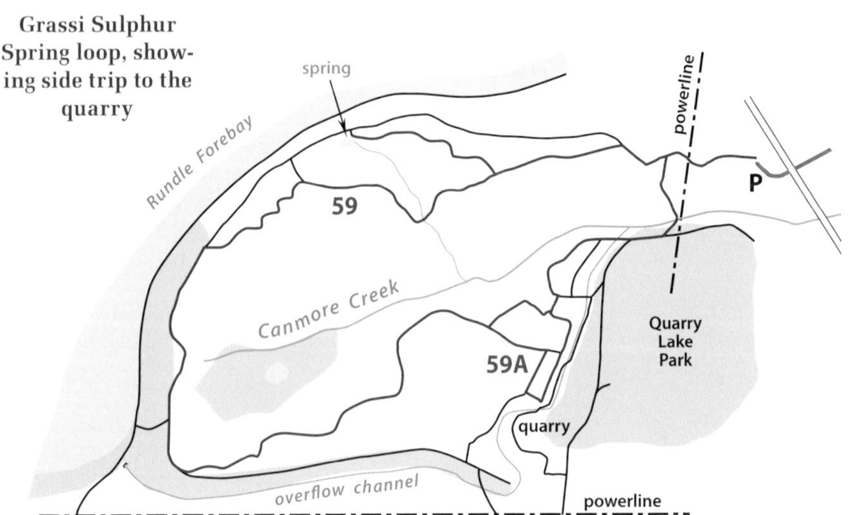

Grassi Sulphur Spring loop, showing side trip to the quarry

#59A The pale cliff band above the quarry.

turn left on a minor trail. (Trail ahead leads to overlooks above the channel. See also SIDE TRIP #59A.)

Your trail heads for a steep, forested bank, then turns right along the top of it. Turn second left at 132598 down the bank to another T-junction. Turn left and walk past various relicts among the trees to the left. At the next junction keep right on the better trail to arrive at Canmore Creek at a partial dam (pool habitat) and man-made waterfall that has something to do with spawning cutthroat trout. Cross the small creek trickling from the overflow channel and climb into meadow on the fringe of Quarry Lake Park. Go left at the T-junction.

Leave this trail at the following junction and descend the bank to a good bridge over Canmore Creek. On the far side is an interpretive sign explaining the cutthroat trout reclamation project of 1997/8.

Follow the track to the Y-junction with your outgoing track at 135600. Turn right and walk 200 m to the gate and parking area.

SIDE TRIP

59A Quarry Overlook

Distance 530 m

At T-junction 131597 continue straight. Turn next right and walk to the edge of a "quarry" above a cliff band.

Everyone calls it a quarry, this widening and deepening of the overflow channel excavated by blasting. It uses in part a creek known way back as Chinks Creek, which is seen to the right. Gord tells me the pale cliff band below you is a "fining upward sequence" of clay/sandstone/siltstone (very soft and easily sculpted into caves) interspersed with at least two thin layers of conglomerate. The breccia layer of angular rocks seen near the caves possibly originated from a rockfall off EEOR.

Circle left and along the west edge of the overflow channel. Keep straight and follow the trail around to the left until you reach junction 132598, then turn right, down the bank.

60 RIDERS OF ROHAN—map 9

Half-day hike
Official trail with maps at junctions
Distance 1.6 km
Height loss/gain 335 m (1100 ft.)
High point 1722 m (5650 ft.)
Map 82 O/3 Canmore

Powerline access at bottom Via #55 Highline trail. Walk 100 m farther to 126594.
Dam access at top Hwy. 742 (Smith-Dorrien/ Spray Trail). From Canmore drive Spray Lakes Road past the Canmore Nordic Centre to Ken Ritchie Way. Continue ahead on gravelled Hwy. 742 all the way up the hill to the dam at Whitemans Gap. The hwy. about the dam is plastered with 10 "No Parking" signs, so carry on for another 300 m to a pullout on the west side of Whitemans Pond (reservoir).
Also accessible from #61 Grassi Lakes with which it is often combined to make a loop.

This steep forest trail runs between Whitemans Gap and the powerline near Quarry Lake. Recently it has been designated a DHS mountain bike trail for experts, which means that for bikers it's one-way as per the sign on the powerline right-of-way.

Hikers can walk it either way. Just stay on full alert to avoid accidents. If hiking uphill, using the easier Highline trail to the upper junction is an option. After this the going gets steeper, its steepness remarked upon by British spies Warre and Vavasour on their way to Oregon in 1845.

TRAIL ACCESS Since the last edition access to/from the dam has gotten a whole lot easier with the removal of the chain-link fence.

TRAIL HISTORY Hard to believe the historic "Oregon Trail" now sports TTFs and banked corners courtesy of the bikers who know nothing of its history. Originally an Indian trail between the western mountains and the plains, it was used by early European travellers, starting in 1841 with James Sinclair, to get from the site of Canmore up to Whitemans Gap and thence over White Man Pass to Oregon territory. At that time the gap was a rocky defile with screes sweeping down from both sides. James Hector described it as a "nick bounded by a very lofty precipice," which is Ha-Ling Peak. Interestingly, when Father De Smet and entourage descended this route in 1845, it took them 6 hours to "trace (the) route across fragments of broken rocks, through an extensive and parched forest and where millions of half-consumed trees lay extended in every direction."

A hundred years later, the Spray Hydroelectric Project changed the landscape irrevocably with the building of the access road to Whitemans Gap (the future Hwy. 742) and of an earth dam and reservoir filling in the nick where the trail had been.

BOTTOM TO TOP

From the one way sign, head into forest, the going easy to the lower 4-way junction with Highline. Cross, and after veering right, climb a winding trail with smooth, banked corners, the loose rocks having been shovelled off to one side or the other. A straight leads to the upper 4-way junction with Highline at 124590. Go straight.

The trail steepens even further to T-junction 120589. Keep straight. (Narrow trail to right is #61A to Grassi Lakes.)

Continue climbing, the trail a little rocky in places, to the upper T-junction with map. Turn right.

(NOTE Trail ahead is the historic trail continued. It climbs a little more, then descends to Whitemans Pond reservoir where it disappears under water, superseded by a ghost trail along the shoreline. All along this stretch, climber's access trails head up the hillside to the north face of Ha Ling and to Little China bouldering area.)

Today's trail descends to the intake, turns left alongside the intake channel, then right along the top of Whitemans Dam to Hwy. 742. Turn left and walk the road for 300 m to the parking area.

#60 Descending Riders of Rohan.

#61.2 A view of the falls below the lakes.

#61 Upper Grassi Lake from the north shore.

61 GRASSI LAKES—map 9

Lower Grassi Lake, looking towards the canyon.

Short-day hikes
Official trails with signs
Distance 1.6 km to lakes; 1.9 km to dam
Height gain 162 m (530 ft.) to lakes; 265 m (870 ft.) to dam
High point 1670 m (5150 ft.) at lakes; 1673 m (5490 ft.) at dam
Map 82 O/3 Canmore

Main access Canmore. Drive Spray Lakes Road. After passing the Canmore Nordic Centre turn next left onto Ken Ritchie Way. Turn first right into Grassi Lakes parking lot.

Dam access Hwy. 742 (Smith-Dorrien/Spray Trail). From Canmore drive Spray Lakes Road past the Canmore Nordic Centre to Ken Ritchie Way. Continue ahead on gravelled Hwy. 742 all the way up the hill to the dam at Whitemans Gap. The hwy. about the dam is plastered with 10 "No Parking" signs, so carry on for another 300 m to a pullout on the west side of Whitemans Pond (reservoir). Walk the road back to the dam.

Also accessible from #60 Riders of Rohan.

Grassi Lakes are two colourful lakes hidden away in a hanging valley between Spray hydro plant and Whitemans Pond reservoir. The hydro plant, Rundle Forebay, dam, reservoir, their access roads, penstock, pipeline and powerlines are background to most views. Nevertheless, Grassi Lakes trail is still the best hike near Canmore—even amid a hundred tourists—known for its varied scenery including waterfalls, lakes, a canyon, cliffs and rock paintings. Most people just go to the upper lake and back. Some continue through the canyon to look at the petrographs and exit at Whitemans Gap, for which you need two vehicles. An alternative to the latter is to make a loop with Riders of Rohan, returning either to the trail or to the trailhead. See the sketch map on the next page.

WARNING Falling rock is something to be aware of on the northwest shore of the upper lake and in the canyon.

TRAIL CHANGES Since the last edition the trail through the canyon to Whitemans Gap has become a lot easier with the building of wooden steps with handrails and staging platforms for climbers, made and maintained by climbers and paid for by donations to TABVAR. (It wasn't so long ago that TransAlta were insisting the climbers' trail-building efforts on the dam face be demolished.) Also new is a summer-only biffy on the TransAlta access road, which, K Country wants me to stress, is NOT a receptacle for garbage.

TRAIL HISTORY NOTE The lakes used to be called Twin Lakes when Canmore miner Lawrence Grassi (best known for his meticulous trail-building at Lake O'Hara) built his trail in 1921. It started from his house on Three Sisters Drive and followed Canmore Creek to the sulphur spring swimming hole before climbing up to the lakes. Since then his beautiful trail has been severed in two by Rundle Forebay, so this is just the upper half. To walk the lower half see ##58 and 59.

GEOLOGY NOTE Along with everyone else and their dogs, geologists run trips here to inspect the Devonian cliffs above the upper lake. They were once reefs formed under warm tropical seas by organisms called stromatoporoids, marine invertebrates of varying shapes and sizes. The centres of bulbous-shaped stromos are often leached, leaving behind vugs (pockmarks), which make excellent hand- and footholds.

ARCHEOLOGICAL NOTE The red ochre pictographs at the upper lake and in the canyon are believed to have been painted well over a thousand years ago, probably by ancestors of the Kootenays as part of a vision quest. Also take a look at prehistoric rock shelters under the cliffs.

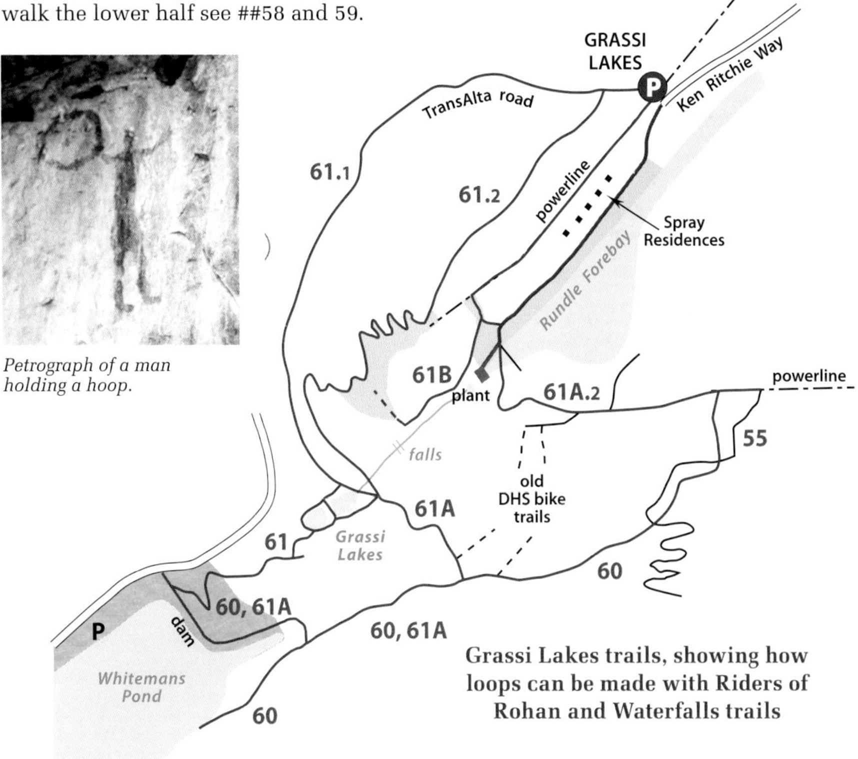

Petrograph of a man holding a hoop.

Grassi Lakes trails, showing how loops can be made with Riders of Rohan and Waterfalls trails

To Lower Grassi Lake

There are two ways to Lower Grassi Lake: the Upper Grassi Lakes trail is an easy walk on a gravelled TransAlta service road; For some people the original Grassi Lakes trail is a little steep.

From the parking lot follow either the TransAlta road or the trail starting at the biffy. The two routes join briefly, then part company after the gate.

1. Via Upper Grassi Lakes trail 1.6 km

Stay on the road, an easy but uninteresting uphill forest plod. The only points of interest are a ruined cabin and a memorial bench near the halfway point. The voices you hear above are mountain bikers zooming down The Reclaimer, built in 2005 by TAG (a group that came out of ROWG and BCEAG) to replace The Claimer that used to cut across the road. A slight descent brings you to the level of the lower lake. Continue past the northwest shore trail to the intersection with Grassi's trail. Turn right.

The steps.

2. Via Grassi Lakes trail 1.4 km

Turn off to the left on Grassi's trail and enjoy a gradual uphill traverse that crosses a number of springs (prime location for butterworts) to a viewpoint with interpretive sign. Look up to Ha-Ling Peak and the magnificent waterfall below the lakes, which not many people realize is Canmore Creek (née Whitemans Creek). Down below lies the Spray hydro plant, the colourful Rundle Forebay and powerline rights-of-way.

Above the viewpoint the trail twists uphill, ultimately climbing rundlestone steps to the right of a weeping wall. (See OPTIONAL DESCENT #61B.) The steps and railing are modern. The original wooden ladder required you to steady yourself on the crag to the right.

Near the top is Grassi's rustic seat where you can rest and read interpretive signs. That done, continue up, then traverse left along a bench above cliffs. A few seconds after crossing Canmore Creek on a bridge, emerge on TransAlta's service road and cross it.

To the lakes 440 m return

Walk past the green biffy. The gleam of azure you see a minute later is *not* Lake Minnewanka as one tourist was overheard to say to another; it is lower Grassi Lake. I love coming here to drool over the clarity and colour of the water.

The trail follows the left shoreline past memorial benches to a junction between the lakes. Should you go to the right here, you would pass Grassi's plaque, then contour around the north shoreline back to the TransAlta road.

Most people save this option for the return and continue along the left shore of the even more beautiful upper lake to its far end. This lake is not seepage from the reservoir above, but is fed by subaqueous springs. At its head, steps lead up into the canyon above.

But first continue around the lake to the north shore, where getting hit by a car was a pre K Country hazard. Because

Hwy. 742 lies directly above at this point, abandoned cars were pushed over the edge into the lake, to be left there and fished out years later. The more obvious danger nowadays comes from falling rocks dislodged by climbers and sheep.

Below the pockmarked cliffs are prehistoric rock shelters you can huddle in out of range of rocks and rain. Look for daubs of red ochre (hand prints?) at the entrance. Grassi built dividing walls and drystone walls on the outside and benches and fireplaces inside. He and his friends would pluck raspberries from bushes near the entrance, then untie the raft to go for a bit of a paddle.

From here you can connect with the "between the lakes" trail and the trail around the north shore of the lower lake without backtracking.

To the petrographs and dam 340 m

No need to flog up scree any more. A well-signposted trail leaves the far end of upper Grassi Lake and climbs steps to a T-junction below Gardener's Wall. Turn right up more steps into the canyon mouth. A little farther on, step right to view the large petrograph boulder. Above an interpretive sign are rock paintings of a man holding what looks like a hoop, a man throwing a spear, a caribou and tally marks possibly used for counting.

Return to the main trail and carry on through the canyon, where at certain times of the year the shortest stream in the Rockies springs forth below the dam face and after watering a few arnicas disappears down a hole below the cliff on the right side. This is the place to look for picas.

From here the latest trail version climbs the earth face of Whitemans Dam via flights of steps up the middle, where you are relatively safe from falling rocks. High up at a T-junction with signpost, the hiker's trail veers left up slippery shales, then (much better) zigs to the locked gate on the dam road at the junction with Hwy. 762.

Climbing into the canyon before steps. A good viewpoint for the two Grassi Lakes.

Signpost en route to Whitemans Dam.

#61B Waterfalls trail, looking upward from the lower falls.

OPTIONAL RETURNS

61A via Riders of Rohan

Distance from dam 1 km via no. 1 to Lower Grassi Lake; 2.7 km via no. 2 to trailhead

There are two ways back from the dam via #60 Riders of Rohan. Route no. 1 takes you back to Lower Grassi Lake. Route no. 2 returns you to the trailhead.

To junction 120589, 700 m
On reaching the dam, turn left and cross it. Walk alongside the intake canal, then at the intake turn right onto a trail and climb to a T-junction with map. Turn left and descend rather steeply to T-junction 120589.

1. To TransAlta road 300 m
Turn left onto a narrower trail that descends a rather beautiful mossy forest past the abandoned DHS trail "itt" and assorted boulders. Duck under the penstock and join TransAlta's service road, which takes you down to the intersection with Grassi's trail near Lower Grassi Lake.

2. To trailhead 2.4 km
At T-junction 120589 keep straight on Riders of Rohan and follow it down an even steeper hill to the upper 4-way junction with Highline trail at 124590. Go straight to the lower 4-way junction. Cross Highline and descend ever more gradually, going either way at a split, to the powerline right-of-way at the one-way sign at 126594.

Turn left and walk the powerline access road, in late June a hot spot for yellow lady's slipper orchids. Keep going straight. (Service road to right runs along the bank of Rundle Forebay; service road to left ends at the penstock.)

Wind down to a bridge crossing Rundle Forebay near the hydro plant. Close by to your right is the $480,000 wildlife-only bridge built as a G8 legacy and hailed as "a significant link in the wildlife corridor between Banff National Park and Kananaskis Country." Grassi's trail wasn't the only casualty when the forebay was built.

On reaching the access road to the plant, turn right and pound pavement past Spray Residences to Grassi Lakes parking lot.

61B Waterfall trail

Unofficial trail
Distance 1.4 km

A rough, often wet trail, in no way suitable for the casual tourist, connects Grassi's trail to the hydro plant area via Canmore Creek. In reverse, this is the route ice climbers use to access the Canmore Junkyard, once called the ultimate practice area. Some junkyard! In summer the waterfalls are spectacular.

Descend Grassi's trail. After the initial steps with handrail, make two more zigs, then turn off to the right on a faint trail.

A gradual descent on scree, often running with water from seeps, leads to the cliff base and the waterfalls. See the photo on page 17.

Still on the trail, descend a little, then traverse left into trees. The trail resumes the descent, steeply at first, then easing off as it heads for the lower falls. After this the creek quietens down and the going is flat and easy. Near a small reservoir, transfer to a service track. Go straight at the first T-junction and walk to the left of a fenced-in area. (En route the abandoned Claimer DHS bike trail comes in from the left.) At the next Y-junction of tracks there is a choice of routes.

If you go right, a track takes you out to the hydro plant access road. Turn left and plod pavement to Grassi Lakes parking lot. If you go left, climb a short, steep hill, at the top turning right, onto a powerline right-of-way with trail. This takes you directly to the end of the parking lot.

62 AM Trail—map 9

Half-day hike
Official trail with occasional numbered junctions, then unofficial trail
Distance 3.7 km one way to EEOR
Height gain 580 m (1903 ft.) to EEOR
High point 2000 m (6562 ft.) at EEOR
Map 82 O/3 Canmore

Access Canmore Nordic Centre, located on Spray Lakes Road. Use the near parking lot.

There is only one designated hiking route at the Canmore Nordic Centre: a strenuous jaunt from the stadium to the north end of EEOR (East End of Rundle). Theoretically, you can walk any combination of ski and bike trail, but who would want to? The trails resemble a pile of spaghetti that's had a plate of spaghettini dropped on top of it. Not only is the network incredibly convoluted, it's almost totally in forest and without interest for people on foot.

AM stands for "alpine meadows." Sounds good, but in fact there aren't any. Also know the upper half of the route follows the line of an abandoned DHS bike trail and is very steep. There are plans in the works to make the trail more walker friendly. NOTE The trail from junction marker 51 up is closed between Dec 1 and Jun 15.

BEAR NOTE Before you go, check the K Country website for grizzly sightings.

AMENITIES NOTE In the day lodge: showers, soft couches and Fresh Trax Cafe, open 9 am–5:30 pm daily.

HISTORY The specific area you are visiting was once a ski hill called "the L" (or backward L), cleared in the mid 1940s and maintained by a group of volunteers, aided and abetted by Lawrence Grassi. A ski cabin at the bottom was fashioned from materials carried up from Grassi's house on Three Sisters Drive. I'm not sure what the L stands for, but maybe it's a more appropriate name for AM.

AM in the shallow gully after Back Door.

Bike trail section 2 km
Head for the day lodge. Cross the cross-country stadium to the left of the lodge, aiming for waxing huts on the far side. To their right is a track climbing diagonally left to right out of the stadium to junction marker 113. Turn left onto Centennial.

Climbing gently all the while, go straight at 3-way junction 114. At the next 4-way, junction 115, go straight onto EKG trail, which is single track. At T-junction 51 turn left onto Killer Bees, which winds around a lot to T-junction 52. Turn left onto Back Door and follow it past T-junction 53 to its high point, where two trails turn off to the left. Take the first one, which has a "No Bikes" sign. There is nothing to indicate this is AM.

So far the going has been easy and pleasant along the fringes of the CNC in a wildlife corridor. Now the route is about to get a lot steeper.

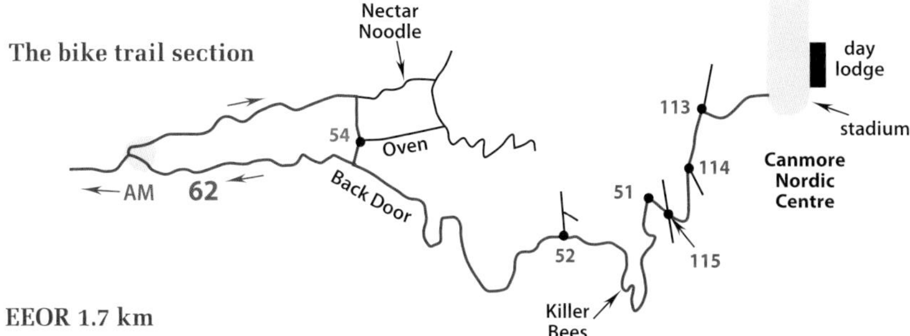

To EEOR 1.7 km

The trail follows the bed of a shallow, treed gully, ultimately turning right and climbing in duplicate onto a ridge. At a junction on the crest at 117610 turn left. (The trail to right descends to Nectar Noodle. See OPTIONAL DESCENT.)

Finally leaving the bikers behind, plod up the steep northeast ridge of EEOR, stopping at all three openings to admire increasingly better views of Canmore. At a Y-junction with blue flagging, keep left. (Good trail to right appears to be making for the gully on your right.) Continue uphill, then climb even more steeply up left OVER a DHS technical feature. Zig back right, going either way at a split. Left is best. (The right-hand split accesses another trail, fainter but cairned, bound for the gully. How come this gully is so popular?)

A left turn leads into a much appreciated traverse across the full width of the ridge to a viewpoint above the east face overlooking Whitemans Gap and Ha Ling Peak. Possibly this is the official ending to the trail, because here you join a climber's access route come up from Hwy. 742.

Turn right and on trail climb up the edge of the east face now steepening into alternating rockbands and treed ledges below the great cliff itself, which towers over everything. Behind you the view expands to include the Bow Valley and the peaks of Ehagay Nakoda.

At the very last you head left through some trees and come to a full stop against rock. Climber's access trails continue. One heads out along a ledge to the left. Another follows the dipping rock base to the right, eventually reaching Rundle's second buttress, which has been in view at odd times during the ascent.

OPTIONAL DESCENT 700 m

Descend the same way to junction 117610 on the ridge crest. Continue straight and descend a long hill of varying gradients and trail widths to Nectar Noodle at a T-junction with no number. Turn right here and continue straight past Oven at marker 54 to Back Door. Turn left and return the same way you came up.

Climbing the last leg to EEOR. In the background at right are Mt. Lawrence Grassi and Ha Ling Peak.

63 CANMORE TRAIL to Canmore Nordic Centre —map 9

Half-day walk return
Official trail with numbered markers
Distance 2.2 km
Height gain 110 m (361 ft.)
Map 82 O/3 Canmore

Access Canmore. Mineside parking lot on the southwest side of the bridge over the Bow River.
Also accessible on foot from the high end of Three Sisters Drive.

Pre Legacy Trail, this is the usual route between Canmore and the Canmore Nordic Centre (CNC).

REFRESHMENT NOTE Fresh Trax Cafe in the day lodge at the Nordic Centre is open 9 am–5:30 pm daily.

The steps at Rundle power plant.

To bluffs 1 km

Walk out to the trail on the bank of the Bow River. Turn left and duck under the road bridge. The trail runs along the diketop to a gate. On joining Rundle Plant Lane turn right.

Just before reaching Rundle power plant, turn left and climb steps to a 4-way junction. (Trail to left comes in from Three Sisters Drive.) Turn right on a dirt trail which climbs to grassy bluffs above incipient hoodoos—a great viewpoint. Here, at T-junction 138610, turn left onto a trail signed "Canmore Trail." (Trail straight on is #64 to Georgetown.)

To CNC 1.2 km

After a dip, the trail climbs onto the banktop above an unnamed creek holding a small reservoir. Disregard numerous bike trails peeling off from left and right at unmarked junctions and at markers 41 and 42. At a Y-junction with marker 43, come to a track and turn right.

Almost immediately step off the track to the right and circle around left UNDER the bridge. The grassy track you join is part of the disc golf course. The next (4-way) junction is staggered. Curve second right—still on the disc golf course—and climb alongside a wooden retaining wall to a wire basket at the top of the rise. Looking up, you can spot the large map of the course at the edge of the CNC access road. Either climb the slope direct or, more easily, continue to follow the track slightly downhill to a kiosk. Then turn left on a trail that climbs to the map.

Cross the parking lot and turn left. The day lodge is the building on the right next to the stadium.

From marker 43 to day lodge, also showing #64.2 in purple

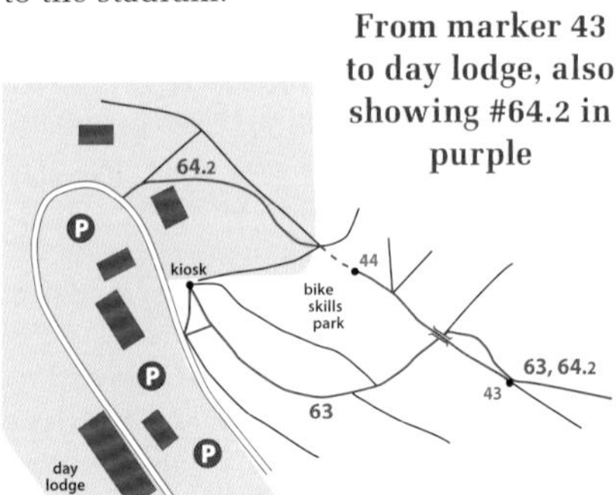

64 GEORGETOWN INTERPRETIVE TRAIL —map 9

Short day
Official trail
Distance from access 1, 3.7 km; loop with Nordic Centre, 8.3 km
Height gain/loss to Georgetown, 50 m (164 ft.); to mine site, 70 m (230 ft.)
Map 82 O/3 Canmore

Access Canmore.
1. Mineside parking lot on the southwest side of the bridge over the Bow River.
2. Canmore Nordic Centre, located on Spray Lakes Road. Park at the far end lot near the biathlon stadium.

An easy forest walk to the site of a mining community called Georgetown. You can start from either Canmore or the Canmore Nordic Centre or do a combo with a stop for lunch at Fresh Trax Cafe. If mazing through the Nordic Centre trails, it's worth picking up a map of summer trails from the day lodge for a small payment.

REFRESHMENT NOTE Fresh Trax Cafe in the day lodge at the Canmore Nordic Centre is open 9 am–5:30 pm daily.

HISTORY NOTE Georgetown mine was developed by the Canmore Navigation and Coal Company in 1912. Because of its remote location north of the Cochrane Mine, miners were accommodated on site in 40 houses supplied with running water and electricity. When the mine closed only three years later, the houses were hauled to Mineside, where a few still stand at the top end of Three Sisters Drive. The company store was dragged down the ice of the Bow River in 1918 into Townside and eventually became Marra's Grocery, which is not the new store built in 1978 that is now Stonewaters on Main Street.

FROM ACCESS 1

To trail from access 2, 1.2 km

Walk out to the trail on the bank of the Bow River, turn left and duck under the road bridge. The trail runs along the diketop

The bluffs.

to a gate. On joining Rundle Plant Lane turn right.

Just before reaching Rundle power plant, turn left and climb steps to a 4-way. Turn right on a trail that climbs onto grassy bluffs above incipient hoodoos—a great viewpoint. Here, at T-junction 138610, stay right. (Canmore trail to left climbs to the CNC.) In another 210 m again keep right. (To left is a single-track bike trail named Sponge Bog and the shortcut used by access 2.)

FROM ACCESS 2

To Georgetown trail 1.1 km

Start from the far end parking lot. Following the sketch map on page 252, head east, taking the paved trail to the left of the wax room building in the meadow. In a few metres the trail splits and downgrades to dirt. Go right. Touch on a paved trail at a bend, then cut right across waste ground to a bench and marker 44. This is adjacent to the bike skills park. A trail starts beyond the marker and is signed "Georgetown

Trail." Follow it over a bridge to Y-junction 43. Keep left.

Keep straight at junction 42, shortly after running along the banktop of an unnamed creek. Note the glint of a small reservoir down in its depths. After passing multiple junction 41, turn left at the next, unmarked junction onto a shortcut that descends and, converging with Sponge Bog, spills onto Georgetown interpretive trail. Turn left.

To Georgetown 2.5 km

The trail descends, then climbs to star-shaped junction 39 with bike trails, including Callaghan, which used to be the road to Georgetown. Stay right on what is now a track and descend a long hill to the flats of the Bow River. A long straight between a steep bank and willowy channels brings you to the site of Georgetown at 125631 in a large clearing infilling with small spruce trees. Apart from interpretive signs at the T-junction, there is absolutely nothing to see. The mine was located up the hillside to the left. The trail ahead can be followed a long way, but eventually you come to a full stop at a channel of the Bow.

Coal Chutes loop ~900 m

At the T-junction turn left up a hill to a 4-way. Turn right onto Coal Chutes bike trail, then left up a winding track. At the next junction follow the track around to the left to its end at the lower mine portal. A seepage of rust-coloured water escapes from the entrance, which has been covered up. Just beyond is a slag heap. Higher up the slope is another portal.

Turn left and follow Coal Chutes bike trail down a steep coal bank. At a flattening look for mining junk in the trees to the left. After another down step, the trail turns right and back left to the 4-way junction.

Go straight down the hill and return the same way.

Alternatively, turn right at the 4-way and climb to the Nordic Centre for some refreshment. Then regain your outgoing trail at the bluffs by following either the route from access 2 or #63.

Interpretive signs at Georgetown site.

The entrance to Georgetown mine before it was filled in.

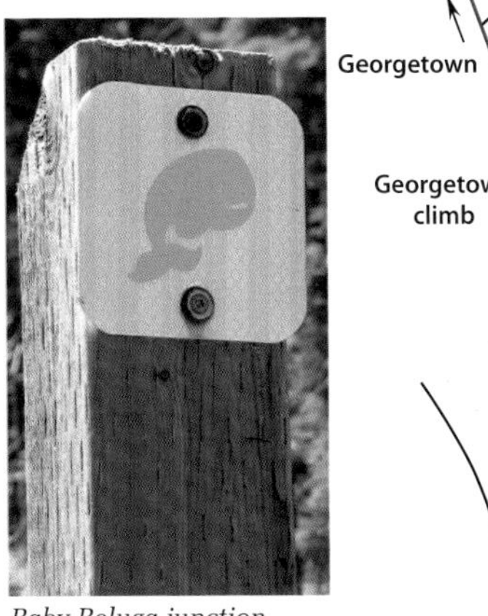
Baby Beluga junction.

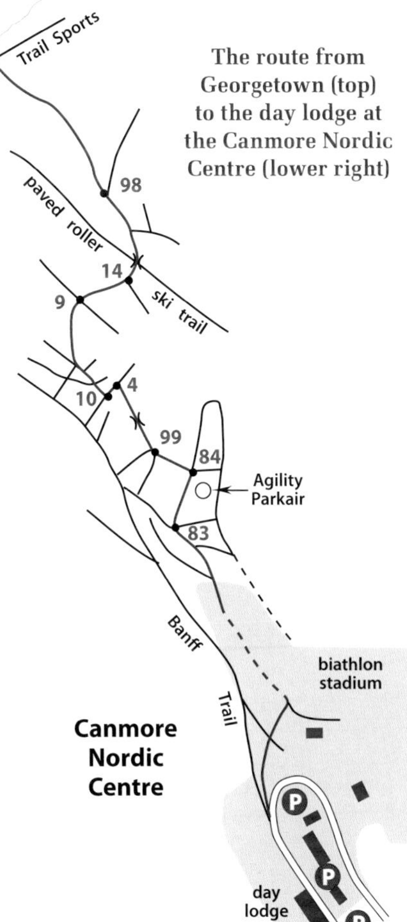

The route from Georgetown (top) to the day lodge at the Canmore Nordic Centre (lower right)

OPTIONAL RETURN

64A to the Nordic Centre

Official trails with numbered junctions
Distance 2.4 km
Height gain 100 m (328 ft.)

If taking in the Nordic Centre, be prepared to navigate a confusion of bike and ski trails with numbered and unnumbered junctions. And just because you see the odd sign pointing the way to the Nordic Centre, it doesn't mean you should follow it. Often that trail goes all around the boonies first.

At the 4-way turn right onto a track and pass the foundation walls of a building. Staying on track, climb Killer Hill, a long, steep hill renamed the Georgetown Climb. At a 4-way with Salt Lake go straight uphill. At the 4-way with EKG at marker 33 go straight uphill. At a T-junction turn left on Salt Lake and parallel the paved roller-ski trail, en route passing 3 trails forking off to the left. Cross the bridge over the roller-ski trail.

At the following marker 14 with Baby Beluga keep right. Cross Get Out at marker 9. Up next is a very convoluted area below Banff Trail: at the 4-way, turn left and, forsaking all other trails, make a beeline to marker 10. Turn left to marker 4 nearby. Turn right on Get In and cross a bridge to marker 99. Turn left to marker 84. Turn right by the side of Agility Parkair to marker 83. Keep going straight into a large open area near the biathlon range where the trail peters out.

Continue ahead and on hitting a paved trail turn right. Go straight at a 4-way and into the far end parking lot. To reach Fresh Trax Cafe in the day lodge, turn right and walk up the road to the building on the right.

If returning to Canmore from the day lodge use #63 Canmore trail in reverse.

65 LARCH ISLAND/POLICEMAN CREEK LOOP—map 9

Engine Bridge over the Bow River. In the background is the Ehagay Nakoda massif: Ha-Ling Peak to right, Mt. Lawrence Grassi at centre.

Half-day walk
Official trails, interpretive signs, walkway signs and km signposts
Distance 7.7 km
Map 82 O/3 Canmore

Access Canmore. Mineside parking lot on the southwest side of the bridge over the Bow River.

Also accessible from downtown Canmore via walkways leaving 10, 13, 14, 15, 16, 17 Sts., 11 Ave., Larch Ave. (various), 8 Ave., 7 Ave., Fairholme Drive, Pinewood Cres., Birchwood Pl., Railway Ave., Main (8) St., Riverview Pl.

A flat, easy walk exploring the flood plain in and around Canmore, using in part a disused railway line and interpretive trails alongside the Bow River and its many channels, including Policeman Creek. The description includes one shortcut and one variation sans shops that are coloured blue in the text.

REFRESHMENT NOTE At the end of the loop you'll pass a wide range of watering holes and eateries.

NAMING NOTE Larch Island is named after the nearby street, which is not named after nearby larches. Policeman Creek used to be called Carey Creek until the NWMP built a barracks in 1893 directly across from Charles Carey's house.

HISTORY NOTE Engine Bridge and the spur line were built by the CPR in 1892 to connect mines on the southwest side of the Bow River to the main CPR track.

Rundle power plant is the last stage of the Spray Lakes hydroelectric project. In brief: the 97 m (320 ft.) drop from Rundle Forebay via an underground penstock drives the generator that produces electricity. Used water flows into the Bow River—temporarily freed until the next go-around at Kananaskis Dam.

To Engine Bridge 1.3 km
Walk out to the trail on the bank of the Bow River and turn left. After a gate turn right and duck under the footbridge and road bridge. The trail runs along the diketop past the Shareholders Cabin built in 1910 by the Canmore Coal Company. Pass plentiful memorial benches. Just beyond Granddad's bench, intersect Rundle Plant Lane at a gate. Turn right. You are now walking the railway spur line to No. 2 mine. Follow it up to a T-junction at Rundle power plant. Behind the plant and the substation rise vertical walls of till.

Keeping rightish, cross the spillway and then a trestle bridge. Back on the spur line, cross a trail. (Trail to left leads

Round-leaved orchids on Larch Island.

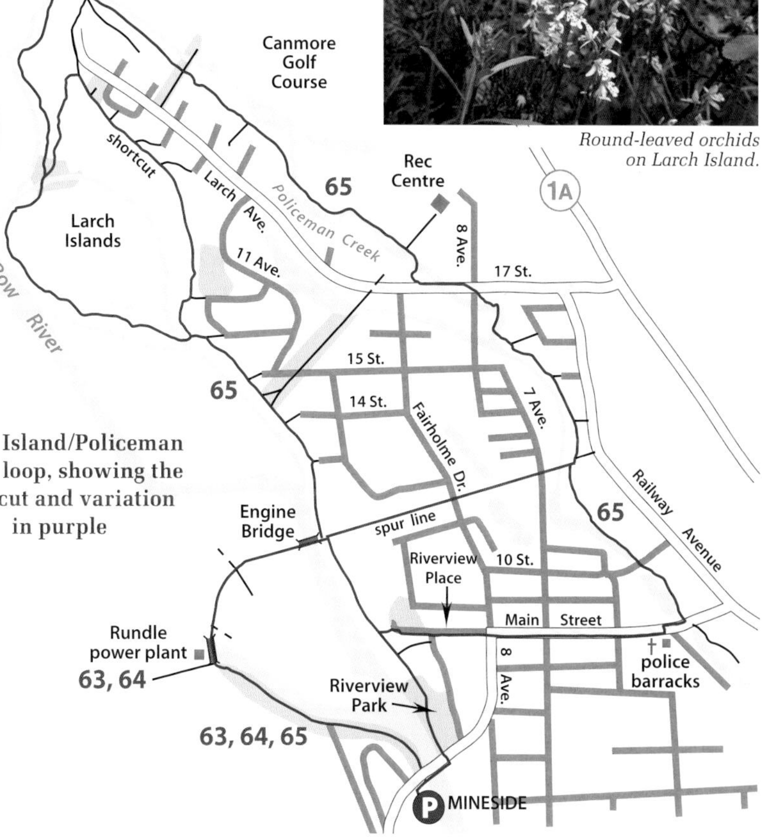

Canmore Golf Course
Rec Centre
1A
65
Larch Islands
shortcut
Larch Ave.
Policeman Creek
8 Ave.
11 Ave.
17 St.
Bow River
15 St.
65
14 St.
Fairholme Dr.
7 Ave.
Railway Avenue
65
Engine Bridge
spur line
Riverview Place
10 St.
Main Street
Rundle power plant
63, 64
8 Ave.
police barracks
Riverview Park
63, 64, 65
MINESIDE

Larch Island/Policeman Creek loop, showing the shortcut and variation in purple

NWMP barracks on Main Street. In summer it is open Wed–Sun 10 am–6 pm; Mon–Tue noon to 4 pm. In winter/spring the hours are noon to 4 pm depending on volunteer availability.

Big Head on Main Street. Designed by Al Henderson, Big Head is a translation of Ceanmore, another spelling for Canmore.

to the old Cochrane mine, which operated between 1888 and 1893, its passages now flooded by seeps.) In the same distance again come to the impressive Engine Bridge over the Bow.

To Larch Island 680 m

At the 4-way junction on the far bank turn left. (Spur line ahead, Riverview Park to right.)

The trail follows the east bank of the Bow and then a narrow channel past six walkways leading to streets 13 through 16. At 138618 is a T-junction. Turn left over a footbridge onto Larch Island. (Trail ahead is shortcut no. 1.)

Larch Island hiking trail 1.6 km

A narrow trail signed "Larch Island Hiking Trail" meanders through wolf willows to the left of sloughs, then parallels the Bow River with side trails off to the shoreline. In spring, all this area is the place to look for round-leaved orchids Franklin's lady slipper and the exquisite bird's eye primrose. Numbers on posts hark back to the time when this was an interpretive trail.

After interpretive No. 4, the trail leaves the Bow and follows the willowy bank of a narrow channel. In a slightly open area, a little boggy underfoot, is unmarked Y-junction 135622 with the shortcut. If not taking the shortcut, skip the next two paragraphs.

SHORTCUT This reduces the loop to 5.4 km. At Y-junction 135622 go straight and back into forest, passing numbers 6 and 7 en route to reaching a T-junction on a dike. At the junction is a sign "Larch Island Hiking Trail." Turn right. (Left connects with the main loop at the head of Larch Avenue.) A good, wide trail runs along the dike to the west of Larch Avenue, offering 4 accesses onto the avenue before passing a hockey rink and the Childhood Development Centre. Shortly after a walkway comes in from 17 Street, you reach the Larch Island footbridge.

Return to Engine Bridge and continue straight to where the walkway comes in from Riverview Place. Now read the last paragraph.

Keep left. The trail continues to follow the bank of the channel to a seat with a clear view of EEOR and Bruno's Buttress on Mt. Rundle. Continue to a wider channel of the Bow, veering right along its bank to a memorial seat at 135628. From it is a good view of the jagged summit ridge of Mt. Princess Margaret.

Policeman Creek 2.7 km

Turn right onto a dike that parallels the beginnings of Policeman Creek. At Y-junction 136627 keep left.

The trail runs between Larch Avenue and Canmore Golf Course, soon between a high fence and back gardens. Cross a footbridge and swing right in spruce trees alongside a creek widening. At a 4-way go straight. (Rec centre to left, powerline trail to right.)

Cross a footbridge over the creek, then turn left. Emerge on 17 Street. Turn left and walk sidewalk across a road bridge to a trail crossing with lights. Cross 17 Street, then 8 Avenue to where the trail continues in the angle between 8 Avenue and 17 Street.

The trail crosses the creek twice en route to the east bank for a stretch through spruce trees. En route three side trails connect with Railway Avenue. Come to a T-junction at 149615 with the railway spur line. This is where the variation takes off. If continuing on, skip the next two paragraphs.

SPUR LINE VARIATION This reduces the loop by 350 m. Turn right, then keep straight across a footbridge and between ponds. Cross 7 Avenue. Beeline between more ponds, the one on the left being Canmore's outdoor skating rink. Cross Fairholme Drive. The trail continues straight as an arrow between recently planted trees, across an alley, then between natural forest to the 4-way at Engine Bridge.

Turn left. A good, wide trail runs along a

Following a side channel on Larch Island.

Policeman Creek.

dike to the T-junction with the walkway from Riverview Place. Now read the last paragraph.

At T-junction 149615 turn right, then immediately left onto 12 Street. Follow it around to the right. The trail continues to the right of a gate and shortly runs alongside a section of the creek supplemented by springs where you'll see lots of mallards. Cross 10 Street. Continue alongside a widening of the creek and along a raised boardwalk to 8 Street, which is also Main Street. Emerge next to The Drake and the Big Head sculpture.

Main Street to Riverside Park 860 m
Turn right across the highway bridge. (NOTE Policeman Creek trail continues beyond 8 Street on boardwalk initially—a very popular 10-minute stroll with tourists. It ends at a T-junction near a footbridge. Going right, one can follow a trail to Spring Creek and cross it to 5 Street, then 3 Avenue where trails end. After this, looping requires much road bashing.)

Cross Main Street to the NWMP barracks. Next door is the United Church, dedicated to the Rev. C.W. Gordon, who under his pseudonym Ralph Connor was a prolific author with connections to the Lesueur family (see #5). Continue down to 8 Street, passing assorted eateries, bars and shops—the most notable of which is the historic Canmore Hotel, the Old Tyme Candy Shoppe and the two best book shops in the Bow Valley.

Cross 8 Street and walk down Riverview Place. At its end a walkway leads through to a T-junction on the east bank of the Bow River. Turn left.

Higashikawa Friendship Trail 560 m
Keep straight and enter Riverside Park with benches and picnic tables and a great view of the Three Sisters. On the right, plaques on a boulder explain the name of the trail. At the Y-junction following, keep left. Cross Bridge Road, then turn right and cross the footbridge over the Bow. Turn first left, go straight, then right into the parking lot.

66 CANMORE BENCHLANDS Harvie Heights trails—map 9

Memorial Bench Ridge, looking toward the Three Sisters, Mount Lawrence Grassi and Ha Ling Peak.

Half-day, short-day hikes
Official & unofficial trails
High point 1570 m (5150 ft.)
Map 82 O/3 Canmore

Access
1. Main access Hwy. 1 (Trans-Canada Hwy.) west of Canmore. Heading west, take exit 86 (signed "Canmore, Bow Valley Trail") and follow the service road west for ~900 m to a parking lot with kiosk on the right side.
2 Hamlet of Harvie Heights Hwy. 1 (Trans-Canada Hwy.) west of Canmore. Heading west, take exit 83 (signed "Harvie Heights") and follow the service road west. Just past Gateway Motor Lodge, turn right onto Blue Jay Road, which leads into this rather private community. At main access points onto the trails, there are "No Parking" signs. Park elsewhere on the verge.
Also accessible from #67 Stoneworks Canyon, from #68 Silvertip trails in a number of places including Montane Traverse and Douglas Fir trail.

The hiking and mountain biking trails of Canmore Benchlands run along the northeast side of the Bow Valley above Canmore between Harvie Heights and the Graymont Exshaw Quarry. Or to put it another way, along the lower slopes of Squaw's Tit, Lady Macdonald and Grotto Mountain. They can be neatly divided up into four sections. Route #66 describes the trails between the hamlet of Harvie Heights and Stoneworks Creek.

Scramblers and climbers use them to access Squaw's Tit and The Alcove sport climbing area.

Not all the trails are described. Johnny's Trail up Stoneworks Creek is written up separately under #67 Stoneworks Canyon. The horse trails developed by Cross Zee Ranch between Meander and Stoneworks Creek have been omitted.

Aside from the loops described, trails can be used in a variety of ways to make shorter loops. Longer days can be had

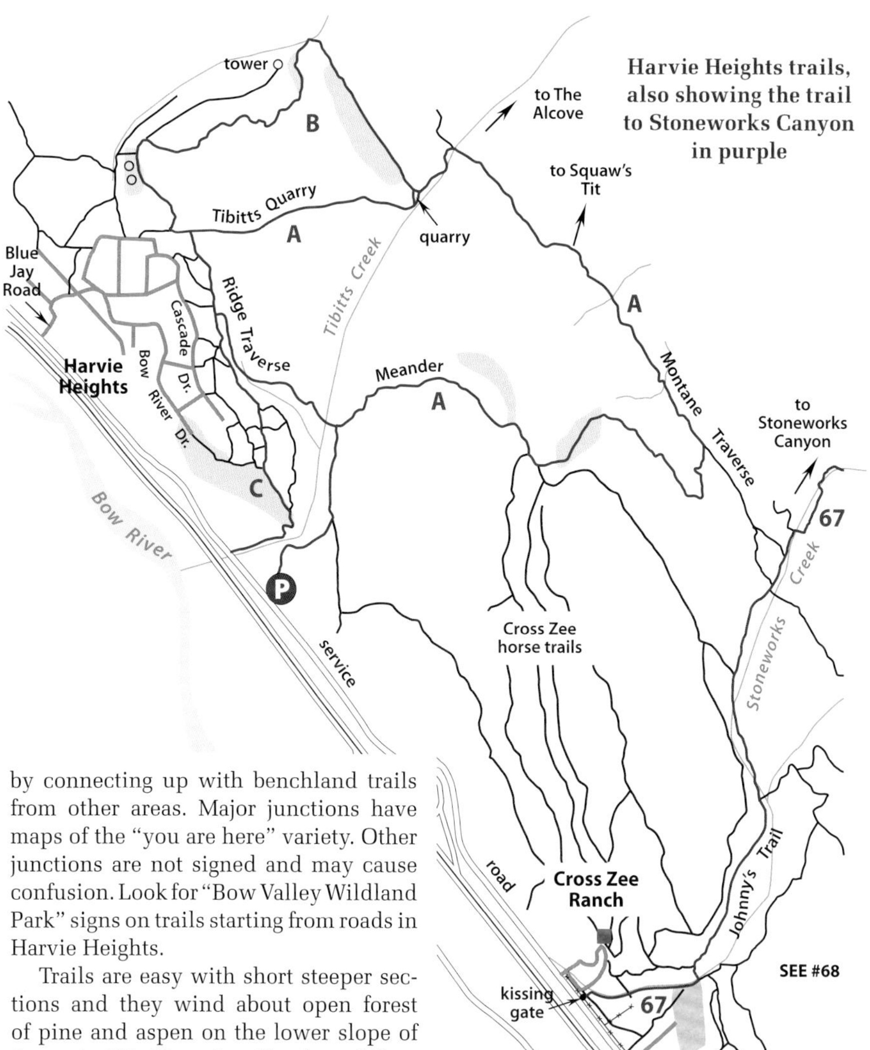

by connecting up with benchland trails from other areas. Major junctions have maps of the "you are here" variety. Other junctions are not signed and may cause confusion. Look for "Bow Valley Wildland Park" signs on trails starting from roads in Harvie Heights.

Trails are easy with short steeper sections and they wind about open forest of pine and aspen on the lower slope of Squaw's Tit. Occasionally they follow benches and small ridges lined with Douglas firs and it's here where you get the views. Located on the sunny side of the Bow Valley, these are especially useful in early spring and late fall when trails across the valley are snowbound.

WARNING Bears and cougars frequent the area. Don't travel solo, and keep dogs on a leash for their own protection.

REFRESHMENT NOTE No refreshments are available in Harvie Heights. In spring there is water in upper Tibitts Creek.

QUARRY NOTE Look for the abandoned rundlestone quarry at the upper end of Tibitts Quarry trail. Guy Tibitts, described as being of slight build with thick glasses and a hot temper, built an access road from the Canmore Ranger Station and in partnership with Jack Summerhays worked the quarry for a brief period in the late 1940s, early 1950s. After the government took away the lease, Summerhays went on to mine siltstone in Cougar Creek. See #71A.

66A Meander loop

Short day
Official trails
Distance 7.2 km
Height gain ~230 m (~755 ft.)

The big loop.

FROM MAIN ACCESS

Meander trail 2.8 km

A trail leaves the west end of the parking lot and crosses the powerline right-of-way. Keeping straight, climb gradually through forest to T-junction 139647 with map. Turn right. (Left is Ridge Traverse.)

A mossy dell opens out into forest. Keep right twice, then left twice around Skull Corner. (The two good trails to right lead to Cross Zee Ranch.) Climb more steeply up the fall line, then traverse right and up left to a T-junction with Montane Traverse. Turn left. (Montane Traverse to right leads to Stoneworks Creek.)

Montane Traverse 1.5 km

Not far along, cross a shallow gully and follow a ridge to its left with views of Mt. Rundle. Cross a stony creekbed. Enjoy more views en route to a sudden steep drop. (The cairn at the top signals the scrambler's takeoff for Squaw's Tit.)

Continue along to another stony creekbed that is Tibitts Creek. Cross it and turn left. (Walking upcreek gets you to The Alcove, a sport climbing area.) Follow the creek to unmarked T-junction 142656 with a track (née Tibitts Quarry Road). Go leftish on the track. (Trail to right is VARIATION #66B.)

Tibitts Quarry trail 1.2 km

Descend past Tibitts Quarry to a T-junction with map. Go straight. (Narrow trail to right climbs through the quarry to join #66B on a bench.) In only a few metres keep straight on the main track (a grassy track to right runs parallel), and curving right, descend into mature forest, the track stony and uninteresting. Note the parallel trail joining in from the right at a bend. Low down, come to T-junction 134654. Turn left. (The track ahead emerges on Grotto Road at a gate. En route VARIATION #66B joins in from the right.)

Ridge Traverse 1 km

The trail crosses a dip. At the T-junction following go straight. Then in thinned forest keep left three times. (Third trail off the right side at 135651 is ALTERNATIVE FINISH #66C Memorial Bench Ridge.)

Enter Weird Woods, a beautiful old-growth forest of fir and spruce where the slow seepage of groundwater keeps watered a forest of mare's tails. On leaving

Tibitts Quarry.

Tibitts Quarry trail.

it, keep straight everywhere and traverse grassy banks of the spring creek, then of Tibitts Creek to T-junction 139647.

Turn right and return to the parking lot.

VARIATION

66B Montane Traverse west

Distance 2 km

This scenic option to Tibitts Quarry trail adds 800 m to the loop.

At T-junction 142656 turn right and gain a bench at the point where the trail through Tibitts Quarry joins in from the left. Follow the scenic bench trail past a rustic seat and ultimately down off the bench to the upper communications tower. The trail continues, veering left, then easily down through open spruce forest to the towers access road. Turn left. In a few metres, at the edge of a meadow surrounding the lower two towers, turn left on a trail that wanders along to a T-junction with Tibitts Quarry trail.

Turn left and shortly join the main loop at T-junction 134654. Turn right onto Ridge Traverse.

Montane Traverse west.

ALTERNATIVE FINISH

66C Memorial Bench Ridge

Distance 1.3 km

A lovely ridge with a steepish drop-off at the end. There are many ways onto this ridge from Harvie Heights via trails leaving Cascade Drive and the end of Bow River Drive.

Leave Ridge Traverse at T-junction 135651 and go straight, following the ridge though open forest. All side trails to right descend to Cascade Drive. Those to left join Ridge Traverse. The main trail arrives at the south edge where grass sweeps down toward the service road. Turn left. (Trail to right follows the edge downhill to Bow River Drive.)

Walk past many memorial benches to ridge's end viewpoint at two picnic tables. (A trail heading left at the tables backtracks along the gradually descending north edge to Ridge Traverse.)

Descend off the point, making two steep zigs down to Tibitts Creek. DON'T CROSS. The trail turns right and can be followed alongside the creek to Palliser trail bike path. Turn left and reach the trailhead in just a few minutes.

Stoneworks Canyon.

67 STONEWORKS CANYON—map 6

Short-day hike
Unofficial trail with old signs, official trail with blue posts, then route; creek crossings likely dry
Distance 2.9 km to canyon
Height gain 341 m (1120 ft.)
High point 1676 m (5500 ft.)
Map 82 O/3 Canmore

Access Hwy. 1 (Trans-Canada Hwy.). Heading west, turn off at interchange 89. At the T-junction turn left onto the service road that parallels the hwy. on the northeast side. Park on the left shoulder of the road between the gated access road into a quarry and waypoint 149626. DO NOT park near Cross Zee Ranch's access road.
Also accessible from ##66 and 68 Benchland trails.

This (almost) subterranean climber's canyon is a terrific choice for stinking-hot days when you're looking for somewhere cool. Most of the route is on good trail through pine forest with a bit of rock-hopping at the end. Since the last edition the pesky barbed wire fences have been removed courtesy of Cross Zee Ranch and volunteers. See sketch map on page 270.

The trail is the climbers access to the canyon. Scramblers use it to access "Princess Anne."

ACCESS NOTE Recently, access onto Johnny's Trail has been made more difficult thanks to a "No Trespassing" notice on the gate to the disused quarry (future subdivision) and the diversion of Stoneworks Creek back onto its original path. There are plans in the works for a new access trail to be built from Palliser Village, but in the meantime locals are using this new route.

WARNING NOTE Most of the year, the creekbed is dry or has very little water in it. But as can be seen by the churned-up stones, it's subject to flash floods, which can affect access, even trap you in the canyon.

NAMING NOTE Access is via Johnny's Trail, named after Johnny Boychuk, "Canmore's Cowboy," who for 45 years ran Johnny's Riding Stables, later to become the Cross Zee Ranch under Jim and Brenda Stanton, though Johnny still lived there until his death in 2006 aged 101.

FLORA NOTE Interestingly, a Canmorite had a thriving sideline going in this valley many years ago, collecting flower seeds of a rare purple sedum and selling them all over the world.

To Johnny's Trail 400 m
At 149626 on the service road, climb the bank to a gap in the fence marked by a cairn and flagging. Cross the powerline right-of-way and a few metres of easy ground to Stoneworks Creek diversion. Turn right and walk a gravel road to a sheet-piling bulkhead designed to keep water in the diversion channel. After the road ends continue on the right bank for a few metres and at 156642 cross the creekbed to the kissing gate and trail sign on the left bank. Only a few steps away is an obvious wide track, which is Johnny's Trail come up from the Cross Zee. Turn right.

Johnny's Trail to the canyon 1.7 km
This track follows the left bank of Stoneworks Canyon, and while stony and a little eroded, is straightforward. Remember the large cross stuck in the ground with the word "Midnight" written on the crosspiece? According to Jim, Midnight was a favourite black horse who was buried here in 1989.

At a signposted T-junction continue straight. (Trail to right crosses the creekbed into the Silvertip trails.)

Shortly, the track runs into the wandering creekbed. Follow cairns, after the third cairn transferring onto the resurrected track. Shortly after, keep straight at a T-junction. (Trail to left is Cross Zee horse trail.) The next T-junction with Montane Traverse is signposted. Go straight.

In just a few metres continue straight. (Trail to left is a well-used shortcut to Montane Traverse.) The track climbs a little more steeply to a third signposted T-junction. Continue straight on a narrower trail marked with a blue post. (Trail to left is Montane Traverse heading west.)

The canyon 800+ m

At a split go right and descend to the creekbed at the start of the valley confines. Walk up the stones a way, looking for a trail starting along the left bank. (There's also a trail on the right at this point, but eventually you have to cross to the left.) In a kilometre you're back in the creekbed. Head to the next cairn, where a very short bit of trail leads back into the bed just before the narrows. The canyon starts suddenly as a deliciously cool tunnel of waterworn rock. Emerge momentarily at The Underworld Crag, featuring climbs with off-putting names like Spider in the Tub, then head back into another narrows, emerging a second time into a bay with a cave on the left wall, a cool retreat reverberating with the noise of running water. After a third narrows the valley opens up and you pass Weird Wall on the left. Cairns guide you up a steeper section of creekbed, then head off right to Arcade climbing cliff. At this point the creek turns left, but you've seen the best it has to offer.

GOING FARTHER

Scramblers can continue to follow the creekbed into the upper valley between Squaw's Tit, Princess Anne and Lady Macdonald. I'm told that Princess Ann, the highest peak of the three at 2758 m (9050 ft.), is an easy scramble via west slope screes and the south ridge.

Johnny's Trail leaving the stony creekbed at the third cairn.

Johnny's Trail beyond Montane Traverse.

68 CANMORE BENCHLANDS Silvertip trails—maps 9, 6

Montane Traverse. Photo Derek Ryder

Half-day, short-day hikes
Official & unofficial trails
High point 1550 m (5085 ft.)
Map 82 O/3 Canmore

Access Canmore.

1. Cougar Creek trailhead, located on Elk Run Blvd. at Cougar Creek crossing. Biffy.

2. Benchlands trail. Parking lot on NE side 360 east of the Hwy. 1 overpass.

3. Silvertip Resort at the end of Silvertip Trail.

4. Stoneworks Creek Hwy. 1 (Trans-Canada Hwy.) Heading west, turn off at interchange 89. At the T-junction turn left onto service road that parallels the hwy. on the northeast side. Park on the left shoulder of the road between the gated access road into a quarry and waypoint 149626. Do NOT park near Cross Zee Ranch's access road. Gives access to the west end of Douglas Fir Bench. See the sketch map on page 270.

Also accessible from #67 Stoneworks Canyon in two places; from #66 Harvie Heights trails at the junction of Montane Traverse and Johnny's Trail: from #71 Horseshoe loop on the SE bank of Cougar Creek (only accessible at low water levels). Also accessible from various streets in Eagle Terrace subdivision (no parking).

The hiking and mountain biking trails of Canmore Benchlands run along the northeast side of the Bow Valley above Canmore between Harvie Heights and the Graymont Exshaw Quarry. Or to put it another way, along the lower slopes of Squaw's Tit, Lady Macdonald and Grotto Mountain. They can be neatly divided up into four sections. Route #68 describes trails between Stoneworks Creek and Cougar Creek.

Trails are easy with short steeper sections that circle around Silvertip Resort, and Eagle Terrace subdivision on the lower slopes of Lady McDonald. Mostly they stay in pine and aspen forest, only occasionally following open ridges lined with Douglas firs. The hoodoos above access 2 are a prominent feature. Located on the sunny side of the Bow Valley, these trails are especially useful in spring and fall when trails across the valley are snowbound.

Aside from the loops described, trails can be used in a variety of ways to make shorter loops, especially if you're parked at access 3. Longer days can be had by connecting up with benchland trails from other areas. Major junctions have maps with "you are here" variety. Other junctions are not signed and may cause confusion.

ACCESS NOTE There are plans in the works for a new trailhead to be built near Palliser Village. This will give a more satisfactory start to Douglas Fir trail.

TRAIL CLOSURE NOTE Douglas Fir trail is closed between Dec. 1 and June 15. The upper bench trail (the most scenic trail of the lot) was closed permanently in 2005 "by ministerial order" after it was realized the spread of urbanization across the Bow Valley and up the sides of Lady McDonald had left no room for wildlife travelling through the area. Fines of $287 are issued if you are caught walking this trail by the conservation officers who patrol it. "Area Closed" signs are displayed at all entrances and exits.

WARNING Bears and cougars frequent the whole area (bears seem particularly attracted to the water features on the golf course). A few years back there was a fatality on Montane Traverse just above the course, so while you may FEEL safe in an area visited by so many people, still carry bear spray and bear bangers and don't travel solo. Keep dogs on a leash for their own protection.

REFRESHMENT NOTE At Silvertip Resort (golf course) in the heart of the trail system: Stoney's Bar & Grill opens mid-May (golf season) for breakfast, lunch and dinner. Down below in Eagle Terrace, the Iron Goat Pub & Grill is fortuitously located across Benchlands Trail from the Cougar Creek parking lot and stays open late. Located on Cougar Creek Drive is Summit Cafe (famous for its all-day breakfasts), French Quarter Café, a bakery and convenience store.

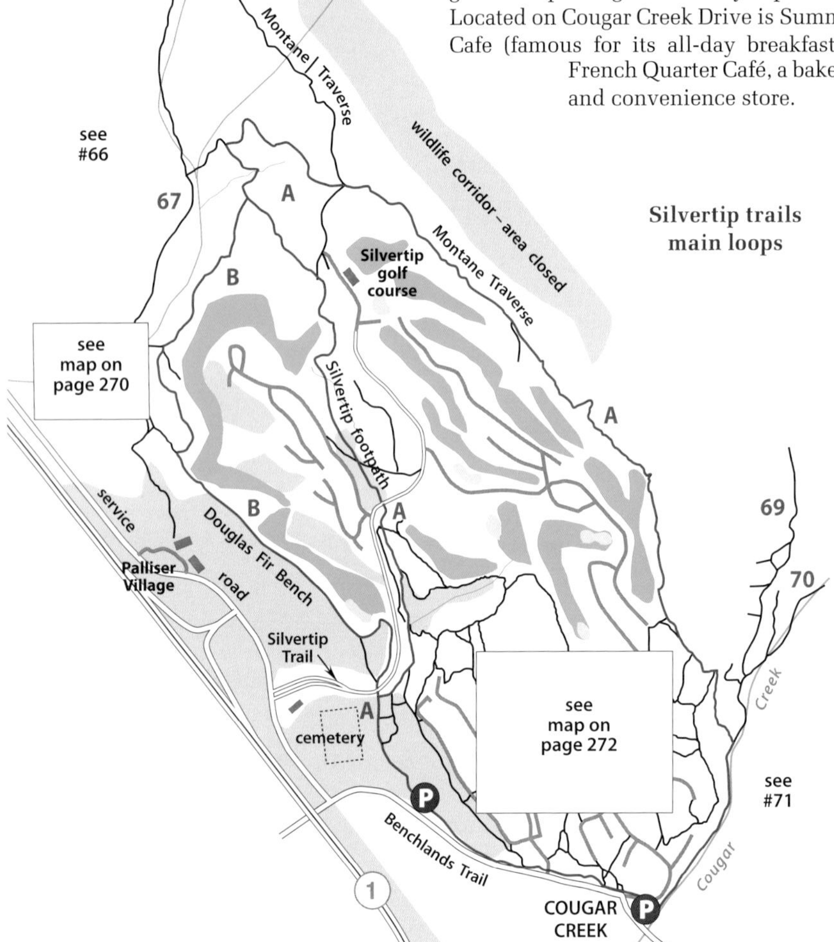

68A Montane Traverse loop

Half-day hike
Distance 7.8 km
Height gain ~200 m (~656 ft.)

A loop around Silvertip Resort taking in the east section of Montane Traverse and Silvertip Footpath. Smack between the two trails lies Stoney's Bar & Grill. (Why not call in for lunch and a beer on the patio?) The loop works well in either direction and can also be accessed from access 2.

TRAIL HISTORY Montane Traverse was built by members of TAG and the BVMBA at the recommendation of ROWG, a working group under BCEAG (Bow Corridor Ecosystem Advisory Group). It's touted as a replacement trail for upper bench trail, and while it works as a connector, it lacks the great mountain views. Silvertip Footpath was built by Trailminders after the building of the paved road to Silvertip Resort.

FROM ACCESS 1, ANTICLOCKWISE

Cougar Creek 600 m

From the parking lot follow the paved Cougar Creek trail along the northwest bank of Cougar Creek. Arriving at the first signposted T-junction with map, turn left.

Montane Traverse 2.8 km

The trail climbs diagonally up the bank, then flattens. Keep straight at two T-junctions, then keep right at the next two. (Trails to left connect with Eagle Terrace trails.)

After Silvertip golf course makes its first appearance, you climb the left side of a gully into the traverse line, wandering along in trees just above the fairways. An aspen meadow offers the only half decent view.

Come to a staggered 4-way junction. Go straight. (Trail to right is Montane Traverse continued. Shortcut trail to left leads in 400 m to junction 159630, with an offshoot to the very end of Silvertip Trail (road).)

To Silvertip Resort 1.4 km

Wind down a pleasant hillside past a seat to a T-junction with map. Turn left. (Trail to right descends to Stoneworks Creek and joins Johnny's Trail.) Traverse (one dip) to T-junction 157633 with map. Go straight. (Trail to right is VARIATION #71B.)

Continue traversing to junction 159630 with map in an opening. The trail continues to the left of a building and across a gravel road. (NOTE To reach Stoney's Bar & Grill, turn left and walk up the road between parking lots to Silvertip Trail (road). Turn right. The eatery is on the left. On a fine day head to the patio which gives a fine view of Lady Macdonald.)

The trail crosses a paved cart path and old track, then descends to a gravel road at a white tree marker. Turn right on the road. Keep straight (paved cart path to right) to a 4-way road junction. Turn left. Just past the gazebo, turn right on a trail with a white marker at the forest edge. Now you're set.

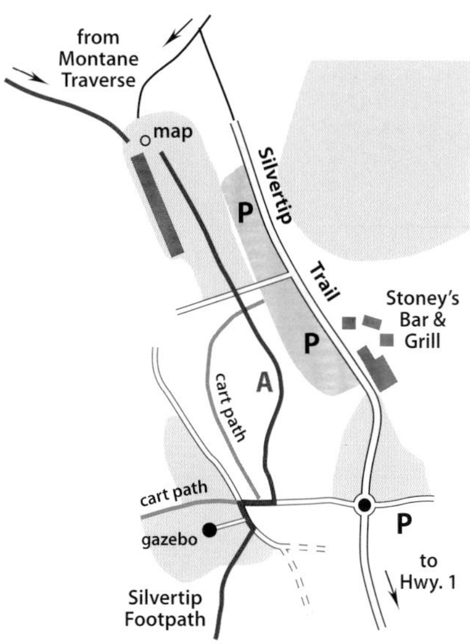

Navigating around Silvertip Resort

Snacking in the gazebo.

Looking down the Devils Staircase.

Silvertip Footpath 1.5 km
The trail zigs down to a gully, then climbs onto a treed ridge and follows it down between the gully on the left and Little Ravine Road on the right. Lower down, the ridge becomes grassy and gives good views. At a 4-way go straight and start a zigzag descent to Silvertip Drive. The trail builders call this section the Devils Staircase.

Cross the road and the paved cart path to the continuation of the trail that heads downvalley. At Y-junction 162620 keep right. (Trail to left is #68D.1.)

Descend a little more steeply. After the cart path disappears into a tunnel below the road, your trail traverses steep, forested hillside to T-junction 162615 with a gravelled track. This is where VARIATION #68B joins in from the right.

To access 2, 370 m
Turn left. Follow the track 'twixt the cemetery and trails leading up to the hoodoos. On grassy ground leave the track that veers right, and continue straight on a trail that climbs to the parking lot off Benchlands Trail (road).

To access 1, 1.1 km
From the far side of the parking lot pick up a paved path that runs parallel to the road, crossing Benchlands Terrace, then Benchlands Trail itself at the junction with Elk Run Blvd. On the far side is Cougar Creek trailhead.

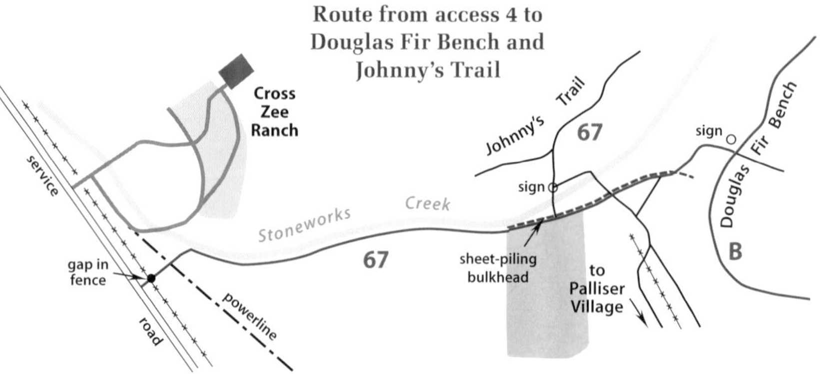

Heading northwest on Douglas Fir Bench.

VARIATION

68B via Douglas Fir Bench

Distance 2.4 km

A slightly longer loop only available after June 15.

Banktop trail 700 m
Turn right off #68A at T-junction 157633.

The trail follows the banktop above Stoneworks Creek, descending in steep steps to a 4-way junction with map at 154627. Go straight. (Trail to right connects with the trail to Palliser Village, Johnny's Trail and access 4 at the service road. See also #67 and the sketch map on page 270.)

Douglas Fir Bench 1.6 km
Climb onto a broad, lightly treed bench trending southeast. A short, steep descent precedes a Y-junction. Keep left. After flirting with the soft grass of the golf course, the bench gets more ridge-like, descending trees to the left, a grass slope dotted with Douglas firs sweeping down to the Trans-Canada to right. Nice views, but noisy.

On arriving at the far end, do not drop off the end. Turn left and descend a less abrupt trail to a paved cart path. Turn right, then right again onto a paved path leading to Silvertip Trail (road). Cross. Continue on gravelled track. A trail coming in from the left is Silvertip Footpath at T-junction 162615.

Continue straight between the cemetery and the hoodoos, following the last two paragraphs of #68A.

68C Hoodoos loop

Hour hike
Distance 1.7 km

A short stroll centred on Canmore's hoodoos.

GEOLOGY & ARCHEOLOGY NOTE The hoodoos have been eroded out of glacial till laid down during the last ice age. Nearby on Benchlands Terrace, Barney Reeves uncovered evidence of two aboriginal settlements going back 1000–2000 years.

FROM ACCESS 2

To Hoodoos 1.3 km
From the upper end of the parking lot follow a paved path alongside Benchlands Trail (road). At a sign turn left onto "Benchlands Ridge Hiking Trail."

The trail climbs to the benchtop, then runs between the grassy scarp and the back gardens of houses facing Benchlands

Canmore hoodoos.

Terrace. There are plenty of memorial seats where you can linger and take in the view across the Bow Valley. Just after triple seats is a Y-junction. Go straight.

Turn first left down a steep, shaley trail at the edge of trees. Cross a 4-way to rub noses with three hoodoos. As the interpretive sign shows, the backdrop looked very different in 1895.

Back to the parking lot 370 m

Head back up to the 4-way and turn right, descending on the diagonal. Either turn first right down to the gravel track, or continue ahead until you hit the toboggan run and follow it down the grass.

Where the gravel track veers right, continue ahead on a trail, or if you've come down the toboggan run, turn left onto the trail, which climbs to the lower end of the parking lot.

Trails in Benchlands and Eagle Terrace

68D Benchlands Ridge

Half day walks
Distance 4.4 km loop 1; 3.9 km loop 2; 4.6 km loop 3

These three loops all start along Benchlands Ridge Hiking Trail, but take different ways back to the parking lot. As you can see by the map on page 272, there are umpteen variations worth trying.

FROM ACCESS 2

Benchlands Ridge 1.6 km
From the upper end of the parking lot follow a paved path alongside Benchlands Trail (road). At a sign turn left onto "Benchlands Ridge Hiking Trail."

The trail climbs to the benchtop, then runs between the grassy scarp and the back gardens of houses facing Benchlands Terrace. There are plenty of memorial seats where you can linger and take in the view across the Bow Valley. Just after triple seats is a Y-junction. Turn right onto Benchlands Terrace (road). Turn left. Just after the road turns right, turn off left onto a trail, which is a continuation of Benchlands Ridge Hiking Trail.

The trail follows the top of the scarp above trees. Keep left, right and straight (main trail is obvious) to a T-junction at 165618. This occurs at the top of a downhill. From here there are various ways back to the trailhead. Three suggestions follow:

1. Douglas Fir Overlook to #68A, 760 m
Basically, you're continuing to follow the scarp to Silvertip Footpath.

Go straight down a hill and up to a T-junction. Go straight. (Trail to right eventually joins the golf course service road.)

Continue to where two fainter trails head left. Take the first one. (Trail ahead climbs past a cabin ruin, then heads right, below the golf course, to the course service road.) The second trail joins in and you cross a gully. Climb up the far side, and above the scarp head left along the fringe of a fairway with dazzling white sand traps. At a trail junction keep left and descend a grass slope to Douglas Fir Overlook. From here a better trail traverses out to Silvertip Footpath at 162620. Turn left and read the last three paragraphs of #68A.

2. Benchlands & Eagle Terrace 2.3 km
At T-junction 165618 turn right. Keep

Douglas Fir Overlook.

straight on a very nice terrace trail through open woodlands. Ignore descending trails to right until you reach junction 166615 on a left-hand bend. (You can identify this junction with certainty because the main trail starts climbing.)

Your new trail descends a bank, crosses a creek, improves dramatically and follows the bed of a slightly descending gully. Go straight at a 4-way. At the next junction keep left under a crag and climb to the end of Wapiti Close. Turn right onto a paved path. After only a few metres turn right onto a trail that swings below Eagle Terrace Road to a T-junction with a paved trail. Turn right. Keep straight past a trail heading uphill and descend to the paved trail paralleling Benchlands Trail (road). Turn right. Cross Benchlands Terrace (road) and continue straight on the paved path back to the parking lot at access 2.

3. Eagle Terrace trails 3 km

At T-junction 165618 turn right and follow the first paragraph of #68D.2.

Instead of turning right down the bank, climb a short hill. Then keep right across a small bridge and climb behind the back gardens of houses off Eagle Point (road). A little farther on, the trail is obvious among many lesser trails peeling off to left and right. Reach the golf course service road.

By turning right on the service road you reach Eagle Heights (road), and can follow assorted footpaths and roads down to Benchlands Trail. I prefer to cross the service road onto a trail headed in the direction of Cougar Creek. Keep straight to Rest Awhile memorial seat at a T-junction on the banktop overlooking Cougar Creek valley.

Turn right (trail to left joins Montane Traverse) and follow the banktop down past viewpoints, then alongside a fence—a big dip rather spoils things—and on down to Eagle Terrace Park playing field. Turn left and reach Benchlands Trail (road) to the left of the field parking lot.

Turn left and walk Benchlands Trail (road). Just after crossing Eagle Landing, cut across to Cougar Creek trail if parked at access 1. If parked at access 2, continue down the road to the junction with Elk Run Blvd. There, turn right and walk the paved path running parallel to Benchlands Trail to the parking lot.

#68D.2 Trail below Eagle Terrace Road.

#68D.3 Trail above Cougar Creek.

69 MOUNT LADY MACDONALD Teahouse site—maps 9, 6

Day hike
Official & unofficial trails, cairns
Distance 4.4 km to teahouse
Height gain 888 m (2915 ft.)
High point 2260 m (7415 ft.)
Map 82 O/3 Canmore

Access Canmore. Cougar Creek trailhead located on Elk Run Blvd. at Cougar Creek crossing. Biffy and picnic tables.

There are two objectives on this hike depending on your fitness level: the site of the former teahouse and the lower summit. Despite improvements by Trailminders, the route to the teahouse up the southwest slope is still a steep, demanding grunt. The trail to Lake Agnes teahouse it is not. Watch for cairns and flagging and intersections with old trails sealed off by branches and rocks. Often it's in condition in the shoulder months of March–April and October–November, even February in some years. Which means that on a regular sunny summer day this slope bakes. Carry plenty of water.

This is also the normal route up Lady Macdonald—a difficult scramble described in Alan Kane's *Scrambles*.

TRAIL NOTE Since the 3rd edition of the present book, the trail has been completely realigned in the middle section.

Top: The teahouse before its 2013 removal.

Below: Teahouse as envisaged by Bob Johnson. Drawing courtesy Bob Johnson

FACILITIES NOTE Awaiting you on your return is the Iron Goat Pub & Grill, located just across Benchlands Trail from the parking lot.

TEAHOUSE HISTORY NOTE In 1988 helicopter pilot Bob Johnson decided to build a teahouse on the south ridge of Lady Macdonald to succour his clients, and for a few years in the mid-1990s helicopters unloaded tourists as often as 15 times a day to the "Highest Tee & Tea in the Rockies," meaning golfers got to tee off the ridge with biodegradable golf balls. Of course, sandwiches, cakes, scones with strawberry jam and Devonshire cream served between 11:30 and 4:30 Thursday to Sunday was something regulars (hikers, that is) soon cottoned on to. The teahouse also attracted the unprepared. Bob would relate how casual walkers, freaking out at the thought of descending the steep, shaley ridge would expect a free flight out or stagger in at dusk and expect free accommodation.

As the helicopter side of the business slipped, Bob decided to make his teahouse a hiking and tenting destination for guided groups. This involved changing the zoning, which the MD of Bighorn agreed to, unlike the town of Canmore, which started legal proceedings against the MD, citing "parking is on town land, helicopter traffic to complete construction goes through Canmore and the tours cut through a wildlife corridor." Meanwhile, Trailminders under Doug Campbell, with official permission, spent 6 years rerouting the upper half of the approach trail, only to have it vandalized a week after its official opening. But before this happened, Canadian Rockies Touring decided to call it quits.

For many years afterwards the half-built teahouse was a come-on to hikers. But finally in 2013 the ESRD ordered its demolition and that of the helipad and gazebo. By the time you read this, the teahouse will have passed into history.

To the lower viewpoint

From the parking lot follow the paved Cougar Creek trail along the northwest bank of Cougar Creek. Go straight at the first signposted T-junction. (Trail to left is Montane Traverse.) At the next signposted T-junction turn left onto Lady Macdonald trail.

The trail takes a diagonal line up the grassy bank into the trees, the latest trail always obvious. Old trails have branches laid across them. Above these "junctions" the trail twists up the easy-angled portion of the south ridge to a viewpoint that requires a short detour to the left.

To the Teahouse site

The trail then steepens, this section ending at a small rock step where the trail traverses left to a junction of old and new trails marked by a rock in the angle between them. This is the start of new zigs that eliminate the steep, shaley section.

Zig right onto the east face, then back left a long way on stones, crossing the old route at the scree slope. A zig right meets the old route again but this time follows it uphill a short way before taking off left

On the new zigs. Photo Gord Dobson

again. This time the zig sweeps nearly all the way across the southwest face, a pleasant section beneath a high-reaching meadow that gets steeper as you re-enter trees.

Slabs ahead force the trail to turn right into a small boulderfield, where it turns left at cairns. After you've navigated the left edge of boulders, the trail charges full steam uphill for the southwest ridge.

When done exclaiming over the view of the Bow Valley, you plod up the shaley ridge and clamber over a few rocks. Not too far below the top of the southwest face, the trail turns right and traverses across it to the south ridge. Meet up with the old route at flagging and turn left. Below you on the right is a low, perpendicular rockband.

After a short climb you cross over the band onto the more verdant east side of the ridge, which is followed up to a levelling where ticks lie in wait for knackered hikers collapsing onto the grass.

The teahouse was located a little higher up the ridge, at treeline, the breezy sun roof of the first-floor roof a tick-safe place for eating our salami sandwiches. (After abandonment, this first floor suddenly became available for shelter, though the roof leaked.) Nearby was a helipad and an inukshuk. The gazebo was located down the right slope, perched dramatically above a 10-metre-high cliff (roped off for the security of tourists), which in its heyday was also available as a rain shelter if nothing else was going on there, like a wedding.

Above: The gazebo in its heyday.

Below: Looking up at Mount Lady Macdonald from the helipad, showing the route up the scree ridge to the lower summit on the centre skyline.

GOING FARTHER

69A Lady Macdonald, lower summit

Easy scramble
Unofficial trails
Distance ~500 m
Extra height gain 239 m (785 ft.)
High point 2499 m (8200 ft.)

A small percentage of walkers will carry on to the lower summit of Lady Macdonald—in 2002, February's "Mountain of the Month." It's a straightforward ascent on good firm rubble with no exposure and takes much less time than you think.

NAMING NOTE Named after Agnes, feisty second wife of John A. Macdonald, first prime minister of Canada, who in these parts is best remembered for riding a CPR train for 1000 km strapped to the front of the locomotive's cowcatcher. That was in 1886.

CLIMBING HISTORY Likely the first person to look over the edge was James Hector on August 16, 1859. Setting out from the site of Canmore he climbed in excess of 3000 ft. in a northeasterly direction to a summit, noting the top of the mountain had a sharp ridge. The view was like a "magnified geological model," but unfortunately, before he could work out the structure of this portion of the Rocky Mountains, he ran out of time.

In our lifetime, Art Davis (who named Midnight Peak down the Kananaskis Valley) climbed the mountain a record 49 times over 28 years. His ashes lie scattered at the teahouse site and a memorial plaque was placed at a secret location known only to his family.

From the old teahouse site, the trail continues on scree up the next rise in the ridge to another flat area with a rusted takeoff ramp for paragliders. Above rises a wall of rubble and small slabs. Rather than be lured by trails starting up the fall line, walkers should follow the yellow scree trail diagonally to the right. It passes BELOW a perpendicular slab before turning uphill. Here I recommend treading the firmer rubble to one side and reserving the runnable scree for a fun descent.

Arrive on the summit ridge of Lady Macdonald and head up left to a cairn. At midnight on December 31, 1999, Ben Johns, Allison Dyck and Josh Duncan set off fireworks from this spot to celebrate Y2K. The actual summit can be seen at the end of a narrow, curving ridge. But unless you're a really proficient scrambler, go no farther. The vertiginous drop on the east side should do the trick. Or to put it another way, if you have to cross the next section of ridge *à cheval* it doesn't bode well for the exposed pitch below the summit.

Summit ridge cairn. High point at far right.

70 COUGAR CREEK—map 6

Cougar Creek just beyond Canadian Forks.

Half-day, day hike, backpack
Official and unofficial trail, route, creek crossings
Distance to valley head 8.3 km
Height gain ~503 m (~1650 ft.)
High point ~1875 m (~6150 ft.)
Map 82 O/3 Canmore

Access Canmore. Cougar Creek trailhead located on Elk Run Blvd. at Cougar Creek crossing. Biffy and picnic tables.
Also accessible from #22C.

The best valley I know of for giving you sore feet! Winding deep into the heart of the Fairholme Range, spectacular and very stony Cougar Creek offers everything from a half hour's stroll to a weekend's backpack. A trail gradually whittles down to nothing and while there's lots of stream hopping, you should be able to keep your feet dry later in the season. The main bed is usually dry past Canadian Forks, and the problem then (for backpackers) is to find water without delving into side valleys.

Experienced hikers with good navigation skills can connect with the South Ghost via the northwest fork to Carrot/Cougar col and via the headwaters to col 197693 on the ridge traverse. Reaching Exshaw Creek is also possible in a couple of places but requires good scrambling ability on the Exshaw Creek side.

SIGN HISTORY A sign at the trailhead once read: "Canmore: A Hiker's Dream. Welcome to Cougar Creek and the Bow Valley." So you eagerly followed the trail only to be met with a spate of signs guaranteed to raise the hackles of people who had been coming this way for donkey's years pre-development and wildlife corridors. Remember the authoritative one beginning with the word "Attention" and inviting us to use this trail, but only from dawn to dusk and don't litter? And the one at Labrador retriever height reading "Attention All Pets!" Thankfully, they're all gone, replaced by a simple sign "Bow Valley Wildland Park Boundary."

EAGLES NOTE During early spring and late fall, you'll see people milling about with binoculars on the first part of the trail. They're eagle counters, and perhaps among them is Peter Sherrington, who is largely responsible for bringing eagle migration to everyone's notice. Hence the name "Eagle Terrace" for the subdivision to your left, which incidentally is laid out in the shape of a stylized eagle and has an eagle sculpture at the entrance.

NAMING NOTE Shamefully, during the 1920s, when the creek was included in Rocky Mountain Park, the policy was to kill all predators, including cougars and eagles, and this is how the creek got its name, from the 18 cougars killed in this valley by predator control officer Ike Mills.

Peter Sherrington in Cougar Creek.

To Lady Mac trail junction 1.1 km
Follow the paved trail along the northwest bank of Cougar Creek, which is lined with rip-rap. The paved section ends and the real trail begins at the sign "Bow Valley Wildland Park Boundary." Stay on the left bank of the creek. Opposite some small cascades, Montane Traverse turns off to the left at a signpost. At the next signpost Lady Macdonald trail turns off to the left up a steep hill.

To Canada forks 2.8 km
Ignoring all other trails climbing the left bank, continue on to the mouth of the canyon opposite a huge mound of rocks — the remnants of a flood control dam washed out in the spring floods of 1990. Descend a little and pick your way over rocks to where the trail resumes. Almost straightaway it crosses the creek to the right (southeast) bank.

During the next few kilometres the trail crosses and recrosses the creek about 12 times, passing below a huge number of sport climbing crags on both sides of the valley. Note evolving hoodoos and inaccessible-looking caves where someone once found a projectile point. The long-lost rock paintings remain lost, but I'm still working on it.

Just after passing an overhanging wall to right, reach Canadian Forks at 195634 below a great cliff. To your right two tributaries head off in the east and southeast directions. See OPTION ##70A and B. It's a good place to camp.

To Northwest fork 2.9 km
The scenery ahead is no less spectacular, with rock ridges winging up to unnamed summits. The trail has more or less given up, leaving you to stumble along an outrageously rough, stony creekbed. En route, a cliff-bound drainage to left is worth venturing up for the superlative view it offers of Grotto Mountain's northern cliffs. A little farther on at 196645 you pass the mouth of a major northwest tributary to left, which is *not* the described route to Carrot/Cougar col, but offers relatively easy going. I've only ever gone halfway, but Alf Skrastins says it's possible to cross the col at its head into the cirque below Princess Anne and make a loop with the northwest fork.

Another 1.5 km of easier progress below Grotto Peak, to right, (first scrambled up by Bob and Dinah in 2001 from the gully at 201657), brings you to a heap of stones spilling out of the side valley to the left at 203660. This one leads to Cougar/Carrot col. See OPTION #70C.

Top: #70 Epic Tower and Mythic Tower from the head of the valley.

Bottom left: #70 The narrows, where cliffs sweep down to the creekbed.

Bottom right: Option #70A The east fork fall. You scramble up the light-coloured rocks to the right of the fall.

To upper forks 1.5 km
At the next bend, you run into boulders and deep pools. Scrabble up them or bypass to left or right. Up next is the narrows where a cliff sweeps down to the creekbed. Note the big triangular rock face up left. The terrain then eases off to the unexpectedly verdant sanctuary of the upper forks at 215667 where valleys spin off like the points of a star.

The second valley to right gives scramblers access to scree ridges overlooking Mt. Fable and the route down to Exshaw Creek via Mythic Creek or Fable Creek. Directly east is Epic Tower and Mythic Tower with the higher Mt. Townsend to their left.

The main fork makes a right-angled turn to the northwest and ends under ruddy-coloured scree slopes criss-crossed with sheep tracks giving very steep routes to col 198692. This is the same col gained more easily perhaps by the ridge route from South Ghost Pass.

EXPLORING FARTHER
All options travel through rough terrain with lots of creek crossings.

70A East Fork

Distance 2.3+ km
Height gain ~277 m (~910 ft.)
High point ~1829 m (~6000 ft.)

A good hot-weather hike at runoff with lots of creek crossings.

At Canadian Forks turn right. A trail runs along the left bank and continues past the confluence with the southeast fork onto a terrace and down to the creekbed. Follow the creekbed below a full-size inukshuk, on the left bank, and through the narrows, en route passing occasional small falls and chutes. Look up right where a side creek rushes down a cliff face. Not far beyond is the valley's highlight, a 10 m high fall into a deep green pool. Scramble easily up the right side to continued creekbed trudging. Gradually the valley opens up, disclosing views of ridges up ahead.

70B Southeast Fork

Distance 1.7+ km
Height gain ~277 m (~910 ft.)
High point ~1829 m (~6000 ft.)

While it lacks the waterfalls of the east fork, this canyon-like fork more than makes up for it in huge overhanging cliffs.

At Canadian Forks turn right and keep right into the southeast fork. The going is easy in a stony creekbed with running water at runoff. The first cliff on the right is called Planet X and features some of the hardest sport climbs in the Bow Valley. Continue past hoodoos, cliffs, caves, even higher cliffs and more hoodoos to where the creekbed widens slightly. This is where we stopped, within view of Grotto Mountain's north face.

The southeast fork.

70C to Carrot/Cougar col

Distance 4.2 km; 11 km from trailhead
Height gain 732 m (2400 ft.);
1082 m (3550 ft.) from trailhead
High point at col ~2454 m (~8050 ft.)

If you're looking for alpine meadows in a creek where stones and dryas mats are the norm, the lovely basin under Mt. Charles Stewart is the place to make for. It is a leg of the Exshaw Creek/South Ghost/Cougar Creek backpack that is usually done in reverse. See ##22 and 22C.

REGULATORY NOTE The meadows are supposedly off limits for backcountry camping.

Using snippets of trail on one side or the other, follow the gently rising valley floor to the rockslide, where big boulders litter the floor. Use the left-slope bypass trail. A section through trees is followed by a long stony stretch below a rubble slope on the left. A prominent white tower on the right signals water for sure if it isn't already flowing, and the beginning of the upper valley.

Re-entering trees, fight your way through willow bushes arching over the stream to the first waterfall. Turn it on the left side. Below the upper fall, be sure to switch to the right bank: for one thing, you enter meadows much sooner. (For another, if you continue to stay on the left bank, you will likely follow the left fork into the cirque below Mt. Princess Anne, which is not where you want to go unless doing a loop with the *other* northwest fork.)

There's still a lot of ankle-aching side-hilling to do before you reach the basin below Charles Stewart. Stay here or climb another 152 vertical m (500 ft.) upmeadow, curling onto the boundary ridge with Banff National Park. The ridge is broad and rounded, with two cols of equal height separated by a small top. Once up there, you can wander along the ridge toward Mt. Charles Stewart or onto Peak 195689 at 2838 m (8650 ft.)—a great viewpoint.

Crossing below the upper fall on the descent. Photo Alf Skrastins

The white tower.

71 CANMORE BENCHLANDS Horseshoe trails—map 9

Horseshoe loop, looking southeast to Pigeon Mountain and Mount Collembola.

Half-day, short-day hikes
Official & unofficial trails
High point 1500 m (4922 ft.)
Map 82 O/3 Canmore

Access

1. Canmore. Cougar Creek trailhead located on Elk Run Blvd. at Cougar Creek crossing. Biffy and picnic tables. (Main access for Horseshoe loop.)

2. Canmore. Various locations in Cougar Creek subdivision: Head of Canyon Road, halfway along Ridge Road, Elk Run Blvd. opposite Lady Macdonald Drive, Elk Run Blvd. opposite Pointe of View.

3. Hwy 1A (Bow Valley Trail). Take Indian Flats Road, signed "Alpine Club of Canada." Keep left at the second bend (Bow Valley Riding Assn. ahead) and park at a road widening on the left side just before the utility buildings. To access lower Horseshoe loop, park en route at the side of the road at the first right-hand bend.

4. Hwy. 1A (Bow Valley Trail). Take Indian Flats Road, signed "Alpine Club of Canada." At the T-junction turn left and drive to the ACC clubhouse parking lot on the right side of the road at the last bend. For ACC members and guests staying at clubhouse and cabins only.

Also accessible from #72 Grotto Mountain via the ACC Route, #73 Horse Meadows trails.

The hiking and mountain biking trails of Canmore Benchlands run along the northeast side of the Bow Valley above Canmore between Harvie Heights and the Graymont Exshaw Quarry. Or, to put it another way, along the lower slopes of Squaw's Tit, Lady Macdonald and Grotto Mountain. They can be neatly divided up into four sections. Route #71 describes trails between Cougar Creek and Echo Canyon Creek.

They give access to #72 Grotto Mountain via the ACC route, to Echo Canyon for sport climbers and to Grotto Mountain via Alan Kane's direct route for more accomplished scramblers.

They connect with Horse Meadows trails via two routes crossing Echo Canyon Creek at the upper level. So while Horse Meadows trails can be accessed from Horseshoe, if you just want a shorter walk around the loops, see #73.

While trails remain easy, expect short, steep hills and many more of them. On the plus side there is more bench walking with better views. Trails are also used for trail riding by the Bow Valley Riding Assn., which has facilities on Indian Flats Road.

This is perhaps the most complex area of all the bench trails. Besides the main trails, there are dozens of minor, interconnecting ones. Some major junctions have maps. Horseshoe loop has blue signs and arrows at some junctions but the signage is nowhere near comprehensive, which is very perplexing if you're not a local.

WARNING Bears and cougars frequent the area, so carry bear spray and bear bangers, don't travel solo and keep dogs on a leash for their own protection.

71A Horseshoe loop

Distance 7.3 km
Height gain ~171 m (~560 ft.)

Based on the old blue trail, it now takes a slightly different line to avoid wet ground. Follow blue markers and arrows and hope they haven't been nicked by the sign collectors. The return leg is still being worked out. In the meantime I have suggested a route that stays high as long as possible.

FROM ACCESS 1

To the return loop 1.1 km
Cross the road bridge over Cougar Creek and turn left onto the trail running along the southeast bank of the creek. After you pass the builders house and a dynamite shed, a relic of the Jensen and Summerhays siltstone quarry, come to a 4-way junction with map. Turn right. (Trail to left crosses the creek to Cougar Creek trail and can be used when the water is low.)

Shortly, the trail turns left, then heads up to the right into forest. Stay on the well-used trail amid minor side trails and climb to T-junction 177612, where you meet your return trail. Turn left. This is a complex area with a multitude of side trails, including Old Blue. See inset map no. 1.

To Leben's Run junction 580 m
Climb to a T-junction signed "Blue Heaven." Go right, and climbing a little, meander along in a dark forest, keeping straight, to another complex junction at 180610. See inset map no. 2.

To Grotto Mountain trail 1.4 km
Veer left here and cross a dip. Keep straight. (Leg Bone trail to left connects with Blue Heaven.) The main trail then runs along a bench above a major gully system. Just after, two trails turning right at signed T-junctions are interconnecting variants, which shortcut with the return route.

Hiker among bikers at Leben's Run junction.

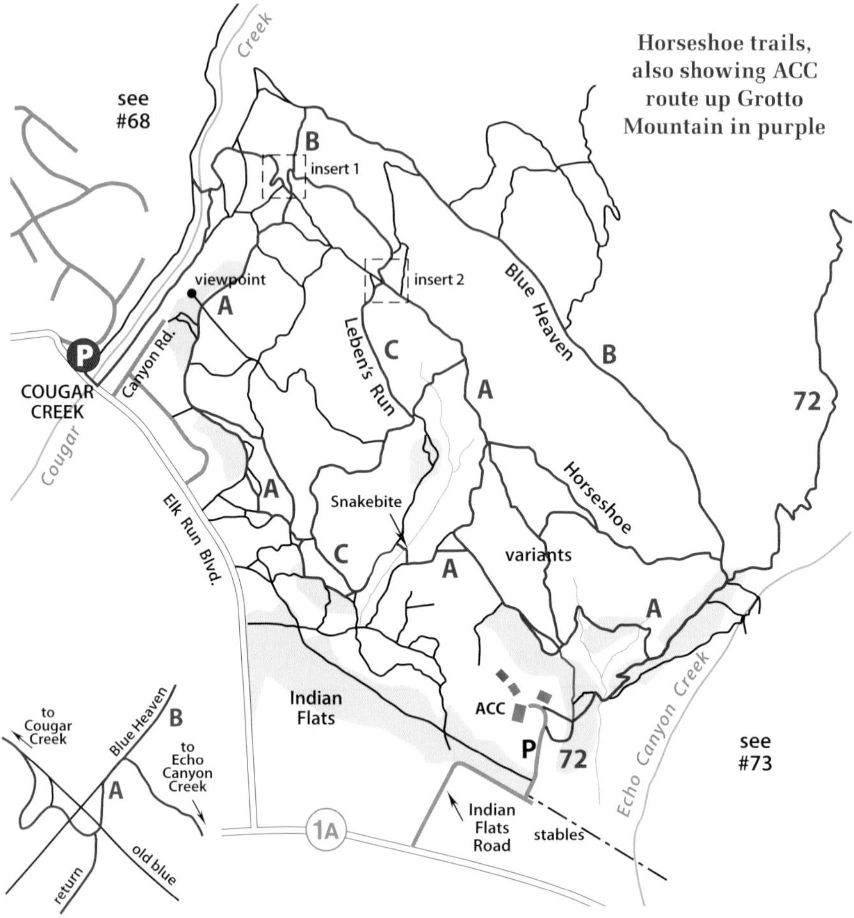

Horseshoe trails, also showing ACC route up Grotto Mountain in purple

Creek
see #68
B
insert 1
insert 2
viewpoint
A
Blue Heaven
B
Leben's Run
C
Canyon Rd.
P
COUGAR CREEK
A
72
Cougar
Horseshoe
A
Snakebite
Elk Run Blvd.
C
variants
A
A
Indian Flats
ACC
P
72
Echo Canyon Creek
see #73
1A
Indian Flats Road
stables

to Cougar Creek
Blue Heaven
B
to Echo Canyon Creek
A
old blue
return

Inset map no. 1: Horseshoe trail near Blue Heaven junction

Inset map no. 2: Horseshoe trail at Leben's Run junction

Horseshoe trail at the meet-up of variants above Cougar Creek subdivision.

Horseshoe then climbs a little. After it flattens, Blue Heaven comes in from the left just before you join Grotto Mountain trail above Echo Canyon Creek. At the 4-way 189602 turn right (trail ahead dipping into the creek connects with Horse Meadows trails).

Descend a ridge to a T-junction with map. Go straight. (Trail to left is the official connector to Horse Meadows trails.) Continue down the ridge to T-junction 187600 with map. Turn right.

To Leben's Run lower junction 1.6 km
The trail undulates across hillside, en route crossing two gullies. Climb more steeply out of the second gully to a T-junction. Turn left (variant to right) and in a minute reach a T-junction in the open. Turn right.

Walk a scenic bench above a grassy slope pictured on page 284. Ignore two trails heading right and one descending the slope to your left at the edge of trees. In trees, turn next left off the bench and diagonal down to a good trail. Turn left and wind gently down the hillside to the left of a major gully.

Rather than follow the good trail all the way down to Indian Flats (which means climbing back up the other side of the gully), it's less hassle to cross the gully on Snakebite trail. So at indistinct junction 180602 on a left-hand curve, head right. The trail descends into the gully—just one short, steep drop—then contours out of it to intersect a trail running along the gully's west bank. An old sign reads "No Shooting or Trespassing."

Turn left and follow the bank all the way down to a 4-way at 179601. Go straight. (Trail to right is Leben's Run.) In a few seconds reach the benchtop above Indian Flats and turn right. (Trail to left drops in loose gravel to Indian Flats.)

Above Cougar Creek subdivision 750 m
Walk the benchtop above Indian Flats, known by the Stoney Nakoda as *Tinda Meemum*, "round clearing," where they camped while travelling between Morley and Banff. Nowadays it's bisected by horse trails and a powerline leading to an electrical substation.

Descending the ridge above Echo Canyon Creek.

Staying on the benchtop, keep right twice. Then, within a very short distance, keep right, straight twice (junctions not marked on map), left and then right. At the following junction go either way. If going straight, keep left. If going left on the more scenic route, keep right most times— just don't descend into the mess of trails above Elk Run Blvd. Both variations meet up in a lovely area of Douglas firs.

Cougar Creek view leg 740 m
Follow the banktop above Cougar Creek until you get back to your outgoing trail. (En route a trail to right leads to a popular dog-walking area; two trails down the bank drop in on Canyon Road; a viewpoint on the left lies opposite a walkable cutline; a shortcut trail plummets down the bank and two trails to right fetch up on old blue.)

At T-junction 177612 turn left and walk another 1.1 km back to the parking lot.

Exploring the side trails above Blue Heaven.

VARIATION

71B Blue Heaven

Distance 2 km

Popular with walkers and runners, this trail takes a slightly higher line than Horseshoe and is the more pleasant trail. Likely named after the cocktail "inspired by changing spring weather."

Leave #71A at the trail sign "Blue Heaven" and climb gently uphill to a T-junction. Turn right, continuing to climb into the traverse line. Keep straight. (Leg Bone trail to right connects with Horseshoe loop.) A long stretch takes in one viewpoint and passes three side trails heading up the hillside. Join Horseshoe loop just before it hits the ACC route up Grotto Mountain.

NOTE You can make loops with the three side trails that climb even higher up the slope and interconnect. From the highest point, the first original trail pointing the way up Grotto Mountain delivers you to open slopes, then fades out.

SHORTCUT

71C Leben's Run

Distance 1.2 km

A DHS trail that cuts the loop in half.

At Leben's Run junction turn second right, then left. Look for the wood sign on the right side of the trail.

After a short uphill, the trail settles into a long, winding descent with a few technical features. En route keep right at a right-hander, then left. After the next left-hand bend the trail steepens and gets stony. Keep straight downhill to staggered 4-way junction 179601 on a benchtop above Indian Flats. Turn right. (Horseshoe trail has come in from the left.)

#71C Seesaw on Leben's Run.

72 GROTTO MOUNTAIN via the ACC route—map 6

Looking toward the summit.

Long-day scramble
Unofficial trail, route, cairns & flagging
Distance 5.3 km
Height gain 1381 m (4530 ft.)
High point 2707 m (8880 ft.)
Map 82 O/3 Canmore

Usual access Hwy. 1A (Bow Valley Trail). From the Trans-Canada Hwy. gain Hwy. 1A from the east exit into Canmore. Turn left (east) on Hwy. 1A, then turn second left onto Indian Flats Road, signed "Alpine Club of Canada." Keep left at the second bend (Bow Valley Riding Assn. ahead) and park at a road widening on the left side just before the utility buildings.
ACC Clubhouse access A trail leaves the residence parking lot and joins the main route at the 4-way atop the first hill.
Also accessible from #74 Grotto Mountain via the Carter route at the summit.

The huge mass of Grotto Mountain towering above the Bow Valley has a route up the sloping west flank that is fairly easy technically, but strenuous. It's a two-piecer: the laborious ascent to the northwest ridge on a twisting trail, followed by an interesting ridgewalk with some easy scrambling and no exposure. Most people return the same way.

DESCENT NOTE Every year, people and their dogs get benighted on this mountain, either by not starting early enough or more usually by attempting a direct descent from the ridge and getting stuck among cliff bands and having to be rescued by helicopter. (There IS a more direct route up the mountain as described by Alan, but it is not for the average hiker.)

NAMING NOTE The mountain was named Pic de la Grotto by James Hector and Eugène Bourgeau on August 12, 1858, while botanizing. They didn't name it after the three massive grottos of the west face, though, but after a cave with a high-arched roof and narrow mouth, the exact location of which appears to have been lost. Could it have been Rats Nest Cave? No one will ever know.

Looking back along the ridge. Photo Shawn Lawrence

Benches section 820 m

Walk up the road to a trail sign on the right side opposite the utility buildings.

From the sign, a trail climbs onto a little ridge. At a 4-way junction go right. (The steep trail ahead is touted as the official Grotto Mountain route, which makes no sense to me. Trail to left is the route from the ACC clubhouse.)

Your trail descends very gently to a valley bottom. At a 3-way junction turn right. (Steep trail to left is the official route down to this point.) Climb up the bank to a T-junction on another ridge. Turn left. (Lovely trail straight on follows Echo Canyon Valley and is the route taken by climbers to Echo Canyon and by scramblers on the direct route up Grotto.)

So you go left past the hiking sign and wind up the open ridge. On its crest join the Horseshoe trails. Go straight uphill, ignoring a trail to left with signpost, a trail to right with signpost and finally an intersecting trail with signpost. (Left is Horseshoe trail; right crosses Echo Canyon Creek to Horse meadows trails.)

For clarification see the sketch maps on pages 286, 293 and 297.

The hole that you walk across quite unknowingly is the narrowest part of the ridge!

To the northwest ridge 3.2 km

You haven't quite left the benches behind. After climbing onto a higher one, you're standing already quite tired with all the mountain in front of you. The good news is that the laborious pull to treeline no longer involves dragging yourself from tree to tree. Give thanks to the Rocky Mountain Section of the ACC, who in 1995 and 2011, with pickaxes, hoes and rakes, scratched out one decent trail featuring cairns, flagging and small switchbacks. It winds about, avoiding slabs and rockbands, even hits a few grassy openings with views of Canmore on its way to treeline, a remarkably clean demarcation of trees and scree at a flattening. Smell the sheep?

The trail continues up the scree slope, angling right to gain the northwest ridge below a minor hump.

Coming back down the final scramble to the summit. Photo Shawn Lawrence

To the summit 1.3 km

The ridge is easy to the second hump. A narrowing precedes the first bit of scrambling courtesy of two parallel rockbands slanting down the west flank. Go over the top of the first one. The second one requires some inward facing downclimbing on the far side. Alternatively, descend the scree gully on the right a short way, then cut left across slabs to the edge of the band. At this point you can scramble down weaknesses.

After this comes a longer, steeper pull up rubble on the right flank to gain the upper ridge, which is wide and grassy with a few scrambly bits to keep up the interest. Amazingly, this is where you walk over an arch without even knowing it (the hole can be seen from Canmore). The final rise to the summit is girdled by innumerable little rockbands, which are so much fun to scramble up you'd be a moron to stagger up the scree to the side.

After signing the register lodged in the cairn, take in the view. In the words of David Thompson, the mountains of the Fairholme Range resemble waves of the ocean in a wintry storm. "Imagination apt to say, these must once have been liquid, and in that state when swelled to its greatest agitation suddenly congealed and made solid by "Power Omnipotent." You wonder what he would have said about the 52-foot-high wireless communications tower blocking up the view of the cement plant. However, it would be hard to ruin the view completely. Most thrilling is the view to the south of Mt. Assiniboine and the Royal Group.

Summit cairn. Photo Rick Green

73 CANMORE BENCHLANDS Horse Meadows trails—map 6

View from G8 loop looking towards Mt. Lougheed, Rimwall, The Orphan and the Three Sisters.

Half-day hikes
Official & unofficial trails
High point 1470 m (4823 ft.)
Map 82 O/3 Canmore

Access Hwy. 1A (Bow Valley Trail).
1. Hwy. 1A (Bow Valley Trail). At 870 m east of Indian Flats Road, just past Echo Canyon Creek, park on the grass verge. No pullout or trail sign. Look for the Bow Valley Wildlife Park sign a little way in. (Best access to G8 loop.)
2. Hwy. 1A (Bow Valley Trail). At 1.4 km east of Indian Flats Road, pull into a small parking area on the left side of the road. (Steep access to G8 loop; climber's access to Bataan.)
Also accessible from #71A Horseshoe loop and #72 Grotto Mountain via the ACC route in two places.

The hiking and mountain biking trails of Canmore Benchlands run along the northeast side of the Bow Valley above Canmore between Harvie Heights and the Graymont Exshaw Quarry. Or to put it another way, along the lower slopes of Squaw's Tit, Lady Macdonald and Grotto Mountain. They can be neatly divided up into four sections. Route #73 describes trails below Grotto Mountain between Echo Canyon Creek and Graymont Exshaw Quarry.

The trails give access to the sport climbing cliff Bataan.

They are connected to the Horseshoe trails by two trails crossing Echo Canyon Creek at the upper level. So while the G8 trails can be accessed from Horseshoe, if you just want a shorter walk around the G8 loops, it's best to start from access 1.

Trails are easy, with steeper hills here and there. On the plus side, these easternmost benchlands are more open and give better views. Trails are used for riding by the Bow Valley Riding Assn., which has facilities nearby on Indian Flats Road.

Bikers know these as the G8 trails, though there is no connection with the G8 Summit held at Kananaskis in 2002.

Most major junctions have maps of the "you are here" variety. Other junctions are not signed.

TRAIL CLOSURE NOTE Horse Meadows trails are closed Dec 1 to May 15.

WARNING Bears and cougars frequent the area, so carry bear spray and bear bangers and don't travel solo. Keep dogs on a leash for their own protection. Bighorn sheep are often seen in the vicinity of the quarry. This means ticks.

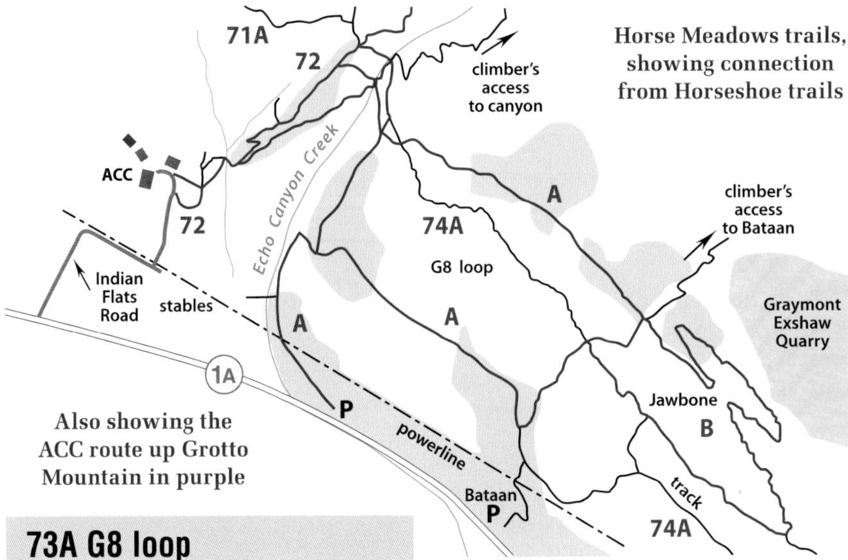

73A G8 loop

Distance 3.9 km

An enjoyable circuit with meadows and views.

FROM ACCESS 1

The trail follows grass to the right of Echo Canyon Creek. After the access trail joins in from the stables, it turns right and climbs to the banktop. At T-junction 188596 with map go straight. (Left is the return route.)

The trail crosses a shallow gully, then gravitates downhill through Douglas fir meadows interrupted by a patch of aspen to a T-junction with map. Turn left. (Trail straight on leads to access 2 and the powerline access road.)

Climb a little to 4-way junction 195594 with ##73B and 74A. Go straight and continue uphill to the upper 4-way at 197595. Turn left. (Right is Jawbone loop, ahead the climber's access trail to Bataan.)

Traverse aspen meadows, going straight at a 4-way (#74 to right and left) just before you hit the 4-way with map on the banktop above Echo Canyon Creek. Turn left. (Trail ahead connects with the Horseshoe trails and the ACC route up Grotto Mountain.)

Descend grassy hillside, enjoying the head-on view of the Three Sisters, to T-junction 188596 and turn right. Descend the same way you came up.

GOING FARTHER

73B Jawbone loop

Distance 2.3 km

A good add-on, named after a jawbone hanging from a tree.

Start from the 4-way 195594. Turn right and head downhill in forest. En route go straight at a T-junction. (Trail to right connects with the powerline access road.) At the top of a slabby uphill, come to a skewed 4-way junction. Bikers use the trail ahead, a DHS twister in a gully that you don't want to walk. I recommend turning left and plodding a straightforward hill to the top of the twists. Go straight, shortly traversing right past the jawbone and back left when you hit the quarry. Reach the highlight of the trail in meadows. Zig down left, then right between crags to upper 4-way 197595, where you can pick up #73A.

74 GROTTO MOUNTAIN via the Carter route—maps 8, 6

Summit ridge from the south (lower Grotto) summit.

Short-day scramble to lookout, long-day scramble to summit
Unofficial trail with cairns & yellow paintmarks to overlook, then route
Distance to overlook 2.6 km; to summit 4.7 km
Height gain to overlook 869 m (2850 ft.); to summit 1442 m (4730 ft.)
High point overlook 2133 m (7000 ft.); summit 2707 m (8880 ft.)
Map 82 O/3 Canmore

Access Hwy. 1A (Bow Valley Trail). Going west: 2 km west of Gap Lake or 400 m west of an interpretive sign turn right (north) into the Rats Nest Cave parking lot (unsigned). Going east from Canmore: the parking lot lies 300 m east of Graymont Exshaw Quarry access road. **Also accessible** from #72 Grotto Mountain via the ACC route at the summit.

The southern route up Grotto Mountain is more strenuous and more complex than the ACC route, despite there being a trail to the halfway point at Buttress Lookout. After that you climb the southwest ridge, which gets you onto the summit ridge, which in turn leads to the top. The alternative to all this hard work is to stop at Buttress Lookout—it's where the trail ends anyway.

It makes sense to pair this route with the ACC route—a muscle-aching grind of up to 11 hours called the "Grotto Mountain Grand Traverse." Which way round? The advantage to starting up the Carter route is that the ACC route is much easier to descend at the end of the day when you're tired. And for those unlucky enough not to have two cars or bikes, it's possible to return to the parking lot via the Horse Meadows trails and the powerline right-of-way. See #74A GETTING BACK and the sketch map on page 297.

Another consideration is the weather. You do not want to arrive at the 52-foot-high communications tower on the summit ridge at the same time as a thunderstorm. This latest piece of metal to desecrate a mountaintop was flown up on Friday, April 2, 2004, with the approval of four agencies of the provincial government and is used for wireless high speed Internet.

TRAIL HISTORY The trail is the brainchild of Canmore's Brian Carter, who spent 30 years working out a route suitable for hiker/scrambler hybrids with friend Leon Blumer. It was scratched out by the local scout troop and finally finished by Trailminders, the opening ceremony being held on October 24, 2001, in pouring rain.

In 2002 the "Grotto Mountain Grand Traverse" was chosen by Trailminders and the ACC as a fitting objective for celebrating "The Year of the Mountains." Over 50 people started out that August 18, the idea being that many feet would make the trail clearer. That evening, among the finishers celebrating at the ACC clubhouse with a beer and burger was Brian, then in his mid-seventies.

GEOLOGY NOTE On this route you not only see oyster fossils, but also a beautiful example of fossil soils called paleosols: ancient soils laid down during the time when the area was tropical and now uncovered by erosion as shales at the bottom of the Etherington Formation.

To Buttress Lookout 2.6 km

The trail leaves the back of the parking lot and climbs to a T-junction with the old trail (branches laid across). Turn right. Shortly, the trail zigs to gain the powerline right-of-way. Whereas the Rats Nest Cave approach turns right along the right-of-way, you cross it onto the end of Fossil Ridge.

The trail follows the broad, treed ridge, low down crossing slabs imprinted with white oyster shells. Brian assures me the ridge name is doubly suitable in that this section was completed by a lot of old fossils. Some old fossils!

Higher up, scramble three easy rock steps. Ahead rises Buttress Overlook, the Great White Tower, seemingly blocking up the way. At a large cairn on a flattish area, the trail leaves the ridge crest and traverses steep, forested hillside on the right side to the bottom of a short gully, which is the crux. (NOTE; If you miss this traverse and carry on up the ridge you fetch up against a short vertical rockband, which Brian at one time thought of overcoming with a wooden ladder. The route above is actually a great deal easier than the new route.)

Back to the gully, you zig left across it and up some scramble steps, then head back right and finally recross it near the top. This gets you into the claustrophobic Rats Nest Valley above the big step. Below you is a small canyon.

The trail traverses a scree slope poised above the canyon, then climbs steeply up left in two main zigs to the base of the white buttress. Turn right. (Trail to left is the abandoned ridge route.)

The trail skirts the bottom of the cliff, then heads right, across a scree gully and up a steep rocky rib on powdery shale with two zigs at the top. Traverse left a long way, finally zigging some more to the flat top of Buttress Overlook. A cairn is perched on the edge of the cliff overhanging Graymont's Exshaw Quarry. What a place to view Canmore and the Bow Valley!

Scrambling the gully.

Route 2 to the right of the rock buttress. Photo Rick Green

Buttress lookout. Photo Rick Green

On the south summit, looking southeast along the ridge to a higher top.

Southwest ridge 700 m

Follow cairns up the shaley southwest ridge, the going easy at first under pines. A rocky step can be avoided by a trail on the right side. Above treeline the ridge narrows and care is needed at one point where scree lies atop slabs dropping off the left side into a gorge called the Inner Sanctuary. Looking above the sanctuary, the eye is caught by exquisitely coloured, slumping "slabs" of pink and pale blue shading to green. This is the paleosol, most easily reached from above. Close in, check for root casts.

Fetch up below a rock buttress. From below it are two ways on to the low point between the main and south summits.

1. Turn the buttress on the left side and follow a trail of cairns across big scree to the low point. Turn left.

2. Turn the buttress on the right side, gradually working your way up large scree back onto the ridge crest. This leads to a cairn on the "south summit" as Brian Carter calls it, though others call it Lower Grotto. (A higher summit exists to the southeast.) Turn left and descend 30 m to the low point.

Summit ridge 1.4 km
Climb straightforward rubble on the edge, the angle easing off where the ridge widens and curves left into your final approach along the ridge crest to—the communications tower with cluster management module, solar panel and sealed, insulated battery box.

A little beyond lies the summit with cairn and register. From here look across Cougar Creek to Lady Macdonald, which the tower was initially slated for. The authorities said no, not because of any aesthetic concern, but because Macdonald was inside a wildland park. Grotto, unfortunately, is not.

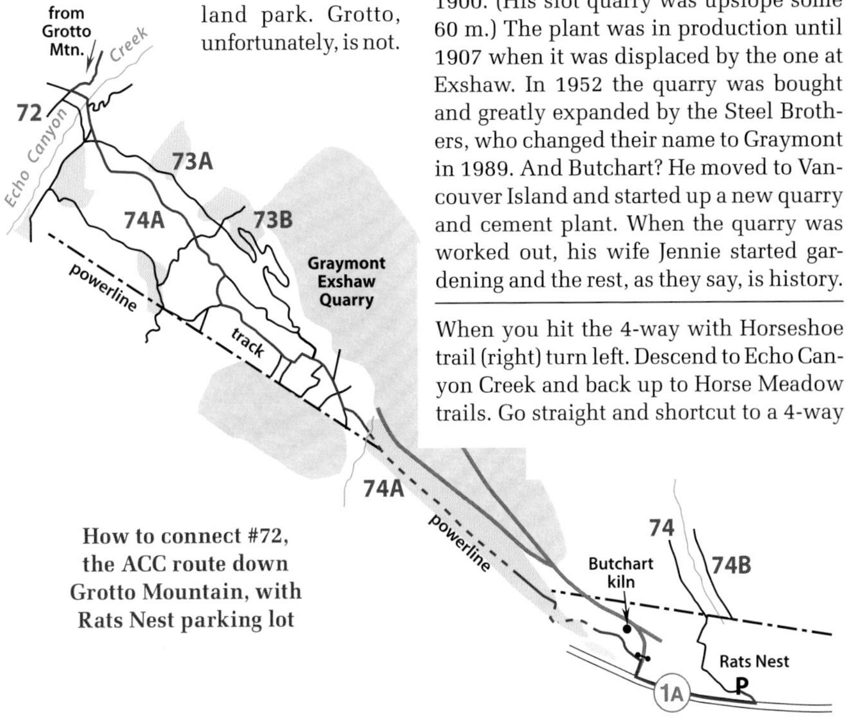

How to connect #72, the ACC route down Grotto Mountain, with Rats Nest parking lot

GETTING BACK FROM ACC ROUTE

74A Grotto connector

Distance 5.1 km

A mostly downhill route using trails, powerline access road and the powerline.

GEOLOGY NOTE The route takes a line below Graymont's Exshaw Quarry. As you will see, the grade of the quarry is much steeper than the grade of the slope above it. This worries naturalist Ben Gadd, who thinks the stripping of limestone from the down-dip edge of the slabs *all along the base* of the mountain could destabilize the slope above and one day send it crashing down like Turtle Mountain. Some say a tremor felt on May 24, 2000, by residents of Cougar Creek subdivision was a precursor.

QUARRY NOTE At the end of the route you pass below the Butchart kiln, the only remnant left of the cement plant started by Robert Pim Butchart sometime prior to 1900. (His slot quarry was upslope some 60 m.) The plant was in production until 1907 when it was displaced by the one at Exshaw. In 1952 the quarry was bought and greatly expanded by the Steel Brothers, who changed their name to Graymont in 1989. And Butchart? He moved to Vancouver Island and started up a new quarry and cement plant. When the quarry was worked out, his wife Jennie started gardening and the rest, as they say, is history.

When you hit the 4-way with Horseshoe trail (right) turn left. Descend to Echo Canyon Creek and back up to Horse Meadow trails. Go straight and shortcut to a 4-way on upper G8 trail. Cross and follow the middle trail. Go straight at the 4-way 195594, then turn next right. On joining a track (powerline access road) turn left.

Follow the track, ignoring all side trails. At a Y-junction of tracks on a bench turn left uphill, in a few metres turning left onto a grassy track identified by boulders at its entrance. When the track fades in meadows below a wall of stones, join the powerline right-of-way and follow its grassy swath eastwards.

At power poles perched above a drop, leave the right-of-way and head to the right along a ridge to a survey post. Descend the right-hand slope, at the bottom contouring back left and in meadow picking up a grassy track that takes you out under Butchart's kiln to the quarry access road at the gate. Turn right and in less than a minute reach Hwy. 1A. Turn left and walk 300 m along the road to Rats Nest parking lot.

OPTION

74B Rats Nest Cave

Half-day hike
Distance 2.6 km return
Height gain ~150 m (~492 ft.)
High point ~1440 m (~4724 ft.)

A short walk up a valley to the gated entrance of Rats Nest Cave, Canada's 8th longest. This is not a walk-in cave like Canyon Creek Ice Cave, but has shafts requiring you to rappel, "shimmy, slide, grovel and thrutch." The rewards are decorated passages with flowstone and draperies, soda straws, rimstone dams, helictites, pearls and moonmilk. To see these marvels, take a guided trip with Canmore Caverns and read *Under Grotto Mountain: Rat's Nest Cave*, by Charles J. Yonge.

Interestingly, 4 km of passages pass right underneath Fossil Ridge at about the 1600 m level. The thinking is the cave extends under Grotto Mountain to Cougar Canyon and farther—Chas guesses as much as 50 km!

The trail leaves the back of the parking lot and climbs to a T-junction with the old trail (branches laid across). Turn right. Shortly, the trail zigs to gain the powerline right-of-way. Turn right. Cross a dry creekbed, then turn immediately left onto a good trail.

The trail heads up the right bank of a steep-sided finger valley. After an up–down on the left bank at a mini-canyon, the route follows dry creekbed the rest of the way to the cave, which is a horizontal slit on the right-hand wall.

(NOTE Going farther up the valley is easy until you hit a big step, sometimes waterfall, that stops all progress.)

On your return to your vehicle you might look for "a mysterious area where the gravel "breathes," indicating a cave passage below.

Also check out Railside Spring below Hwy. 1A. Start from the interpretive sign "Railside" on the eastbound lane and walk east. The spring in question joins some general seepage immediately below the access road to Bighorn Meadows and flows all year round into a channel of the Bow. It's speculated that this is the resurgence of the creek that flows through the lowest level of the cave.

Rats Nest Cave entrance.

75 EAST END OF RUNDLE (EEOR)—map 9

EEOR, showing the ascent route and summit. Photo Rachel Oggy

Day scramble
Unofficial trail & route, cairns, blazes, yellow discs low down
Distance 2.6 km to summit
Height gain 875 m (2870 ft.)
High point 2545 m (8350 ft.)
Map 82 O/3 Canmore

Access Hwy. 742 (Smith-Dorrien/Spray Trail) at Whitemans Gap. Use Goat Creek parking lot.

Here's a chance to impress your non-climbing friends. EEOR at 107598 is the easternmost peak of Mt. Rundle, the one that looms over Canmore. What your friends don't know is that above the cliff there's a pretty good trail following the south ridge all the way to the shoulder. After that it's an easy scramble on scree and rock, with one or two steps requiring concentration. Overall, a much more serious route than Ha Ling, with route-finding challenges.

NOTE the upper section is *not* the Kane route as described in *Scrambles in the Canadian Rockies*, and Alan's summit and my summit are different tops. That's okay, because a lot of people nowadays are combining the two routes to make a loop.

TRAIL HISTORY The present start omits the old south ridge trail, which is for "sheep and goats," says Brian Carter, who with Trailminders refashioned the first part of the route and marked it with yellow discs.

NAMING NOTE The acronym EEOR stands for East End of Rundle and is pronounced almost the same as the character in Winnie-the-Pooh books, Eeyore. Interestingly, the name of a sport climbing crag on its southeast face is Kanga, another A.A. Milne creation. During the great Canmore name shuffle of 1998/9, EEOR was almost renamed Miner's Peak. It is also the name of an "environmentally friendly" cleaning company in Canmore.

To the south ridge

Walk back along the highway toward Whitemans Pond. In between the first two power poles turn left onto a trail and climb up to the right above the second power pole. Shortly, turn left and in trees climb easily up a twisty trail onto the south ridge. En route, keep right at a boulder, then right after the next uphill. (Old trails have branches laid across them.)

To the saddle

The south ridge trail is fun, flattish treed sections alternating with progressively

Typical section of trail below the open slopes. Photo Geoff Williams

higher slabby risers with route options for scramblers of all ability.

Reach a flat that marks the top of the lower ridge. Sheltered from the westerly blast by trees, but with a tremendous view of Ha Ling Peak, this is a logical place for a breather or a turnaround. It's here we once stumbled on two red and white striped lawn chairs arranged around the firepit with a neatly folded Sunday newspaper on one seat. Let me tell you, leaving was not easy once I'd started on the crossword.

Up and off again, enthusiasm returns. For one thing, you're near treeline and the summit is in view. Surmount two more risers to the right of slabs, then plod scree to the shoulder. This is a large meadow with spruce thickets, gently inclined toward the southwest and bounded on the east by a profound precipice of Palliser limestone which dares you to look over the edge.

To the summit

From the meadow you can spot Alan's route in loose scree, heading up and left and around rockbands. I kind of like the more solid ridge route myself, and if *I* can do it without whimpering for a rope, anyone can.

Follow the top edge of the meadow as it swings round to the left and assumes the form of a scree ridge. Luckily, by this point the immediate drop-off to the right is not the scary cliff, but much less vertiginous rubble. Bypass the pinnacle easily on

The meadow. From here you can peruse the two routes to the summits. Alan's summit is to the left, mine to the right. Photo John Miller

the right side to a notch. The rock ridge above intimidates the inexperienced, but in reality the rocks are very safe and in-sloping. It's a bit like walking up stairs with different-sized steps. Near the top, circle around to the left on a ledge above a drop-off, then head up right and cross a neck. Up next is the only iffy part of the route: the few steps to the left across fine, runnable scree poised above the black gash of a gully. Once you're past that, head uphill, climbing scree and rubble to the summit. On top is a cairn, shelter wall and summit register in a green box. Look across the head of a gully to the second peak of Rundle and the start of the climber's traverse.

From here you're in position to pick off Alan's summit at 103598, connected by a broad ridge with a pesky rock band right across the middle.

Return option

If visiting Alan's top, or even if not, you can descend his ascent route to make a loop. The problem is to find the right exit gully from above. The photo to right should help you find the right route.

Top and middle: Scrambling the rock ridge. Photos Rob Eastick

Bottom: Starting down the descent gully. Photo Bob Spirko

76 HA LING PEAK—map 9

Miner's Peak (left) and Ha Ling from Canmore.

Day scramble
Official trail, then route
Distance 3 km to summit
Height gain 737 m (2417 ft.)
High point 2407 m (7897 ft.)
Map 82 O/3 Canmore

Access Hwy. 742 (Smith-Dorrien/Spray Trail) at Whitemans Gap. Park in the Goat Creek parking lot on the west side.

A muscle-aching grind up the back side of Ha Ling Peak takes you to the saddle between the mountain and Miner's Peak from where Ha Ling—Canmore's Mountain of the Month for April and Best Day Hike in Best of the Bow 2012—is an easy scramble up scree. Don't expect to be alone on this popular ascent.

Other, less crowded options are Miner's Peak and "Three Humps," both minor bumps on the ridge toward Mt. Lawrence Grassi. All three can be climbed on the same day. See OPTION ##76A and B.

NAMING HISTORY Originally Ha Ling was called "The Beehive." Then, in 1896, Ha Ling, a Chinese cook working in the Oskaloosa Hotel in Canmore, was bet 50 dollars he couldn't climb up and down within 10 hours. Starting at seven on a Saturday morning with a small flag to place on the summit, he was back in time for lunch. Of course, no one believed him; the time was ridiculous and they couldn't spot the flag. So on Sunday Ha Ling led a group of doubters to the top and next to the original flag "proudly flapping in the breeze" set up a 12-foot-high flagpole with a six-foot-square scarlet banner that could be seen from Canmore with "The Naked Eye."

"As the peak has no name let it henceforth be called Ha Ling Peak in honour of his daring intrepidity" was the proclamation. It wasn't, and the name "Chinaman's" came into use and was declared official in 1980. Then, during the Great Canmore Influx of the 1990s, a Calgary lawyer of Chinese descent declared the name "derogatory." So in 1998 the name was officially changed to Ha Ling (but not before the Monarchist League of Canada suggested the name "Princess Diana.") To this day there are pockets of resistance to the new name by long-time locals. But Ha Ling surely deserves the kudo. How many people can climb up and down Ha Ling in 5 hours from Canmore? Without trails. I'm only surprised that a race up Ha Ling "to plant the flag" has not become an annual event on the Canmore calendar.

TRAIL HISTORY The story of the winding trail built in 1997–99 by "The Ghosts of Lawrence Grassi" (Trailminders), under Brian Carter's direction, was almost as much of a saga as the name change. Curiously, some individuals who chose to remain incognito seemed to prefer the hideously eroded up-and-down trails of yore and did a spot of trail vandalizing and tool pilfering. In one instance a wheelbarrow chained to a tree was stolen and tracked down by the RCMP to people who thought it had been abandoned by hikers. "Okay Allan. Have you got the wheelbarrow all packed for the trip up Ha Ling?" Hardly likely. Anyway, when the story broke in the *Canmore Leader* donations of tools and wheelbarrows poured in, a result surely not anticipated by the anti-trailists (who may or may not be the same as the anti-cairnists).

But the grinch was still at work. On Miner's Day, July 17, 2004, a plaque was bolted to the trailhead post and with miners in attendance the trail was dedicated to Canmore's mining heritage. Six weeks later the plaque was stolen and never recovered.

Even before the upgrade, this trail was always popular. One miserable October Wednesday several years before Alan's *Scrambles*, I counted six parties besides ourselves on the summit. On Trails Day in June 1998 there were 70 people in one party. On Canada Day in 2012 there were 500 people bound for Ha Ling's summit, including school groups from as far away as Winnipeg and Detroit. Among them was "super senior" Richard Guy, aged 95. He and his wife had been up about 20 times before, the last time in 2009 when Louise was 90. On this occasion (not his last, he says) he was on a mission to scatter her ashes among the summit rocks. A loving and hard-won gesture to a remarkable woman.

The original trail across the slab.

The final ascent to the summit.

The summit.

To the saddle 2.6 km
Cross the highway, walk up the trail to a gravelled track and turn right. Cross the bridge over the canal to the start of the trail in the trees. A large black rock with a plaque marks the spot.

Initially the trail meanders through beautiful mossy forest to a slabby gully at the base of steeper slopes. Then, after a few preliminary zigs, it makes a long zig to the left, then back right, en route crossing the notorious slab now made secure by park authorities using heavy timber and gravel. This is followed a short time later by the crossing of the "rib." This brings you back to the gully. (Originally it was intended to take the trail across the gully to an open area suitable for a viewing seat, but then "leg 3 would have had to cross a humongous slab.") Instead the trail makes another long zig to the left, then zigs right and corkscrews up to treeline.

Turn right, into Leon's Traverse (carved into the scree slope by a ghost from BC), that crosses numerous up-and-down trails and gives foreshortened views of Ha Ling Peak up left and "Three Humps" up ahead. Ultimately the trail short zigs up the scree and sweeps left to the saddle between Ha Ling on the left and Miner's Peak to the right.

To Ha Ling Peak 400 m
Keep left and pick your way up the rocky southeast ridge to the top. There's no one route; just innumerable trails etched in scree winding about the slabs. The cairn is perched right on the edge of the great eastern abyss—a climber's playground featuring the longest sport climb north of Mexico.

For a bird's-eye view of Canmore this summit can't be beat. It's also the ideal location for studying the entire route up EEOR. In the western direction lies Goat Valley and Goat Pond where the great Welsh actor Anthony Hopkins got a touch of hypothermia while filming the movie *Bookworm*. To the south you can check out Miner's Peak and Three Humps, both looking totally insignificant against the huge shadowy mass of Lawrence Grassi.

OPTIONS
The two options are easily visited on the same trip and well worthwhile.

76A Miner's Peak

Distance from saddle 300 m
Height gain from saddle 46 m (150 ft.)
High Point 2438 m (8000 ft.)

A smaller point along the ridge between Ha Ling and Mt. Lawrence Grassi named in honour of Canmore's miners.

At the saddle turn right and follow the trail along an easy-angled ridge. The peak is the promontory to the left. It looks a ton more impressive from Canmore, but wait... the promontory narrows near the end, giving a feeling of exposure as you look across a great gulf of air to the east face of Ha Ling. To your right the steep basin narrows into Town Gully (also called Canmore Gully and Stones Creek Canyon), an iffy ski descent in early spring.

Top: Trail from the saddle to Miner's Peak at left and Three Humps at right.

Bottom: Ha Ling from Three Humps.

76B Three Humps

Distance from saddle 400 m
Height gain from saddle 67 m (220 ft.)
High point 246 m (8070 ft.)

Another small point along the ridge, completely overshadowed by the cliffs of Mt. Lawrence Grassi zooming above it. But what a marvellous viewpoint for Ha Ling!

At the saddle turn right and follow the trail along an easy-angled ridge. Instead of turning left for Miner's Peak, turn right and walk across flat ground toward a three-humped summit of brown scree. A trail bypasses the first top, leaving you to scrabble rubble to the other two tops. Look down cliffs to the trail seen winding its way up scree to the saddle.

Left: #76B The second summit of Three Humps.

Middle: #77 The narrow part of the southwest ridge just below the summit. Photo Eric Coulthard

Bottom: #77 The optional scramble summit, which is the same height as the main summit. Photo Bob Spirko

77 MOUNT LAWRENCE GRASSI—map 9

Looking up the endless southwest ridge to the two summits. Photo Bob Spirko

Day scramble, bike 'n' scramble
Unofficial trail, then route, cairns & flagging
Distance 4.8 km
Height gain 1027 m (3370 ft.)
High point 2688 m (8820 ft.)
Map 82 O/3 Canmore

Access Hwy. 742 (Smith-Dorrien/Spray Trail). Drive south of Goat Creek parking lot to where the hwy. turns left and crosses the bridge over the canal. Immediately turn left off the hwy. onto the canal access road (track) and park just before the gate.

The high point of Ehagay Nakoda is easily scrambled up from the west via a route of about the same difficulty as EEOR, but lacking the latter's route-finding problems. Conversely, there is much more vertical height to climb.

NAMING NOTE The first two times I climbed the mountain it was nameless. Finally in 1991 it was officially named after Canmore's Lawrence Grassi, a coal miner, climber, guide and trail builder who, to paraphrase, enjoyed sharing the beauty of the mountains with others.

Canal section 2.3 km

Heading north, walk or bike the canal road (gravel and grass). At ~113557 a cairn and flagging indicate a right turn on trail into the forest.

To summit 2.5 km

The trail veers right to a side creek, then back left and onto the southwest ridge, taking you all the way to treeline. Look for cairns and flagging.

Snippets of trail continue on open ground. The wide ridge of grass and stones tapers as you climb higher and gets more scrambly with a few little downsteps. Still easy, though. The only place requiring care is where it pinches in with drops on both sides. As a friend of mine, a keen housekeeper, said: the slabs, perilously scattered with pebbles and shale, need a good vacuuming! Be especially careful on the descent not to go for a slide.

A bit more rubble and you reach the summit. Luckily there are two tops of the same height. I say "luckily" because the summit to your right is a rocky nubbin requiring greater scrambling skills. From its summit you look south to more summits of Ehagay Nakoda. The traverse, which looks a doddle on the topo map is scuppered by rockbands, many of which you can't see.

78 THREE SISTERS PASS—map 9

Looking from one of the viewpoints towards Little Sister and Middle Sister (right).

Day hike
Unofficial trail & route with cairns, creek crossings
Distance 3 km to viewpoint
Height gain 610 m (2000 ft.)
High point 2270 m (7450 ft.)
Map 82 O/3 Canmore

Access Hwy. 742 (Smith-Dorrien/Spray Trail). Park 6.8 km south of Goat Creek parking lot. To put it another way, just north of your creek at 128520 is a loop on the west side of the hwy. where you can park.

When driving along Hwy. 742 you have to be quick to catch a glimpse of the pass between Big Sister and the southernmost peak of Ehagay Nakoda. It's reached via a narrow valley with intermittent trail, the going frequently rough and stony with a tad of optional scrambling thrown in.

Though experienced bushwhackers can combine this trip with Three Sisters Creek, there isn't much point to it unless you're being pursued down Hwy. 742 by the KGB and just happen to know of this secret pass through to Canmore and the Bow Valley. Anyway, the best part is the pass itself—its viewpoints and meadows.

The pass 2.3 km
Walk south along the highway to the creek. Start up the stony creekbed, shortly transferring to the left bank where good time can be made to the valley entrance.

Continue up the left bank past side gullies to a little canyon where you're forced to the right bank, then back left below waterfall steps. Scrabble up slabs beside pools and chutes. I love this part, especially the tub at the left-hand bend. Beyond the next right-hand bend, cross to the right bank, then, all scrambling at an end, move back to the left bank for good. All of this is made easier when the water's not running. If none of this appeals, use the bypass trail high on the right bank.

Coming up is a long rough stretch along the left bank, all stones and boulders from rock slides, the whiff of wormwood mixing with the sulphur smell of rocks. At one point the trail is forced way up left to get above steps in the bed. On regaining the streambed, note that the water in the creek emanates from falls pouring down the right-hand slope, so the final stretch of creekbed is dry, right to the base of the watershed ridge that rises up like the face of a dam.

At the final Y-confluence under Big Sister turn left with the trail into a stand of spruce that reaches almost to the pass, a totally unexpected and easy finish. On the far side of the grassy ridge cliffs plummet into Three Sisters Creek.

To the viewpoints 700 m
So how do you get into Three Sisters Creek without a paraglider? Turn left. Even if you aren't going right through there's viewpoints to visit before returning. No need to climb much higher. Traverse a terrace of grass and stones below Ehagay Nakoda to a notch marking the high point of a huge basin sloping gently down to timberline in the southwest fork of Three Sisters Creek. The right side of the basin tilts upward, supported by cliffs, and it's along its undulating edge—really a ridge—where you'll find superlative viewpoints. Just know you'll be heading downhill and must climb back up!

While Canmore was visible from Three Sisters Pass, you can now see all Three Sisters and look across the basin to the summits of Ehagay Nakoda, their huge eastern buttresses put into proper perspective from this vantage point.

Third Sister looms above the pass.

The rubbly creekbed above the canyon. Photo Dinah Kruze

79 "BOULDER PASS" & "THE ORPHAN "—map 8

Boulder Pass, looking south up the west ridge to Rimwall.

Day hike & scramble
Unofficial trail, mainly route
Distance to pass 2.5 km
Height gain to pass 655 m (2150 ft.)
High point at pass 2362 m (7750 ft.)
Maps 82 O/3 Canmore, 82 J/14 Spray Lakes Reservoir

Access Hwy. 742 (Smith-Dorrien/Spray Trail). Park at Driftwood day-use area.

Boulder Pass is the pass between unnamed and unclimbed peak 166512 and Rimwall. Getting there is a fairly easy walk with no boulders to clamber over, just an easy valley to follow, then meadows. It's an easier objective than Three Sisters Pass and more enjoyable if you're a flower buff. While the pass sees few visitors, quiet it is not. Helicopters use it as a route back to Canmore from the Mount Shark helipad, so expect about 7 or 8 flights per weekend afternoon, and plan your pee breaks accordingly.

From Driftwood parking area cut through to the highway, turn left and walk alongside the road to the intersecting stony creekbed at 158496.

Turn right, following the left bank of the creekbed. A trail materializes and takes you under some cliffs and past a fire circle with rock seats to the narrows. From both sides, screes punctuated by crags sweep down to the creekbed. Framed in the V are the meadows you are making for.

Continue upvalley, using either intermittent trails on the left bank or the creekbed itself, which may or may not have water. Pass an extremely large cairn. Who knows what it indicates! After trees make an appearance, the valley wends right. At the second side creek on the left, leave the valley. This is before the valley curves back to the left.

Follow the right bank of the second side creek a short way, then climb up to the right onto a wide billowy ridge. Simply follow the ridge up through meadow, then open trees, then steeper meadow laced with scree. It was here I once found clumps of frilly white dryas, with extra sets of petals.

The gradient gradually eases and you angle up left to the pass, which is broad, a mix of grass, scree and tiny rockbands. This is the place to find alpines, including alpine cinquefoil, roseroot and my favourite, woolly fleabanes.

The northeast side of the pass drops off sharply in boulders. It looks a terrible route down into Stewart Creek. To your right rises the alluring west ridge of Rimwall, displaying three small tiers of rockbands just below the summit. To your left, gentler slopes extend to the col below "The Orphan," the summit itself visible atop an impressive line of cliffs.

OPTION

79A "The Orphan"

Route
Distance from pass 700 m
Height gain from pass 213 m (700 ft.); from trailhead 869 m (2850 ft.)
High point 2576 m (8450 ft.)

From the pass an easy scramble takes you to the top of "The Orphan" at 174516. Like Windtower, it's an easy scree walk up the back side with just a few feet of rubbishy ridge at the very end. Apart from the satisfaction of climbing a small peak that looks absolutely spectacular from Stewart Creek and Wind Ridge, the summit is an exceptional viewpoint for the Three Sisters.

NAMING NOTE The northeastern point of peak 166512 was named "The Orphan" by climbers because until 2000 its steep walls went unnoticed between the bigger cliffs of Rimwall and the Three Sisters.

From the pass head left (west) up a broad, easy-angled ridge above cliffs. Where the gradient eases off, traverse right on a scree bench, then climb up left at the demarcation of orange scree to the col west of the summit. This is the way the animals come. You can see the trail carrying on above the top of a fearsome cliff, just part of a vast network of via ferrata routes for ungulates.

At the col turn right and climb the short rise to the lower top. Stop here or continue over the connecting ridge to the true summit. It's narrow enough for you to be aware of drops on both sides, so take care treading the totty rubble.

The summit is a grandstand seat for the Three Sisters, and with a kind of perverse enjoyment you watch people toiling up all that scree to the summit of Middle Sister.

The easy slope above the col, with Two-headed Peak 166512 in the background.

The summit from the lower top.

80 WEST WIND PASS—map 8

Day hike
Unofficial trail with cairns & flagging
Distance 3 km
Height gain 375 m (1230 ft.)
High point 2088 m (6850 ft.)
Map 82 J/14 Spray Lakes Reservoir

Access Hwy. 742 (Smith-Dorrien/Spray Trail). Park 4.6 km south of Three Sisters Dam on the right (southwest) side of the road. The trailhead is identified by "Bow Valley Wildland Park" signs on both sides of the hwy.

A trail, come into being by the passage of many feet over the years, climbs to a low "pass" between two dramatic pieces of rock: Rimwall to the left and Windtower to the right. Nowadays it's a very popular trail to a viewpoint. Scramblers use the trail to access Rimwall and Windtower.

HISTORY NOTE Prior to the 15th Olympic Winter Games, the pass was earmarked for a tunnel to convey the access road to alpine venues at Tent Ridge and Sparrowhawk, so desperate was the government to avoid reconstruction of the highway between Canmore and Whitemans Gap.

NAMING NOTE It's a bit worrying that some people are calling the usually dry valley you hike alongside "Spurling Creek" and calling the trail the "Spurling Creek Trail." It's not. K Country has it right. Some 100 m south of the parking area, a sign "Spurling Creek" indicates a creek with copious water. It's this creek that was named after Calgary Power's J.E. Spurling, who was chief of the initial survey for Spray Lakes Hydro Development in the early 1920s. You can imagine the surveyors on their travels stopping at this convenient spot to fill up their canteens. You too can find the source of its warm water by following a trail on its left bank to the spring.

The trail starts opposite the parking area and follows the left side of the unnamed creekbed a short way before heading up left onto the banktop. The trail keeps to the edge of grassy bank for the lower quarter of the route, then moves away onto steeper hillsides in open forest. As you progress it's all too easy to climb uphill with the lay of the land and end up on the backside of Rimwall with several tiers of rockbands between you and the pass. Of course, the summit of Rimwall may be your intention, but it wasn't mine when I guided some friends up to the pass on my third visit. The result of this humiliation was to build a very large cairn at the point where you actually *descend* a little, the trail undulating across rough, slabby ground.

The trail runs under a rockband, then climbs steeply out of the trees and across scree to the meadows of West Wind Pass. Just below the pass, a side trail heading right is the route to Windtower. See #81.

The pass is a heavenly spot overlooking West Wind Valley and Wind Ridge. On this side the ground drops away as if sliced by a knife, and is criss-crossed with vertiginous goat trails. Growing in a crevice at the very edge of the precipice you'll find a solitary larch—still there?—that by some fortuitous quirk of the wind is the only one of its kind in this valley.

Opposite: The slabby traverse on the approach trail. Photo Geoff Williams

Above: West Wind Pass and Windtower at the height of summer. Photo Geoff Williams

81 WINDTOWER—map 8

Long-day scramble
Unofficial trail & route, cairns
Distance 5 km one way from Hwy. 742
Height gain 616 m (2020 ft.) from West Wind Pass;
975 m (3200 ft.) from hwy.
High point 2688 m (8820 ft.)
Map 82 J/14 Spray Lakes Reservoir

Access Hwy. 742 (Smith-Dorrien/Spray Trail). Via route #80 to West Wind Pass.

Windtower. Tower of the Winds. Elegant ridges dividing dark overhanging walls explored by hard men overnighting in hammocks slung from pitons. From Wind Valley it certainly looks impregnable. The back slope, though, is a hiker's walk-up, hardly qualifying as a scramble at all. The views are terrific, and the exposure is nil until on the summit you look over the edge and "get frozen in fear," as one hiker put it. Carry water all the way up from the highway.

TRAIL NOTE Since the last edition a fairly good trail has developed with lots of little cairns at regular intervals.

NAMING NOTE The name Wind originates from Wind Mountain (Pic du Vent) as named by Eugène Bourgeau in 1858, but later renamed Lougheed after Peter's grandfather. Why this was done is inexplicable, as the second peak is the higher point of the Lougheed massif by just a few metres and no. 1 peak could well have retained its original name. Anyway, the name Wind was transposed to the fifth peak above Ribbon Creek, despite the best efforts of William E. Peters, the rationale behind the name having been completely lost sight of. I think I'm going to start a Protection Society for Original Names (PSOM).

To Windtower/Lougheed Saddle 1.2 km Start from just below West Wind Pass, about halfway between the trees and the drop-off. Windtower at this point is

Windtower is an awesome sight from Wind Valley.

a jumble of cliffs. The idea is to bypass the cliffs by traversing a long way south to where the west face smooths out into grass and easy-angled scree.

The game trail you want is the obvious one that can be seen climbing left to right across a scree patch. In the rising traverse at treeline, it's soon evident you're cutting across the strata.

In detail: Step up two rockbands, then avoid the third (steeper, higher with no obvious break) by an uphill climb to a cairn at a junction. Turn right and resume traversing. The fifth band has a few awkward steps. Then comes the easy sixth, grass, a few token trees, a seventh band and another cairn indicating the bottom of the obvious ramp leading to the Windtower/Lougheed saddle.

The trail climbs the ramp, a gently inclined slope of grass and scree between the seventh band and a line of low cliffs high up to the right. Stop often to look at increasingly fine views of Spray Lakes Reservoir, obscured now and then by travelling clouds of highway dust. At the top of the ramp slip through the left-hand break in the cliffs and join an intersecting sheep trail leading right to the shale saddle. Sheep, it seems, take a rather steeper route to this point.

To the summit 600 m

The saddle is broad and flat, overlooked by the first peak of Lougheed. From here it's such an easy stroll up the broad south ridge to the summit you can carry on a serious conversation with a friend without once gasping for breath.

Tower of the Winds. As you will have gathered by the names hereabouts, the west wind hurls itself over this part of the range into the Bow Valley at Dead Man Flat and is funnelled through the Gap, rocking cars as they round the bends at Lac des Arcs. It's been my experience that no matter how calm it was at West Wind Pass, by the time you near the summit it will be blowing a gale and I'd be cautious when approaching the summit cairn and shelter that is perched near the edge of a 760-vertical-metre drop-off. I stop here, but traversing to the lower summit is an airy option for sure-footed scramblers.

It's satisfying to look down on West Wind Pass and across to Rimwall and the Three Sisters. And surely that's Mt. Assiniboine off to the west!

Top: The final, easy slope to the summit from the saddle. Photo Matthew Clay

Bottom: Spray Lakes Reservoir from the summit. Photo Matthew Clay

82 OLD GOAT GLACIER—map 9

Day hike
Unofficial trail with cairns and flagging, then route
Distance 4.7 km to viewpoint
Height gain 701 m (2300 ft.)
High point 2408 m (7900 ft.)
Map 82 J/14 Spray Lakes Reservoir

Access Hwy. 742 (Smith-Dorrien/Spray Trail). Cross Three Sisters Dam (signed "Spray Lakes West Campground"). At the end, turn left and drive West Side Road to where there are places to park in a borrow pit at the campers registration box and water pump 1.8 km in from Hwy. 742. This is start no. 1. Alternatively, drive another 200 m down the road where there are one or two parking places opposite start no. 2.

This route has three parts: easy valley stroll to the waterfall, which is popular with campers; a steep grunt on rough trail up the headwall into the hanging valley; and the long trudge on lateral moraine to the viewpoint for Old Goat Glacier. Overall, a fairly strenuous trip if you go all the way.

Waterfall from the trail.

WARNING While the route described is perfectly safe, going off trail can be hazardous. In 2005 two inexperienced hikers were killed by a fall into a gully.

FACILITIES Spray Lake West unserviced campground lies opposite the trail and stretches far down the lakeshore. The overflow is located near the dam.

HISTORY & NAMING NOTE Driving along on the east side of the reservoir, I was always fascinated by the waterfall splashing down the headwall of this otherwise quite ordinary-looking valley in the Goat Range. The amount of water fluctuated tremendously and seemed greater when the day was stinking hot, which meant... Grabbing the first colour air photos of K Country as soon as they were issued, Pat Ronald, the then district ranger, and I bubbled over with excitement when we met, because hidden behind high rock walls a glacier was revealed, *almost as long as the Robertson*. The topo map outdoes itself here in not showing even a hint of ice.

Actually, quite a few people knew of this glacier long before Pat and I cottoned on to it, like Banff Heli Sports, who for a few years used it for heli-skiing trips. It was during this time that it received its name. Let's just say it's named after a Banff celebrity who has since passed over the Great Divide...

So this not so secretive glacier below the highest peak in the Goat Range is the true north fork of the Spray River. It used to be. Nowadays it's just another contributor to the hydro scheme, passed by undetected as you drive down the highway.

The valley 2.1 km

There are two starts.

1. A trail beginning behind the water pump joins a NE–SW cutline. Turn right and uphill, then shortly downhill and left off the cutline to join start no. 2. Turn right.

Top: Snow fills the draw leading to the glacier viewpoint.

Bottom: Looking down on Old Goat Glacier.

2. Even if you're not parked opposite start no. 2, I recommend walking farther along the road for 200 m. Then turn right on a good trail that runs alongside bubbly Old Goat Creek.

After start no. 1 comes in from the right, continue alongside the creek. Join the cutline briefly, then meander along in fir forest to its right, Nearing the headwall the trail climbs a little and wends a little left following cairns and flagging across stony ground with willow bushes where the creek is travelling underground. Reach the bottom of the headwall at avalanche debris. Up right is the waterfall. You're going to be climbing the open slope far to its left, separated from it by a belt of forest.

The headwall 700 m
The trail continues in the same line and climbs to the right of big boulders. Then more obviously twists up the fall line on shale and scree. Halfway up the headwall be alert for where your trail forks right across rocks (flagging, cairns) on its way over to the forest edge. (The trail to left leads to problems.) From here on, the trail follows the forest edge all the way to the top. En route is one ugly section of slabs and shale.

Top out on a grass ridge, likely an old lateral moraine, scattered with trees including the odd larch.

To glacier overlook 1.9 km
The trail heads left along the ridge a way, then drops steeply down grass into a draw between two lateral moraines. Turn left. If you are lucky the draw will be filled with snow. Alternatively, get onto the crest of the far lateral moraine and follow that. An awfully long way down to your right is wavy blue ice, concealed lower down by scree.

Both routes end at a moraine overlook at ~150449, a viewpoint for the upper, snow-covered part of the glacier. View the col at its head and the black-streaked east wall of "Old Goat Mountain," at 3109 m (a 10,000er) the highest summit of the Goat Range. Perhaps it is time now to call it Mount Bruno Engler?

SIDE TRIP

82A Tarn

From where you first gained the ridge, experienced hikers can head right and using sheep trails explore some lovely country of spruce, larch and meadow below the glacier. One trail leads to a seasonal tarn, green in colour, that is the reservoir from which the waterfall draws its water.

Following the right bank of the waterfalls all the way down to the trail is not recommended, although it is impossible to take a header through the dense scrub.

#82A The tarn. Photo Alf Skrastins

83 SPENCER CREEK — map 8

The valley head under Nopasseron Col.

Day hike
Unofficial trail & route
Distance 4.6 km to valley head
Height gain 579 m (1900 ft.)
High point ~2286 m (~7500 ft.)
Map 82 J/14 Spray Lakes Reservoir

Access Hwy. 742 (Smith-Dorrien/Spray Trail). Park 4.2 km south of Driftwood day-use area at the creek crossing.

A generally good trail at a moderate grade leads into the dead-end valley between Mt. Lougheed (summits 2, 3 and 4) and Mt. Sparrowhawk. The lure is fine rock scenery and meadows below the spectacular north face of Sparrowhawk. After the trail ends expect one small stretch of bushwhacking. A GPS is useful when looking for the trail on the return; no need to spend 3 hours stumbling down the rocky creekbed like one climber I know! This trail sees use as a climber's and scrambler's access to Mt. Lougheed the easy way up, and as the escape route from peaks 3 and 4.

To trail's end 2.2 km
A small cairn by the highway marks the start of the trail into the trees of the left bank. Keep left twice and come to small rivulets lined with moss — a perfect Japanese garden. At the "spring" itself the moss is starred with one-flowered wintergreens.

Not far beyond, the trail starts its ascent, most often following the top of the left bank 50 m up from the creek, occasionally heading inland or traversing the bank's steep slope on shale. At a questionable junction in trees keep right. Near trail's end you cross two little gullies. Then the trail deteriorates and at white flagging it more or less ends. Record a waypoint here.

To head of the valley 2.4 km
At this point there is the option of heading down to the stony creekbed (red flagging at creek). Otherwise, follow an

The springs near the start of the trail.

Flower meadows below Mount Sparrowhawk.

indistinct trail uphill to where it disappears in grass (perhaps pointing the way to the col between "Little Lougheed" and Lougheed 2.). At this place head right and for the next 300 m or so push through a mishmash of shrubs, trees and grass and cross two shallow grassy gullies.

Emerge in meadows, much of the "green grass" discovered to be dryas or kinnikinnick. Up left is a view of "Little Lougheed," renowned for its boulders, and of Lougheed 2, the summit out of sight above cliffs. To your right is a long line of cliffs that make up the shadowy north face of Mt. Sparrowhawk. A black dripping seep may be the WI 6 ice climb Golden Showers, a beautiful chandelier curtain first climbed by Eric Dumerac and Guy Edwards in 1997. (I'll leave you to look up the meaning of the name.) As Bob Spirko has shown on his camcorder, it lies smack in the path of huge avalanches.

At a narrows use the creekbed, then grass on the right side of it. Cross to the left bank before a short section of chutes and pools and walk up slabs to a windbreak of stones—a possible bivy spot. Continue through meadows and cross the side creek between peaks 2 and 3. From here you finally get an unobstructed view of no. 2, the highest summit of Mt. Lougheed, showing the relatively easy route up its south face.

Continue to meadow's end. Stop here or walk up the wide creekbed, which harbours a few scree plants like the miniature mountain dandelion (*not* a weed), and the exquisite alpine campion, which has as many scientific names as common names. Arrive under Nopasseron Col, as Pete calls it. To your right the north face of Sparrowhawk reaches its greatest height at 823 m (2700 ft.). To your left is the side creek from 3/4 col with waterfalls.

The return

The only problem is finding the end of the trail. Some people get into the stony creekbed when the going gets pushy, and at red flagging they head uphill at 10 o'clock until they intersect the trail.

84 SPARROWHAWK TARNS—map 8

On the lip of the cirque, looking to Mount Bogart.

Day hike
Unofficial trail & route, minor creek crossing
Distance 5.7 km
Height gain 671 m (2200 ft.)
High point 2408 m (7900 ft.)
Map 82 J/14 Spray Lakes Reservoir

Access Hwy. 742 (Smith-Dorrien/Spray Trail) at Sparrowhawk day-use area.

The head of Sparrowhawk Creek is wild, open country with at least 5 little paternoster tarns to delight in. Just don't go in fall or you'll be disappointed.

Since the last edition and the blowdown of August 21, 1999, a good trail has been re-established all the way to the rockslide and a little above. Former trails have branches laid across them. After this, the way is mostly a navigational exercise through bumpy terrain with the added complexity of finding ways up tiers of rockbands between tarns. Nevertheless, many people count it as one of their favourite places and make it a yearly trip. Look for marmots and pikas.

CAMPING NOTE Camping in the cirque is by permit only.

To Reads Ridge trail junction 1.1 km
From the loop road walk through to the highway, cross and on trail climb the bank to a survey marker. Enter trees and climb steadily along the left (north) bank of Sparrowhawk Creek. Shortly after the creek and trail bend to the right, the narrower Reads Ridge trail turns off to the left at a broken tree used as a signpost.

To Tower Gap junction 2 km
Straightaway the trail dips, then settles into a mainly flat, forested trail with the occasional split. Pass below a scree slope, then circumvent a large blowdown area using the latest trail. For a while you travel close to Sparrowhawk Creek, here descending in small falls through mini-canyons. The next point of interest is a fast-flowing spring on the right side, which is possibly the resurgence of the creek from Tower Gap. A little farther on, a short, steep uphill leads to a stony rib out of the trees. Here, cairns indicate the turning-off place to Tower Gap between Reads Tower and Mt. Sparrowhawk. The grassy headwall below the hanging valley is obvious. See #85B.

To the tarns 2.6 km

These cairns also indicate an alternative trail to the rockslide that crosses Sparrowhawk Creek straight off.

The main trail stays on the north bank and re-enters trees, then crosses the creek in willow brush. Come to a grassy draw running around the base of a massive rockslide that thundered down the mountainside from the left. Your entry is marked by cairns on both sides.

There's only one reasonable way up the impasse. Walk right along the draw to the cairn marking the alternative trail's entry into the draw. Turn left here and climb a grassy slope with a scattering of trees and rocks to the right of the boulder field and to the left of a bouldery draw that is the ski route.

On reaching a flat grassy draw, turn left and follow it a short way, staying alert for where a trail climbs onto the ridge to the right—the ridge bounding the bouldery draw—and follow it up, the going easy on grass with larches and the odd rock.

At the lip of the cirque it's worth detouring up left to a high point where all becomes clear. There are actually two cirques. The left-hand cirque, backdropped by Mt. Bogart, has a creek running down it into a sink lake, likely the main source of Sparrowhawk Creek. To the right, half-hidden, lies another cirque and this is the one you are making for.

Drop right and follow a sinuous wet meadow below the cliffs of Red Ridge to a rockband, the first of several to be scrambled up. The first one is tackled at its low point and leads into another swale, this one a flowery paradise where the creek from the tarns sinks underground. Come to a second rockband. Climb up the right side of the creek, then halfway up cross to a trail that circles up left and through the third rockband. On the terrace above is a reflecting tarn edged with clouds of Red-stemmed saxifrage bobbing over the inlet stream. After sweating your guts out to reach this heavenly spot, it's galling to find it a put-down place for heli-hikers.

After checking out a nearby chocolate-coloured pool, continue up two smaller bands to a narrow blue tarn almost completely enclosed by rock. Higher yet are two tarns that lap against the red screes of the "Red Peak."

You might think the screes and cliffs a dead end. Not so. See #87.

The rock-bound tarn.

#84 The lower tarn in the cirque of Sparrowhawk Creek. In the background is Mt. Bogart. Photo Alf Skrastins

#85A The head of Sparrowhawk Creek from Read's Tower. Red Ridge and Red Mountain to right, Mount Bogart to left.

85 READ'S RIDGE—map 8

Plodding up Read's Ridge. To left is Mount Sparrowhawk, Tower Gap and Read's Tower.

Half-day hike
Unofficial trails, cairns, flagging
Distance 2.5 km
Height gain 646 m (2120 ft.)
High point 2353 m (7720 ft.)
Map 82 J/14 Spray Lakes Reservoir

Access Hwy. 742 (Smith-Dorrien/Spray Trail). Park at Sparrowhawk day-use area.

An unrelentingly steep bash gains you the ridge below Read's Tower. This same route accesses three different trips in reverse order of strenuousness: Mt. Sparrowhawk (#86) which is described separately, Read's Tower (#85A) and Tower Gap loop (#85B). The fourth alternative is to call it quits on Read's Ridge and spend the afternoon doing absolutely nothing.

NAMING NOTE Harry Connolly named the ridge and tower after Ken Read, a member of the Crazy Canucks, world champion skier and one of the originators of *Own the Podium.*

To Read's Ridge 2.5 km

Start out on #84 Sparrowhawk Creek Tarns trail. From the loop road walk through to the highway, cross, and on trail climb the bank to a survey marker. Enter trees and climb steadily along the left (north) bank of Sparrowhawk Creek. In 1.1 km turn left onto the narrower Read's Ridge trail at a T-junction at ~190441, which is identified by a broken tree used as a signpost.

The trail follows cairns and flagging. Keep left. (The trail with branches laid across it is an earlier edition that threads its way through a welter of small crags.) After this the trail winds about a bit and steepens considerably below another junction where the trail-before-this-one joins back in. Again keep left, twisting up the fall line and up a shale slope that's gotten very slippery and is equally unpleasant on the descent. (It *needs* zigs.) Top out onto gentler slopes of heather with views of Spray Lakes Reservoir looking remarkably like a fjord.

Gain grassy Read's Ridge and follow it above larches, stepping down into Forbes Creek. As you climb, Sparrowhawk and Read's Tower come into sight ahead. Reach the top of the ridge at a levelling with cairn.

GOING FARTHER

85A Read's Tower

Day hike
Route
Distance 600 m from Read's Ridge
Height gain 277 m (910 ft.) from Read's Ridge; 924 m (3030 ft.) from trailhead
High point 2630 m (8630 ft.)

Read's Tower, a prominent feature on the west face of Mt. Sparrowhawk, is a moderately angled scree ascent via its west slope.

Start from the cairn on Read's Ridge. Descend a little and then follow the trail, climbing scree that takes you onto the west slope of the tower. Rather than head straight up, it's easier to traverse a bit before turning uphill, so as to take advantage of islands of dryas. When they give out, head up left and follow the left edge to the summit cairn.

Of course, the view to the east is blocked by Mt. Sparrowhawk, but in all other directions the views are glorious.

DESCENT TO #85C Hikers have got into trouble when descending off the south ridge too early. The lower route through the cliffs is the better bet.

GOING FARTHER STILL

85B Tower Gap loop

Day hike
Unofficial trail, route, cairns
Distance 2.8 km from Read's Ridge to Sparrowhawk Creek trail; 8.4 km loop from trailhead
Height gain 244 m (800 ft.) from Read's Ridge; 890 m (2920 ft.) from trailhead
High point 2576 m (8450 ft.)

The loop behind Read's Tower and down to Sparrowhawk Creek is becoming a popular trip with experienced hikers who can hack the steep climb to the gap and the route finding down to trail #84.

#85B Tower Gap below Read's Tower.

To Tower Gap 1 km
From the cairn on Read's Ridge descend left into the basin at the head of Forbes Creek, a delightful pocket of larch meadow with marmots.

The trail is faint but followable as it climbs the scree slope to the foot of a narrow rocky step. Down it falls the infant Forbes Creek, which then travels via the underground for some way down the valley. The trail negotiates this impasse by joining up patches of scree on the right-hand slope. Near the top you cross Last Chance Springs, where you can fill up the water bottle. NOTE Snow lingers on this slope until about mid July, masking the trail. At such times expect to do some step kicking.

The gap is a flat area of scree below Read's Tower, which looks absolutely spectacular from this vantage point.

To Sparrowhawk Creek 1.8 km
The payoff is the descent to Sparrowhawk Creek, ALL ON MEADOW below the eastern rock band of Read's Tower. Enjoy continuous views of the cirques of Sparrowhawk encircled by Mt. Bogart, Red Peak and Red Ridge.

In detail: Head south down grass to the left of the scree, lower down transferring to meadow on the right side of a creek that drips down slabs from high up on Sparrowhawk. Descend steep grass, aiming for a boulder, then bear left with the creek and drop more steeply into a flat hanging valley. Cairns guide you along the right side of the flat and through low willow bush to the valley lip. At the end you cross the creekbed, which is dry.

Descend the somewhat steep headwall to the left of the creekbed, which is enclosed by crags, en route detouring left to avoid the stray outcrop. Low down, the gradient moderates and faint trails appear, taking you out to Sparrowhawk Creek trail, reached at one or other of two cairns.

Turn right and follow #84 out to the trailhead.

#85B Red Ridge from the lip of the hanging valley.

86 MOUNT SPARROWHAWK—map 8

View from the summit of Read's Tower of Mount Sparrowhawk, showing the long scree slope and the col at far right.

Long-day scramble
Unofficial trails, route
Distance 4.7 km
Height gain 1439 m (4720 ft.)
High point 3124 m (10250 ft.)
Map 82 J/14 Spray Lakes Reservoir

Access Hwy. 742 (Smith-Dorrien/Spray Trail) at Sparrowhawk day-use area. Via #85 Read's Ridge.

Sparrowhawk's an easy scree ascent until the final steep scrabble up the loose rubble of the southeast face, which feels a mite exposed if you're not used to such places. A consideration: while the west slopes may be free of snow (usually by about mid-July), the southeast face could well be plastered with the stuff, ruining your chances of reaching the summit. If coming from Calgary, drive Hwy. 40 so you can look up Ribbon Creek and assess conditions. And start early: the height gain is humongous!

HISTORY NOTE Now I come to why Read's Ridge is named after Ken Read. It is interesting to speculate whether, had a decision in 2000 gone the other way, you would be walking up an easy cat track to Read's Ridge and perhaps enjoying an after-scramble beer and fine dining at a Mid-Mountain Lodge before making a leisurely return to the parking lot near the tour boat launch. To explain: Harry Connolly's Assiniboia on nearby Tent Ridge, together with Mt. Sparrowhawk, formed part of the bid that won Calgary the Olympic 15th Winter Games. Ken Read, who designed the downhill runs on Sparrowhawk, called the courses "absolutely phenomenal," while the Association of Canadian Mountain Guides took the line that it would "take a nuclear blast to turn it into a recreational slope." Regardless, the Alberta government decided to build their own ski resort on Mt. Allan.

After Sparrowhawk was scotched as an Olympic mountain, Kananaskis Pathways Corporation (Harry again) applied to operate a heli-cat skiing operation, featuring five warming huts up and down the west face, none of which, I hasten to add, would have been available in the summer for beer and shelter like the rest houses up Mt. Fuji. Genesis Land Development Corporation later took over Kananaskis Pathways, but the tide of public opinion was turning and in 2000 "Genesisland" at the head of the Spray Lakes Reservoir was turned down by the Minister of the Environment and the area became a provincial park instead.

As for Harry, after spending 30 years on this project, he very graciously said "c'est la vie" and moved out to live in the Ghost.

First of all, ascend 646 m (2120 ft.) to Read's Ridge at 2.5 km, whose high point was earmarked for Mid-Mountain Lodge.

To Tower Gap 1 km

Descend left into the basin at the head of Forbes Creek, a delightful pocket of larch meadow with marmots. The trail is faint but followable as it climbs the scree slope to the foot of a narrow, rocky step down which falls the infant Forbes Creek. The trail negotiates this impasse by joining up patches of scree on the right-hand slope. Near the top, cross Last Chance Springs—birthplace of Forbes Creek—which is the very last place to fill up the water bottles. The gap is a flat area of scree once slated for a warming hut with a view of Read's Tower.

To the col 700 m

The long scree slope above the gap has a gradient of only 18–23 degrees, but in the time it takes you to reach the col at ~218443 you can work out the meaning of life.

On the col between Sparrowhawk's head and a formidable line of cliffs circling around to Mt. Bogart is an RCMP transmitter station put up during the 15th Olympic Winter Games. It has a definite design fault in that the doors open outwards. Should snow pile up against it during a blizzard, Harry worried that any-

The summit block from the col, showing the trashy ridge. The southeast face is to right.

one inside it would be trapped. He fully expected to open the door some summer and have a skeleton fall out!

To the summit 500 m

You can't see it from the col, but the cliffs guarding the summit have a couple of weak spots around the back side. Start off up the broad, trashy ridge above the col. Then take one of the "trails" heading around to the right, aware as you gain height of a deepening gulf below you that climbers never seem to notice. Gaining the steeper ground of the southeast face, you stagger at the pace of a tortoise toward the summit cliff band, much reduced this side. The scree is horrible and you suffer. Look for sharp points of bedrock poking through to help in upward propulsion. Possibly there's a bit of a trail by now.

As mentioned there are two gaps in the cliffs. I recommend traversing right, under the rock to the rightmost gap where a fan of easier-angled scree gives access to the summit ridge. Turn right and reach the cairn in less than a minute.

The summit. Photo Blake Edwards

Relief is replaced by wonder, first at the communications tower, sadly becoming commonplace on our mountains (this one belongs to Alpine Helicopters), and then at one of the best views in the Canadian Rockies. Mt. Assiniboine can be seen, of course, and a huge array of peaks including Mt. Joffre, the Royal Group and the nearby summits of Lougheed, where you can trace the route taken by climbers doing the traverse. Looking back down the southeast face you're treated to a view of colourful second and third Memorial Lakes. The summit may not be quiet. Kananaskis Heli Tours likes to circle the summit on their Signature Rockies Tour.

Scrabbling up the southeast face. Photo Rob Eastick

87 "RED RIDGE"—map 8

Upper ridge, looking toward the high point and col below Red Peak at right. Photo Roy Millar

Day hike
Unofficial trails, mostly route
Distance 4 km; to col 4.7 km
Height gain 1036 m (3400 ft.)
High point 2636 m (8650 ft.)
Map 82 J/14 Spray Lakes Reservoir

Access Hwy. 742 (Smith-Dorrien/Spray Trail). Park at Spray Lake day-use area.

This rocky ridge (highest point is at 211417) looks red from the highway. Not a good sign, you think, and sure enough it has a rotten rock section. But don't let this deter you; the rest is great walking, rather rough in places but neither narrow nor exposed. Overall, a strenuous trip with bushwhacking and optional scrambling for experienced hikers. Can be combined with #84 Sparrowhawk Tarns to make a 12.2 km loop.

To the ridge ~1.6 km

From Spray Lake day-use area walk out to the highway and cross the road to the unnamed creek at 181427. Follow the left bank on a so-so trail that keeps left of the old stream channel. At the point where the creek bends right and the ground rises up ahead, leave the valley trail at about 186428 and head diagonally up left on an indistinct trail. While you can continue on this line and hit the ridge low down, fit impatient people turn off right at some point and bushwhack up the fall line, which gets a little steep. Go too far to the right and you hit a boulder slope. Wherever you top out, turn right.

The ridge ~3.1 km

Initially the going is easy through trees with bit trails. Reach open ground and clamber up mounds of big scree onto a flattish area of dinner plate rocks coated with black lichen. I'm not sure what the very large cairn signifies, but the view of Mt. Sparrowhawk is fabulous.

Next comes the undulating grass 'n' spruce section. From a low point before the last bump, traverse the right slope on game trail and drop into a deep gap. This is where the Red Ridge becomes the Rotten Red Ridge.

Climb the big step (photo to right), which looks as if a giant-sized bucket of boulders had been tipped onto it. Keep well on the right flank, which has smaller-sized rocks and strips of terra firma.

At the top, the character of the ridge changes once again to turf and gentle slopes rolling down to the valley on the right. One final climb gains you the summit, a small cairn perched on the brink of the northeastern cliffs.

Continue along the ridge—watch for the bite—to the col at 214410 between Red Ridge and the Red Peak at 214404. Now you can look down on Sparrowhawk Tarns.

Looking up the big step.

OPTIONAL RETURNS

1. Via Sparrowhawk Tarns

At this level, the northeast face of the Red Peak is a band of scree hanging over a line of cliffs with a most fortuitous break in the middle. Follow a sheep trail on a downward traverse some distance above the cliffs to the break. DON'T try descending the gullies en route; wait until you reach the break, then descend straightforward scree to the two uppermost Sparrowhawk Tarns. Read #84 for the route back to Sparrowhawk trailhead. Then walk south on Hwy. 742 for 1.3 km.

2. Unnamed valley

At the col turn right, and heading northwest descend an easy valley on strips of grass. Turn cliffs on the right side. Keep left of the first rockfall area and scramble down the creekbed to a second rockfall area below the rotten red ridge. Switching banks, descend more steeply to the forks with Red Basin's creek. Don't go the creekbed route. Rather, traverse the steep right bank using bits of game trails. As you'll find out, the trail you started out on is a lot farther down than you think.

Undoubtedly this is a messy way out. However, just above treeline is one of best flower gardens I have ever seen in the Rockies.

Flower meadow in unnamed valley used as a descent route.

1
camp
940
Waiparous Valley Road
NORTH FORK
Cow Lake
camp
WAIPAROUS
1.2
Waiparous
Horse Lake
dunes
1A
1
Aura Creek
MAP 2
940
4808
1.1
Creek
Cadet Camp
4836
S A L T E R
IMPROVEMENT DISTRICT 8
BIGHORN MUNICIPAL DISTRICT
6A
LESUEUR RIDGE
6
Lesueur
Creek
5
to Hwy. 1A
Dump
940
G H O S T
4451
TransAlta Road
7
Richards Road
STONEY INDIAN RESERVE 142-143-144
STONEY INDIAN RESERVE 142-143-144
RÉSERVE INDIENNE STONEY 142-143-144
RÉSERVE INDIENNE STONEY 142-143-144
South Ghost River
MAP 5

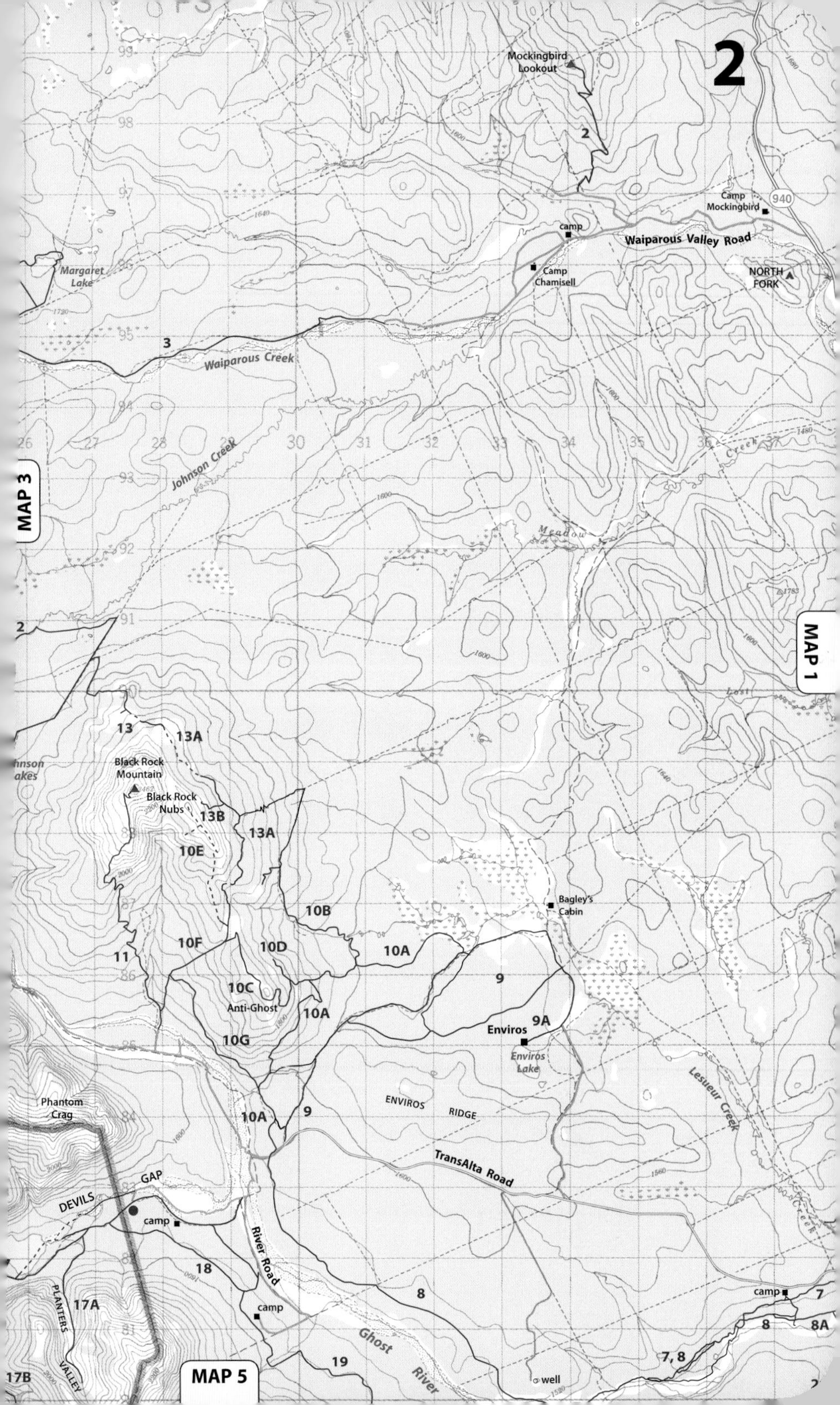

2
Mockingbird Lookout
Camp Mockingbird
940
camp
Waiparous Valley Road
Camp Chamisell
NORTH FORK
Margaret Lake
Waiparous Creek
Johnson Creek
MAP 3
MAP 1
Meadow
Lost
Black Rock Mountain
Black Rock Nubs
13
13A
13B
10E
10F
11
10B
10D
10A
10C
Anti-Ghost
10G
9
9A
Enviros
Enviros Lake
Bagley's Cabin
ENVIROS
RIDGE
TransAlta Road
Lesueur Creek
Phantom Crag
GAP
DEVILS
camp
18
River Road
17A
PLANTERS
VALLEY
17B
MAP 5
19
Ghost
River
8
7, 8
7
8A
well

3
Mount Davidson
3A
chasm
The Prow
north fork
Waiparous Creek
3
Sunrise Wall
Margaret Lake
4
3
12
Devils Head Meadow
MAP 2
Castle Rock
14
JOHNSON CANYON
12
Johnson Creek
16.3
14B
14A
Poltergeist Peak
MALAMUTE VALLEY
Devils Head
BASTION RIDGE
16.2
12A
16
MAP 4
15B
DEVILS HEAD VALLEY
15A
VALLEY OF THE BIRDS
16.1
Johnson Lakes
12
Black R
Mount
13
Claw Creek
16
11
Ghost River
15
15
Ghost River
Phantom Crag
15C
Mount Costigan
Costigan's Boil
DEVILS GAP
PARC NATIONAL
BANFF
Lakes
15D
17
17A
PLANTERS VALLEY
HOODOO HALL
17B
Ghost
Lake Minnewanka
MAP 6

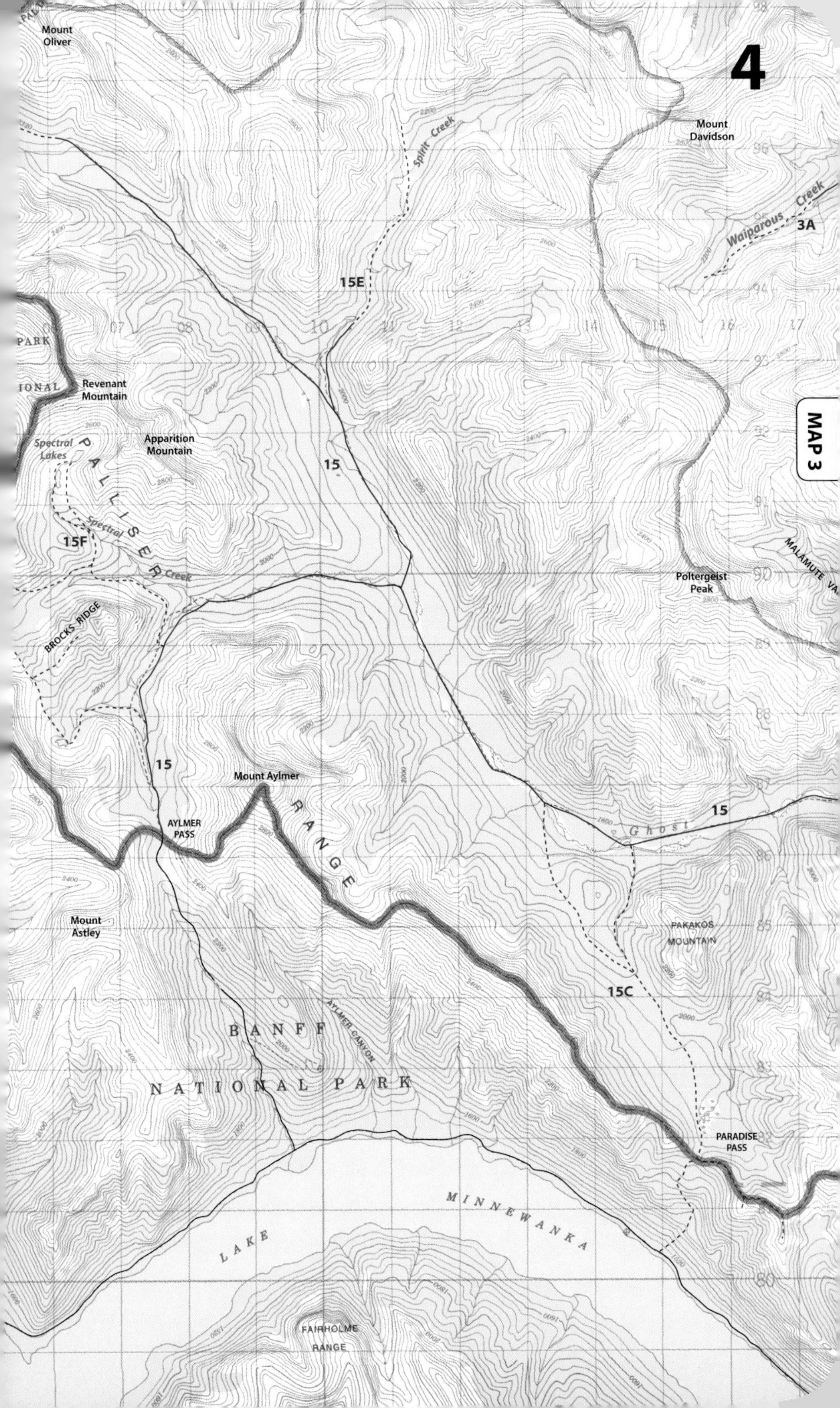
4
MAP 3
Mount Oliver
Mount Davidson
Spirit Creek
Waiparous Creek
3A
15E
15
Revenant Mountain
Apparition Mountain
Spectral Lakes
PALLISER
Spectral Creek
15F
BROCKS RIDGE
Poltergeist Peak
MALAMUTE VA
15
Mount Aylmer
AYLMER PASS
RANGE
Ghost
15
Mount Astley
PAKAKOS MOUNTAIN
15C
BANFF
AYLMER CANYON
NATIONAL PARK
PARADISE PASS
LAKE
MINNEWANKA
FAIRHOLME RANGE
PARK
IONAL

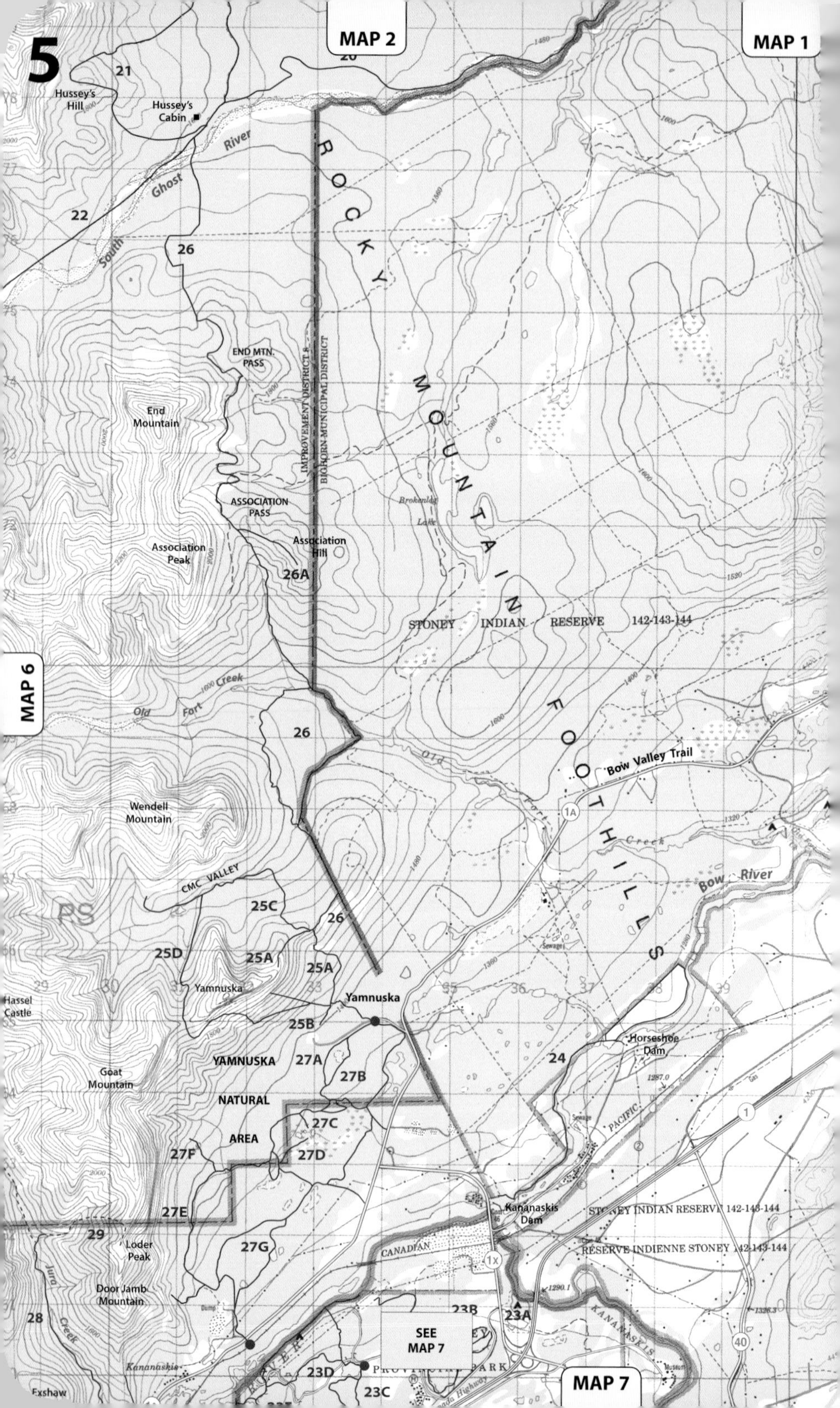

5
MAP 2
MAP 1
MAP 6
MAP 7
SEE MAP 7
Hussey's Hill
Hussey's Cabin
South Ghost River
ROCKY MOUNTAIN FOOTHILLS
END MTN. PASS
End Mountain
IMPROVEMENT DISTRICT 8
BIGHORN MUNICIPAL DISTRICT
ASSOCIATION PASS
Association Peak
Association Hill
STONEY INDIAN RESERVE 142-143-144
Old Fort Creek
Bow Valley Trail
Wendell Mountain
CMC VALLEY
Bow River
Yamnuska
YAMNUSKA NATURAL AREA
Hassel Castle
Goat Mountain
Horseshoe Dam
Kananaskis Dam
Loder Peak
Door Jamb Mountain
Jura Creek
Kananaskis
Exshaw
CANADIAN PACIFIC
STONEY INDIAN RESERVE 142-143-144
RESERVE INDIENNE STONEY 142-143-144
KANANASKIS
PROVINCIAL PARK
21
22
26
26A
25A
25B
25C
25D
27A
27B
27C
27D
27E
27F
27G
24
28
29
23A
23B
23C
23D

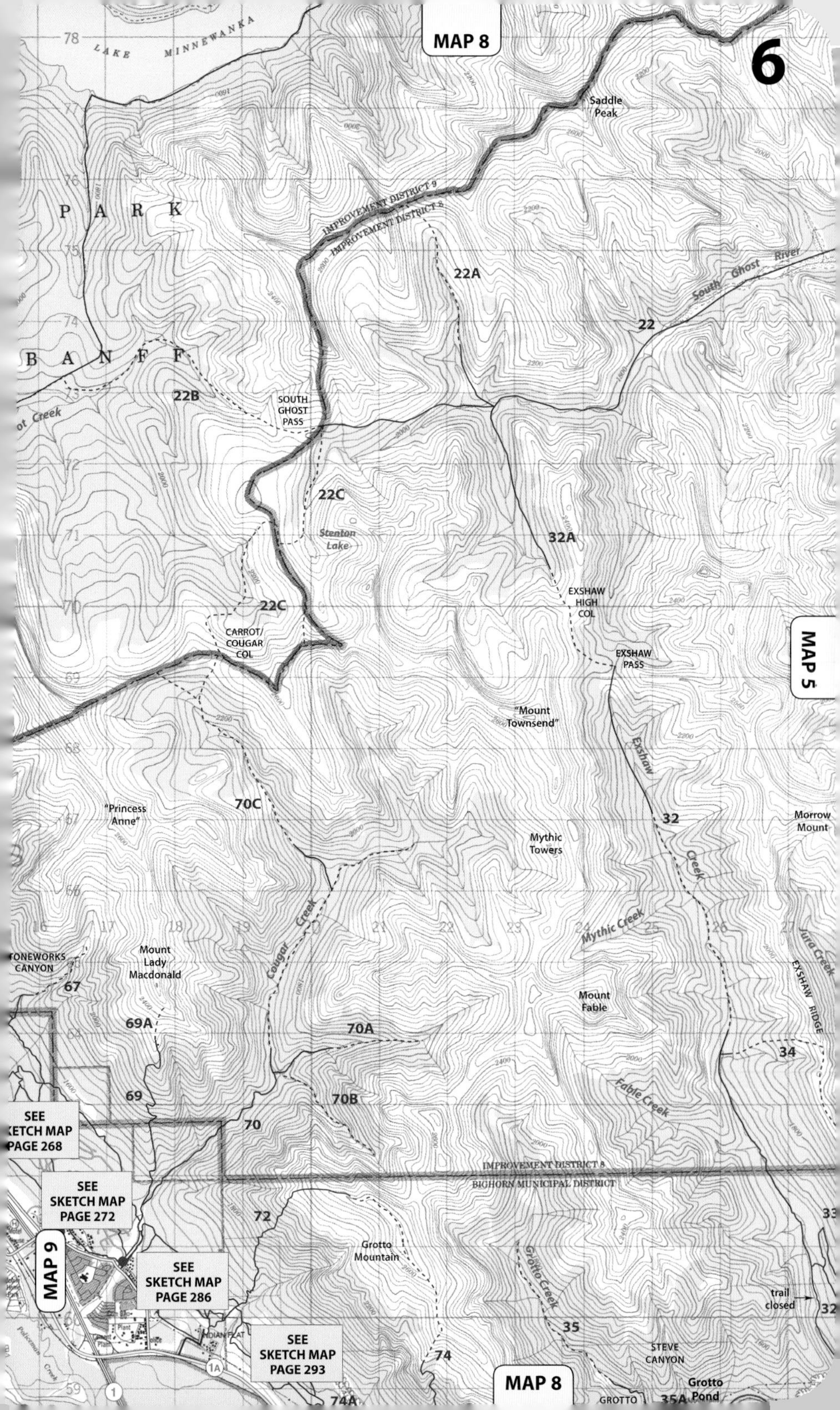
MAP 8
LAKE MINNEWANKA
P A R K
B A N F F
Saddle Peak
IMPROVEMENT DISTRICT 9
IMPROVEMENT DISTRICT 8
22A
South Ghost River
22
22B
SOUTH GHOST PASS
22C
Stenton Lake
32A
EXSHAW HIGH COL
22C
CARROT/ COUGAR COL
EXSHAW PASS
MAP 5
"Mount Townsend"
Exshaw
70C
"Princess Anne"
32
Morrow Mount
Mythic Towers
Creek
Cougar Creek
Mythic Creek
STONEWORKS CANYON
Mount Lady Macdonald
67
Jura Creek
EXSHAW RIDGE
Mount Fable
69A
70A
34
69
70B
Fable Creek
SEE SKETCH MAP PAGE 268
70
IMPROVEMENT DISTRICT 8
BIGHORN MUNICIPAL DISTRICT
SEE SKETCH MAP PAGE 272
72
33
MAP 9
Grotto Mountain
SEE SKETCH MAP PAGE 286
Grotto Creek
trail closed
32
35
SEE SKETCH MAP PAGE 293
74
STEVE CANYON
MAP 8
Grotto Pond
74A
GROTTO
35A

7
MAP 5
SEE MAP 5
SEE MAP 5
Mountain
28
29
Loder Peak
Door Jamb Mountain
32
33
34
Jura Creek
Exshaw Mountain
31A
32
31
30
Exshaw
Lac des Arcs
Lac des Arcs
Lac des Arcs
Kananaskis
Bow River
CANADIAN
PACIFIC
Kananaskis Dam
STONEY INDIAN RESERVE 142
RESERVE INDIENNE STONEY
23A
23B
Flowing Water
Bow Valley
23D
BOW VALLEY PROVINCIAL PARK
23C
Middle Lake
23E
Many Springs
Trans-Canada Highway
Chilver Lake
KANANASKIS
Rafter Six Resort
38
39B
39
McConnell Point
39A
Qualte Valley
37
38
37
camp
camp
SEE SKETCH MAP PAGE 163
Yates Mountain
Heart Creek
43
42
43B
40
Quaite Creek
41
41
Heart Mountain
JEWELL PASS
Barrier Lake
Stoney Creek Provincial Recreation Area
SEE VOLUME 1
Barrier Lake
42A
Grant MacEwan Peak
Heart Creek
MAP 8
45
Mount McGillivray
"Twin Towers"
BARRIER LAKE PROVINCIAL RECREATION AREA
Mount Baldy
"Skogan Peak"
BARRIER LAKE PROVINCIAL RECREATION AREA
46
SKOGAN PASS
SKOGAN PASS PROVINCIAL RECREATION AREA
Mount Lorette
PORCUPINE CREEK PROVINCIAL RECREATION AREA
WASOOTCH CREEK PROVINCIAL RECREATION AREA
Mount Lorette Ponds Provincial Recreation Area
SEE VOLUME 1
SEE VOLUME 1
EVAN-THOMAS PROVINCIAL
1A
1X
1
40
40
68

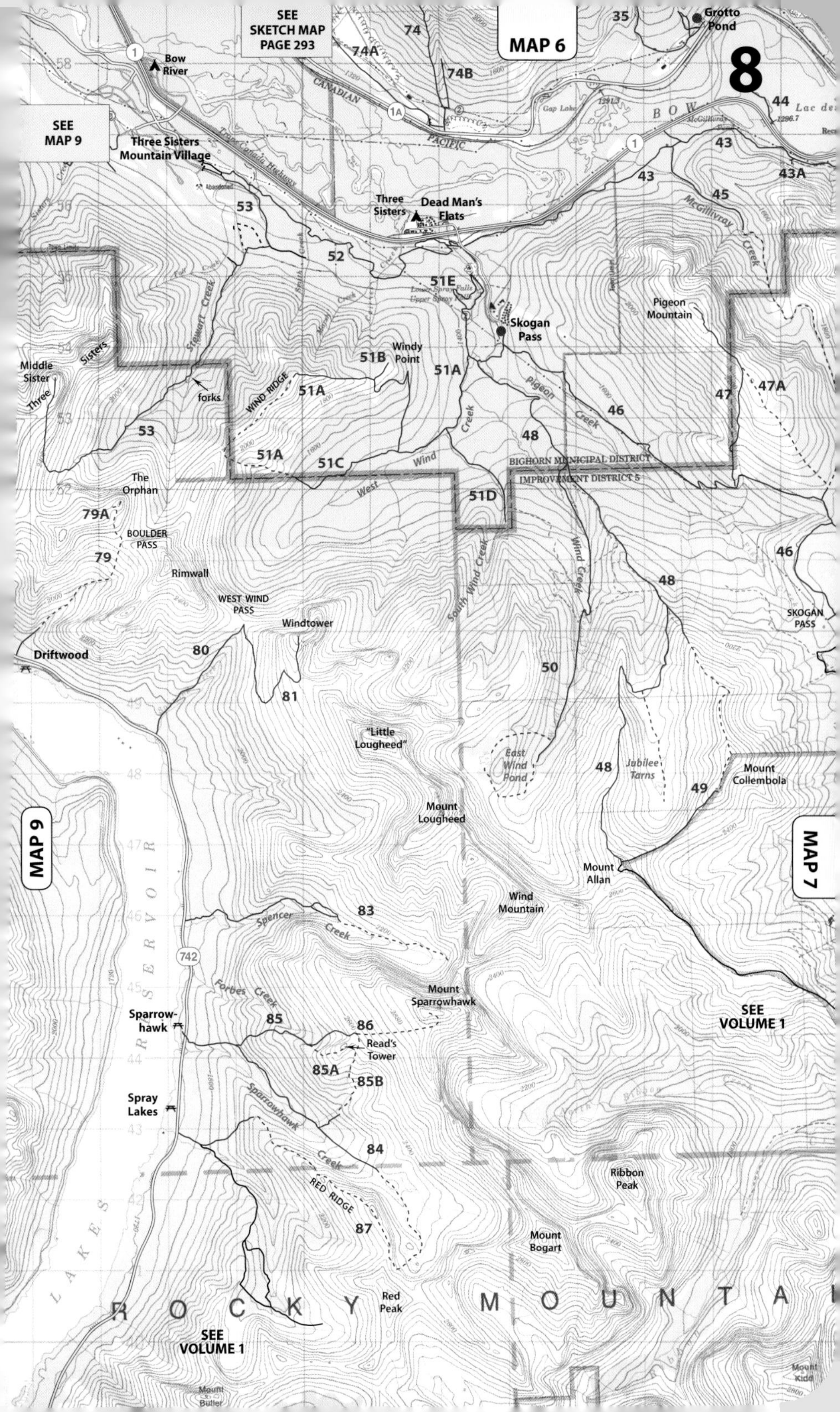

8
MAP 6
SEE SKETCH MAP PAGE 293
SEE MAP 9
MAP 9
MAP 7
Bow River
Three Sisters Mountain Village
Grotto Pond
Dead Man's Flats
Three Sisters
Skogan Pass
Windy Point
Pigeon Mountain
Middle Sister
Three Sisters
WIND RIDGE
forks
Stewart Creek
Pigeon Creek
Wind Creek
West Wind
BIGHORN MUNICIPAL DISTRICT
IMPROVEMENT DISTRICT 5
The Orphan
BOULDER PASS
Rimwall
WEST WIND PASS
Windtower
Driftwood
South Wind Creek
SKOGAN PASS
"Little Lougheed"
East Wind Pond
Jubilee Tarns
Mount Collembola
Mount Lougheed
Mount Allan
Wind Mountain
Spencer Creek
Forbes Creek
Mount Sparrowhawk
Sparrowhawk
Read's Tower
Spray Lakes
Sparrowhawk Creek
RED RIDGE
Ribbon Peak
Mount Bogart
Red Peak
ROCKY MOUNTAI
SEE VOLUME 1
SEE VOLUME 1
Mount Kidd
Mount Butler
CANADIAN PACIFIC
BOW
Trans-Canada Highway
Gap Lake
McGillivray Creek
Lac des
RESERVOIR
LAKES
74 74A 74B 35 44 43 43A 45 53 52 51E 51B 51A 51C 51D 47 47A 46 48 79A 79 80 81 50 49 83 85 86 85A 85B 84 87

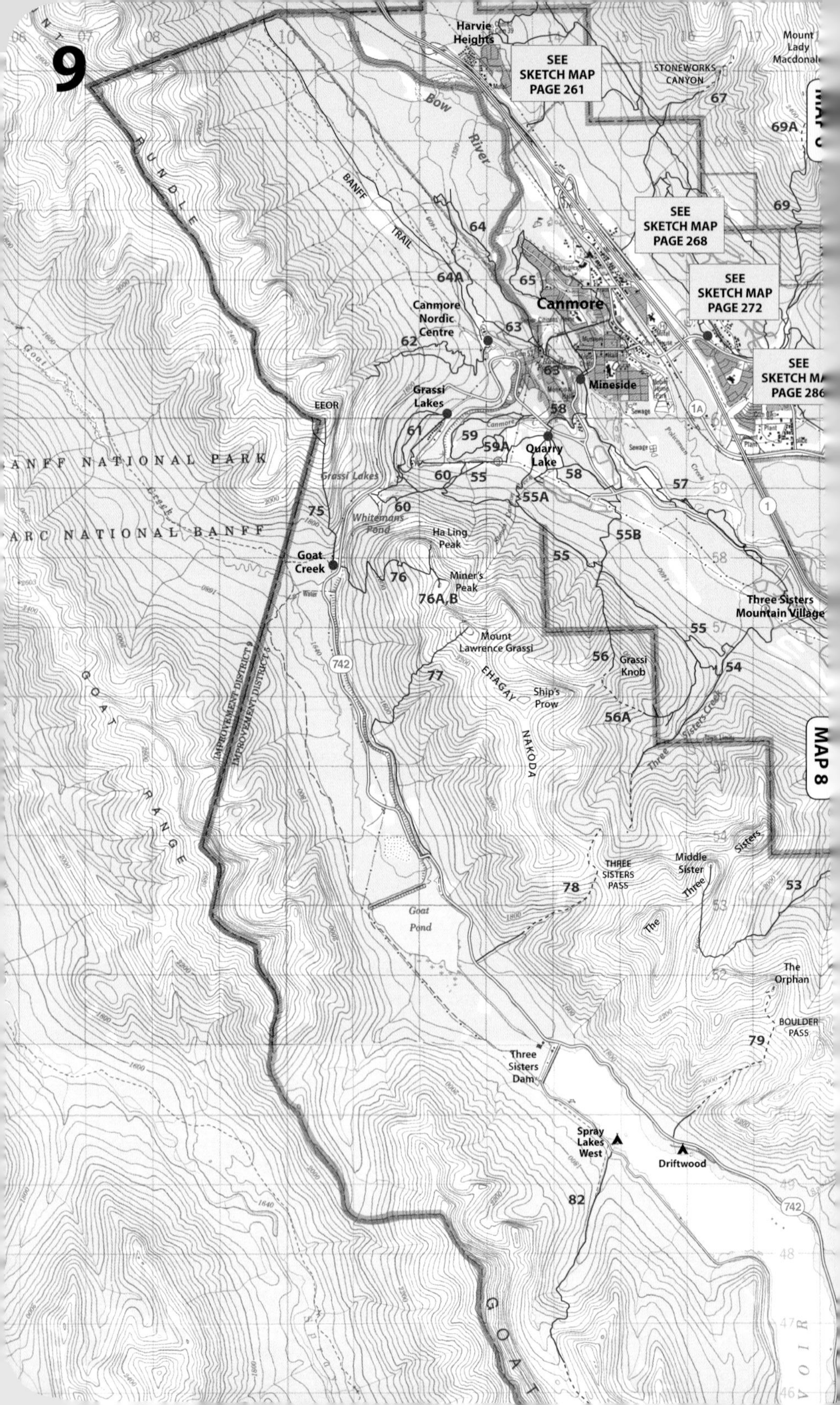
9
Harvie Heights
SEE SKETCH MAP PAGE 261
STONEWORKS CANYON
Mount Lady Macdonald
67
69A
69
SEE SKETCH MAP PAGE 268
SEE SKETCH MAP PAGE 272
SEE SKETCH MAP PAGE 286
MAP 8
Bow River
RUNDLE
BANFF TRAIL
64
64A
65
Canmore
Canmore Nordic Centre
63
62
Mineside
Grassi Lakes
61
58
59
59A
Quarry Lake
60
55
55A
57
EEOR
BANFF NATIONAL PARK
PARC NATIONAL BANFF
Goat Creek
Grassi Lakes
75
Whitemans Pond
Ha Ling Peak
Goat Creek
76
Miner's Peak
76A,B
55B
Three Sisters Mountain Village
Mount Lawrence Grassi
56
Grassi Knob
54
742
77
EHAGAY
Ship's Prow
56A
NAKODA
Three Sisters Creek
IMPROVEMENT DISTRICT 9
IMPROVEMENT DISTRICT 5
GOAT RANGE
THREE SISTERS PASS
Middle Sister
The Three Sisters
78
53
Goat Pond
The Orphan
BOULDER PASS
79
Three Sisters Dam
Spray Lakes West
Driftwood
82
GOAT

INDEX

CONTACT NUMBERS

NOTE: for government establishments use the toll-free line 310-0000

Kananaskis Country Head Office (Alberta Tourism, Parks & Recreation) in Canmore 403-678-5508

Alberta Environment & Sustainable Resource Development in Calgary 403-297-8800

The Friends of Kananaskis Country 403-678-5500 ext. 288 www.kananaskis.org

On-line info
Kananaskis Country and trail reports www.Kananaskis-Country.ca

Gillean and Tony Daffern's blog site KananaskisTrails.com

Information Centres
Tourism Canmore & Kananaskis 907 7 Ave., Canmore 403-678-1295
Canmore Nordic Centre 403-678-2400
Bow Valley Provincial Park 403-673-3663

Campground reservations
Ghost Area Campgrounds Mark & Ingrid Tannas 404-637-2198

Bow Valley Park Campgrounds 403-673-2163 www.bowvalleycampgrounds.com

Kananaskis Camping Hwy. 762 (Spray Lake West) 403-591-7226, kancamp@kananaskiscamping.com

Other useful contacts
Kananaskis Guest Ranch 403-673-3737

Rafter Six Ranch Resort 403-673-3622, toll free 1-888-267-2624

Cross Zee Ranch 403-678-4171

Canmore Nordic Centre 403-678-2400

Bike 'n' Hike Shuttle 403-762-4453, www.bikeandhikeshuttle.com

Canmore Caverns 403-678-8819, toll free 1-877-317-1178 www.canmorecavetours.com

In an emergency DIAL 911 and tell the operator you have an emergency in Kananaskis Country. Or contact Kananaskis Country Emergency Services at 403-591-7755.